THE GROWTH OF AFRICAN CIVILISATION

# The Revolutionary Years
## West Africa since 1800

(New Edition)

J. B. WEBSTER BA PhD
A. A. BOAHEN BA PhD
with
MICHAEL TIDY BA Dip Ed

THE GROWTH OF AFRICAN CIVILISATION

# The Revolutionary Years
# West Africa since 1800

(New Edition)

LONGMAN

*Longman Group Limited*
London

Associated companies, branches and representatives throughout the world

First published 1967
New edition 1980

ISBN 0 582 60332.3

---

Webster, James Bertin
   The revolutionary years. — New revised ed.
   — (The growth of African civilisation).
   1. Africa, West — History
   I. Title II. Boahen, Albert Adu
   III. Tidy, Michael IV. Series
   966     DT475     79-40566

---

Printed in Hong Kong by
Sheck Wah Tong Printing Press Ltd

# Contents

*List of maps and diagrams*     vii

**Part One**    *States of the western Sudan in the nineteenth century*

1   The jihad of Uthman dan Fodio and the Sokoto caliphate     1
2   The Islamic revolution in Macina, the Bambara states and Senegambia     15
3   The Islamic revolutions of Maba and Samori     26
4   Revival and decline in Borno     35
5   Changing trade patterns—the western Sudan and the Sahara     46

**Part Two**    *Coastal states in the nineteenth century*

6   Changing trade patterns—the coast and the Atlantic     55
7   Collapse of the Oyo empire and Yoruba wars     62
8   Dahomey—a centralised and planned economy     74
9   The Asante empire in the nineteenth century     85
10   Igboland—a segmentary political system     98

**Part Three**    *West Africa and Europe 1800-1900*

11   Sierra Leone and Gambia in the nineteenth century     111
12   Liberia 1822-1914—the love of liberty kept us free     123
13   City-states of the Niger Delta     137
14   The fall of southern Ghana     153
15   Partition and conquest     166
16   Collapse of independence     177

**Part Four**    *Response and resistance to foreign rule 1900-45*

17   Colonial government (1): indirect rule and the chiefs     197

18    Colonial government (2): the Western-educated elite    212
19    The colonial economy    223
20    Responses to colonialism (1): the early period    237
21    Responses to colonialism (2): the inter-war years    252

## Part Five    *Independence regained 1945-60*

22    The independence movement    275
23    From Gold Coast to Ghana    284
24    Nigeria—the path to independence    298
25    French West Africa—the path to independence    313

## Part Six    *Independent West Africa 1960-78*

26    Ghana since independence    326
27    Nigeria since independence    344
28    Sierra Leone, Gambia and Liberia    361
29    French-speaking West Africa since independence    374
30    West Africa and African unity    382

*Further reading*    390
*Questions*    394
*Index*    397

# List of maps and diagrams

1   The western Muslim world in the nineteenth century   2
2   Major kingdoms of the Sudan in 1800   3
3   Gobir at the beginning of the nineteenth century   4
4   The Sokoto caliphate in the mid-nineteenth century   8
5   The western Sudan in about 1863   22
6   Senegambia in the mid-nineteenth century   27
7   The Mandinka empires *c.* 1875-98   31
8   Borno and its neighbours before the jihad   36
9   Saharan trade routes of the central Sudan   43
10   Trans-Saharan trade routes   47
11   The Oyo empire and its neighbours in 1800   63
12   Yorubaland 1840-60   68
13   Yorubaland 1877-93   70
14   The kingdom of Dahomey   75
15   The kingdom of Dahomey and the partition   77
16   The Asante empire   86
17   The Fante states   87
18   The Igbo and their neighbours in the early nineteenth century   98
19   Igbo clan organisation   100
20   Plan of a typical Igbo village   101
21   Trading systems of Igboland in the nineteenth century   109
22   The foundation of Sierra Leone   112
23   The colony of Sierra Leone during the 1830s   114
24   Liberian settlements in the early nineteenth century   124
25   The growth of Liberia 1847-1900   127
26   The Niger Delta in the mid-nineteenth century   142
27   The Fante Confederation 1868-73 and British Crown Colony 1874   162
28   Alien domination of the import-export trade of West Africa in 1880   166
29   The Suez Canal: a British commercial lifeline   168
30   The French conquest of the western Sudan   180

| 31 | Sierra Leone: colony and protectorate after 1896 | 195 |
|----|--------------------------------------------------|-----|
| 32 | West African cocoa production to the 1950s | 228 |
| 33 | Groundnut production in Nigeria and Senegal before 1939 | 228 |
| 34 | West African trade patterns 1900-39 | 229 |
| 35 | The growth of West African cities before 1950 | 230 |
| 36 | Peoples of Northern Nigeria in 1952 | 307 |
| 37 | Religious conviction in Northern Nigeria in 1952 | 308 |
| 38 | Independent West Africa | 324 |
| 39 | The twelve Nigerian states created in 1967 | 351 |

# Acknowledgements

The publishers are grateful to the following for permission to reproduce photos in the text:—

Professor G. Atkins, SOAS Library for page 33; Robert Brain for page 16; British Museum for pages 66, 103 (Museum of Mankind), 139 and 203; Cadbury Schweppes Ltd for page 235; Camera Press Ltd for pages 89 (John Bulmer), 115, 256 left, 323 (United Nations), 333, 338, 349 (Courage Photo), 352 (David Robinson), 360 left, 357 right (Mike Wells) and 366 (Christine Osborne); Clarendon Press for page 264; Edinburgh University Gazette for page 163; Mary Evans Picture Library for pages 12, 23, 41, 58 and 170; Foreign and Commonwealth Office for pages 94 and 118; Ghana Information Services for page 288; Werner Forman Archive for page 64; Mr & Mrs J. Hilton for pages 105 and 106; Agence Hoa-Qui for pages 184, 347; Alan Hutchinson Library for pages 6, 226, 354, 355 and 387; IC Magazines for page 359; Keystone Press Agency Ltd for pages 248, 304 and 309; Akinola Lashekan for page 299; Musée de l'homme for pages 72, 76 left, 76 right, 80 and 186; Photo Documentation Française for page 320; Popperfoto for pages 134, 151, 294, 297, 316, 339, 363, 368, 371 and 380; Radio Times Hulton Picture Library for pages 48, 92, 165, 169, 193, 195, 201, 207, 253 and 318; Royal Commonwealth Society Library for pages 30, 39, 116, 125, 129, 214, 220 and 256 right; Syndication International for page 382; West Africa Magazine for pages 69, 148, 155 (Central Office of Information), 199, 227, 276 and 312 (Western Nigeria Information Service); F. Willett for page 203 left.

The publishers regret that they are unable to trace the copyright holders of photographs on pages 145, 191, 242 and 257.

The cover photograph was kindly supplied by Alan Hutchison Library.

# PART ONE

# States of the western Sudan in the nineteenth century

# The jihad of Uthman dan Fodio and the Sokoto caliphate

## The Muslim world at the beginning of the nineteenth century

At the beginning of the nineteenth century the Muslim world, which had once been famed around the Mediterranean for its military skill, learning and government, was in decline. The Muslim countries and the Middle East were threatened by the growing power of Christian Europe. In the western Sudan the Muslim empires of Songhai and Borno had collapsed, and by 1800 there were only small minority groups of Muslims in non-Muslim states. Scholars of the western Sudan believed this was because most Muslims had abandoned the simple living habits and purity of faith of the earliest Muslims. Therefore during the nineteenth century they formed a number of reforming movements to restore the Muslim world to its former greatness by renewed devotion to the ideals of Islam. The most important of these movements were the Wahhabiya of Arabia (in the eighteenth century), the Sanusiyya of Cyrenaica, the Mahdiyya of the eastern Sudan and the three jihads of the western Sudan led by Uthman dan Fodio, Ahmad Lobbo and al-Hajj Umar.

## The western Sudan at the beginning of the nineteenth century

At the beginning of the nineteenth century Borno was the most thoroughly Muslim of the states of the western Sudan, under its Mai (king) of the thousand-year-old Sefawa dynasty. The Hausa states, of which Gobir and Katsina were the most powerful, were ruled by traditionalists, or Muslims in name only who mixed traditionalism and Islam. South and west of the great bend of the Niger the Bambara

1

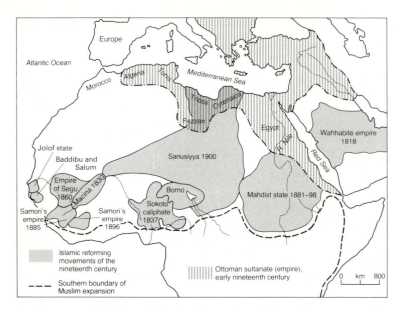

*1 The western Muslim world in the nineteenth century.*

people of Macina and Segu and the powerful Mossi federation were under non-Muslim rulers. However, in the Senegal area three Muslim states—Futa Toro, Futa Bondu, and Futa Jalon—had been founded as a result of Islamic revolutions in the eighteenth century.

The Fulani who lived all over the western Sudan were inspired by these revolutions as they looked on the Futas as their homeland. Most of them were nomadic herdsmen and were often traditionalists in religion, or Muslim in name only. They lived among the Hausa and Bambara farmers who valued the Fulani cattle's manure. There were also a number of town-dwelling Fulani who had settled in the cities in the Hausa states, married Hausa wives and spoke the Hausa language. Some were wealthy traders, while others, because of their education and knowledge of the outside world, held high positions as teachers, judges, scribes and advisers to the Hausa aristocracy, and in the courts of the Sultans or Sarkuna.

Education was highly valued by devout Muslims in the western Sudan. A young child began his education in the local Koranic school, and then as a promising young man he would move about the country seeking more qualified teachers. In time he might begin to gather pupils of his own while at the same time continuing to study under more learned men. Agades, on the caravan and pilgrimage route to the north, was a famous educational centre where mallams (scholars) from North Africa, Borno and Hausaland gathered to discuss law, philosophy and the affairs of the Muslim world. Occasionally Sudanese mallams moved on to the educational centres of North Africa and the Middle East. The majority of Sudanese scholars were either Fulani, Tuareg, Kanuri or Shuwa Arab, though there were some scholars from other peoples like the Hausa. There were two types of scholars. Some settled in the cities of the western Sudan and enjoyed high positions in the courts. Other scholars preferred to wander from place to place alone, or with the Fulani or Tuareg nomads. They had no connections with the governing classes and frequently became the spokesmen for the people, criticising the abuses of the rulers.

## Muslim grievances in Hausaland

The Muslim community in Hausaland, both Hausa and Fulani, had many grievances against the mainly non-Muslim ruling aristocracy. These were religious, political and economic. Muslims objected to having to fight in non-Muslim armies against brother Muslims; they hated the practice of selling Muslims into slavery; they despised the Sultans for their sacrifices and belief in spirits, for the luxury and sinfulness of court life as well as for the way they treated the commoners. They complained about judgements in the courts, and

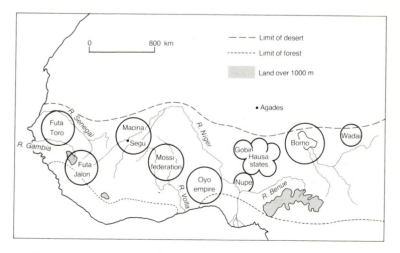

*2   Major kingdoms of the Sudan in 1800.*

bribery and corruption in appointments to office. Most important of all, the merchants disliked the heavy market taxes, while nomads hated the tax on cattle. Muslim scholars pointed out that all these things were illegal by Koranic law. They preached reform, and attracted not only Muslims but also traditionalists ready to support reform even if they did not like the Muslim religion. What the reformers now needed was a leader.

## Victory for the jihadists in Gobir

The most famous of the wandering scholars, whose influence eventually spread throughout the western Sudan, was a Fulani from Gobir named Uthman dan Fodio. Uthman and his brother Abdullah studied under various teachers and finally ended up at Agades under the famous scholar Jibril b. Umar. Eventually Jibril was forced to leave Agades after announcing an unsuccessful jihad (holy war) among the Tuareg. Dan Fodio returned to Hausaland at the age of twenty, to begin teaching and preaching in Kebbi, Zamfara and Gobir. He soon attracted student-disciples, who then returned to their homes to teach and preach in Hausaland and beyond. Dan Fodio continued to write to his former students, to improve their knowledge and keep their faith strong.

Dan Fodio always preferred conversion and reform to violence and bloodshed to achieve Muslim aims. He successfully negotiated an agreement with the powerful Sultan Bawa of Gobir, which granted Muslims freedom of religion and guaranteed respect for the turban, which was the symbol of Islam. Taxation was lessened and

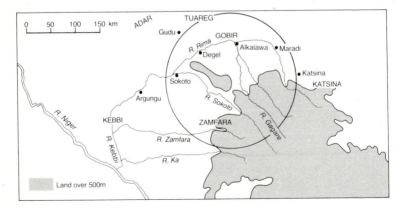

*3   Gobir at the beginning of the nineteenth century.*

4

Muslim prisoners were released from jail. However, the non-Muslim aristocracy disapproved of this agreement and after Bawa's death they persuaded Sultan Nafata (1796–1802) to withdraw the privileges. Nafata also ordered all converts to return to the traditionalist religion. Many Muslims, of whom the most outspoken was Abdullah, wished to oppose Nafata by force, but dan Fodio was against this.

On Nafata's death his son Yunfa became sultan, and it was he, not dan Fodio, who first resorted to force. He turned against the Muslims, and tried to assassinate dan Fodio in Alkalawa, the capital of Gobir, but failed. As tension rose, Abd al-Salam, a leading Hausa scholar and disciple of dan Fodio, forcibly struck the chains from a group of Muslim slaves belonging to Yunfa. Gobir was seriously divided and civil war could not be avoided. It was not merely Muslim Fulani against traditionalist Hausa; some Muslims, Fulani and Hausa were loyal to Yunfa while some Fulani and Hausa traditionalists sympathised with dan Fodio.

Dan Fodio and his companions at Degel, including his father, his brother Abdullah, his son Muhammad Bello, Abd al-Salam and a number of scholars and disciples withdrew from Degel to Gudu on the western frontier of Gobir. This was the hijra (flight) in imitation of the Prophet Muhammad's hijra from Mecca to Medina. Supporters began to arrive in the following months both from Gobir and from all over the western Sudan. Most of the Shehu Uthman's companions were Fulani, followed by Tuareg and Hausa. At Gudu, dan Fodio reluctantly accepted election as Amir al-Muminin (Commander of the Faithful) and proclaimed a jihad against the unbelievers as the Prophet had done at Medina. Since dan Fodio was middle-aged, and not a warrior but a scholar, his lieutenants Abdullah and Bello took charge of military operations.

The first defeat of Yunfa's army at Gudu increased dan Fodio's supporters. The jihad army was then defeated in its attempt to capture Alkalawa, but when it turned south into Zamfara and Kebbi, it was welcomed as bringing freedom from the oppression of Gobir. Dan Fodio won much support by issuing two manifestos, *Wathiquat Ahl al-Sudan* and, later, *Kitab al-Farq*. In these he pointed out the duty of Muslims to resist traditionalist religion and the evils of governments led by non-Muslims. Finally, in 1808, Sultan Yunfa was killed at the fall of Alkalawa, and serious resistance collapsed. The Gobir army and aristocracy withdrew to the north. The major parts of Gobir, Kebbi and Zamfara were occupied by the jihad army and were governed from the new capital of Sokoto, built by Bello in 1809.

### The spread of the jihad

Even before the fall of Alkalawa made victory certain in Gobir, Muslims had gained control in a number of other Hausa states. Immediately after the hijra, Muslims from far away had travelled to dan Fodio to receive his blessing on their plans to start the jihad in their home states. The Shehu gave flags to his representatives in the various states to show that they had his blessing and authority. The following jihads were successful:

### 1   *Zaria, Katsina and Kano*

The Shehu's flag bearers had gained control by 1809. The Hausa rulers of Zaria and Katsina fled into exile and set up new states at Abuja and Maradi respectively.

### 2   *Macina*

Ahmad Lobbo, a disciple of dan Fodio and a poor wandering mallam, preached among the Fulani and Bambara. He made the hijra to Hamdullahi where he built a new capital after overcoming traditionalist rule. For some time he was considered to be under the authority of Sokoto but was finally proclaimed Amir al-Muminin, and was thus the head of an independent Muslim state.

### 3   *Nupe*

A Fulani, Mallam Dendo, chief court adviser to the Etsu (king of Nupe) had earlier received a flag from dan Fodio. In a dispute

*Hausa trumpeters during the Salah Day celebrations in Katsina.*

between two Nupe as to who should succeed to the throne, Dendo, leader of the local Fulani, held the balance of power and supported first one candidate and then the other. In the end his son, Uthman Zaki, seized the throne of Nupe and founded an emirate, and his two rivals fled.

## 4 *Adamawa*
The emirate of Adamawa was founded by a Fulani educated in Borno, Mallam Adama, who visited Sokoto in 1806 and received a flag. He united the Fulani on the Benue and conquered a large area which before had been ruled by many small chiefs. He founded Yola as the capital of the emirate in 1841.

## 5 *Ilorin*
Further to the south across the Niger the once-powerful Oyo empire of the Yoruba was suffering from instability and decay. In 1817 Afonja, the Kakanfo or commander of the Oyo army, revolted against his overlord, the Alafin, and set himself up as a ruler of Ilorin. In order to keep his independence from Oyo he asked for help from the Fulani, and took Mallam Alimi into his service as adviser. Alimi's son secretly obtained a jihad flag, and when Afonja tried to free himself from Fulani domination he was assassinated and Alimi's son took the throne. Ilorin was therefore brought within the caliphate. The Fulani-Ilorin army sacked the Oyo capital, killing the Alafin and spreading the jihad south among the Yoruba until it was halted by Ibadan's firearms at the battle of Oshogbo in 1839. The Yoruba then fought a series of civil wars, when various Yoruba states tried in vain to re-establish the unity lost by the collapse of Oyo.

At the time of dan Fodio's death in 1817 the frontiers of the caliphate were roughly established. Borno was the only place where the jihadists had failed to overthrow the old rulers.

## Resistance to the caliphate

However, in the ten years after dan Fodio's death, the caliphate fought for its very existence. When his son Bello was elected Amir al-Muminin, he faced a leadership struggle, a strong Hausa rebellion, and attacks first from Gobir and the Tuareg and later from the powerful army of Borno. The quality of Bello's leadership between 1817 and 1827 decided the fate of the caliphate.

Before dan Fodio's death the emirate had been divided for administrative purposes, so that Abdullah, at Gwandu, was placed in

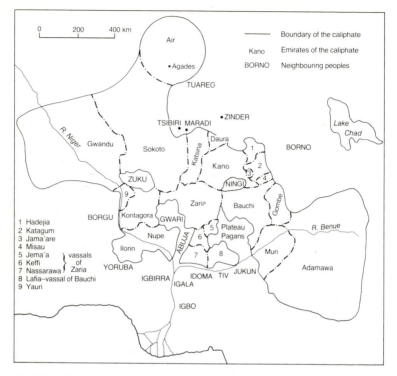

*4　The Sokoto caliphate in the mid-nineteenth century.*

charge of the west, including Nupe and Ilorin, while Bello, at Sokoto, controlled the east. When Bello and Abdullah disagreed over policy this division became permanent, though it probably was not meant to be so at first. Abdullah disliked the way the military leaders were becoming more powerful than the scholars. He was particularly worried about the cruelty of the army to the Hausa peasants, especially in seizing food in the dry season, and the fact that the Hausa scholars were no longer supporting the movement.

While this disagreement was going on between Bello and Abdullah, a rebellion broke out led by the Hausa scholar, Abd al-Salam. This was followed by traditionalist uprisings in Kebbi and Zamfara. Abd al-Salam said that the Hausa were getting an unfair share of booty and that the Fulani, including those not interested in Islam, were gaining all the benefits of the movement. Although Bello agreed with this, he also believed that internal revolts and external attack must be overpowered before reform could be carried out; although he wanted to negotiate with the Hausa rebels, he eventually was forced to declare Abd al-Salam an apostate (someone who has given up the faith).

The rebellion was particularly dangerous since at the same time the Gobir army from the north, and its allies among the Tuareg, were trying very hard to crush Sokoto. It was a tribute to Bello's leadership and military tactics that he succeeded both in defending the northern frontier and in crushing the Hausa rebellion.

These two dangers were hardly overcome when the Borno army under al-Kanami invaded the caliphate from the east. Borno wanted to reconquer some emirates on its western border with Sokoto. These emirates had been captured by Sokoto earlier, when the Fulani in Borno had rebelled against the Mai in 1808 and called in the Fulani of Sokoto to help them. Borno's capital had been sacked and the Mai had fled into exile. However, the scholar al-Kanami rallied the scattered Borno army. He won victories against the Fulani and also strengthened his position by carrying out religious and social reforms, such as removing injustice in the law courts and making the government more efficient. This put Bello, in Sokoto, in the embarrassing position of fighting against a reformed Muslim state, for al-Kanami's reforms had removed the excuse for a holy war against Borno. However, it was now al-Kanami's turn to invade Sokoto, as he attempted to win back the lost emirates. His army advanced to within 100 kilometres of Kano city, but was thrown back through the efforts of Emir Yakubu of Bauchi. The caliphate retained the emirates, and an uneasy though permanent peace was brought to Sokoto's eastern frontier after 1827.

Sultan Mayaki of Gobir also attacked the caliphate ten years after Bello's death, but after his defeat the last serious crisis for the caliphate was over. There was now little possibility that it would be overthrown, for, although external enemies remained, they were no longer able to organise large-scale revolts inside the caliphate. This was because Bello and his successors had managed to settle the grievances of the Hausa people, which were the major internal problem of the caliphate.

## Organisation of the caliphate

### Improvement of Hausa-Fulani relations

Bello did various things to win the support of the Hausa people.
1   He weakened the power of the Fulani military leaders and thus strengthened his own power. He could then stress the importance

of the reforming rather than the military side of the movement, of the scholars (whether Fulani or Hausa) rather than the soldiers. Military chiefs were gradually replaced in local administration by well-respected mallams.

2 He encouraged better relations between the army and the Hausa peasants by stationing the army well away from Hausa settlements. He built ribats (walled towns or fortresses) on the caliphate's frontiers where the army was stationed.

3 He encouraged better relations between Hausa peasants and Fulani herdsmen by persuading the latter to settle down around the ribats. He also taught them agriculture and educated their children.

4 He encouraged education as a key to efficient administration as well as conversion to Islam. He also encouraged the better education of the mallams and he himself provided hospitality for scholars at his court, so that Sokoto became a widely respected centre of education and enlightenment.

5 He did not enforce Islam as this might have caused rebellion. According to normal Islamic practice traditionalist Hausa peasants were allowed to pay special taxes, in return for protection against conversion to Islam by force. Even the famous traditionalist Choka shrine in Kano was left untouched.

6 He made sure there was an impartial administration of justice. He checked the courts, and frequently overruled decisions which he believed were unfair. He encouraged greater links between Fulani and Hausa, and himself married one of Yunfa's wives, entrusting her son with the command of a ribat on the northern frontier. Later caliphs continued to give Hausa positions of trust, and a Muslim Hausa, dan Hakima, was encouraged to set up and administer a protective area on the frontier of the caliphate facing Gobir and Maradi.

## Relations between Sokoto and the other emirates

Bello took care that there were good relations between Sokoto and the other emirates and did not interfere much in their internal affairs. The emirs had won their thrones with little assistance and ruled almost independently of Sokoto. Besides, Sokoto had no standing army large enough to compel the emirs to obey its will and was fully occupied in dealing with internal revolts and external aggression. The Sokoto leaders never intended to create an empire, ruled by force.

Rather they wished to create a caliphate, a confederation of states held together by common aims and religious allegiance to the Amir al-Muminin.

Although the emirates were mainly self-governing, they were not completely independent. The Amir al-Muminin had a number of important powers, among them the authority to confirm the appointment of the emir chosen by each emirate. This gave him considerable power, especially in Zaria and Nupe where three dynastic lines competed for the throne, and the caliph could decide which candidate was chosen. Sokoto also confirmed the appointment of the emir's chief ministers.

Sokoto advised the emirs on how to convert the Hausa administrations which the emirs had inherited to Islamic methods and policies. Apart from a great deal of correspondence in Arabic, there were regular tours of inspection by Sokoto officials to oversee the practical application of these policies. Inter-marriage between the Sokoto aristocracy and emirates was also encouraged, with a view to linking the two through family ties.

The emirates sent two kinds of regular tribute to Sokoto:
1  produce and goods (this included an annual amount, part of the booty taken in war, gifts on the Muslim festivals and gifts from individuals on appointment to office);
2  military levies (mainly slaves for the army).

Every year all the emirs joined their armies with that of Sokoto to extend the frontiers of Islam into traditionalist territories, but after 1880 the campaigns became less frequent, for religious enthusiasm had declined. There was little desire for war anyway, especially among the peasants and merchants who found trade more profitable. Most important of all, no serious threat remained to the caliphate. Rather than join the campaign the emirs preferred to increase their tributes of produce.

## Influence on Sudanese society

The success of the jihad and the establishment of the Sokoto caliphate had a profound influence on the nineteenth-century western Sudan.

### Economic progress

Economically, the success of the jihad brought a great deal of prosperity because of the establishment of peace and order.

*Kano in 1850, drawn by J. M. Bernatz from a sketch made by the German traveller, Heinrich Barth.*

In the mid-nineteenth century the Sokoto caliphate was probably the most prosperous area of the Sudan. Prosperity was built upon a thriving agriculture. Major cash crops included cotton, indigo and tobacco. Cotton and indigo provided the raw materials for the caliphate's major industry, the manufacture of cloth. The four most important manufacturing towns were Kano, Bida, Argungu and Ilorin. Cloth was woven, dyed and embroidered in Kano for sale all over the Sudan and Sahara. Bida, Argungu and Ilorin manufactured cloth quite distinct from that of Kano. While Kano specialised in embroidery, Bida and Ilorin produced most attractive woven designs. In addition, European cloth was also imported, dyed and embroidered to make it acceptable to African taste.

Another major industry was the smithing of silver, brass and iron. Kano was again the major centre specialising in agricultural implements, weapons, bits and stirrups and ladies' ornaments. Bida also possessed guilds of brass and silver smiths noted for the quality of their designs and workmanship. Bida was unique in the Central Sudan for its guild of glass-workers who produced bangles and beads which found a ready market. Sokoto was first and foremost a centre of learning, but it also produced and exported, particularly to Kano, the best quality iron to be found in the caliphate. Sokoto was, however, most noted for its tanners and leather-workers who produced leather known in Europe as 'Morocco' because it was obtained from that country. Almost every ethnic group had a distinct pottery style, but the peoples most famous for their pottery were the non-Hausa along the Niger-Benue, especially the Gwari and the small ethnic groups in Abuja, Keffi, Nassarawa and Jema'a.

In value the cattle trade was probably the most lucrative for supplying the domestic demand for meat, milk and hides. Bauchi, Yola and Zaria, located close to the traditionalist peoples, were the major markets for slaves, while Yola also dealt in ivory. A brisk trade in gold and kola nuts came into Kano from Asante. Kola was also very profitable. It was reputed that while an onion might be bought in Kano market for one cowry, a kola nut from the new season's crop sold for 120 cowries.

One major economic change in the nineteenth century was the centralisation of trade and commerce in Kano, which became the undisputed commercial and financial capital of the caliphate. Its industry, the stability of its currency and the fact that the trans-Saharan routes gradually shifted from the Borno markets to Kano, were important in the city's growing commercial dominance.

## Political progress

Politically, large political units in place of numerous small competing units were created. Islam spread throughout the western Sudan and led to an increase in education and learning, which in turn led to better administration, expanded trade and prosperity. The jihad united the Hausa states politically for the first time in their history, and, while they were the centre of the caliphate, there were also a number of non-Hausa in it, such as the people of Adamawa, the Nupe, Gwari and the Ilorin Yoruba. The caliphate was the largest political unit in nineteenth-century West Africa, made up of fifteen major emirates spread over 466,000 square kilometres, which required four months to cross from east to west and two months from north to south. The boundaries of the caliphate and Borno included rather more than the boundaries of present-day northern Nigeria.

Areas outside the caliphate were greatly affected by the jihad. It brought temporarily renewed vigour and a change of dynasty to Borno, while it challenged Borno's commercial supremacy in the central Sudan. It inspired Ahmad Lobbo to create the independent Muslim state of Macina, and influenced al-Hajj Umar who built up the Tokolor empire which was only a little smaller than the Sokoto caliphate. Indirectly it also influenced the career and policies of Samori Touré in his empire-building among the Mandinka people.

13

## Cultural and religious progress

More important than its economic and political results was the jihad's stimulus to learning, education and the spread of Islam. The leaders were primarily scholars, and from their pens poured a stream of books (more than 200 known works from dan Fodio, Abdullah and Bello alone) to educate administrators in the Sudan about the kind of society they should aim at creating, and to explain Islamic law to the judges. Great libraries grew up at Sokoto and Segu; high officials had to be able to read and write; Arabic became the official written language; and in many areas Hausa became the common spoken language among peoples of different languages.

In 1800 Islam had been the private religion of a small minority in the Sudan; by 1850 it was the official religion of the majority. Islam replaced loyalties to individual ethnic groups with loyalties to the Brotherhoods (the Qadiriyya was the dominant Brotherhood of the Sokoto caliphate while the Tijaniyya was favoured in the Tokolor empire, in the Futas and in Borno).

Although some conflict and violence continued around the frontiers of the larger emirates, internally there was peace, order and good government which increased prosperity and encouraged trade.

Many criticisms have been made of the caliphate. Some said the old Hausa administrations were not reformed properly, and some of the evils of the old Hausa dynasties continued under the new Fulani aristocracy. Others said that Islam became mixed with traditionalism, that even learned scholars made charms and magic, and that the annual expeditions turned into slave raiding. Dan Fodio feared, 'When I am gone the whole country will go back to Paganism'. Still others claimed that the caliphate lacked unity, and that the British found it falling apart, with the Hausa so oppressed that they welcomed the British as liberators. Finally the caliphate is blamed for the fall of old Oyo and civil strife among the Yoruba.

But successes outweighed failures. Other religions such as Christianity have been just as unsuccessful at abolishing all traces of earlier traditionalist beliefs. The British criticised the caliphate administration at first but later used it as a basis for their system of indirect rule and strongly defended it. Some people argue that the Yoruba caused their own confusion, for they failed to find unity, even after 1840 when the caliphate was no longer a threat in Yorubaland. The leaders of the caliphate were in the main devout and sincere. In general they did a solid job of nation-building, uniting under Islam one of the most culturally mixed areas of West Africa.

## CHAPTER TWO

# The Islamic revolution in Macina, the Bambara states and Senegambia

## The theocratic state of Macina

Uthman dan Fodio's teaching and the success of the Sokoto jihad had an important influence on the history of Macina in the nineteenth century. Macina lies west of the great bend of the Niger in its inland delta where the river breaks up into numerous branches and passes through a dozen or so small swampy lakes. It is a fertile area, one of the best agricultural areas of the western Sudan, though wasteland and desert lie close to its frontiers.

At the beginning of the nineteenth century the people of Macina were non-Muslim Fulani and Bambara. The rulers were Fulani from the Dyalo clan, the most important king being the Ardo of Macina. The area paid tribute to the Bambara king of Segu. Within this non-Muslim world there were Muslim minorities of Fulani, Soninke, Songhai and Kenata Moors. Two cities were noted centres of Islamic learning, Jenne and Timbuctu. In the late eighteenth century a devout Kenata Moorish scholar, al-Muktar, had preached to the Muslim communities of Macina and under his influence the Qadiriyya Brotherhood had gained many members.

Al-Muktar prepared the way for the Islamic revolution in Macina which was led by Ahmad Lobbo (sometimes known as Hamad Bari or as Seku Ahmadu). Ahmad studied under various teachers: his father, scholars at Jenne, possibly al-Muktar or his disciples, and dan Fodio at Degel. The teachings of dan Fodio had a great influence on Ahmad. He took part in the early stages of the jihad in Gobir and this made him want to change his own society in Macina. He and his followers were influenced by the Sokoto scholars and they used the Sokoto writings to settle their own disputes (tried according to the laws of God).

Ahmad went to Sokoto to consult dan Fodio about the timing of the jihad. He then settled in a small village under the authority of the Arma (ruler) of Jenne, who later expelled him because of his

*Bambara wearing Chi-wara headdresses in the shape of male and female antelopes. The headdresses commemorate the mythical half-man half-antelope who taught the Bambara their agricultural skills.*

popularity. He resettled at Sebera under the Ardo of Macina, teaching and gathering disciples as dan Fodio had done at Degel. His fame as a scholar, reformer and devout Muslim spread until the Ardo, who felt his own position threatened, asked his overlord, the Bambara king of Segu, for help to defeat Ahmad. Ahmad performed his hijra to Hamdullahi, received dan Fodio's blessings and possibly his flag, proclaimed the jihad and was elected Amir al-Muminin by his followers.

Ahmad defeated the Segu army, and as a result the scholars of Jenne invited him to take over authority in that city. When the army refused to step down and killed Ahmad's representative, the jihadists besieged and captured Jenne. Next, the Fulani Sangare revolted in Macina, overthrew the Ardo and like the people of Jenne invited

Ahmad to take over. Elsewhere Fulani chiefs, in order to hold their positions, declared their support for the jihad. This was a political rather than religious move as these chiefs were not true Muslims, and Ahmad spent a number of years in overthrowing them. In 1819 he made his capital at Hamdullahi.

Ahmad conquered Timbuctu (1826-7) and stationed a Fulani garrison in the city not only to keep it loyal but also to defend it from Tuareg raids from the north. Although the people of Timbuctu were Songhai, the scholar class was Kenata. After Ahmad's death in 1844 Timbuctu, under al-Bakkai, rebelled because the Fulani, not Songhai or Kenata, held the top posts in its government. Ahmad's son and successor, Ahmad II, was therefore forced in 1846 to come to an agreement with al-Bakkai. This agreement stated:

1  Timbuctu would pay tribute to Macina;
2  Songhai and Kenata would be favoured over Fulani in appointments;
3  the Fulani garrison would be withdrawn from Timbuctu.

Ahmad Lobbo divided Macina into five emirates, each under an emir and qadi. The state was governed according to Islamic law by a Grand Council of forty scholars and a Privy Council. Any disputes between the Grand and Privy Councils were settled by forty independent scholars. In religion, in law and in daily life the Islamic code was strictly enforced. The Censor of Public Morals made sure that everyone, regardless of their religion or status, had no more than four wives and did not drink or dance. This clean-up of vices partly caused the rebellion in Timbuctu. Because it was on the edge of the desert, many visitors came from across the Sahara, especially young men free from the watchful eye of their elders seeking the immoral pleasures which the city offered. Ahmad's clean-up of vice reduced the attraction of the city and its merchants' profits suffered from the decline in the number of visitors.

Macina was a theocratic state. It was theocratic because it was ruled by the laws of God as laid down in the Koran. It was a state because it was highly centralised, and the government legislated for the entire nation. The emirates here were like provinces and were ruled by the central government, unlike the emirates of the Sokoto caliphate which practically ruled themselves. As in Sokoto, however, unity was maintained more by the shared ideals and aims of the educated leadership than by the threat of a powerful army.

The jihad in Macina, as in the Hausa states, was at least partly a revolt of the people against the ruling classes. If the non-Muslim masses had loyally supported their rulers, the small Muslim communities could not have achieved success. Many of the ordinary people were oppressed by heavy taxes, injustice and corruption, and were therefore anxious for reform of the system even if they were not Muslims. They joined the jihadists to gain a better life. In Macina, the jihad was not a war of conquest by an outside army. It was more a series of civil wars in each state where the Muslim minority won not so much the military battle as the battle for men's loyalty. It was the loyalty of ordinary people that made Ahmad's victory against the ruling classes (the Arma and the Ardo) possible.

We have seen how in Gobir the Fulani almost came to dominate the Hausas. This was because the non-Muslim Fulani nomads were welcomed into the Muslim armies in order to win military victories and they fought more for Fulani gain than for the good of Muslim brotherhood as a whole. The Hausa scholars and masses resented this, as is shown by the revolt of Abd al-Salam.

In Macina this did not happen. The military were not as powerful, and so Ahmad did not have to reassert the influence of the scholars as Bello had done. Not as many non-Muslim nomads joined the army as they had in Gobir. Moreover, the split in Macina was not mainly between non-Muslim Fulani and Muslim Hausa, as in Gobir, but between non-Muslim Fulani and Muslim Fulani. The split was therefore not along ethnic lines in Macina. The Fulani were divided not only on religious but also on political grounds. For example, the Fulani Sangare (under Ahmad), aided by minorities such as the Kenata Moors, overthrew the Fulani Dyalo (former rulers).

On the whole, the theocratic state of Macina was intolerant of immorality and 'paganism' but tolerant of minority peoples. For example, although the Fulani at first occupied the best posts, this was corrected after the rebellion when the Songhai and Kenata were generously treated. The resulting national unity was demonstrated in the resistance of Fulani, Kenata and Songhai to the Tokolor conqueror, Umar, and support for Ba Lobbo's revolt against Umar.

Although the people resented the activities of the Censor of Public Morals, on the whole Macina was remarkably stable. The succession passed smoothly from father to son, Ahmad II (1844-52) and Ahmad III (1852-62). Ahmad III was killed by the Tokolor conqueror, al-Hajj Umar, but two years later a rebellion under Ba Lobbo, uncle of Ahmad III, and supported by al-Bakkai and the Kenata of Jenne, killed Umar and repelled his Tokolor armies. After a long struggle al-Tijani, nephew of Umar, brought Macina again under Tokolor rule. Al-Tijani and his succeeding sons maintained the political system and strict morality laws of the Ahmads.

# Al-Hajj Umar before the jihad

Between Macina and the Atlantic, in the Niger-Senegal area, were the non-Muslim Bambara states of Segu and Kaarta; the Tokolor Muslim states—Futa Jalon, Futa Bondu and Futa Toro—each ruled by an Almami; a number of coastal kingdoms (the Wolof state of Cayor was the most important); and a few European settlements on tiny islands off shore—the French at St Louis and Gorée and the British at Bathurst. South of the Niger-Senegal were the non-Muslim Mandinka people, divided into numerous small independent towns or village groups.

The man who revolutionised this area was a Tokolor, al-Hajj Umar Tall, born in Futa Toro in 1794. Umar left his homeland on the hajj in 1820 and did not return for almost twenty years. During his travels he witnessed two of the greatest Islamic reform movements of the nineteenth century: the Wahhabi struggle against the Turks in Arabia and the efforts of Mohammed Ali of Egypt to adapt the industrial techniques of Christian Europe to a Muslim country. Umar visited al-Kanami in Borno, married into his family and was so impressed with this scholar-reformer that he wrote a poem in his praise. He also remained with Muhammad Bello in Sokoto for seven years, reading the Sokoto books and playing a part in the political life of the caliphate. Umar married two wives from Sokoto, one the daughter of Bello whose son became one of his military commanders, and another who bore him Ahmad, his successor. When he left Sokoto he was followed by many Hausa who later held prominent positions in his empire. On his way back to the Futa Jalon where he settled, he visited Ahmad Lobbo in Macina.

An even more important influence on Umar was the Tijaniyya Brotherhood. The ancient Qadiriyya had emphasised that spiritual fulfilment came through scholarship, and as few men were born with great intellectual powers only those few—the elite—ever approached the ideal. The Qadiriyya was therefore favoured by the educated classes and did not spread widely among ordinary Muslims who were never likely to attain a high level of scholarship. The Tijaniyya, however, believed that the faith was basically simple and easily understood by all men. Salvation came not through the intellect but through action, strict adherence to the moral code of Islam and zeal for the spread of the faith. There was no elite. All brothers of the Tijaniyya were equal and superior to those outside the movement, as long as they obeyed the moral code and spread the faith. It was a Tijani's duty to show others the way to salvation. These beliefs appealed to the ordinary people, the young and the soldiers to whom action was more attractive than study.

The Tijaniyya had been founded at Fez by Ahmad Tijani in the late eighteenth century. The brotherhood spread in Arabia and from Morocco to the Futas. Umar was probably initiated into the Tijaniyya before he left on the hajj. In Mecca he was appointed khalifa (head) of the order in the western Sudan by the supreme head of the brotherhood. Between 1839 and 1848, from his base in Futa Jalon, Umar made tours among the Mandinka and Tokolor to spread news of the Tijaniyya. Most of his followers came from the Tokolor or the Futas but, as Samori Touré's career was later to show, Umar also influenced the Mandinka. In 1846 on a preaching tour of Futa Toro, his homeland, Umar followed the example of dan Fodio and Ahmad Lobbo by preaching to the people an appealing message of social reform: 'You are like the unfaithful eating and drinking oppression and your chiefs violate God's law by oppressing the weak'.

As Umar's popularity spread, many Muslims left the Qadiriyya (led by the almamis of the Futa kingdoms) and joined the Tijaniyya. In 1848 the Almami expelled Umar from Futa Jalon. Umar performed his hijra to Dinguiray and supporters flocked to him there. He began to make preparations for war, buying guns and ammunition in exchange for gold dust.

## Al-Hajj Umar establishes the Tokolor empire

On his tour of Futa Toro in 1848 Umar had made a proposal to the French who for many years had been trading from posts on the coast of Senegal. This proposal was that the French should sell firearms to nobody but Umar and in return they could move freely in Umar's empire. Umar returned inland and from 1852-4 his army conquered the Bambara states of Bambuk and Kaarta. In a second tour of Futa Toro he had more military successes. Thousands joined his army, including a large number of educated and skilled artisans from the French-ruled port of St Louis who helped him build his stone forts and man and repair his guns. The ruling classes of the entire Senegal area feared for their positions and were alarmed at Umar's influence over their subjects and at his proposal to the French, which he repeated on his tour in 1854.

In 1854 Umar invited Ahmad III of Macina to help him to wipe out traditional religion in the western Sudan, but Ahmad refused.

Ahmad was a member of the Qadiriyya Brotherhood and opposed Umar and the Tijaniyya. So Umar marched against the Bambara king of Segu, who was a traditionalist in religion. However, Ahmad made a defensive alliance with the king of Segu, provided he became a Muslim. Umar felt this alliance with unbelievers was apostasy (betrayal of religion).

In 1861 Umar captured Segu, mainly because of skilful use of firearms and a good supply of ammunition manufactured by his army blacksmiths behind the battle line. The king of Segu fled to Hamdullahi secretly carrying the traditional family religious images which he had promised to destroy. In 1862 Umar entered Hamdullahi and executed Ahmad. He also produced the images of the Bambara king before the assembled scholars of Macina to justify the attack on Macina and his execution of Ahmad as a traitor to the faith. Umar's forces then captured Timbuctu and this was the highest point of the Tokolor empire.

## Al-Hajj Umar and the French

The French said they wanted to open trade routes for the St Louis merchants, yet twice they failed to respond when Umar offered them interior routes and markets in exchange for guns. This was because they did not want a powerful neighbour like Umar, nor, as Catholics, did they want to aid the spread of radical Islam. They knew, too, that the abuses practised by the rulers Umar had overthrown were also found under French rule. In the French settlements Christians ruled and Muslims served. When people began to leave the French settlements to join Umar, the French and the former ruling groups formed an alliance, based on their common fear of Umar.

In 1854, as Umar's popularity reached its peak, the Frenchman Faidherbe arrived as governor of the French settlements along the coast. He was not anti-Muslim and he liked the idea of co-operation with a powerful African state in the interests of commerce. However, he was determined that the Tokolor empire should not extend to the coast and threaten the tiny French settlements. Instead he wanted the French to expand into the Senegal interior. Faidherbe now had an ideal opportunity to extend French rule by posing as the protector of the previous rulers against radical Islam.

In 1855 Faidherbe built Fort Medina on the edge of the Tokolor empire to show how far he aimed to extend French power. He said that Umar could create his empire east of Medina and if Umar

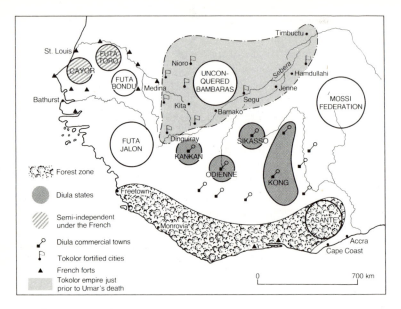

5   *The western Sudan in about 1863.*

accepted this, he was ready to welcome Umar's proposal for Franco-Tokolor co-operation. Umar and his advisers were divided as to whether to accept this division of the country. Some favoured destroying Medina, conquering the Futas and forcing the French to accept their terms. Others, including Umar himself, wanted to accept the Medina boundary. Umar thought (mistakenly as it happened) that the French were only interested in trade, not in building an empire, and so there was no conflict between Tokolor and French aims. To compromise with his anti-French opponents, Umar made a half-hearted attack on Medina in 1857. The French repulsed the attack and Umar concentrated on enlarging his empire to the east.

## The succession of Ahmad

Soon after the capture of Timbuctu, Umar lost his life in 1864 in a rebellion in Macina. The rebellion was led by Ba Lobbo, who resented the way Umar forced Qadiriyya members to become Tijaniyya. Umar was succeeded by his son, Ahmad.

Upon his succession as Tokolor ruler Ahmad immediately faced a number of problems inherited from his father.

22

*Ahmad, the son of Al-Hajj Umar.*

## 1   Rebellions

Umar had placed his sons, brothers and favourite slaves over the conquered emirates and they had little respect for Ahmad. Macina revolted and two emirs (Ahmad's half-brothers) declared their independence. Large areas of Bambara right inside his empire had still not been conquered, and there was real danger that a revolt of the Bambara under Ahmad's control would be joined by attacks from Bambara areas outside the empire.

## 2   The Tokolor army

The Tokolor army did not support Ahmad alone, but divided its loyalty among members of Umar's family. The army was foreign, recruited not from the conquered areas as in Sokoto, but from outside the empire. It was disliked by the people for its cruelty and immorality which discredited Islam. The soldiers did not pay taxes and, as they owned horses and guns, were almost impossible to discipline.

By 1873 Ahmad had defeated his half-brothers; his cousin reconquered Macina. Ahmad began to disband the army and rely more upon the subject people for support. However, he really needed a strong army to check the French advance.

## Comparison between Umar and the other Islamic reformers

There are various opinions about Umar, who differed from the other Islamic reformers. Umar has been accused of being a military adventurer more interested in extending his personal power than spreading Islam. Some people say that the jihad was not a holy war but Tokolor imperialism resulting in a Tokolor empire, for unlike Muhammad Bello or Ahmad Lobbo, Umar led a foreign army into states where there were no uprisings against traditionalist rule. Others say that Umar was a great preacher who appealed to the common people in a way previous reformers had never done. However, Umar's preaching tours were more outside the empire (among the Mandinka and Tokolor) than inside (in the Bambara states and Macina). So his preaching was really separate from his military campaigns, not closely allied as with Uthman dan Fodio.

Unlike his predecessors dan Fodio and Ahmad Lobbo, Umar did not have the support of all devout Muslims. In the Sokoto empire Muslim minorities had themselves rebelled against their rulers in support of dan Fodio, but Qadiriyya Muslims resented Umar as leader of the Tijaniyya and sometimes rebelled against him, e.g. Ba Lobbo's revolt. There were no spontaneous uprisings by Muslims outside the Tokolor empire in support of Umar.

The difference between Umar and the other reformers was basically the difference between the Tijaniyya and the Qadiriyya. The Qadiriyya believed that scholarship was more important than war. The jihad in Gobir was only a means of creating the ideal state through education. Dan Fodio himself retired from the business of war and politics to write books and educate the officials of the caliphate, for he, Abdullah and Bello were primarily scholars and not warriors.

Umar, however, as a Tijani, did not stress the intellectual side so much. The Tijaniyya stressed action in the cause of Islam, and the quickest kind of action was war. So Umar quickly turned Dinguiray into a military camp in preparation for the jihad. In his empire, active soldiers were more important than scholars. However, his methods were certainly effective for, although his empire collapsed, the Tijaniyya, not the Qadiriyya, became the dominant brotherhood in the western Sudan. Umar had the problem of an external power, unlike Sokoto or Macina. It is strange that Umar did not overthrow the former ruling classes in the Futas, then negotiate with the French from a position of strength. Although Umar has been accused of using Islam to arouse anti-European feelings, the opposite is true.

Umar and Tijaniyya elsewhere made great efforts to meet French demands. In Algeria and Tunisia, for example, the Tijaniyya helped French expansion and colonialism.

Like his father, Ahmad did not make a strong attack on the French despite the unrest in Senegal. This was because
1   he was a religious not a military leader;
2   he had reduced the army and taken away the privileges of the Tokolor who fought against him;
3   he could not rely upon the subject peoples.
In the early eighties Ahmad was the obvious leader of an anti-French coalition of African states; but not only did he reject alliances, he also estranged Samori (even though he was also a Tijani) and actually assisted French troops to suppress the Medina revolt. This failure to form an alliance with Samori meant the end of the Tokolor empire.

## CHAPTER THREE

# The Islamic revolutions of Maba and Samori

We have seen how the jihad of Uthman dan Fodio in Hausaland influenced first Ahmad Lobbo and later al-Hajj Umar to carry out jihads further west. Umar, in his turn, influenced new jihads in Senegambia and among the Diula Mandinka.


## The Mandinka

The Mandinka or Mandingo lived in an area of the western Sudan with the Futa Jalon and Gambia valleys on the west, the forests on the south, the Tokolor empire on the north and the Mossi and Asante kingdoms on the east. In 1800 there were no large states nor any central authority in this area but just hundreds of town or village groups. The Mandinka did, however, have a pride in their common origin and history under the great empire of ancient Mali.


### The jihad of Maba Diakhou Ba

Maba's jihad in the Gambia valley in the 1850s and 1860s was, like other nineteenth-century Islamic reform movements in the western Sudan, an attempt to purify Islam, to spread Islam, and to unite separate ethnic communities under the banner of a universal religion.

In the Gambia the main ethnic group—today forming 40 per cent of modern Gambia's people—were the Mandinka. They were spread throughout the valley but were particularly concentrated in the Barra-Baddibu region along the north bank of the lower river. The Mandinka were divided into numerous small kingdoms. Groundnuts became an important item of export in the 1840s, especially from the Mandinka kingdom of Baddibu. By 1860 exports reached almost 10,000 tonnes. The exports passed through the small British colony of Bathurst (Banjul) at the mouth of the river.

The causes of the jihad in the Gambia valley were similar to the causes of the jihad elsewhere. The Mandinka kings, including those

26

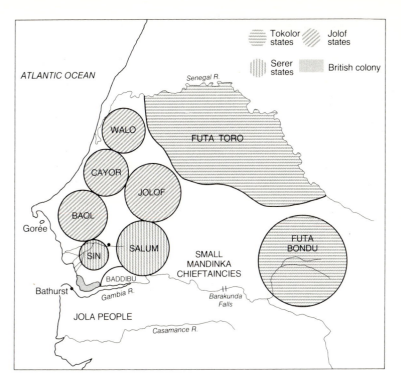

6   *Senegambia in the mid-nineteenth century.*

of Baddibu, were called 'Soninke' or 'drinkers' by devout Muslims. This meant that like so many of their contemporaries, for example the Hausa Sultans before dan Fodio's jihad, the Mandinka kings of the Gambia were 'mixers' of Islam and traditional religious practice. The Muslim marabouts or mallams complained of the kings' heavy taxation, illegal slave trading and oppression which fell hardest on the Muslim traders. A situation much like that of an earlier period in the Hausa state of Gobir was developing as a preliminary to jihad.

The leader of the jihad was Maba Diakhou Ba, the son of a Tokolor mallam who had been educated in the Wolof states and married the king of Jolof's niece. In 1850 Maba met and prayed for three days with al-Hajj Umar who had not yet begun his military conquests. Umar instructed Maba in the Tijaniyya way of salvation. Following Umar's example Maba established his headquarters at Kir Mab (Maba's town) in Baddibu where talibes (disciples), mainly Wolof, came to study under him. However, in contrast to Umar and much like dan Fodio, Maba was not primarily a warrior. He taught

27

and prayed and allowed others to lead in war. At one time he sought unsuccessfully to retire totally from the political and military activities of the jihad. In 1861 the Baddibu ruler's oppressive activities again interfered with the groundnut trade and damaged European traders' riverside property. The British sent an expedition. In the confusion which followed the British withdrawal, Maba declared a jihad and drove out the chiefly elite who had maintained their authority, in his words, 'by plundering the property of others'. Baddibu now became a reformed Muslim state.

The jihad spread all along the river with Muslims calling for Maba's assistance and involving all the Gambia's ethnic groups. Many Mandinka joined the jihad. The Serahuli, the largest national group on the upper river—today forming seven per cent of Gambia's population—sold their services as mercenaries to both sides. Maba's armies attempted to carry the jihad into the country of the Jola in the Foni district south of the river. The Jola (who today form another seven per cent of the Gambia's population) were thoroughly traditionalist and unwilling to accept Islam; they succeeded in repulsing the jihadist armies. Both the British at Bathurst and the French in Senegal under Faidherbe professed to desire stable government for commerce but neither were prepared to see this happen under Islamic leadership. They feared a strong Muslim state might expand to the coast. Faidherbe sent three expeditions against Maba and his Wolof allies, defeated them, and checked the advance of the jihad towards Senegal.

The major national groups in Maba's wars were the Mandinka and Wolof. Like the Fulani in Sokoto and Ahmad Lobbo in Macina, Maba set up a theocracy, a government led by religious leaders. His new state was dominated largely by the Wolof talibes who had gathered around him in Kir Maba. The Mandinka resented this Wolof domination and in 1865 rose in a massive revolt. It was temporarily crushed. Maba was killed in 1867 and his grave became a place of pilgrimage. His successors were unable to hold Mandinka, Wolof and Serahuli in a single state. The larger unity the reformers sought to create through Islam was destroyed. Although political unity was not achieved, Maba's influence did much to spread Islam more thoroughly. Through his influence both Lat Dior Diop, the Damel (king) of Cayor, and Ali Bouri Ndiaye, the Bourba-Jolof (king of Jolof), were converted. The Wolof, the Mandinka and other ethnic groups of the Gambia, with the exception of the Jola, became thoroughly Islamised. As a result, the Gambia today is almost 90 per cent Muslim.

# The Mandinka empire of Samori Touré 1870-98

## The Diula

One group of Mandinka—the Diula— were long-distance traders. They were skilled craftsmen (weavers and blacksmiths) and they travelled widely, trading among the Mossi, with French merchants on the Senegal and on the coast at Monrovia and Freetown. The Diula were Muslims. They settled in villages, some of which grew into towns and they insisted on their independence from the local people. They built mosques and schools and attracted scholars to their towns. Kong, one of the famous Diula towns, was famous not only for its trade, its weavers and dyers, but also for its mosques, schools and scholars.

The Diula towns were Muslim islands in a sea of traditionalism. However, the Diula compromised with their traditionalist neighbours (they were both Mandinka), intermarried and practised traditionalist rites along with their Muslim faith. The circle of Muslims widened around the towns, but the Diula were not missionaries, and even less jihadists, for they were unwilling to upset their commercial activities by rousing traditionalist hostility. They were the 'nominal Muslims', 'compromisers' and 'sacrificers to many gods', condemned by the Islamic reformers of the nineteenth century.

By the 1850s some of the Diula towns were expanding into large states. The Muslim reform movement in the Sudan aroused some of the Diula Muslims to spread their faith more vigorously and form larger Muslim settlements. Diula traders saw the commercial advantages of large political units. Kong's expansion was to gain control of the horse trade from the northern savannah and the kola nut trade from the southern forests. By 1860 it had become the largest of all the Mandinka states. Kankan, on the other hand, expanded to spread Islam, and was led by Mamadu, a Mandinka, and former disciple of al-Hajj Umar. Two other Diula towns, Odienne and Sikasso, had also expanded into large states by 1850.

## Samori Touré

Samori Touré was born in 1830, the son of a Mandinka peasant farmer who practised traditional religion. As a young man Samori joined the Diula trading community. Samori traded in gold from Wassulu and cattle from Futa Jalon, and he probably visited Freetown and the Tokolor empire. He was converted to Islam under

*Samori Touré.*

a scholar-chief of Wassulu. Samori also knew the teachings of al-Hajj Umar, and joined Umar's brotherhood, the Tijaniyya. Many of the Diula belonged to the Tijaniyya. Later Samori gave high positions in the empire he created to disciples of Umar and one of Umar's nephews.

Samori's home was on the border of the Sise kingdom, a Mandinka state created by a jihadist Diula trader, Mori Ule, between 1835 and 1845. Mori Ule was killed in battle in 1845, but the Sise state continued to expand under his son, Sere Burlay, who ruled from 1849 to 1859. Samori's mother was captured by a Sise raiding party in 1853. Samori surrendered himself to Sere Burlay to take his mother's place, and he was put into the Sise army. Samori soon proved to be a skilful soldier, and he quickly rose on merit to be a commander. He became a master of tactics using guns and cavalry.

In 1857 Samori broke away from Sise with his unit of soldiers and became an independent warlord. From 1857 to 1867 Samori built up his original small following into an army, winning the support of his traditionalist clansmen and the Muslim Diula traders.

Then from 1867 to 1881 Samori went on to create his own state and empire. His motives were a blend of religion and economics. He believed God had specially chosen him to spread the faith. As a Diula

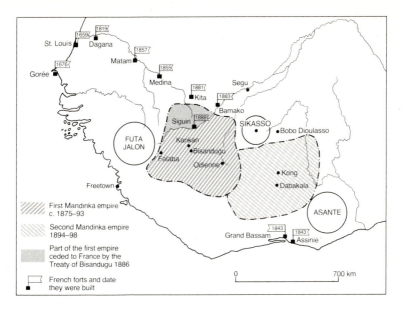

**First Mandinka empire**
c. 1875–93

**Second Mandinka empire**
1894–98

**Part of the first empire ceded to France by the Treaty of Bisandugu 1886**

**French forts and date they were built**

7   *The Mandinka empires* c.*1875-98.*

he hoped to control more trade routes, and also establish a political order in which trade and Islam could flourish. He started by conquering Sanankoro in 1867. Then he gradually absorbed many small Mandinka states. The once powerful Sise kingdom, now ruled by Sere Brema, was forced to recognise Samori's dominance. In 1873 Samori established his capital at Bisandugu. In 1875 he captured Kumban after a long siege, defeating the Sankaran traditionalists. Between 1870 and 1878 he overran a large area in the upper Niger valley, from Kouroussa to Siguiri. From 1879 to 1881 Samori was occupied in suppressing a revolt by the Sise, who were finally defeated. In 1881-2 he extended his authority to Kangaba and to a part of the Bambara country north of the Niger, which had seceded from the Tokolor empire.

Samori did not always expand his empire by force. Sometimes he made marriage alliances with groups like the Touré of Odienne, or diplomatic alliances with men like the Tijani around Dinguiray, led by Agibu the rebellious brother of the Tokolor emperor Ahmad.

By 1888 Samori's empire (298,000 square kilometres) was the third largest political unit of the western Sudan, after the Sokoto caliphate (466,000 square kilometres) and Tokolor empire (388,000 square kilometres). Samori wanted political unification and revival of

31

Mandinka greatness, and he also wanted his new state to be based on Islam. Surprisingly, people did not resent the ruthless way he attacked traditional religion; indeed, many of them seem to have approved. Al-Hajj Umar's preaching tours in Mandinka country probably helped to prepare the way for Samori. In Kankan the religious activities showed Umar's preaching had had an effect. Umar and Samori were both Tijaniyya members, and the Tijaniyya emphasis on equality had a special appeal to the Mandinka whose traditional culture emphasised the dignity and equality of men.

Samori was born one of the common people, unlike the other great nineteenth-century reformers who had been born into the scholar class. He went much further than Umar in attacking and destroying the position of the ruling class. He did not go to the same extremes as Umar and Ahmad Lobbo to enforce all the moral commandments of Islam, which the people had resented. Instead he stressed education and in newly conquered villages his first concern was for the mosque, the school and the teachers. He took a personal interest in the schools and made education compulsory for the children of state officials. The army was also a means of converting and educating people, and soldiers were taught the faith and basic literacy.

The Diula commercial states of Kong and Sikasso resisted Samori, but it is not true to say that the merchant class opposed Samori, since the commercial towns of Kankan and Odienne supported him (Odienne was his most faithful ally). Samori abolished a great number of customs charges among the small states and so made trade easier. The merchants resented the tight economic control Samori had over agriculture and markets, but at the same time they benefited from the increased exports which Samori encouraged in exchange for weapons and ammunition. In fact, the Diula traders acting as his spies far away among the French in the Futas, the British in Freetown and the Tokolor on the Niger helped to make Samori's international diplomacy so successful.

## Samori's political organisation

The Mandinka empire was divided into 162 districts of twenty or more villages each. The districts were grouped together to form ten large provinces. The empire was governed by three parallel lines of unity, the traditional, the military and the religious, all headed by the Almami and his state council. Village heads were chosen by traditional methods. Their power was limited by the village religious leaders (the Imam or learned man and the Qadi who administered the law) and the sofa (professional military officer appointed by Samori). The sofa was responsible for raising troops and supplies for the army and harvesting and selling produce from the Almami's field which was farmed communally in each village. District chiefs of Samori were assisted by a war chief who had 200 to 300 sofas under his command, and a scholar. The Almami was the supreme political, judicial and religious head of the empire as well as its military commander. He was assisted by a state council composed of provincial heads of three lines of authority: political, religious and military.

The Mandinka empire was probably the most efficiently governed of the larger West African empires of the nineteenth century. It was much more united and centralised than the Tokolor empire. Two groups were given power at different levels—chiefs at the village level and Samori's friends and relatives at the higher level. Both groups were checked and reduced in power by the religious leaders and sofa administrators. The sofas were especially important as they were appointed directly by the Almami. They had no traditional claim to office, so they could be promoted, transferred and dismissed at will by the Almami. Samori's empire has been called a military state because

*Mandinka harpists from eastern Senegal. Travelling musicians have played an important part in Mandinka culture from earliest times and are widely admired by Muslim and non-Muslim alike for their performance of epic tales.*

the sofas were so important. The empire was at war for most of its existence and so the army had to be strong. Samori was able to appoint the best men, regardless of their origins, to high positions in the army. Since education, discipline and national rather than local loyalty were taught in the army, it was a good training ground for political officers.

Samori's major aim was to destroy ethnicism and promote national loyalty among the Mandinka. He placed less emphasis on the village groups and more on the canton which united villages. At each level of government he saw to it that men of different families and ethnic groups worked together. He also tried to abolish distinctions between privileged and non-privileged classes by giving everyone the chance to rise through the army to the highest places in the state.

Mandinka unity was based on the law, way of life and thinking of Islam. Religious leaders were as important as the political and military. Images, ancestors' houses and sacred groves were replaced with mosques and schools. Taxation and law were reformed according to Islamic practice. Judicial matters were usually settled in the alkali's courts at the village, district or provincial levels, but very serious matters could be brought before Samori and his state council.

Samori introduced great changes and did not just preserve old customs and institutions. He created a complex administration with political officers appointed by the central government and an efficient and loyal army to carry out the government's will—both essential for a modern state. He also aroused a feeling of national pride, without which a state is not likely to last for long. Samori was a diplomatic and military genius who was helped by the Mandinka's pride in their history (the empire of Mali). Samori, therefore, appeared as a modern Mansa Musa. What happened to this great empire and its great leader Samori during the 1880s and 1890s will be discussed later (see Chapter 16).

CHAPTER FOUR
# Revival and decline in Borno

Borno lies between the western and eastern Sudan and has close connections via the Fezzan with North Africa, and during the nineteenth century Borno was strongly influenced by developments in these three areas. Dan Fodio and the Sokoto caliphate had the greatest influence of the three, and their effect on Borno was probably as revolutionary as on the Hausa states. Another important influence was the Sanusiyya order which was established in North Africa and spread into the Sudan. It allied with the military power of Wadai to the east and created a challenge to Borno's control around Lake Chad.

## Political organisation

During the eighteenth century the Borno empire was more powerful than any other state of the central Sudan. Neither the divided Hausa states to the west, nor Wadai, a vassal (subject) state of Darfur, to the east, were strong enough to challenge Borno. The empire consisted of Borno proper, the small chieftaincies to the south and west, e.g. Bedde, the nomadic peoples, the vassal states of Kanem, Zinder, and Bagirmi and the Hausa states of Kano, Katsina and Zaria which were independent apart from having to pay annual tribute. Borno proper, the heart of the empire and home of the Kanuri, was ruled directly by administrators responsible to the Mai. Areas other than tributary states were governed through their own chiefs, but they were supervised by a Kanuri resident.

The Mai of Borno was regarded as semi-divine. There was an elaborate court ritual and the Mai was hardly ever seen; he gave audience hidden from view. Because he had to remain in hiding most of the time, he took little part in practical politics, and spent his time in study, excessive religious devotion, or in his harem. However, although he always remained hidden in peacetime, he did come out of

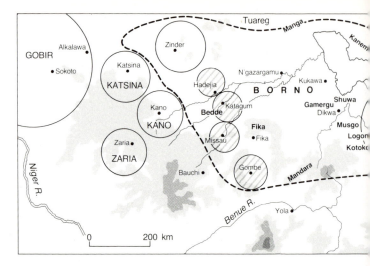

8  *Borno and its neighbours before the jihad.*

hiding when the empire was in danger and used his wide powers to save the empire.

The Mai governed through a State Council of Twelve, made up of the nobility and Kokenawa (administrators). The nobility held military titles which gave them responsibility for certain parts of the empire. They lived in the capital, not in the areas they were responsible for where they might encourage rebellion against the Mai. Administration, tax collection, the raising of military levies, and supervision of local chiefs, were done by the Kokenawa, either the Kambe (freeborn commoners) or Kachela (slaves). Commanders of the army were titled nobles, but officers and lesser ranks were Kachela.

The high court of twelve judges presided over by the Mainin Kanendi (Chief Justice and second in rank to the Mai) sat in the capital. Judgements of local magistrates (Mallamai) could be appealed in the high court.

Because of this political organisation Borno was very stable—the Sefawa dynasty ruled uninterruptedly for one thousand years. Succession disputes were few and, once in power, the Mai was unlikely to be challenged. The Kokenawa, who in practice governed Borno, could be promoted, transferred, demoted or executed on the orders of the Mai and State Council, so they were powerless to rebel. The system was strengthened by the Kanuri idea of a centralised state and loyalty to the Mai.

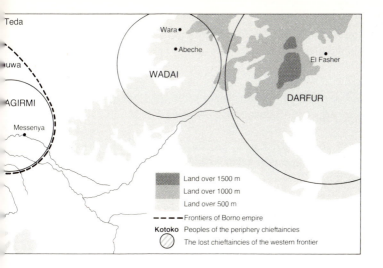

Other kingdoms to the east were also organised much like Borno. The Kolak of Wadai and Mbang of Bagirmi held a similar position to the Mai.

## Borno and the Sokoto jihad

Borno had tried to keep the Hausa states divided and weak. The Sokoto jihad aimed to unite these states into a strong caliphate, thus weakening Borno. Borno was weakened not only by the expansion of the caliphate in the west, but also by Wadai in the east:

1 *Kano, Katsina, Zaria*
An army sent by the Mai to aid the ruling chiefs against the jihadists was defeated and the three states became emirates of the caliphate.

2 *Hadejia, Katagum, Missau and Gombe*
A number of leaders, among them the Fulani mallams Gwani Muktar and Ibrahim Zaki, led rebellions in these western chieftaincies and founded emirates.

3 *Borno proper*
Muktar, having received a flag from dan Fodio, attacked Borno proper and sacked Birni Gazargamu, the capital, in about 1808. The Mai fled to Kanem.

### 4　*Zinder*

Because the jihadists were causing such confusion in Borno, Zinder declared its independence.

### 5　*Wadai*

Wadai, led by Kolak Sabun, also took advantage of Borno's weakness, conquering Bagirmi and invading Kanem.

No longer undisputed master of the central Sudan, Borno was being crushed between two great expanding powers, the caliphate from the west and Wadai from the east.

But at this stage an important development took place. Mai Ahmad called upon al-Kanami, a scholar of Borno, to take command and rescue the state from the jihadists.

## Al-Kanami

Al-Kanami, like dan Fodio, was really a Muslim scholar, who came from an influential family in Kanem. He had spent some time in the Fezzan because it was his mother's homeland, and his father, who was also a scholar, had taught there. Al-Kanami had been on the hajj and had lived for long periods in Egypt and Arabia. He had married into royalty in Kanem, and was friendly with the large Shuwa Arab scholar class in the Lake Chad region.

When Muktar took the capital of Borno, Mai Ahmad asked al-Kanami to rescue Borno from danger. Al-Kanami retook the capital and killed Muktar. When Ahmad died he was succeeded by his son Dunama, who was driven from the capital in 1811 by another Fulani mallam and flag bearer, Ibrahim Zaki. Like his father, Mai Dunama turned to al-Kanami, and offered him half the revenues of the provinces Zaki had taken if he would take control of the army and drive Zaki out of them. Al-Kanami accepted, and drove the Fulani from Borno proper, forcing Zaki to return to his emirate of Katagum.

Al-Kanami was the hero of Borno. He insisted that his followers should show the greatest respect for the Mai, the court ritual went on as before, and the Mai controlled the nobility. But the real power behind the throne was al-Kanami. He was like a prime minister and the king had to take his advice, because he was chief justice and army commander. To increase his own influence he surrounded himself with Shuwa advisers and raised the Kambe and Kachela in the military and civil administration at the expense of the nobility. He

*Al-Kanami, from a drawing by the British traveller, Major Dixon Denham.*

also had a large revenue from the provinces according to his agreement with Dunama, and enjoyed the complete loyalty of his Kanembu soldiers who settled with him in Borno. Al-Kanami took no title and was known as the Shehu until his death in 1837.

The Sokoto jihadists had said the Mai allowed non-Muslim practices and persecuted Fulani Muslims and that was why they attacked Borno. Al-Kanami replied that though Borno was not perfect it was a Muslim state and the Fulani were really seeking power and wealth and only pretending to be fighting for Islam. Al-Kanami himself showed that Borno was not a traditionalist state by carrying out Islamic reforms (like Bello in Sokoto). He enforced Islamic law, tightened control over the Kokenawa administrators and expanded education, so that by 1850 two to three thousand people were studying in the capital. In 1814 he built his own capital, Kukawa, which became the largest city of the kingdom. Borno now had two capitals: (1) the *ceremonial*, inhabited by the Mai and nobility, and (2) the *administrative*, controlled by the Shehu and Shuwa. This symbolised the widening division in Borno society between the ceremonial (Mai) and the administrative (Kanami).

**Why the jihad failed**

1 The Fulani nomads came from the western chieftaincies, and both Muktar and Zaki found it impossible to keep their forces together after the conquest of Borno proper. The nomads returned to their homes after an early victory.

2 While in Hausaland the jihadists were mainly nomads and scholars, in Borno the Shuwa nomads fought against it and the scholars, mainly Shuwa, Kanembu and Kanuri, also remained loyal to the Mai; this left the movement without solid support or intelligent direction. The loyalty of the Shuwa was very important for like the Fulani they were nomads, scholars and warriors.

3 The Kanuri political system was very strong. While the Hausa peasants often did not care who they supported, the Kanuri remained loyal, and there were no rivals or discontented groups to take advantage of the Mai's weakness.

4 Hausaland produced no leader of the military and administrative qualities of al-Kanami, whose reforms quickly removed possible causes of discontent.

Al-Kanami was only part successful in his efforts to recreate the Borno empire of the eighteenth century. He reconquered Zinder, Kanem and Bagirmi, but, after an unsuccessful invasion of the caliphate, he recognised Fulani sovereignty over the western chieftaincies in 1826 in order to gain peace on Borno's western frontier. After this the caliphate and Borno remained at peace, but were still hostile and suspicious of each other.

In Borno, as in Hausaland, the jihad transferred power from secular (non-religious) to religious leadership and from one ethnic group to another: from Sarkin to Emir, and Hausa to Fulani in Hausaland; from Mai to Shehu, and Kanuri to Shuwa Arab in Borno. In Borno the jihad created two leaders which divided the society and weakened the kingdom, while Wadai was becoming more and more powerful.

## Internal divisions in Borno

The divisions caused by the two leaders in Borno led to civil wars in 1819 and 1846. Mai Dunama (1808-19) had always resented the power of the Shehu even though al-Kanami was loyal to him. However, when vassal states began to send tribute to al-Kanami at Kukawa rather than to Dunama at Gazargamu, the Mai declared

*Borno warriors, the bodyguard of the Shehu, from a nineteenth-century drawing.*

war on the Shehu. Mai Dunama was killed in the battle that followed. Al-Kanami, however, did not make himself king, but arranged for Dunama's younger brother, Ibrahim, to become Mai. When Umar became Shehu after his father al-Kanami in 1837, he reduced Mai Ibrahim's revenues and used his power much more openly than his father had ever done. The Mai and new Shehu hated one another personally and the Kanuri nobility were jealous of the power of the wealthy Shuwa and Kokenawa.

There was a revolt in Zinder, and while the army were busy there, Mai Ibrahim opened secret negotiations with the ambitious Kolak of Wadai. Umar executed Mai Ibrahim, but the Kolak invaded Borno. The Wadai army, supported by the Kanuri nobility, burnt Kukawa, drove Umar into exile, and installed a puppet Mai, the seventeen-year-old son of Ibrahim, on the throne. However, the Kolak withdrew his army, in return for 10,000 silver dollars, and possibly for Umar's recognition of Wadai's supremacy over Bagirmi and Kanem. The young Mai, the last representative of the thousand-year-old Sefawa dynasty, was killed in battle. Umar was therefore the sole ruler of Borno.

41

Umar took over the position of Mai though he kept the title of Shehu. He kept the elaborate court ritual and remained in seclusion as the Sefawas had done before him. Power was entrusted to his Waziri (prime minister), al-Hajj Bashir, son of a Shuwa who had been adviser to al-Kanami. Bashir became the real power behind Umar just as al-Kanami and Umar had been behind the Mais. However, the nobility hated the dominating Shuwa and in particular the greedy and corrupt Bashir.

In 1883, Abd al-Rahman, the brother of Umar, gained the support of the nobility and led a revolt against Umar and the Shuwa. Bashir was executed and Umar was forced to give up the throne. But then Umar regained his throne through the loyalty of the army, and lived until he was very old and blind. When he died, three of his sons ruled in turn. Another Shuwa, Waziri Abd al-Karim, became very powerful and so from 1875-1900 the Shuwa were still the ruling class. However, the rivalry between Shuwa and Kanuri divided Borno society and was one of the main causes of the decline of Borno in the last half of the nineteenth century.

## External factors in the decline of Borno

Borno also faced serious problems outside its frontiers. It now had powerful neighbours to the east and west who wanted to control the trans-Saharan trade. The growing importance of Wadai was shown by the burning of Kukawa in 1846 just as the rise of the caliphate had been shown by the Fulani's capture of Borno's capital forty years earlier. In the early nineteenth century Borno lost its western vassals (Kano, Zaria, Katsina, frontier chieftaincies) to the Fulani; in the middle of the century it lost territory (Kanem and Bagirmi) to the Wadayans.

Trade was very important and a strong empire was needed to control trade. Thus the struggle for 'empire' between Wadai and Borno was also a struggle for control of trade. The brotherhoods played an important part in controlling trade; they were not only religious societies but also trading organisations.

During the eighteenth century Borno had been the meeting point of the two greatest trade routes of the central Sudan. The Saharan caravan route led from Borno through the Teda country and Fezzan to Tripoli. Slaves were exchanged with the Tripolitanians for luxuries and firearms, and wheat was exchanged for salt with the Teda. (A European traveller in the 1850s described how he travelled to the

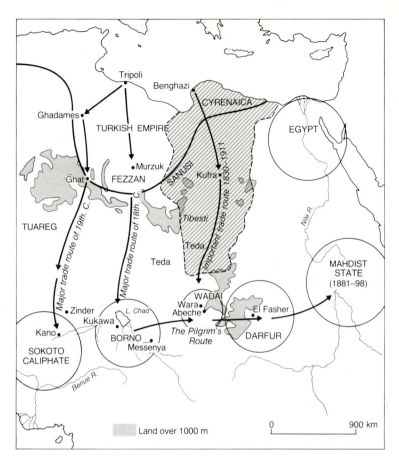

9  Saharan trade routes of the central Sudan.

central Sudan in a salt caravan of 3,000 camel loads.) The Mai usually married a Teda wife to remain on good terms with the people who lived along the route and were responsible for the safety of the caravans.

Borno also lay in the middle of the pilgrim route between Kano and Darfur. Darfur copper was exported to Nupe, and Lake Chad potash to Hausaland and to Bida where it was used in the glassmaking industry. Kola nuts were exported from Kano to Darfur and the area north of the Sahara.

The Fulani invasion ruined trade in Borno and so al-Kanami had to restore Borno's position as the leading trading power. He was born and brought up at the important caravan stopping point of

Murzuk in North Africa and he used his connections in the Fezzan to get the caravans moving again. But, although Kukawa became a busy commercial centre attracting fifteen to twenty thousand traders on market days, Borno never regained its eighteenth-century monopoly of trade for two reasons.

1 The Kano-Tripoli route became the major caravan route of the early nineteenth century, and Zinder, on this route, became a very important vassal of the Borno empire. But Umar did not remain friendly with the Teda, and Zinder revolted, so Borno's commercial position declined. The Shuwa families used to make their fortunes in currency speculation (dealing with money), so the value of the Maria Theresa dollar changed from day to day. Traders began to prefer the Kano market where the state maintained a stable currency.

2 During Umar's reign Wadai became a serious trading rival. Kolak Sabun, 1803-13, opened a new caravan route through Teda country to Benghazi, and trade later expanded rapidly during the political stability provided by three great, long-reigning Kolaks (al-Sharif 1835-58, Ali 1858-74, and Yusuf 1874-98). The Kolaks also established industry in Wadai to attract traders. For, while the leather workers, weavers and smiths of Kano attracted traders, Wadai, like Borno, lacked artisans. There were artisans in Bagirmi, and so Kolak Sabun in 1806 and Kolak Ali in 1870 invaded Messenya, capital of Bagirmi. They captured thousands of artisans, who were taken to Wadai and given special privileges in the royal court.

The Sanusiyya became the major religious brotherhood of Wadai under Kolak al-Sharif, who was converted to the order before he became king in 1835. In the 1840s the Sanusiyya headquarters was established in Cyrenaica. The zawiyas or lodges of the order spread through the oases of the Fezzan, Borku and Tibesti, and the Teda were converted by the 1870s. In 1874 there was a dispute about who should succeed to the throne of Wadai. The head of the Sanusiyya was called to decide and chose his own candidate—Kolak Yusuf.

By about 1875 the Sanusiyya had created a unique trading and religious 'empire' suited to the desert people it controlled from Cyrenaica in the north to Bagirmi in the south. The zawiyas acted as local government centres, carrying out the orders of the Grand Sanusi. The nomadic chiefs were under the authority of the zawiyas, who were responsible for law and order. Wadai, under Kolak Yusuf, was like a vassal state of the 'empire'. The Sanusiyya financed its activities through trade, and every zawiya head was a trader, so a flourishing caravan trade was vital to the brotherhood. The Wadai-Benghazi route, hardly known in the early nineteenth century, became the most profitable of all the caravan routes by the late nineteenth century because of the co-operation of the Teda and Wadayans under Sanusiyya leadership.

Brotherhoods and empires were closely related in the central Sudan. In Borno, possibly because of the Fulani connection with the Qadiriyya, the Mai and Kanuri belonged to the Tijaniyya. The Sanusiyya, who spread around Lake Chad with the rise of Wadai, made it a policy to free slaves, teach them in the zawiyas of the Fezzan and Cyrenaica, and send them back inland to establish zawiyas as trader-missionaries. In Bagirmi and Kanem the zawiyas strengthened the position of the Wadai.

The Wadai invasion of Borno in 1846 was the beginning of the decline of Borno and the rise of Wadai. The crisis of 1846 had been on the one hand an internal struggle between different groups for control of Borno, and on the other an external struggle between Borno and Wadai for control around Lake Chad. Between 1846 and 1890 Wadai steadily gained economic and political control of Kanem and Bagirmi with the aid of the Sanusiyya. Borno, in 1800 the most powerful state of the central Sudan, was by 1890 little more than a small state between two empires, the Sokoto caliphate and Wadai.

# Changing trade patterns—the western Sudan and the Sahara

## The Sahara and Atlantic trades

During the nineteenth century the pattern of West Africa's international trade changed rapidly, in two ways. Firstly, the camel caravan trade across the Sahara declined sharply, and finally stopped completely during the first two decades of the twentieth century. The Atlantic trade, which by 1800 was already much more important than the Sahara trade, became steadily more important after 1800. Secondly, the Atlantic trade changed from being largely a trade in slaves to being largely a trade in vegetable oils, because European nations suppressed the slave trade for a mixture of humanitarian and economic reasons.

### Caravan trade routes

At the beginning of the nineteenth century, the caravan trade across the Sahara had become concentrated on four main routes:
1   One began in Morocco and ran through Taodeni to Timbuctu on the Niger, which was the main trade centre.
2   A second began in Tripoli, and ran through Ghadames and the oasis of Air to the Hausa states of Katsina and Kano, which were the main trade centres.
3   A third route also began in Tripoli, then ran through the oasis of Murzuk in Fezzan to the kingdom of Borno and eastern Hausaland. Birni was the main trade centre.
4   A fourth ran from eastern Tripoli (or Cyrenaica) through Kufra to the kingdoms of Wadai and Darfur. Wara and Abeche were the main trade centres.

From these trade centres other routes ran through the savanna to towns and cities of the forest areas to the south. (See the sketch map on page 47). Particularly important junctions of trade were at Timbuctu, Katsina, Kano, Kuka, Wara and Abeche just south of the

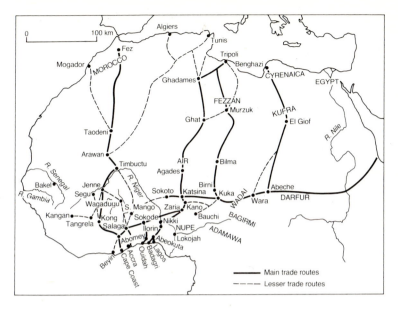

10    Trans-Saharan trade routes.

desert, Jenne, Salaga and Zaria further south in the savanna, and Kumasi, Abomey and Abeokuta in the forest zone. There were further routes from these forest towns to the coast.

Some of these routes were busier than others. Throughout the eighteenth and at the beginning of the nineteenth centuries, there was more trade along the two routes from Tripoli to Hausaland and Borno than along the Morocco-Timbuctu and Cyrenaica-Kufra-Wadai routes. The Tripoli-Ghat-Kano route was busier than the Tripoli-Fezzan-Birni route, according to the European explorers of the period (Denham, Clapperton, Richardson and Barth). By the 1880s, trade along the Morocco-Timbuctu route and the Tripoli route had almost stopped, but there was still quite a lot of trade on the Kufra-Wadai route. By 1900, the traditional caravan trade had ended on all the routes except the Wadai-Kufra route where it continued for another fifteen years or so.

Bringing goods to the Sudanese and forest ends of the routes never stopped completely, though it suffered changes in fortune. By the beginning of the nineteenth century very few goods were exported northwards from Ghana, Ivory Coast or Guinea to Timbuctu, and beyond to Morocco and Tunis, and trade declined steadily. By the 1860s, if not earlier, trade in those areas had become mainly a one-way affair. The produce was sent mainly from north to south, and in the Senegal and Gambia area from east to west; there was little traffic in the reverse directions, and the regions of Timbuctu, Walata and Jenne were no longer centres for trade going to and from all directions. The two-way traffic along the north-eastern routes from Ghana through Togo continued throughout the century, and during the first half of the nineteenth century it was particularly important, and trade between Hausaland and Salaga reached its peak during the nineteenth century. This trade has been continuing to this day, the only difference being that, instead of bullocks and asses, lorries are used to transport goods.

## Some commercial centres of the western Sudan

Timbuctu, which had been the main commercial and educational centre of the region of the Niger bend in the sixteenth century, had declined by the beginning of the nineteenth century. The French traveller, Caillié, who entered Timbuctu in 1837, reported that he

*The city of Timbuctu in 1837, an engraving based on a sketch prepared by the French traveller, René Caillié.*

found it 'neither so large nor so populous' as he had been led to expect. Barth, who visited Timbuctu in 1853, reported that it did recover some of its former position as a trading centre in the 1840s; he estimated its population at 10,000. Though this figure is probably exaggerated, it is only a fraction of the population in the days of Leo Africanus in the sixteenth century.

This very small recovery did not last and Timbuctu steadily declined throughout the second half of the nineteenth century. When Félix Dubois, a French writer, entered it in 1894, Timbuctu was a ghost of its former self. Its role as a trading centre for goods from the north and south had long ceased, and Dubois found in its once famous market, where traders from Morocco and Egypt, and from Ghana and Hausaland had met, only 'women with little baskets, little calabashes and little mats, selling insignificant little things, red, green, white, drab and black spices and vegetables for infinitely little money, just as in any, no matter what little market, in no matter what little town of the Sudan'.

In Hausaland, Katsina was the main commercial centre at the beginning of the nineteenth century. But the town never recovered from the wars of the Fulani jihad. From about 1815 onwards, Kano became the main commercial and industrial town of Hausaland. The population of Kano was estimated by the British explorer, Clapperton, who visited it in 1824, at between 30,000 and 40,000. Barth, a German who was there in 1851, estimated it at 30,000, but added that the figure doubled itself during the main caravan season between January and April each year. The markets of Kano were reported by both travellers to be crowded 'from sunrise to sunset every day', and some of the traders came from as far as Tripoli in the north and modern Ghana and Togo in the south. The nineteenth-century European explorers were particularly impressed that Kano was not only a market town and a trading centre, but also an industrial centre. As Barth put it, 'the great advantage of Kano is that commerce and manufactures go hand in hand, and that almost every family has its share in them'. Its main products were the famous Kano cloth woven on looms from locally grown cotton and usually dyed blue, sandals, and tanned hides. These products, particularly the cotton goods, were exported as far north as Ghat, Fezzan, Tripoli and Morocco, as far west as Timbuctu and the shores of the Atlantic, and as far south as Kumasi and Lagos. Towards the end of the nineteenth century, Kano, unlike Timbuctu, lost only its role as entrepot: but it remained as it has been ever since, an important commercial and industrial centre of northern Nigeria.

In the Chad area, the old capital of Borno, Birni Ngazargamu, was destroyed in the Fulani wars and Kuka or Kukawa, the town built by al-Kanami in 1841, had, by the middle of the nineteenth century, become the main commercial and trading centre. It supplied the states of Bagirmi, Bauchi and Adamawa with goods brought from North Africa.

## Decline of the traditional trade

At the beginning of the nineteenth century trade with the Sahara and North Africa was still going on in traditional products, such as exports of gold, ivory, gum, 'morocco' leather, ostrich feathers and slaves, and imports of North African goods like salt, clothing, carpets and horses and European textiles and hardware. However, this traditional trade declined steadily throughout the nineteenth century. By the 1820s no gold was being exported northwards along the Hausa-Borno-Tripoli routes, and, as Barth found when he visited Timbuctu, only a very little gold was going northwards to Morocco. Exports of ivory and gum northwards also became very small. However, goods were still sent southwards or westwards to the Atlantic coast. Indeed, in the nineteenth century the main exports northwards were kola nuts, Kano cloth and above all, slaves and ostrich feathers. The demand for kola nuts in particular throughout the western Sudan and the Sahara kept trade busy on the route from Ghana to Hausaland.

The demand for slaves in North Africa and in the Muslim states of the Middle East also continued throughout the nineteenth century, but the number of slaves exported from the western Sudan was relatively small, not more than an average of about 10,000 per year during the first half of the century. Of these, about 5,000 were exported to Tripoli, and from there about 2,500 were re-exported to Turkey. Slaves were practically the only export to the north at the end of the nineteenth century and during the first ten years of the twentieth century. The slaves were exchanged mainly for guns and ammunition which began to be imported in large quantities into the Sudan for the first time.

The Trans-Saharan trade actually increased after 1840 to meet a sudden European demand for ostrich feathers. The trade reached a peak in 1875, when it was worth about £1½ million. However, the European demand for ostrich feathers was short-lived, and so the boom in trans-Saharan trade was short-lived too. After 1875 the steady decline in trans-Saharan trade resumed.

# Decline of the trans-Saharan caravan trade

The decline in trans-Saharan trade was due to three main factors.

## 1   The changing political conditions in the Sahara and western Sudan

Trade depends largely on political conditions. The more unstable and disturbed the area was politically, the less trade there was. After the overthrow of the famous Songhai empire by the Moroccans at about the end of the sixteenth century, there was rivalry for the political control of that area among the Moroccans, the Songhai, the Tuareg and the Fulani. This resulted in chaos and insecurity in the region of the Niger bend throughout the seventeenth and eighteenth centuries. This chaos continued, particularly in the western Sahara, during the nineteenth century and so trade along the western routes steadily moved to the more stable eastern routes leading from Tripoli.

The importance of the Tripoli-Hausa routes during the first half of the nineteenth century was due to the establishment of law and order in most of the regions of Hausaland—especially in the Sokoto half of the empire—by the new Fulani rulers. The Tripoli-Fezzan-Borno route became important during the first thirty years of the nineteenth century, when the Karamanli dynasty of Tripoli and al-Kanami of Borno were able to maintain peace and order throughout the route. However, with the overthrow of the Karamanli dynasty in 1835 by the Turks, and the wars in southern Tripoli, and with the death of al-Kanami in Borno in 1837, the caravan trade on that route declined.

Farther to the east, however, the Cyrenaica-Tripoli route enjoyed more stable conditions throughout the nineteenth century than had ever been known before. This was mainly due to the expansion of Wadai in the Sudan during the first half of the century, and the spread of the Sanusi order from Cyrenaica, along the route of Kufra and Wadai, during the second half of the century. In 1905 the great French travellers and scholars, Gautier and Chudeau, saw large caravans still leaving Benghazi, the main town of Cyrenaica, for Wadai, whereas traffic on all the other three routes had ceased. The French occupation of Wadai, Tibesti and Borku between 1906 and 1914, and the Italian occupation of Cyrenaica in 1911-12, finally broke the last of the commercial links between the Mediterranean, the western Sudan and the Guinea coast.

## 2   The abolition of the trans-Saharan and trans-Atlantic slave trades

The trans-Atlantic slave trade was legally abolished by most of the

European powers between 1807 and 1820. The attack on the slave trade across the Sahara and the Mediterranean, however, was not begun until 1840. In theory, by 1857 the slave trade had been abolished throughout the Ottoman empire and the Barbary states except in Morocco. In practice, however, the trade went on illegally until the Italian and French occupation of Tripoli and Morocco during the last years of the century. Partly to see that the trans-Saharan slave trade was stopped and partly to promote trade, the British Government established two vice-consular posts, at Murzuk in Fezzan in 1843 and at Ghadames in 1850, and maintained them till 1860 and 1861 respectively. There is no doubt that the anti slave-trade pressure by the British from 1840 onwards greatly reduced the trade in slaves, and helped to end the traffic on the Tripoli-Ghat-Hausa and the Tripoli-Murzuk routes during the last forty years of the nineteenth century.

However, European nations should not take all the credit for suppression of the trans-Saharan slave trade. Sidi Muhammad al-Sanusi, founder of the Sanusiyya Brotherhood, began a programme of buying and freeing slaves from the trans-Saharan caravans. Some of the freed slaves settled around his headquarters in Cyrenaica. Others, after conversion and training, returned to the central Sudan as Muslim missionaries, in much the same way as slaves liberated in Sierra Leone by the British squadron became Christian, and returned to their homeland as Christian missionaries.

### 3    The European advance into the western Sudan from the coast

The Europeans had originally wanted to gain direct control over the sources of the supply of gold which came across the Sahara to the North African countries. The Europeans made a few unsuccessful attempts (mainly from the Senegal and Gambia regions) to push inland in the sixteenth and seventeenth centuries, and then decided to stay on the coast. They did not even know until 1830 that the rivers which flowed into the Bight of Biafra together formed the mouth of the Niger. If the Europeans had stayed on the Guinea coast, the overland trade routes would most probably have remained in use. From 1783, however, a private scientific society, the African Association, and, from 1805 onwards, the British and French Governments, organised expeditions into the interior. By 1830, the entire western Sudan and the Sahara, the Senegal, the Gambia, and the west coast had been explored and reported on by Europeans approaching from North Africa. The problem of the mouth of the

Niger, and of its connection with the Nile of Egypt, which had haunted geographers and historians for well over a thousand years, had also been solved.

The exploration of the Senegal and the Niger rivers raised great hopes among traders and imperialists in Europe. As one of them, Laird, wrote, on hearing of the solution to the Niger problem, 'The long sought for highway into central Africa was at length found. To the merchant it offered a boundless field for enterprise, to the manufacturer an extensive market for his goods'. The discovery of the mouth of the Niger came at the same time as the abolition and suppression of the trans-Atlantic slave trade, when new commodities and new markets had to be found to replace the lost ones. The Europeans therefore tried to fill this gap by trading along the trails on the Senegal and the Niger left by the explorers. Between 1817 and 1840, for example, the French tried to establish plantations along the Senegal, and between 1818 and 1821 they built forts on the River Senegal at Bakel, Dagone and Richard-Toll. In 1832 the British and the Americans also each sent out an expedition to travel up the Niger and set up trading stations on its banks 'for the purpose of collecting the various products of the country'. Other expeditions by British merchants followed in 1836 and 1840; and in 1841, the abolitionists (led by Fowell Buxton) persuaded the British government to send a carefully prepared expedition to establish legitimate trade and set up experimental farms in order to overthrow the slave trade.

All these efforts by the French, the British, and the Americans to push up the Senegal and the Niger failed, because of the opposition of the African rulers, middlemen, and traders, and above all because of the high death rate of the crews of the ships. The British Government thought that the climate of the west coast and the lower Niger basin was so deadly that from the late forties onwards they turned northwards to the Sahara and established two vice-consular posts. The now famous Richardson-Barth expedition was then sent from Tripoli to Borno and Timbuctu in 1849.

However, in the 1850s the French successfully advanced from the Guinea coast inland up the Senegal and the British advanced up the Niger. Mainly as a result of the energy and drive of General Louis Faidherbe, the governor of the Senegal from 1854 to 1861 and 1863 to 1865, the French had gained full control of the Senegal River by 1865. French traders followed their armies, and all trade was soon going from the regions of Timbuctu down the Senegal to the coast instead of towards the north. Only the strong resistance of al-Hajj Umar (see chapter 2), in the 1850s, and the defeat of the French in Europe by the

Germans in 1870 temporarily halted French political expansion inland, but this was resumed in 1879. Four years later they occupied Bamako on the Niger and pushed on to Timbuctu, which they captured in 1894.

The British advanced up the Niger from the 1850s onwards. Baikie, the commander of the expedition sent up the Niger in 1854, discovered that by taking regular doses of quinine, Europeans could become immune to malarial fever which had been their greatest hazard. The British Government agreed not only to subsidise the development of trade up the Niger, but also to send warships against African coastal traders and middlemen who were stopping the development of inland trade. British merchants led by Laird began, from 1857 on, to establish trading stations up the Niger, and by 1859 had reached the confluence of the Niger and the Benue and established a station at Lokoja. By the late 1860s five British companies were operating on the Niger. Rivalry soon broke out among the British traders. But this ended in 1879 when Goldie Taubman (later Sir George Goldie) united all of them in the United Africa Company, which was given a charter in 1886 under the name of the Royal Niger Company. The activities of this company won northern Nigeria for the British during the rivalry among European powers to gain colonies in Africa in the last twenty years of the century.

Once European goods began to reach the markets of Hausaland, and, from the late fifties onwards, at cheaper prices and in larger quantities, it was obvious that the caravan trade was bound to collapse. The camel was no match for the steamship. The increased supply of European manufactured goods in the interior from the late 1850s onwards, and the occupation of the entire western Sudan as well as the Sahara by the French and the British finally put an end to the northern or Saharan trade routes that had been used for well over 2,000 years.

# PART TWO

# Coastal states in the nineteenth century

CHAPTER SIX

# Changing trade patterns—the coast and the Atlantic

## The suppression of the Atlantic slave trade

The British action in abolishing the Atlantic slave trade ranks with the Islamic revolutions of the western Sudan and the later conquest and partition of Africa by European powers as one of the three most important events in the nineteenth-century history of West Africa. The end of the slave trade brought revolutionary changes in the social structure and economic activities of many African states. It led to the establishment of Sierra Leone and Liberia, whose influence extended far beyond their borders. The replacement of the slave trade by the palm oil trade brought Europeans steadily into the political life of the coastal kingdoms, and led finally to conquest and partition.

### Why it was suppressed

Britain abolished the Atlantic slave trade for both economic and humanitarian reasons, because of the industrial revolution and the evangelical revival.

In the eighteenth century the British West Indies were the most valuable possessions of the British Empire, because they produced sugar for Europe and America. Sugar was a luxury food of high price which brought large profits to British slave plantation owners in the West Indies. However, in the last quarter of the eighteenth century the French West Indies began to produce cheaper sugar, and Europe was less interested in the declining sugar trade of the West Indies and more interested in the new cotton and palm oil trades which supported the industrial revolution taking place in England after 1750.

The triangular trade was out of date by 1800. The British industrialists wanted ships to go directly to the USA and return with raw cotton, and wanted ships loaded with British manufactured cotton to go to West Africa and return directly with palm oil. Raw cotton was needed for Britain's new textile factories and palm oil was needed to lubricate factory machinery. The slave trade interfered with the palm oil trade in West Africa. Since European slave-traders paid higher prices than oil-traders, African kings often made oil-traders wait as long as a year for a cargo, while they rushed to meet the slave-traders' requirements. This pushed up the cost of oil which the industrialists in Britain had to pay, and it reduced their profits. However, if the slave trade was abolished, then the price of oil would drop, and industrialists in Britain would make higher profits. Also, the industrialists wanted the slave trade to be abolished for another reason. They wanted Africans to labour in Africa at harvesting and preparing palm oil for the factories of Britain, rather than to be slaves working in sugar plantations in the West Indies. Moreover, West African farmers could become customers for British manufactured goods. In other words, trade *with* Africans was now considered to be more profitable than trade *in* Africans.

So British industrialists had strong economic motives for the abolition of the slave trade. But it was by no means certain that they would be able to force their policy on the British Government in the early nineteenth century, for the sugar plantation owners and slave traders were still powerful in the political parties. However, in the last quarter of the eighteenth century an evangelical revival took place in Britain. There was a new concern among many British Christians for the welfare of all mankind, and this new spirit of humanitarianism supported the industrialists. Influenced by evangelicalism, many British people began to regard slavery and the slave trade as evil.

**How it was suppressed**

The abolitionists, led by Granville Sharp, Thomas Clarkson and William Wilberforce, carried out a brilliant propaganda campaign which so aroused British public opinion that it made the British Parliament abolish the slave trade for British subjects in 1807. In 1833 another Act of Parliament abolished slavery itself in British possessions. These measures did not stop the Atlantic slave trade. Other nations rushed in to take over where the British left off, and between 1807 and 1845 the trade flourished as never before. However, the British Government, backed by industrialists, humanitarians and missionaries, was determined that the slave trade should end entirely. A British naval squadron was therefore stationed off the coast of West Africa to seize slave ships and take the slaves to Sierra Leone, where missionaries could teach them Christianity.

Unfortunately, the 'Preventive Squadron' had very limited success for many years. It did manage to free 150,000 slaves in the Atlantic and land them at Freetown, but this was only a small fraction of the two million Africans who were carried across the Atlantic as slaves in the nineteenth century. Indeed, in the 1830s the Atlantic slave trade was at its height, a quarter of a century after its abolition by Britain.

There are many reasons for this. The coastline was too long for the British Navy to patrol effectively. There were very many lagoons and creeks where slave ships could hide. There were few British warships available for the expensive patrols. But the main reason was the continuation of the trade by Portugal and Brazil, Spain, France and the USA. Brazil (which had won self-governing status from Portugal in 1822) was the main culprit. In the early nineteenth century Brazil expanded her coffee and sugar plantations and obtained vast numbers of African slaves to work in them. Spain developed sugar plantations in Cuba, also with African slaves. France and the USA had abolished the slave trade for their subjects at about the same time as British abolition, but they did little to enforce abolition. Both countries kept naval patrols in West Africa, but they were smaller than Britain's—French slave traders smuggled slaves into various countries in the Americas, and American slave traders took many thousands to the southern slave-owning states of the USA to supply labour for cotton, tobacco and sugar plantations.

The British Navy could, by law, only stop British ships. An important breakthrough came in the 1845 Anglo-Brazilian Treaty, which gave the British Navy the right to stop Brazilian slave ships. Thereafter, there was a definite decline in the Atlantic slave trade. However, even after 1845 the trade persisted on a fairly large scale. Smuggling of slaves into the Southern USA continued until the South's defeat in the American Civil War (1861-5) and the abolition of slavery in the USA by President Abraham Lincoln in 1863. The trade continued to Cuba until 1866.

**African resistance to abolition**

Between 1814 and 1850 the British Navy imposed treaties on various African kings along the west coast, giving it the right to seize slave ships while they were loading in port. The treaties were not very

*The British gun-boat* Teaser *(left) capturing the slaver* Abbot Devereux *off the West African coast in 1857.*

effective, because most kings ignored them. Ports such as Kalabari, Nembe and Ouidah, located on a mass of creeks with numerous exits, could still load the slave ships which slipped away to sea unnoticed.

Bonny (see Chapter 13) resisted enforced abolition because of national pride. Her leaders and people resented the way the British disregarded her sovereignty, seized ships, entered and bombarded the port, created puppet rulers, used naval action to defend British trouble makers, and overrode the authority of Bonny's courts. The British acted like this in Bonny not just because of opposition to slavery; they wanted to secure a privileged position for British oil traders as well. To Bonny the rights and wrongs of the trade in slaves became less important than the right of independence.

Dahomey refused to sign an anti-slave trade treaty with Britain. Unlike Bonny, which faced the open sea, Dahomey was in a position to refuse. The palace and capital were far inland, and the port of Ouidah was on a lagoon, so that the British squadron could not turn its guns on it either. The lesson of Lagos was not lost on Dahomey. The king of Lagos had signed a British treaty and banned the slave trade, but in spite of this he was the first ruler on the coast to lose his independence. This convinced Dahomey that a British treaty was the first step to subjugation.

### African support for abolition

It would be wrong to give Britain all the credit for suppressing the Atlantic slave trade. Africans also played their part, as did governments of other countries in Europe and the Americas. Some liberated ex-slaves took part in the abolitionist campaign in England.

One of them, Olaudah Equiano, an Igbo, pointed out in his autobiography in 1789 the profit British traders would make if they treated Africans as customers rather than goods. Ottobah Cugoano, a Fante ex-slave, in his *Thoughts and Sentiments on the Evil of Slavery* (1787) called upon the British to station a fleet in West Africa to suppress the slave trade.

In Africa itself there were abolitionists. Those African states and communities who found substitutes for the slave-trade were often as actively abolitionist as the British. Neither the people of the Ivory Coast nor the Kru boatmen of Liberia had ever engaged in the slave-trade to any degree, and supported abolition. Again, Calabar and the Cameroons, which were unable to compete with slave-trading Bonny, had never prospered on the export of slaves.

When the British began looking for palm oil, the Efik of Calabar quickly organised plantations for its production. Indeed Calabar was exporting palm oil before British abolition in 1807. Like Britain, Calabar found that the slave-trade interfered with the palm oil trade, and the Efik became vigorous abolitionists. They acted as informers to the British Navy in reporting the movement of slave ships. In 1843 they refused to supply a cargo of slaves to the French even though a French warship threatened to bombard Calabar.

In Sierra Leone a Muslim Mandinka scholar, Momodu Yeli, opposed slave-trading among his own Muslim brethren and the Christians of Freetown, and suffered persecution from both communities for his beliefs. Without his assistance the Freetown courts would have found it difficult to stop secret slave trading in the city.


## The rise of trade in vegetable oils

Though the Atlantic slave trade did not die easily, by about 1850 it was in serious decline. It was being replaced by 'legitimate commerce' – the term nineteenth-century Europeans used to describe the legal trade in goods rather than slaves. The illegal trade in slaves was replaced by legitimate trade in a wide range of exports, including goods which had been exported for centuries, such as gold from the Gold Coast, gum from Senegal and ivory from various parts of the forest zone. But the most important exports in legitimate trade were the new products, palm oil and groundnut oil.

The palm oil trade arose in the eighteenth century, before the abolition and suppression of the slave trade. In the nineteenth century it expanded to meet the greater demand for palm oil in the industrialising continents. As modern industry grew in Europe and North America, palm oil was needed not only to grease factory machines but also to lubricate new railway engines and to make soap and candles. The palm oil belt stretched from Sierra Leone to the Cameroons, though the most important producing area was east of Asante, comprising Dahomey, Yoruba and Igboland and Old Calabar. The Niger Delta came to be known as 'The Oil Rivers' because of its new concentration on exporting palm oil. The rapid expansion of the palm oil trade can be seen in the following table, which lists Britain's palm oil imports from West Africa, 1810-1855.

| 1810 | 1,000 tonnes (nearest thousand) |
| 1830 | 10,000 | (nearest ten thousand) |
| 1843 | 20,000 |
| 1853 | 30,000 |
| 1855 | 40,000 |

A similar economic revolution took place in the groundnut belt of Senegal and Gambia. Groundnut oil was needed for manufacturing cooking oil and soap. The expansion of the groundnut oil trade is seen in the figures of exports from Senegal. In the 1840s Senegal exported virtually no groundnut oil, but by the late 1880s it was exporting 29,000 tonnes annually.

The industrial revolution in Britain between 1760 and 1850, and the industrialisation of other European countries and the USA, could not have taken place without the West African trade in vegetable oils.

The change-over from trade in slaves to trade in vegetable oils along much of the West African coast was largely a response to changing European demands. However, the development of this new pattern of trade was mainly an African affair, carried out by Africans in independent African states. African achievement is seen in the creation of large plantations for palm oil and groundnut production, in the further growth of towns which handled the oil trade, in the expansion of palm oil-producing states like Dahomey and the emergence of new ones like Ibadan and Opobo, and in the rise of able 'new men'—traders and rulers of commoner or even slave origin —like Alali and Jaja in Bonny and Olomu and Nana in Ebrohimi.

The new economic pattern did not always bring improvement. One of the unexpected results of the suppression of the Atlantic slave trade and the expansion of 'legitimate' trade was an increase in the trade in slaves *within* West Africa. A new kind of slave trade developed in the palm oil belt because of the demand for abundant cheap labour to produce the palm oil. Palm oil production required huge gangs of men for harvesting and head porterage to the coast, and slave labour supplied this need most easily. Unfortunately, the increase in the slave trade in West Africa also led to an increase in war. Dahomey, in particular, raided the neighbouring Yoruba states to seize both palm oil-producing land and people who could be turned into slaves to grow the palm oil. The humanitarian abolitionists had not envisaged this.

Another unexpected result of the suppression of the slave trade and the rise of trade in vegetable oils was the increase in the amount of European political intervenion in West Africa. This prepared the way for the conquest of Africa at the end of the century. The abolitionists had not intended or foreseen this either. The main reason for French expansion into the interior of Senegal in the 1850s and 1860s during the governorship of Faidherbe had been to secure control of a much larger groundnut-producing area in the colony's hinterland.

British political intervention also tended to be economic in motive. At the coast, for example, Britain imposed a puppet king in Lagos in 1852 and made the city a British colony in 1862, partly to suppress the slave trade but largely to help British palm oil traders. British intervention in the Niger Delta, such as the making and unmaking of kings in Bonny between 1836 and 1861, had been for the same reason. In the interior, the British push up the Niger was spearheaded by the palm oil traders Laird and Goldie. Goldie's career provides a clear example of a trader playing a prominent part in Europe's economic and political invasion of Africa.

It should be noted that the Europeans always claimed they were liberators freeing Africans from slave-trading and slavery, even when they were seeking economic profit.

## African and European roles in the slave trade

Slavery and the slave trade are still emotional subjects. Europeans and Americans often feel guilty about their countries' participation in the slave trade; but, as an excuse, they point out the humanitarian role of such men as Wilberforce and Lincoln. On the other hand, Africans are also ashamed of the role they played and tend to blame all the ills of their continent on the 'European-sponsored' slave trade. They defend themselves by saying that if Europeans had not bought slaves, Africans would not have sold them.

The slave trade was a crime committed by humanity against humanity. But to apportion blame or praise between European and African or between one nation and another is not the historian's task.

## CHAPTER SEVEN

# Collapse of the Oyo empire and Yoruba wars

West African states are often divided into two groups according to geography and culture. There are the states of the western Sudan in the area of savanna vegetation and attached to Islam, particularly following the Islamic revolutions of the nineteenth century. There are the coastal kingdoms situated in the tropical forest and traditionalist in their religious beliefs and organisation of society. Both areas were influenced in the nineteenth century by many of the same historical events. The best examples are the Yoruba states, usually classed as coastal, although some were situated in the savannah and some in the forest. Like the western Sudan generally, the Yoruba country was profoundly influenced by the Islamic revolution in the Hausa states inspired by dan Fodio and northern Yoruba areas became part of the Sokoto caliphate. At the same time the Yoruba, like other coastal peoples, were greatly influenced by European activities on the coast, the change from the slave trade to palm oil trade, the availability of guns and powder, and the missionary and cultural influences from Sierra Leone and Liberia, Europe and America.

## Decline of the Oyo empire

In 1800 many Yoruba people lived in the Oyo empire, bounded on the north by the Niger, on the east by Benin, on the south by the Gulf of Guinea and on the west by Dahomey. This empire had begun to crumble in the late eighteenth century and it collapsed in the early nineteenth, because of external pressure from Sokoto, the revolts of ambitious vassals, the loss of its commercial supremacy, and weaknesses in its system of government. At the head of the Oyo political system was the Alafin or king. He was considered semi-divine, but in practice political power was shared with the Oyo Mesi or Council of Notables, comprising seven prominent lineage chiefs of the capital. The Oyo Mesi acted as a check upon the Alafin's powers in several ways. They were appointed by their lineages, not by the

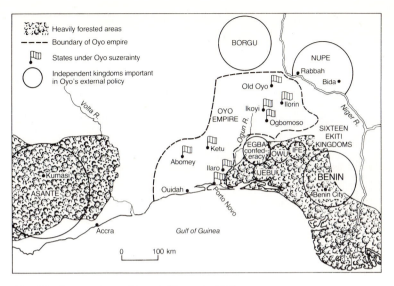

*11    The Oyo empire and its neighbours in 1800.*

Alafin. They shared judicial power with the Alafin in the capital. They acted as mediators for provincial and vassal chiefs in their dealings with the Alafin. Finally, the army was responsible not to the Alafin but to the Oyo Mesi who appointed and promoted its officers.

This system prevented the Alafin from being an all-powerful dictator. However, it gave too much power to the Oyo Mesi, especially to their leader, the Bashorun or prime minister. The Bashorun was high priest controlling all the cults except Sango and Ifa, and he could proclaim that the ancestors and heaven had lost confidence in the Alafin and could order him to commit suicide. Also, in earlier centuries the Alafin used to train his chosen son, the Aremo or heir apparent, in the art of government so that the succession might pass to him smoothly and without dispute. However, the succession rule was altered so that the Aremo did not succeed but died with the Alafin, after which the Oyo Mesi chose a successor from the number of candidates. This increased the Bashorun's power since he could now virtually choose his own favourite for the throne. Ambitious Bashoruns passed over the strong and pushful and chose weak, poor candidates. Furthermore, since the Bashorun could choose the Alafin, he became increasingly tempted to command the death of a troublesome monarch. For example, in the late eighteenth century, Bashorun Gaha raised five Alafins to the throne and

*Wooden figures from a shrine to Shango, the Yoruba God of Thunder, at Ede. Some of the figures are surmounted by the double axe motif, thought to represent the thunderbolts hurled down from the sky by Shango.*

destroyed four of them, while he and his family ruled despotically and unchecked, until at last Alafin Abiodun overthrew and killed him. Taking advantage of civil war, the Egba under Lishabi 'the Liberator' proclaimed their independence.

Alafin Abiodun, who ruled from 1774 to 1789, proved a strong ruler and his reign was remembered as a golden age, but decay set in again after his death. Six Alafins followed one another in rapid succession, an Oyo invasion of Nupe met disastrous defeat, and Dahomey assaulted Ketu, the westernmost Yoruba district, without fear of the imperial Oyo army.

## Collapse of the empire

In 1817 the final blow fell. It was delivered by Afonja, a slave-born child of the royal family who had risen to become Kakanfo, or commander of the Oyo army. Afonja was unsuccessful in his claim to be Alafin, so when he discovered a plot against his life by the Alafin he raised a revolt in Ilorin, a town founded by his great-grandfather. If the empire had been strongly united, Afonja would have been quickly suppressed, but important chiefs sympathised with him.

Mallam Alimi, Afonja's Fulani adviser, encouraged warriors from dan Fodio's jihadist armies in the north, as well as certain Muslim Yoruba from Oyo itself, to come to the Kakanfo's support. In addition thousands of Hausa and Fulani slaves in the empire revolted and fled to Ilorin, where they swelled Afonja's rebel army. Ojo, the only surviving son of Bashorun Gaha, supported the Alafin and led an army to attack Afonja. However, few were anxious to see the empire again ruled by a man from the family of Gaha. The Onikoyi of Ikoyi, the largest provincial town of the empire, marched with Ojo on Ilorin but changed sides in the battle which followed and gave the victory to Afonja.

Afonja's ex-slave supporters roamed the country pillaging and taking vengeance on their former masters. Because their excesses were turning the Yoruba against him, Afonja ordered them to stop. This action was regarded as hostile to Islam and as a result Afonja was killed. Abdul Salami, son of Alimi and his Yoruba wife, then mounted the throne as Emir of Ilorin and gave his allegiance to the Sokoto caliphate. A long war followed, between the Alafin of Oyo and the Emir of Ilorin. Perhaps the Alafin would have won if he had been given united support by his chiefs. However, the provincial chiefs wanted independence from the Alafin. Like slippery fish they fought on one side and intrigued with the other, accepted bribes from both, made promises they never intended to keep, and like the Onikoyi changed sides in battle. The disunity in the Oyo Empire gave an advantage to Ilorin, whose Fulani warriors captured Oyo city, the capital of the empire, and totally destroyed it by sacking and burning in about 1835.

In the turbulent years between Afonja's revolt and the destruction of Oyo's capital almost every major city of the empire had been sacked. Farming was difficult and famine and disease swept the land. Armies looted everything of value and carried thousands into slavery. Each new defeat or destruction of a city in the north sent refugees pouring south into Ogbomoso, Oshogbo, Ife, Owu and Egbaland.

Some of the southern kingdoms began to look upon the refugees as potential slaves for farm work or sale at the coast. Before this, the Yoruba had sold few of their brethren to the Atlantic slave traders but now the slave markets of the coast became overcrowded with Yoruba for sale. Ife and Ijebu were accused of capturing Oyo people as slaves. Owu, supported by the Oyo refugees, attacked Ife, the holy city of the Yoruba. In the war the kingdom of Owu was destroyed, and new hordes of refugees were created. The victorious Ife and Ijebu armies swept into Egbaland turning the Egba into refugees as well. The wars and the refugee problem produced by them, created bitterness and suspicion between the branches of the Yoruba family, and prevented the Yoruba from uniting against external foes.

*A brass figure of the Oni of Ife in coronation dress. The figure was excavated in 1957 and dates from the eleventh to fifteenth centuries.*

Dahomey, under its new king, Gezo, who began to rule in 1818, took advantage of the Yoruba civil wars by declaring independence from Oyo, and stopping the payment of tribute to the Alafin. Dahomey even began to expand and attack Yoruba country, with raids on towns such as Abeokuta and Ketu.

## The rise of new Yoruba states

Civil authority had collapsed and in a search for security the refugees began to cluster around talented warriors. This marked the beginning of the great cities which arose in the 1830s.

1   *New Oyo*
A band of refugees from old Oyo under Alafin Atiba founded a new city a few years after the destruction of the capital by the Fulani. New Oyo was further south than old Oyo.

2   *Ijaye*
Another band of refugees under Kurunmi founded Ijaye in Egba territory.

3   *Ibadan*

Another band, led by a group of warriors, made a settlement which became the city of Ibadan. Ibadan became increasingly important because of its strong army and its central position in the palm oil belt which gave it much trade.

4   *Abeokuta*

Egba fled south from the Oyo refugees and established Abeokuta, where they later welcomed Owu refugees.

Since Ibadan attracted the largest number of refugees, it had to organise the resistance to Ilorin. The problem was one of military technique. The old Oyo army had been built on the strength of its cavalry but Ilorin now controlled the northern routes and the horse trade. Somehow Ibadan infantry had to stop Ilorin cavalry. The Ijebu were the first of the Yoruba to use firearms but it was the Ibadan warriors who perfected their use in warfare. In 1839, at the Battle of Oshogbo, Ibadan infantry armed with Dane guns decisively checked Ilorin cavalry. Thus Ibadan stopped the southward expansion of the Sokoto caliphate.

## The rise and fall of the Ibadan empire

Ibadan greatly increased in size and prestige after the Battle of Oshogbo. It had already grown and become strong because it accepted as citizens anyone who would fight for it. After Oshogbo, many ambitious warriors from all over Yorubaland flocked to Ibadan, and it grew into the largest city in nineteenth-century tropical Africa. A modern Nigerian poet, J. P. Clark, has immortalised the city:

> Ibadan,
>      running splash of rust
> and gold—flung and scattered
> among seven hills like broken
> china in the sun.

The major aim of Ibadan's policy after 1839 was the restoration of Yoruba unity, under its own leadership. In 1855 Ibadan called a conference of the Oyo towns. Resolutions were passed rejecting war as a method of settling disputes between each other, recommending the voluntary payment of tribute to the Alafin of new Oyo, and

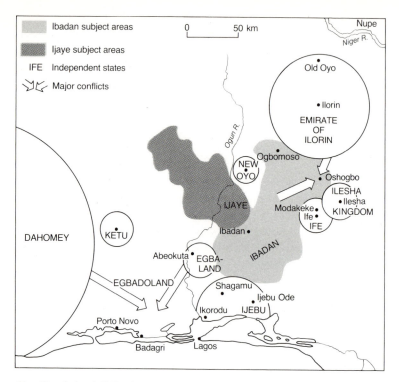

*12    Yorubaland 1840-60.*

proposing peace and friendship with the Egba and Ijebu. Meanwhile, Ibadan acquired an empire, partly by conquest, and partly by the voluntary submission of cities desiring protection and partly by the reconquest of some of the Ekiti states in eastern Yorubaland from Ilorin. By 1860 Ibadan controlled Ife, Ifesha, Ekiti, Oshun, Akoko, and Igbomina. Ibadan paid tribute to new Oyo and encouraged others to do likewise, but Kurunmi in Ijaye and the Egba and Ijebu were upset because Ibadan continued to accept tribute from its own subject towns while she encouraged towns subject to Ijaye to send their tribute to the Alafin. They were also upset because the Alafins of new Oyo favoured Ibadan in their policies.

When Alafin Atiba died in 1859, his son succeeded to the throne, in accordance with the ancient Oyo practice that had been abandoned in the eighteenth century. Ibadan supported this action because Atiba's son, like Atiba himself, was a friend of Ibadan. Kurunmi of Ijaye, however, opposed it on the grounds that the succession of the Alafin's son was contrary to tradition. He hoped to secure the election of a

*Ibadan in the 1850s, from a sketch by Anna Hinderer, an Anglican missionary who spent seventeen years in Yorubaland.*

candidate more favourable to himself. When he failed he withheld his allegiance to the Alafin, causing the outbreak of the Ijaye War 1860-4.

Ibadan decided to force Kurunmi to acknowledge the new Alafin, otherwise the Oyo might split up again. Kurunmi held the title of Kakanfo, and was acting very much like a second Afonja. But Ibadan's attempt to coerce Ijaye did not preserve Yoruba unity. Instead, it brought on the very split it was intended to avoid. The Egba of Abeokuta and the Ijebu in southern Yorubaland feared the rise of Ibadan and wanted to prevent it becoming the undisputed master of the interior. Ibadan also wanted to secure routes to the coast through Egba and Ijebu country, in order to export her palm oil more easily. Once the war began Ibadan was also harassed by her old enemy the Emir of Ilorin who saw Ibadan as the principal obstacle to his intention of carrying the jihad to the sea.

The Ijaye war was indecisive. The Ibadan armies closely blockaded Ijaye to starve the people out. The town fell in 1862 and Ibadan stood astride the Yoruba country like a colossus. But Ibadan was unable to defeat the Egba and Ijebu, Yorubaland remaining disunited.

The Ijaye War was a turning point in Ibadan's history. Ibadan was no longer seen by other Yoruba as their saviour from Fulani invasion, but as an invader itself. Ekiti, Ilesha and other eastern vassal states of Ibadan groaned under the oppressive demands of Ibadan's provincial administrators for high tribute. The Ijebu and Egba continued to fear Ibadan's search for routes to the sea, and Ibadan's growing friendship with the British at Lagos.

The British wanted to buy from Ibadan its abundant palm oil, grown in fertile soil by a constant supply of slave labour from wars of

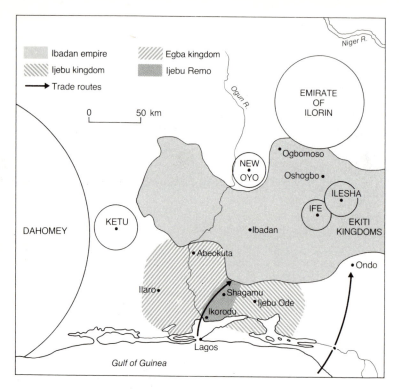

13    *Yorubaland 1877-93.*

conquest. Ibadan wanted to buy guns from the British, but the Egba and Ijebu refused to allow guns to be sold through their territory to a powerful enemy who could use the guns against them. The Egba and Ijebu attempts to stop direct trade between Ibadan and Lagos led to war again, a sixteen-year struggle which Balogun (commander) Latosisa of Ibadan described as 'a war to end all wars'.

The Ijebu and Egba, later joined by Ilorin, declared war on Ibadan in 1877, setting out their war aims as (1) the capture of Ibadan, (2) the forced suicide of Latosisa, its famous Balogun, and (3) the permanent weakening of Ibadan under the joint administration of the Egba, the Ijebu and the Oyo.

In 1882 the allies received unexpected aid from a revolt of the Ekiti vassal states within Ibadan's empire. The rebels formed an alliance, the Ekiti-Parapo, which both Ilesha and Ife joined and chose the Ibadan-trained Ilesha general, Ogedengbe, as its leader. An Ekiti-Parapo Committee was formed among Ekiti people in Lagos, and it

70

provided the alliance with Schneider rifles, superior to, and faster-loading than, the guns used by Ibadan forces. The revolt was proof that Ibadan's imperialism was not beneficial to its subject peoples. Ibadan had exploited the Ekiti states as a source of wealth and cheap labour, had ignored local feelings, had imposed unpopular rulers and had permitted its representatives to enjoy great privileges.

Although Ibadan was now ringed with enemies, it was able to survive by exploiting divisions among its enemies. Ibadan paid high prices to traders from the enemy states to smuggle in arms. Ibadan paid them by selling Ijesha and Ekiti slaves in its southern markets to the Egba and Ijebu, and Egba and Ijebu slaves in its eastern markets to the Ijesha and Ekiti.

In these circumstances the war could not be fought to a conclusive finish. In 1886 two Anglican clergymen, Samuel Johnson, an Oyo, and C. Phillips, an Egba, sponsored by the British who wanted to see trade restored, negotiated a cease-fire. Ekiti's independence was recognised by Ibadan and the Egba and Ijebu opened the roads for trade. However, in 1890 the Egba and Ijebu again closed the roads in protest against the British occupation of Ilaro, an Egba subject town. But the scramble for Africa was now well advanced. Governor Carter of Lagos manufactured an incident with the Ijebu and in 1892 a British force smashed the Ijebu army with such force that the remaining war-weary Yoruba states negotiated treaties which placed them under British protection. Ilorin alone remained independent, until it was conquered by Britain in 1897. Thus the Yoruba wars were ended, but only by British occupation. Yoruba disunity had made Yorubaland an easy prey for European imperialism.

**The western frontier**

King Gezo secured Dahomey's independence from Oyo between 1818 and 1822, and then turned his attention to solving his country's economic problems. Dahomey was not as well situated as the Yoruba for securing control of either of the exports—palm oil or slaves— which the coastal traders wanted. So he began a policy of expansion to the east into the country of the Egbado people from where Dahomey could tap both the slave and oil markets of the Yoruba.

Gezo watched with alarm when the Egba of Abeokuta began to penetrate Egbado country in the 1840s with the aim of securing Badagri as a port under their exclusive control. Gezo determined to stop Egba expansion and marched against Abeokuta in 1851. The Egba were able to defeat Dahomey's army before the walls of

Abeokuta because they had the support of Britain. British missionaries had settled in Abeokuta in the 1840s and they believed that Abeokuta was the hope of Christianity in Yorubaland. Many Egba who had been freed from slavery by the British Navy had returned home from Sierra Leone and settled in Abeokuta, and helped to spread Christianity and to trade in their homeland. British traders at the coast considered the Egba their trading partners. British missionaries and traders persuaded the British Government to supply arms and ammunition to the Egba, who used them to defeat Dahomey. In 1864 Dahomey attacked Abeokuta again, hoping to take advantage of the Egba's involvement in the Ijaye War against Ibadan. But again the Egba won.

Gezo's successor, King Glele, was more successful than Gezo in his invasion of Yorubaland. The westernmost Yoruba kingdom of Ketu, on the borders of Dahomey, was caught between the rival imperialisms of Ibadan and Dahomey. In 1883 Ibadan soldiers occupied Ketu's eastern territory from where they hoped to attack the Egba. While Balogun Hungbo was leading the Ketu army to the east to fight the Ibadans, Glele suddenly attacked Ketu, killed the Alaketu (king) and marched home with thousands of prisoners, leaving the city a blazing ruin. Hungbo hurriedly returned, took civil and military power into his own hands, and rebuilt the city and its walls. Glele led his army back to Ketu in 1886 and settled in for a long starvation siege. Finally, as hunger and disease weakened Ketu's resistance, Glele offered peace with honour. Hungbo suspected the

*Daghisso, a famous warrior portrayed in a bas-relief which commemorates the Wild Antelope Regiment created by King Glele, from the Royal Palace at Abomey in the Republic of Benin.*

offer was a trick but, bowing to the will of the people, he went out with all his generals to negotiate. Glele treacherously seized the Ketu generals, had them put in chains and stormed the walls of the city. Ketu refugees fled to Lagos, Abeokuta and even Ibadan. Glele returned for a triumphant march through his capital, leading Hungbo captive with the largest catch of slaves in Dahomey's history, in street scenes much like the victory parades of the Roman emperors.

## The eastern frontier

At the beginning of the nineteenth century, the Oyo empire stretched far to the east, incorporating all of eastern Yorubaland like the Ekiti states and Ondo, which had once paid tribute to Benin. The ancient kingdom of Benin had declined so much that the Oba could hardly control the original heartland of the state, inhabited by the Edo-speaking people. Large areas like eastern Yorubaland, western Igboland, and the lands of the coastal Itsekiri and Urhobo to the south, had become independent of Benin.

When the Oyo empire collapsed after 1817, the way was clear for Oba Osemwede, who ruled from 1816 to 1848, to revive the fortunes of Benin. Osemwede reconquered the eastern Yoruba states of Akure and Ekiti, forcing them to accept him as Oba and pay tribute to him. Osemwede also regained control of Igboland west of the Niger and Itsekiri and Urhobo country for Benin.

Benin's gains under Osemwede were lost under Oba Adolo (1848-88). Adolo had to fight a long civil war before he became Oba. The succession struggle weakened Benin as outlying vassal states asserted their independence again, or changed allegiance to other rulers. Ekiti, for example, passed under the control of the rising power of Ibadan. Some of the northernmost vassal states came under the Fulani emirates of Nupe and Ilorin, and the Itsekiri became independent again under wealthy trader-rulers such as Olomu Ologbotsere.

The last Oba of Benin, Ovonramwen (1888-97), managed to recover some of the ground lost by Adolo. He solved the succession quickly and ruthlessly by ordering the execution of many prominent chiefs who opposed his accession. He forced Akure to pay tribute to Benin again, and expanded the Benin army.

It is possible that, if the Scramble for Africa had not taken place, both Dahomey to the west and Benin to the east of Yorubaland would have taken more advantage of the Yoruba 'war to end all wars' than they did. However, Dahomey, Yorubaland and Benin all fell to the European invaders instead.

## CHAPTER EIGHT

# Dahomey—a centralised and planned economy

The history of Dahomey (now the Republic of Benin) throws light on one of the major themes of West African history in the nineteenth century: the deliberate attempts of a state to change from economic dependence on the slave trade to an economy centred on the production of palm oil. Dahomey was a rare example in West Africa of a state in which there was extensive development of plantation agriculture. It was also remarkable as an example of a monarchy with a highly organised central government. This made it possible to plan and carry out the change in the economy from the slave trade to the trade in palm oil.

Dahomey was created in the early eighteenth century when King Agaja conquered the small Aja states and Ouidah and amalgamated them into one kingdom under the Aladaxonu dynasty. But Agaja was unable to secure his country's independence, and Dahomey's tributary status to Oyo was confirmed in the treaty of 1730. This provided for heavy annual payments to Oyo but, in return, Dahomey was permitted to keep its army and was not subject to the supervision of resident Oyo officials. This meant Dahomey could largely develop in its own way.

It is surprising that one of the great states of West Africa should have arisen in Dahomey at all, for it is situated in one of the poorest of the West African coastal area. It had neither the gold resources of its western Asante neighbours nor the advantages of the forest-savannah economy of Oyo to the east. It is located in poor savannah and its capital, Abomey, was on a plateau which frequently suffered from drought and famine. Dahomey's achievements are thus something of a triumph of man over geography. Dahomey was one of the few states of West Africa which owed her rise to the profits of the slave trade. She organised the trade efficiently and built up a well-drilled and well-led army which raided north and west, in search of captives to be sold at Ouidah for guns and powder. In the last quarter of the eighteenth century King Kpengla had to organise slave-worked plantations to feed the growing population of the capital and its army regiments. There was growing centralisation of the king's power, caused by the

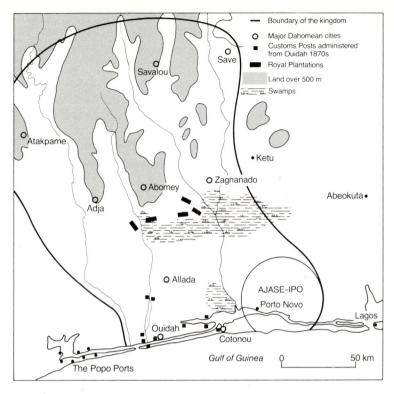

*14   The kingdom of Dahomey.*

slave trade, the conscription of men for the full-time army, and the organisation of plantations.

In 1818 Gezo overthrew King Adandazan and seized the throne of Dahomey. The Oyo empire was split by internal strife after the rebellion of Afonja, and was unable to prevent Gezo declaring Dahomey's independence, which was nurtured by a strong national sentiment, developed under the long subjection to Oyo imperialism. Gezo began his reign by starting Dahomey imperialism, by conquering the small state of Ajase-Ipo, a former vassal of Oyo, and its port of Porto Novo.

## The army

The Dahomean army increased in size and efficiency until the mid-nineteenth century. In 1726 the army was estimated to consist of

3,000 regulars and 10,000 militia who could be called upon at short notice. In 1820 the regulars had increased to between 5,000 and 6,000 and by 1845 to 12,000, about 5,000 of whom were in the women's corps, plus a militia of 24,000.

The regulars were uniformed in blue and white tunics, short trousers and caps decorated with distinctive regimental symbols. Pride and rivalry were particularly intense between the male and female corps. The march-past of the army was a spectacular sight which always impressed visitors to Abomey. The combat units were supported by a carrier corps of young men in training from which replacements were drawn. Arms, ammunition, food rations and uniforms were provided by the state.

The kingdom was small, with a population of possibly a quarter of a million, and the army was also small though well-drilled and famous for its tactics. The poorly organised peoples of the north and west, who were denied firearms by Dahomey's rigid monopoly, were no match for it. However, Dahomey was wise enough not to challenge either Asante or Ibadan, both of which were larger and had firearms. Dahomey made a mistake in attacking Abeokuta in 1851 and 1864, because the Egba army had firearms and probably outnumbered the Dahomean army by two to one.

*Fon wooden figures of King Gezo (left) and King Glele (right), who is represented with the head of a lion.*

The army did not have political power in Dahomey. It was subject to the king and his officials. Dahomey was not a military state, even though many leading official positions were filled from among the army generals.

## The officials

Next to the king the state officials were politically the most powerful group in the kingdom. They were appointed from the commoner class of ordinary people who were not related to the king or former kings. They were appointed, transferred or dismissed by the king.

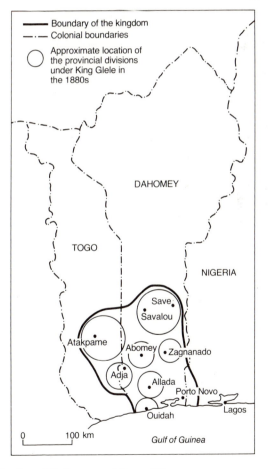

15   *The kingdom of Dahomey and the partition.*

Their officers were not hereditary, but a son had a good chance of succeeding his father if the father had proved efficient and loyal. The officials were the instrument of the monarch's power. As commoners they could never attract a following of rebels nor hope to gain the throne. Top officials were provided with large estates and they had residences in the major cities and occasionally rest-houses along important roads. These officials held all positions, from councillor-ministers and provincial administrators to village chiefs and customs officers.

The king was advised by a council whose members were in charge of certain government posts. Among the councillor-ministers were the Mingi, chief magistrate and superintendent of police; the Meu, collector of revenue; and the Tokpe, minister of agriculture. The kingdom was divided into the metropolitan area of Abomey and six outlying provinces. The provincial administrators were equal to the councillor-ministers in power. The Yevogan, or provincial administrator of Ouidah province in charge of overseas trade and European relations, was one of the three most important officials in the kingdom. The Yevogan, the Mingi and the Meu formed the inner core of the council and on state occasions they occupied positions next to the king.

Another group of the officials were the Naye, often called the king's wives. A few may have been so, but mainly they were older women past child-bearing, or slave women of exceptional ability. Each Naye was assigned a male official whose department she was expected to know as well as the man himself did. The Yevogan was watched over by a Naye called the Yevogana. When a male official reported to the king his Naye was always present. Each Naye had a large number of workers directly under her control to check upon the male officials. For example, the sale of salt was a royal monopoly. The Yevogan was required to send one pebble to the royal court for every bag of salt produced in the salt pans of Ouidah province. The Yevogana kept a record of these pebbles and sent her inspectors to check the salt pans. She also stored the salt. The Yevogana ensured that the Yevogan was honest and efficient.

## National unity

The kings of Dahomey were a symbol of Dahomeyan national feeling and national unity. They commanded respect bordering on worship. But the people as well as the kings had their parts to play in national unity. We can see this clearly in the special ceremony whereby foreigners, mainly Yoruba and Europeans, could become citizens of Dahomey. The state was represented by a perforated calabash filled with water which represented the national spirit or the king. Each citizen symbolically had a finger in a perforation and a candidate for citizenship actually placed his finger in such a hole during the citizenship ceremony. The responsibility for the nation was laid upon each individual, for it was believed that if even one citizen withdrew his finger by an act of treason the spirit of the nation would drain away. During ceremonies when commoners were raised to chiefships the following words were used: 'Dahomey is great and must come before all else . . . a country must be loved by its people'.

State control of religion helped national unity. The king licensed the chief priests of all religious societies. The gods of conquered peoples were absorbed into the Dahomean group of gods. All the religious societies had to recognise the place of the king at the head of human society just as the supreme God was responsible for order in the universe. The king forbade secret societies because they might prove a threat to royal power. The ancestors were important to the well-being of each Dahomean family, but the royal ancestors were especially important because the well-being of the whole nation depended on them. The royal ancestors were honoured annually and in this celebration officials and people from the whole nation gathered at the capital. This celebration was not only a religious occasion. It was also a political occasion when the monarch displayed his wealth and power and the people renewed their loyalty to the throne.

Little is known about the relations between the king and his council. Most visitors felt that the king was all-powerful, but a few believed that he required the consent of his council before deciding on a new policy. However, even if he can act alone, it is a foolish ruler who appoints officials and ignores their advice. Both Gezo and his son and successor Glele were sensible men, and it seems likely that they tried to get general agreement on major issues discussed in their councils. Such general agreement or consensus would help to maintain national unity.


## The law

The king's word was the law, yet he was not above the law. Dahomeans like to recount how King Glele was fined for breaking the law. When gangs of men were working co-operatively either on state roads or building a house for one of their members, it was the law that a passer-by must approach the leader and make an excuse as to why he could not break his journey to assist in the work. Permission was almost always given for the passer-by to continue his journey because the law existed mainly to encourage good manners. King Glele's procession passed one such group without asking to be excused. He was stopped by the headman and fined many cases of rum and pieces of cloth for breaking the law. This story shows that the kings of Dahomey had to obey the laws and their power and position rested on the will of the people. The success of the Aladaxonu kings can be measured from the way the people voluntarily supported the royal family. Many citizens of the Republic of Benin even today look back to the 'great century', their golden age under the Aladaxonus, and this suggests there was good government under the dynasty.

The system of justice was highly developed. There was a Royal Court of Appeal, usually presided over by the Mingi. Severe judgements were given so that the king, if he wished, could show his mercy by reducing or abolishing sentences.

The king's powers were limited during wartime. He was the commander of the army and often accompanied it to war, but did not

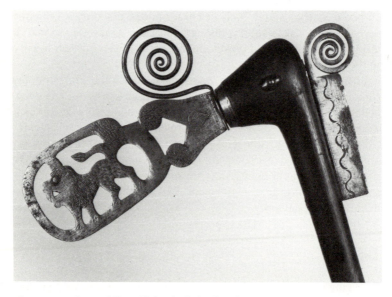

*A ceremonial axe of King Glele which displays his emblem, a lion.*

80

dictate military tactics. The Gao (general) was fully in charge. On the battlefield the Gao occupied a higher stool than the king and was permitted to smoke in the king's presence, an action that was normally the height of disrespect. The king of Dahomey was not an absolute monarch. He had to keep to the customs of the people, and could not just do as he liked.

## From slaves to palm oil

The tax on the export of slaves was the major financial support of the kingdom of Dahomey in the eighteenth century. In 1807, when the British stopped trading in slaves, they abandoned their depot at Ouidah. The slave trade on the Dahomey coast, however, continued almost uninterrupted until 1839 when the British began to seize Portuguese and Brazilian slave ships. 1840 to 1850 was a period of economic uncertainty for Dahomey. Two oil firms, Regis (French) and Hutton (British), established themselves in Ouidah while the Brazilians and Portuguese were still smuggling out slaves to the new world. There was some doubt as to whether the oil or slave interests would triumph. But the British established themselves in Lagos in 1851 and began to blockade the Dahomey coast, and Gezo became convinced that the economic future lay with palm oil alone.

Gezo had already, in the 1840s, begun to encourage palm cultivation on his own plantations and those of his officials. He had also diverted slaves from export to plantation labour. At the same time his army was directed away from the slave-raiding grounds of the north towards securing a hold upon the Yoruba palm belt in Egbado and Egbaland. This was the major aim behind Dahomey's attacks upon Ado in 1844 and Abeokuta in 1851 and 1864. During the sixties King Glele sought to extend his customs posts along the Porto Novo beach up to the British posts in the Badagri area. However, the Egba foiled Dahomey's designs on the palm belt, and the kings had to solve Dahomey's economic problems by internal organisation instead of by external aggression.

Porto Novo and Ouidah began to ship oil in quantity in the 1850s, as the slave trade shrank into insignificance. By the 1870s it was estimated that Dahomey was shipping palm products worth about £500,000 annually. This compared favourably with the £160,000 worth of slave exports shipped annually in the 1830s. It also shows that Dahomey had fully and successfully made the transition from a slave to an oil-centred economy.

Dahomey faced a crisis when Porto Novo broke away and accepted French protection in the 1860s. French firms followed the French flag and tried to load from the Porto Novo beach but Dahomey acted. With the Dahomean army in attendance, Dahomean officials completely sealed the city off from the sea by a string of customs posts. The French were then forced to withdraw and their firms dispersed to other ports. Some went to Lagos, which was under British rule, but most French firms went to Dahomey's other ports, Ouidah and Cotonou.

In spite of the change-over from the slave to the oil trade, the army's raids for manpower continued. The new palm oil economy needed more and more cheap labour. This probably accounts for the destruction of Ketu in Yorubaland in the 1880s, when the entire population was led into slavery. The slaves were now nearly all kept in the country, and only a few were smuggled abroad. The nature of slavery in Dahomey changed. The old domestic slavery, where slaves were usually treated as members of the owner's family, was changed. The profit motive was strong, and owners like the king and officials had no personal contact with their plantation slaves. The powerful Dahomean plantation owners demanded maximum yields from their overseers who in turn drove the slaves harder. Thus slavery in Dahomey in the second half of the nineteenth century became more like slavery in the new world or Calabar, and changed from slavery as it was known in neighbouring West African societies.

Household slaves or those working for small farmers were generally treated in the traditional manner. In the royal household, for example, the king often chose as his heir one of his sons by a slave wife, because it was felt she must be superior to her freeborn colleagues to have risen so high. Traditionally, slaves born in Dahomey—second generation slaves—were assimilated into free-born society. They had grown up with the same language and customs as the Dahomeans in whose homes they had been born. However, the development of plantations must have made it very difficult for slaves to accept Dahomean ways.

By the mid-nineteenth century slaves were being treated more harshly in the new plantations, and Gezo felt they required more legal protection. All deaths had normally been reported to the capital in order that the census might be kept up to date. Gezo placed officials in the provinces with instructions to report whether deaths were natural or violent. This change was designed to protect the slaves from brutal owners and overseers. All cases of violent death of slaves were now brought before the Royal Judicial Court in Abomey.

## A planned economy

One of the spectacular achievements of Dahomey in the nineteenth century was the planning of agricultural production by the state. Originally it had begun in a small way to feed the growing population, the royal family and the army. When the slave trade ended, planned agricultural production became much more organised. Plantation owners and small farmers were encouraged to produce oil. All palm trees in the kingdom were counted and a constant check kept on their annual yield. About one-third of the total production was taxed. The oil tax was the largest single source of state revenue after the 1850s, and it was used at Ouidah for guns and powder.

The production achievements of King Gezo and Glele may best be seen in comparison with the later French colonial period. The general trend of palm oil production in the twentieth century has been static or downward. At the French conquest there were 40 million palm trees in Dahomey. By the 1950s there were only 32.5 million, most of which were old, having been planted before the conquest.

Livestock and food crop production were as closely controlled and regulated as palm oil. The basis of planning was the annual census which provided figures for the total population and its distribution by sex, occupation, province and village. Originally the census was used for conscription and other military needs—for instance all blacksmiths were licensed and each forge had its trade mark registered in the capital because of the importance of the industry to the army. Later the census came to be employed for other purposes, like taxation.

The state tried to keep a balance between production and consumption of livestock. There was a census of all goats, cows, sheep and pigs and strict account of slaughtering. Each village chief reported the number of pigs slaughtered. The butchers' guilds kept all the skulls of pigs sold in the market. Both reports went to the Tokpe and Naye in Abomey. The Naye, in addition, sent out market inspectors to make periodic checks. If sales were running ahead of production the king might forbid the slaughter of cows or all pigs for a year. During the ban, pigs could not be taken past the toll gates on the public roads.

Food crops were controlled in a similar way. Each province concentrated upon certain crops. Abomey specialised in beans and maize, Zagnanado in millet, Allada in maize and cassava, Save in groundnuts and maize and Adja in maize. During a shortage of one crop the Tokpe could order one or more districts to switch cultivation to the crop in short supply. Condiments—honey, red and black pepper, and ginger—were royal monopolies produced in restricted areas under close government supervision. Pepper, for example, was allowed to be grown only by seven villages near Allada. The result of all this centralised planning was greater taxation. There were the export taxes, and annual agricultural and palm oil taxes. Livestock was taxed every three years. Artisans paid an income tax and the wealthy paid death duties (a proportion of the wealth they left when they died was paid to the government). In addition there was a market tax and toll charges on all major roads.

When the French conquered Dahomey they did not set up advanced administration. They destroyed the advanced administration they found there already, and replaced it with a different kind of their own.

Gezo and Glele showed themselves to be capable rulers, quick to change and to adapt to the economic crisis of the nineteenth century. They may rightly be remembered as the rulers of the best organised state on the West African coast in the nineteenth century.

## CHAPTER NINE

# The Asante empire in the nineteenth century

At the beginning of the nineteenth century the Asante empire had expanded to include virtually the whole of modern Ghana and parts of modern Ivory Coast and Togo. The only state of modern Ghana that had not been incorporated into the empire by that time was the relatively small kingdom of Fante which stretched along the coast from the mouth of the Pra to the borders of the Ga kingdom and about twenty miles inland. But even within this stretch was Elmina which was directly under Asante. The rise and expansion of Asante between about 1680 and 1750 was due largely to the state-building genius and military skill of Osei Tutu and Opoku Ware whose reigns covered the period.

## The government of the Asante empire

The empire consisted of two parts, each with its own system of administration. The first part was metropolitan Asante, and the second was provincial Asante. Metropolitan Asante consisted of the Kumasi state or division directly under the Asantehene ('Asante-king'), and all the states within about 30 to 40 miles' radius of modern Kumasi. All these states recognised the Golden Stool created by Osei Tutu as the symbol of their soul and unity, the king of Kumasi state or division (Oman) as their paramount king or Asantehene, and all of them recognised the great oath 'Ntam Kese Miensa' as their supreme oath. The central government of metropolitan Asante consisted of the Confederacy Council made up of all the kings or Omanhene of the various divisions, presided over by the Asantehene. It also had an executive council or cabinet made up of a few of the principal chiefs of the Kumasi division and some of the divisional kings. Each of the states of metropolitan Asante had its own king or Omanhene, and its own State Council. It must be noted that neither the Asantehene nor any Omanhene enjoyed absolute dictatorial powers. On the contrary

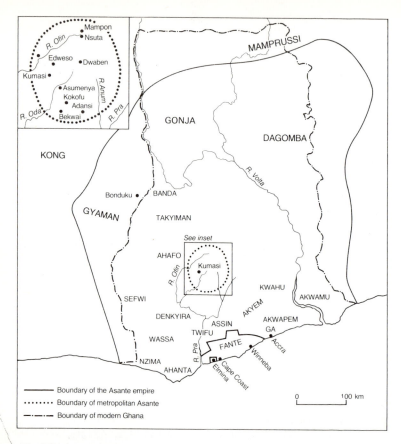

16   *The Asante empire.*

each of them could be destooled whenever he abused his powers, or failed in his duties.

Provincial Asante consisted of all the outer circle of states conquered and annexed by Asante during the eighteenth century. Until about the middle of that century, all these states continued to govern themselves in exactly the same way as they were doing before their conquest and annexation. All they were expected to do was to accept one of the chiefs of Kumasi, who seldom visited the provinces, as a friend at court, to pay annual tribute and contribute a contingent to the army when called upon to do so. The Golden Stool was of little importance to them.

After 1750 the Asantehenes introduced some changes in the government of provincial Asante. For example, they tried to tighten

86

their control over the provinces by stationing regional and district commissioners in these states. In 1776, for instance, Osei Kwadwo established a regional commissioner in Akwapem to be responsible for Dutch, English and Danish Accra. However, these changes in the provincial system did not go far enough, and most of the vassal states made a bid for their independence. The superior military techniques and the bravery of their army enabled the Asante to crush all these rebellions and to preserve the empire intact.

## Relations between Asante and Fante

The only state within modern Ghana that had been able to dam the tide of Asante imperialism was the Fante kingdom, a confederation of Fante states. The Fante Confederation arose between 1670 and 1730, mainly to provide a united front against the Asante and the Akyem (who were driving towards the coast and would thus be able

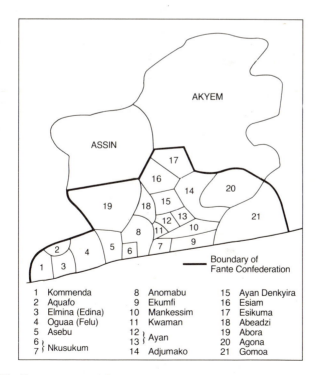

*17   The Fante states.*

to control the flow of arms and ammunition inland). Up to the 1730s the Fante states formed quite a closely knit group under the joint rule of the Brafo, who was probably the king of the central Fante state of Mankessim, and the High Priest of the national god. But after 1750 the Confederation broke up into two parts, western or Bore Bore Fante, and eastern or Ekumfi Fante, each of which established its own government.

Throughout the eighteenth century, relations between the Asante and the Fante remained largely hostile. The Asante attacked the Fante on three occasions, in 1727, 1756 and 1776. The main reason for this state of enmity was economic: the persistent refusal of the Fante to allow Asante traders direct access to the European forts and castles situated in their land. The Fante wanted to ensure their 'middleman' position between the European traders and the Asante. The Asante never abandoned their determination to gain direct access to the Fante coast, and the conflicts between them over routes in the eighteenth century continued into the nineteenth. Indeed, the new century opened on a note of Asante-Fante dispute. In October 1800, the British governor of the forts reported that 'the trading paths have for many months past been shut up by a misunderstanding between the Fantees and Ashantees'. And his successor also stated in 1807 that the Fante had 'always thrown impediments in the way of the Asante so as to prevent their intercourse with us'. The situation was made worse because the Fante were often dishonest in their dealings with the Asante traders. Osei Bonsu told the British diplomat Bowdich in 1817 that the Fante obtained pure gold from the Asante and mixed it with other base metal before selling it to the Europeans on the coast.

The second main Asante grievance against the Fante was political. First of all, to defend their huge empire and suppress all internal revolts the Asante needed a regular supply of firearms. One of the main reasons for the Asante drive to the coast in both the eighteenth and nineteenth centuries was to ensure a regular supply of firearms to Kumasi, especially from the Dutch in Elmina and the Danes in Accra. For the same reason they steadfastly held on to Accra and Elmina, their two principal coastal outlets. But the Fante did everything to prevent this flow of arms inland. Moreover, throughout the eighteenth and nineteenth centuries, the Fante assisted Asante's southern tributary states wherever any of them rose in rebellion. Here the motives of the Fante were mainly to safeguard their 'middleman' position and to ensure that there were strong buffer states between them and the Asante.

## The rule of Osei Bonsu

Such was the state of Asante and Fante, and such was the nature of the relations between them when Osei Bonsu was enstooled as Asantehene at the beginning of the nineteenth century. What policies did he pursue during his long reign from 1801 to 1824, and with what consequences? His policies were, firstly, to continue the centralising reforms begun by his predecessors; secondly, to maintain intact the empire that he had inherited; and, thirdly, to extend its frontiers even further. Osei Bonsu continued the constitutional changes of the last two rulers of the eighteenth century, Osei Kwadwo and Osei Kwame. They had begun to change the hereditary offices or stools of the Kumasi division into offices held by appointment. Also, they created new stools with the aim of increasing the personal powers of the king.

Osei Bonsu created three more stools or departments in the Ankobia stool or Ministry of Home Affairs. He improved the Gyasewa Stool or Ministry of Economic Affairs by co-ordinating the activities of the various sections and employing literate Muslims. He developed a real chancery whose records were kept in Arabic. He completed the conversion of the cabinet from a fixed body of hereditary members to one to which members were invited according to the nature of the business to be transacted. The diplomatic service

*An Asante chief wearing the traditional gold ornaments appropriate to his status and authority.*

became fully appointive. Finally, Osei Bonsu continued the changes in the system of provincial administration by appointing more district commissioners, one at Cape Coast and another at Elmina.

Osei Bonsu's constitutional reforms greatly increased the powers of the Asantehene in both Kumasi and the provinces. As the European traveller Dupuis observed, 'The king rules with unrivalled sway; every king, chief, and unconditional vassal as tributaries or not and most of them holding their governments by virtue of an appointment from the court.' Membership of the new administrative class or bureaucracy depended now on talent and ability rather than on birth, so the administration became more efficient than before, and peace and order reigned. As one European observer wrote in 1816, 'Law and order is just as great in the Asantee Kingdom as with Asiatic peoples. There exist no palavers between one town and another...'

Osei Bonsu's second policy was to preserve intact the empire that he had inherited from his predecessors. This meant that he had to suppress all revolts, and, as he told Dupuis, 'to eradicate the seeds of disobedience and insubordination'. It should not be forgotten that in spite of the considerable improvement in the system of provincial administration, revolts and rebellions for independence continued in the nineteenth century. Indeed, at the time of Osei Bonsu's accession, Gyaman or Abron to the north-west was in revolt, and shortly afterwards Gonja to the north also rebelled. In 1806 the rulers of Assin to the south openly defied the Asantehene, killed his messengers and took refuge in Fante. Akyem and Akwapem also raised the standard of revolt in 1811, Gyaman again in 1817, and Wassa, Denkyira and Assin in 1823.

Fortunately for Asante, Osei Bonsu was able to carry out his policy. He suppressed all these rebellions. In 1808 he defeated the Fante who had helped Assin in 1806. His final campaign against the Wassa and the Denkyira in 1824 ended with the defeat not only of the rebels but also of the British and Fante contingent sent to their aid under the command of Sir Charles Macarthy, the then Governor-in-Chief of the forts. Indeed, during the final and decisive battle of this campaign, at Bonsaso on 21 February 1824, Macarthy was among those killed.

But Osei Bonsu did not aim merely at preserving what he had inherited; he sought also to add to it. He achieved this by conquering and annexing the hitherto independent Fante Confederation. The Fante had assisted all the rebellions by Asante's southern vassal states between 1806 and 1823, so at the same time as Osei Bonsu was reconquering these vassals, he was also conquering Fante. It was Osei Bonsu's personal ambition to rule all the coast. Two of his predecessors whom he admired most were Osei Tutu and Opoku Ware. The former had conquered Denkyira and thereby acquired the note for the rent of Elmina Castle. The latter had conquered Akyem and the Ga kingdom and won the notes for all the European castles in Accra. The acquisition of the notes for the other castles at the coast, then held by the Fante rulers, must have proved an irresistible attraction for ambitious Osei Bonsu.

Osei Bonsu died in February 1824, shortly after the arrival of the news of the decisive victory over the combined forces of Wassa, Denkyira, Fante and Britain. His death coincided with the pinnacle of Asante power and greatness, due largely to his own organising ability, diplomatic skill and bravery. He certainly deserves the title of 'the great', and was easily the foremost of the nineteenth-century Asante kings—a most worthy successor of Osei Tutu and Opoku Ware.

## Decline of Asante power

However, by 1874, only fifty years after the death of Osei Bonsu, the Asante empire had completely broken up. All the southern states had first reasserted their independence and then lost it again to the British, who formed them into a crown colony. The northern states had also declared themselves independent. Indeed, the Asante empire had shrunk to that area formerly occupied by metropolitan Asante alone, and even that was in a very much weakened condition. What brought about this unexpected turn of events? The collapse of Asante between 1824 and 1874 was due partly to the weakness of the Asante system of provincial administration, but above all to the intervention of the British.

Despite the work of Osei Kwadwo and Osei Bonsu, the Asante system of provincial administration never became completely effective. The vassal states were never fully incorporated into the empire. The Golden Stool was never important to them. Their desire to regain control over their own affairs remained strong. The continued loyalty of all of them to the Asantehene depended purely on the military strength of metropolitan Asante. Unfortunately for Asante, this force binding the two parts of the empire together was destroyed. Asante's military strength was smashed by the British and their allies in 1824, 1826 and 1874. Indeed, from 1824 onwards, the wars between the Asante and their southern subjects became primarily wars between the Asante and the British. What were the causes and the course of these wars?

First, the causes. The main concern of the Asante after 1824, as before, was to preserve their great empire. Osei Yaw Akoto, who succeeded Osei Bonsu, lost all the southern states except Elmina, but neither he nor his successors ever abandoned the hope of winning these territories back. In 1873, almost half a century later, Kofi Karikari, the then Asantehene, told the British that the only step that would appease him would be the restoration of the Denkyira, the Akyem and the Assin to their former position as his subjects. The Asante were particularly determined to hold on to Elmina. This was for sentimental as well as political reasons. Elmina was the only one of the southern states whose acquisition was associated with the revered Osei Tutu, the founder of the Asante nation, and for that reason no Asantehene was ever prepared to abandon it. Apart from sentiment, there was a very practical reason why the Asante were determined to keep Elmina. Their hold on the fort ensured them a regular supply of guns and powder, on which depended the very survival of even metropolitan Asante. There is absolutely no doubt that the Asante invasions of the coast between 1867 and 1873 were primarily to stop the British from taking possession of Elmina. From the Asante point of view, then, these wars were for the survival and preservation of their empire.

What about the British? They became directly involved in these age-long conflicts between the Asante and their southern subjects for four main reasons. The first reason was one of self-preservation and

*A nineteenth-century painting which depicts the defeat of the Asante by the British in 1824.*

security. The Asante occupied the entire coastal area between 1807 and 1824. This worried the British because an over-strong Asante would dominate the British traders at the coast.

The second reason was economic. The British traders were convinced that if Asante power could be broken, a vast field for commerce in the interior would be open to them. As one of them wrote to his brother in London in 1823, 'We could then have direct and free access and intercourse with the Bontookos in fact with Kong and leading from there, with Timbuctoo, Houssa, etc.' The British also feared that if a powerful state like Asante controlled the coast, then it could control trade and increase the prices of goods sold to Europeans.

The third reason was humanitarian. The British wanted to introduce Christianity and Western education into Ghana, but were convinced this could never be put into effect until Asante power was destroyed or humbled.

The fourth and last reason for active intervention of the British was the contempt most of them on the coast had for Asante institutions. The British governor's contempt for Asante law and custom precipitated the Asante invasion of the coast in 1863.

The Asante fought two wars with the British in 1824. The first ended in Macarthy's defeat and death in February. The second began in July, when the British sent an expedition to avenge Macarthy's death. This time the Asante army was defeated and driven back to Asante, and the southern vassal states began to assert their independence.

The Asante-British War of 1826 ended in a second decisive Asante defeat at the battle of Dodowah, where the British used Congreve rockets. The main reason, though, for Asante's defeat was that the new Asantehene, Osei Yaw Akoto (1824-34) plunged his army into the battle without adequate preparation. The Asante were driven out of the southern vassal states which became independent. The British controller of the forts, George Maclean, imposed a treaty on the defeated Asante in 1831. The Asante were forced to recognise the independence of all southern vassal states south of the River Pra, including Denkyira, Akyem and Assin. The Brong states to the north and north-west, as well as Dagomba and Gonja, also took advantage of the weakened power of the Asante to break away.

The Asante-British War of 1863 broke out because the British governor of the forts, Richard Pine, did not understand Asante law. An Asante, Kwesi Gyanin, kept a gold nugget he found instead of handing it over to the Asantehene as the law decreed. He fled to a

British fort at the coast to escape justice. The Asantehene, Kwaku Dua I (1834-67), demanded that the British hand over the criminal, but Pine treated Kwesi not as a criminal but as a refugee, and gave him asylum at the coast. Pine misunderstood Asante law and feared the Asantehene would execute Kwesi. Kwaku Dua was a peace-loving ruler, but he felt he had to uphold his authority over his subjects. So he sent the Asante army to invade the coast. The Asante defeated the Fante, destroyed many towns and villages, and besieged the British forts. While the British waited for reinforcements, the Asante army was defeated not in battle but by disease. The Asante soldiers were hit by an epidemic of dysentery, and withdrew to the interior. The British punitive expedition, when it arrived, failed to advance into Asante because it, too, was hit by disease. The war of 1863-4 was indecisive.

The Asante-British war of 1873-4, however, gave the Asante military power a blow from which it never recovered. The Asantehene, Kofi Karikari (1867-74), invaded the coast to recover Elmina, 'given' by the departing Dutch rentees to the British in 1870. Another epidemic hit the Asante army, which withdrew. This time, however, the British reinforcements under Sir Garnet Wolseley invaded the heart of Asante, used their breech-loading rifles to destroy the Asante army with its old-fashioned muzzle-loading Dane guns, and burnt down Kumasi. Wolseley's force withdrew, and Asante was not annexed by Britain, but Asante's losses were enormous.

*Elmina castle.*

Under the Treaty of Fomena imposed on Asante by Britain in 1874, Asante had to recognise again the independence of the coastal states, to give up its claim to Elmina to Britain, and to promise to pay an indemnity (war fine) of gold to Britain. Many of Asante's former southern vassal states were incorporated in the Gold Coast Colony, created by Britain in 1874. More of the northern states broke away. Worse still, even metropolitan Asante was shaken. Some of the member states like Dwaben and Adansi asserted their independence of Kumasi, while Kokofu, Bekwai and Nsuta began to quarrel with Kumasi. To add humiliation to defeat, Kofi Karikari was destooled for theft after he stole gold from the tombs of dead kings. It was quite clearly a dismembered, disunited and demoralised remnant of an empire that Mensa Bonsu inherited in 1874.

However, Mensa Bonsu and his two successors Kwaku Dua II (1884) and Agyeman Prempe (1888-1931) did not despair and accept the collapse of their empire. On the contrary, they set themselves the task of reuniting metropolitan Asante and even winning back provincial Asante. Mensa Bonsu tackled the problem of metropolitan Asante first. By diplomacy and personal appeals, he soon won back Kokofu and Bekwai. However, the Dwaben, who were being supported by the British, rejected these peaceful approaches, and even went on to persuade the neighbouring states of Afigyaase, Asokore and Oyoko to join them. Therefore, in October 1875 Mensa Bonsu resorted to force. He invaded Dwaben and routed her forces. The Dwaben and their allies fled as refugees to Akyem. There, on a stretch of land bought for them by the British, they founded new towns which they named after their old towns in Asante.

This victory greatly strengthened Mensa Bonsu's position as well as the authority of Kumasi and the Golden Stool. However, in 1875, probably with a view to winning the friendship of the British, Mensa Bonsu abandoned the use of force in favour of diplomatic missions. He sent one to Adansi, and sent another to Gyaman in 1878 under a European, Karl Neilson. However, Gyaman was not won over by diplomacy, and attacked Asante's ally, Banda. Bonsu refused to raise an army to assist Banda, and because of both this refusal and his avarice, he was deposed in February 1883.

## The rule of Prempe

This deposition led to a series of civil wars among the metropolitan Asante states and the Kumasi chiefs. They were not brought to an end until Kwaku Dua III or, as he became better known, Agyeman Prempe I, was sworn in as the Asantehene in March 1888. By the time of his accession, the fortunes of Asante had clearly reached the lowest possible point. The Brong states had taken advantage of the anarchy in Kumasi and consolidated their independence. Further south, the Dwaben were still in Akyem. The Adansi had been chased south of the Pra after their unsuccessful war with Bekwai in 1886. To add to Prempe's problems, the states that had not supported him during his contest for the stool—Kokofu, Mampong and Nsuta—rose up in rebellion soon after his enthronement. It looked, then, as if even the very creation of Osei Tutu, the hard core of the former Asante empire, was at long last really cracking up.

However, this did not happen for two reasons. The first was that the magnetic pull of the Golden Stool proved irresistible in the end. After all, most of the troubles and civil wars that raged in Kumasi were the result of clashes of personalities and interests rather than withdrawal of loyalty to the Golden Stool. The second and even more important factor, however, was the quality of Asante's new leader. Agyeman Prempe, the last of the nineteenth-century rulers of Asante, was, like the first, a political genius, a natural leader of men and an able commander. He rebuilt the shattered Asante confederacy and reconquered parts of the Asante empire.

How did Prempe manage to accomplish this? He used two main weapons: diplomacy and war. His first concern was to repair the cracks in the core of the confederate states, and he began by attacking and defeating Kokofu. He then turned his attention northwards and in November 1888 his army crushed the Mampong and Nsuta revolts. The Mamponghene sought refuge in Atebutu but most of his subjects deserted him and returned home. With the support of the Asantehene, they deposed him in favour of his younger brother who promptly returned to Prempe's fold. This incident shows the natural desire of the Asante people to be united in loyalty to the Golden Stool, and their rejection of leaders who opposed the Asantehene for petty reasons such as personal disputes. Nsuta also joined Prempe.

Within months of his accession, Prempe had succeeded in repairing most of the cracks in the confederacy. Next he turned his attention outwards. He wrote a letter to the British governor of the Gold Coast in November 1889 objecting to the extension of British protection to Kwahu, which he claimed was his. He followed up this letter in July 1890 with a large mission to the governor to ask for his assistance in re-establishing Asante's authority over the old outer ring of states, and he demanded the return of all the Asante refugees in the British

Crown colony. He also appealed directly to those Dwaben who had moved to Akyem in 1875, and the Kokofu who had also moved across the Pra after their defeat in 1888, to come home; most of the Dwaben people began to return.

By this time the British had become so alarmed by this steady revival of the confederacy and by French advances in modern Ivory Coast that in 1890 they declared a protectorate over Atebutu. Then in March 1891 they sent an officer to Kumasi to invite the Asantehene to place his country under British protection. Prempe, as one would expect, rejected this invitation politely but firmly. To quote his own words, 'My kingdom of Asante will never commit itself to any such policy. Asante must remain independent as of old, at the same time to be friendly with all white men. I do not write this with a boastful spirit but in the clear sense of its meaning.'

After sending this reply to the British, Prempe turned his attention to the north-west, to try to subdue the Brong states. In 1892 and 1893, he attacked and defeated the Nkoranza and their allies the Mo and Abease, and only the timely arrival of a British force saved Atebutu. In the south, the Kokofuhene Asibe decided in 1893 to return to Asante, but he was prevented from doing so by the British who arrested him and detained him in Accra. In March 1894, Prempe rejected the British request for the establishment of a resident at Kumasi, for fear that would lead to the establishment of a British protectorate over his rapidly reviving empire. Three months later, full of hope and confidence, Prempe was formally installed on the Golden Stool with great pomp and pageantry.

This ceremony, however, marked the height of Prempe's achievements. Barely twenty months later, in March 1896, the British army invaded Asante and overthrew Prempe, and his country became a British colony (see chapter 16).

## CHAPTER TEN

# Igboland—a segmentary political system

The Igbo people live in the area between Benin and Igala, the Cross River and Niger Delta city-states. They were divided into five major cultural groups: the western or Riverain, northern or Awka, Owerri, Cross River, and Ogoja Igbo. These cultural groups did not possess a central government. None of them was a political organisation, so none of them co-operated politically with other cultural groups.

Regardless of cultural differences between the groups, there were certain features typical of Igbo society everywhere. The Igbo respected age, and leadership came from the elders. Respect was not

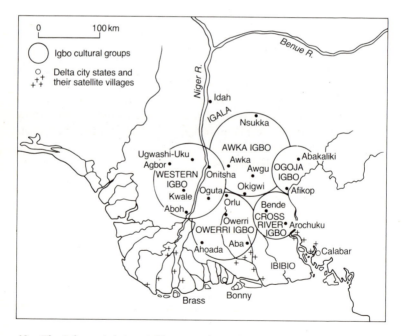

18   *The Igbo and their neighbours in the early nineteenth century. The five major cultural groups of the Igbo are indicated.*

servility and was balanced by the belief that birth did not grant privilege to any man. The Igbo were individualistic and egalitarian, every man considering himself as good as everyone else and demanding a voice in his local affairs. Everyone had a right to rise in the society.

Igbo culture emphasised competition; competition between families, between lineages and between clans. Competition was promoted by sports like wrestling and mock battles. Although men were born equal they could rise to positions of prestige through a combination of wealth and a record of service to the clan. Igbo society was, therefore, intensely democratic. But it also suffered from the failings of wasted uncoordinated effort, slow decision-making and lack of unity.

The Igbo were not unique in the type of government which they created. In West Africa the Kru of Liberia, Tallensi of Ghana, Konkomba of Togo and Tiv of Nigeria, to mention but a few societies, possessed political organisations whose characteristics were closer to those of the Igbo than to the centralised Yoruba, Dahomey or Asante systems. The following discussion of a segmentary political system can be applied to both the Igbo and Ibibio.

Segmentary is the word used to describe the political organisation of societies without a central government. In pre-colonial Africa a central government was usually headed by a single person (king, emperor, sultan, almami, etc.) Segmentary societies are different from 'stratified' societies which usually have royal or noble families who pass on high political office from generation to generation within the family. In segmentary societies stable government is achieved by balancing small equal groups against each other and by the ties of clanship, marriage and religion.

Among the Igbo each cultural group was divided into a number of clans (diagram 1). Usually the clans in one cultural group spoke a similar dialect and had certain customs, traditions and institutions which made them different from clans of other cultural groups. There were hundreds of patrilineal (tracing descent through the father) clans in Igboland averaging in population between 5,000 and 15,000 people (consult diagram 1 frequently as you read on). Of the hundred or so clans which make up the Owerri Igbo, let us say that one is called Umu Nna (the children of Nna). This means that all the people of Umu Nna clan claim descent from their ancestor Nna. All within one clan are considered relatives.

Umu Nna is made up of eight villages. In Igboland there were no large cities but thousands of villages, so closely packed that Igboland

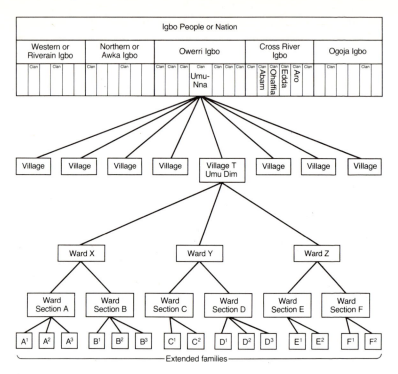

*19   Igbo clan organisation (diagram 1).*

had an overall density of population greater than anywhere else in West Africa. The eight villages were founded by the eight sons of Nna. One of the sons was called Dim who founded village 'T' (diagram 2) whose people call themselves Umu Dim (the children of Dim), as well as Umu Nna. Umu Dim is called a lineage. It is also a village. The lineage or village was the political unit of pre-colonial Igboland. There was no governmental organisation over the clan or cultural group. We will therefore look at the government of an Igbo village and see its relationship to the lineage.

## Village government

The Igbo village was divided into wards. The wards were grouped around the large village market which operated every four or eight days depending on its size and importance. Each ward was made up of sections and each section of a number of extended families whose

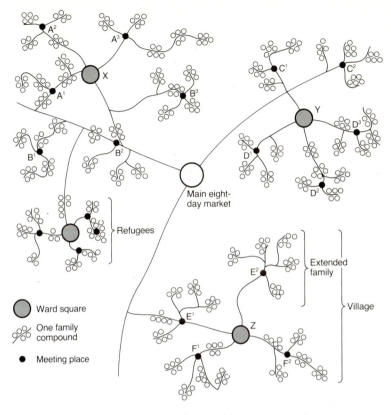

Legend within figure:

- Ward square
- One family compound
- Meeting place

Main eight-day market

Refugees

Extended family

Village

20   *Plan of a typical Igbo village (diagram 2).*

compounds were close together. A meeting of the village would be held in the main market, a meeting of the ward would be held in the ward square and a meeting of the extended family would take place in a cleared area, near its compounds or inside an elder's compound. Diagram 1 shows an Igbo village composed of three wards X, Y, Z (the three sons of Dim). Each ward was made up of extended families descended from X, Y and Z.

Village government consisted of two basic institutions, the Ama-ala (Council of Elders) and the village assembly of citizens. In village 'T' the Ama-ala consisted of fifteen heads of the extended families. However, any adult male held the right to sit on the council. Normally this right was not exercised, but if a decision was to be taken which vitally affected the individual he could insist on his right. This was an important check on elders who might otherwise

101

take decisions without proper consideration. In routine matters the elders ruled by decree and proclamation, but where decisions likely to produce disputes were to be taken the Ama-ala could assemble in the ward square.

At the assembly the elders laid the issues before the people. Every man had a right to speak. The people applauded popular proposals and shouted down the unpopular ones. Decisions had to be unanimous and it was here that young or wealthy men with records of service and dedication to the village could influence policy. If the elders tried to enforce an unpopular decision, the young men could prevent any decision through preventing unanimity. If the Ama-ala made an unpopular decision and refused to call the assembly, the people could force the elders to call an assembly by completely ignoring them and bringing village life to a halt. An unpopular elder would be ignored and no one would speak to him. No-one in the market place would sell to his wives. This social pressure would compel the elder to bend to the popular will. The village assembly was considered the Igbo man's birthright, the guarantee of his rights, his shield against oppression, and the means whereby the young and progressive members of the village society impressed their views upon the older and more conservative ones.

The basic unit of Igbo and Ibibio government was therefore the ward. Above the ward was a council for the governing of the village. The council possessed an equal number of representatives from each of the village wards. Again, decisions had to be unanimous. No ward could be compelled to accept a policy against its wishes. In fact ward representatives on the village council were only delegates since they could not commit their ward to any policy which had not been approved by their respective Ama-ala. The village council normally held full control over the central or main market. Thus at the ward level democracy was direct while at the village level it was representative, but it was still subservient to the popular will. The administration of justice was also democratic. Quarrels between individuals of different families in the ward were settled before the people, the ward elders acting as arbiters. Quarrels between wards or serious crimes such as theft would come before the full village assembly. The danger of the system was that the people, acting as a mob, sometimes took justice into their own hands and the person accused of a particular crime or misdemeanour did not have a proper opportunity to defend himself.

The Igbo judicial system was noted for its lack of set rules. A man might attempt to settle with the individual who had aggrieved him. If

*An Igbo ceremonial pot from Ishiagu, near Afikpo.*

this failed he could ask a respected elder to intervene or call members of the two families together. He could also ask the ward or village elders to solve the case. There were no set rules as to where he should begin his appeal for justice, but he could appeal against the decision of the families to the ward elders and finally to the Ama-ala of the village.

Individuals always conducted their own case. They might call witnesses, or anyone in the assembly might speak. If an elder who was a powerful and persuasive speaker could quote history or an earlier similar case for either side, it had an influence on the assembly. If, however, there was a suspicion that the elder was in any way connected with the individual he was speaking for, instead of helping, he might hurt the case for which he spoke.

Once both sides of the case had been heard the two men withdrew and the Ama-ala and assembly argued the pros and cons. When the decision had been taken, one elder was asked to give judgement when the two parties to the case had returned. It is important to note that in arriving at a decision the assembly acted like a large-sized jury which had to agree unanimously. The Ama-ala could not push a decision against the will of the assembly.

Respect for the elders was not entirely because of their age but also because of their priestly functions. The family, ward and lineage heads were responsible for rituals and sacrifices to the founder of the family, ward or lineage. The rituals reminded the people of their common origin and helped maintain their unity.

## Features of the cultural groups

The segmentary political system so far described was fairly typical of the Owerri Igbo. The other Igbo cultural groups employed the same basic system but added certain features to it. Almost all groups had age-set organisations. Age-sets varied from one group to another but only in a few areas such as Ogoja were they important in village government. Every so many years young people of a certain age were initiated into an age-set in which they remained all their lives, so that the whole population was arranged in two parallel male and female age-set organisations. Each age-set chose a leader and after it had proved its service to the community, it was given a special name by the elders, signifying that it had passed to adulthood. The age-sets competed among themselves in sports and in rendering service to the village, and they promoted and strengthened competition in society.

Age-sets, apart from being societies for mutual help and for discipline, were convenient for organising public works. Younger age-sets were responsible for keeping the village tidy, older ones for clearing the bush for new markets, providing night watchmen, guards or market police. The age-sets performed a valuable function: fostering unity. They brought together people of similar ages from all the segments of the lineage. Through working together, helping each other and competing with other age-sets the members developed a loyalty to the age-set leader which was a strong bond of unity in the village.

In Ogoja the age-set leaders occupied equal positions on the Ama-ala with the lineage elders. This gave the younger men a formal and constant voice in the government. In Asaba the oldest age-set was retired with an honorary advisory status, the next age-set providing the members of the Ama-ala. By retiring the oldest group, government came into the hands of younger, more progressive elements.

Among the Awka and some Niger Igbo such as Onitsha, graded title societies were more important than age-sets in government. In Awka Town, Oguta and Onitsha the title societies were called Ozo

*An Ozo title holder standing beside a carefully carved door to his home.*

while in Nsukka they were called Ama and their meeting places Ozo or Ama lodges. Any freeborn male who could afford the initiation fee might take a title. Upon further payments he proceeded up the grades to the top where he shared in the fees paid by lower grades. So the fees system was a kind of pension scheme for the highest ranking members. The Ozo or Ama members shared seats on the Ama-ala with lineage elders. To a greater degree then the age-sets, title societies encouraged competition and individual achievement, brought government into the hands of ambitious men, and made wealth an important mark of success.

The Cross River clans and Ibibio were famous for their secret societies, the Ekpe being the most popular. Like the Ozo and Ama they conferred titles, were graded with initiation fees and provided pensions. But unlike the title societies they possessed a secret ritual

*Ekpe masquerader at the installation ceremony of the Ntoe of Big Qua Town, Calabar, the late Ndidem Edim Imona, May 1975.*

which they claimed gave them special powers from the gods. Major political decisions were taken by the top grades of the Ekpe, while the lower grades carried out administrative duties. The age-sets were also well organised among the Cross River clans, and also helped in administrative duties. The will of the ordinary people, expressed through the village assembly, was reduced. A small ruling group was created, and gave the Cross River clans more unity and direction than the other Igbo groups had. Perhaps this is one of the reasons why the Aro, a Cross River clan, were able to achieve trading leadership over much of Igboland.

The Igbo living on the Niger river as well as at Nri near Awka had kings who were in some ways considered godlike. Here we see the political influence of the kingdoms of Benin and Igala on the Igbos who lived near them. These western Igbo kings ruled over centralised states rather than villages under segmentary political systems. The king was chosen by and from a royal lineage. His council might either be Ozo title holders, lineage elders or age-set leaders whom he appointed to the council. In Onitsha the Obi (king) was chosen by and from the royal lineage of Eze Chima while his council consisted of the Ndichie (Red Cap chiefs), all senior Ozo title-holders.

The weakness of the Igbo system is found in the thousands of small independent villages, each jealous of and competing with others, quarrelling with each other, going to war and disturbing the peace. However, this lack of unity can be given too much attention, because there were in practice many links which promoted clan co-operation over a wide area.

A major link within the clan was that many Igbo were forbidden by custom to marry within their lineage, so Igbo men sought their wives in neighbouring lineages which created a complex interlocking web of marriage relationships throughout an entire clan. Men were unwilling to engage in war with their wives' relatives. Age-sets were frequently co-ordinated over a number of villages and age-set loyalty could be as strong as the bonds of the lineage. Ozo, Ama and Ekpe operated the same way. An Ozo might travel far outside his own clan and receive hospitality and respect from his brothers in other Ozo lodges.

One of the major forms of inter-clan co-operation was the oracle system. Some clans possessed an oracle for the settling of disputes when there was no clear evidence of guilt. A dispute between two villages might be referred to an oracle. There were famous national oracles which specialised in settling interlineage disputes.

## The Arochuku oracle and trade

Oracle consultation was a method of strengthening the segmentary political system. Some oracles became nationally famous for their impartial judicial decisions, especially the Agbala oracle at Awka and the oracle at Arochuku.

Awka was famous for its blacksmiths whose guilds took turns touring Igboland, settling temporarily in various places and manufacturing iron farming tools, swords and spears. Because of their superior products they were welcomed in all the clans. If an interlineage dispute arose, the visiting Awka blacksmith might suggest that it be referred to Agbala. He would offer, for a fee, to take the contestants to his home town.

More famous than Agbala was the oracle at Arochuku, 'the voice of Chukwu', the high god, and its agent the Aro who traded over three-quarters of Ibibioland and Igboland. An Aro trader might recommend his oracle, take the contestants to it and house them in his family compound at Arochuku for a fee. Since he had been a trader among the people of the disputing villages he was able to provide the oracle priests with a detailed and impartial view of the dispute. When the oracle delivered its decision it was able to show a deep knowledge of the history and conditions of the two villages which impressed the contestants, and convinced them of the oracle's supernatural insight.

Since Arochuku was on the edge of Igboland, it was far away from most Igbo clans, so it could be impartial in a dispute. This impartiality made it very popular. The guilty party or both sides were fined so many slaves according to their degree of guilt. The slaves were supposedly sacrificed to Chukwu to appease his wrath for the offence committed. In fact the slaves were not sacrificed. They were taken into the oracle and then sold. This was deception, but it was more humane than execution. The Igbo and Ibibio generally believed the slaves were sacrificed, but whether the Aros as a whole or just the priests and highest grades of Ekpe knew the truth is not certain.

The Aro employed mercenary soldiers from other Cross River clans as Chukwu's agents, to sweep down upon any village which refused to obey the oracle. Such villages were burnt and their people carried off into slavery. Many people took their disputes to the oracle because they knew its decisions were final and would be enforced.

The Arochuku oracle was popular even outside Igboland. Many Ibibio consulted it. Even the wealthy and powerful kings of the Niger Delta city-states carried their disputes to Chukwu.

The Aro's main concern, however, was not their oracle but the organisation of a complex trading system. They held a monopoly of the sale of slaves to the traders of the eastern Delta city-states, especially Bonny and Calabar. In return they secured firearms to equip their mercenaries. Under the protection of Chukwu's mercenaries the Aro opened up long-distance trade which the numerous small Igbo political units normally made very difficult.

The Aro organised three major trade routes from the north over which the slaves were brought to the central market at Bende, from where they were marched to the Bonny markets on the Imo River.

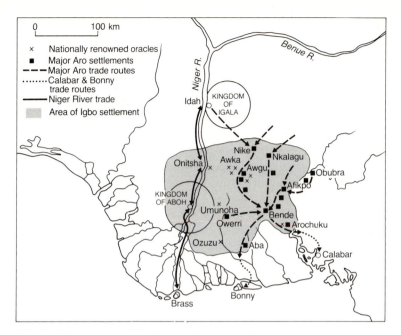

*21   Trading systems of Igboland in the nineteenth century.*

The Aros responded quickly when the British decided to buy only palm oil in Bonny and stopped its export of slaves. They helped to organise the new oil trade among the Igbo and Ibibio so that Bonny became the largest African exporter of palm oil. At the same time the Aro slave trade actually increased, because although slaves were no longer in demand for overseas export, they were required in larger numbers within Igboland for the harvesting, collection and transport of palm oil to market.

Along the trade routes the Aro settled in colonies which were used as resting and feeding stops for the slave and goods caravans and the mercenary troops. By the end of the nineteenth century there were four times as many Aros living in the colonies as in Arochuku. The Aros seldom engaged in the actual slave-raiding. They kept the routes open and safe, purchased in the markets and transported the slaves southward to Bende.

People have assumed that most of the Aro slaves came through the oracle. The oracle and the slave trade were two separate businesses both carried on by Aro agents. The majority of slaves were brought via the trade routes not via the oracle. However, the oracle was a vital part of the Aro trading system, because the Aro people were widely regarded as oracle-protected persons, supported by mercenaries. This gave the Aro the freedom to establish colonies, trade in the markets and travel unmolested over long distances through numbers of jealous, hostile clans.

The Aro were not imperialists. They were interested in peaceful trade along their trading routes, not in ruling the clans who lived along these routes. It should be remembered that the Aro were merely a clan of the Igbo people. They had the same political system and it was little suited for political imperialism. Imperialism required highly organised central rule by a single person or group. The Aro did not have a central government of their own, so they could not impose it on others.

The Aro tried to act in partnership with other communities. Ambitious and able Igbo of other clans were taken into trading partnerships. The Aro had trading agreements with some Igbo groups especially the Ozo title-holders of Awka with whom they intermarried. It is not clear whether there was an informal division of Igboland into Awka and Aro spheres of influence, but the Aro trading system penetrated very little into areas of the other major national oracles.

The British claimed to have 'destroyed' the Aro oracle in 1901-2. They did destroy its physical setting but since it was believed to be supernatural not even British guns could destroy it. Many Igbo believed that it had fled and taken refuge in a cave in Okigwi where it was consulted in colonial times.

Another important trading system to the west of the Aro on the Niger was organised by the Igbo kingdom of Aboh. Traders from the Delta city-states of Brass came as far as Aboh market from where they carried slaves or palm oil in their canoes to be sold to Europeans at the coast. The Igbo of Aboh, like the Aro, were in the strategic position of middlemen between the interior producers and the Delta buyers. As a result the kingdom of Aboh was the largest Igbo political unit of the nineteenth century.

# PART THREE

# West Africa and Europe 1800-1900

CHAPTER ELEVEN

# Sierra Leone and Gambia in the nineteenth century

## A black settler colony 1787-1807

The colony of Sierra Leone was inspired by humanitarian opposition to slavery and was nurtured by the British determination to end the slave trade in West Africa. Sierra Leone was founded in the late eighteenth century by three groups of black settlers from England, Nova Scotia and Jamaica. During the American Revolution a number of black slaves and freemen fought for the British empire. Following the defeat of the British, black loyalists along with their white compatriots fled either to England or Nova Scotia as refugees from American persecution. In England and Nova Scotia life was hard for both black and white loyalists but particularly so for the blacks, because of the unwillingness of the white population to permit their entry into society or recognise in practice the freedom and equality which British law granted them in theory.

Granville Sharp, in co-operation with the British Government, undertook to send 400 of the unwanted blacks of England to establish a colony in Africa. In 1787 the colonists settled on the Sierra Leone peninsula and named their pioneer camp Granville Town, in honour of Granville Sharp. To pay for the expense of the new colony, a group of merchant-humanitarians organised the Sierra Leone Company of which both Sharp and Wilberforce were directors.

When the black loyalists of Nova Scotia heard of the new colony, they sent one of their number to England to interview the directors of the Sierra Leone Company. The delegate was Thomas Peters, an Egba who had been sold into slavery in America, escaped and joined the British army in the revolution and fled with the loyalists to Nova

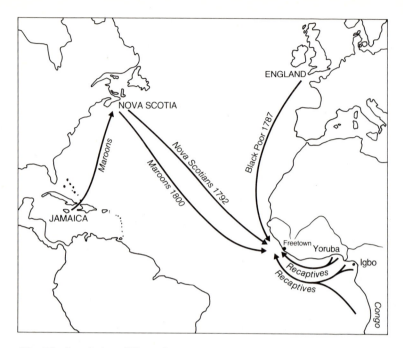

*22   The foundation of Sierra Leone.*

Scotia. Peters met the company directors who promised his people freedom from discrimination and free land in the new colony. As a result about 1,000 black loyalists left Nova Scotia and arrived in Sierra Leone in 1792.

The third pioneer group were the Maroons, free blacks from Jamaica who had revolted from slavery a hundred years before and maintained their independence in the mountains, until conquered in 1796 by the British who deported a large number to Nova Scotia. They requested transfer to Africa and arrived in Sierra Leone in 1800.

The pioneer colonists experienced major problems of survival. Some of them arrived at the beginning of the rains. Many died of malaria. They did not know how to farm in Africa. The food crops they knew would not grow and they did not know how to eat the crops Africans planted. At first most of their food was imported from England. The Napoleonic wars between Britain and France resulted in the destruction of the supply ships from Europe and, in 1794, the French navy destroyed the new settlement of Freetown. In addition the local people—the Temne—like most West Africans, feared settlers. They did not intend to sell their land permanently and gave it to the settlers 'for use only' which by Temne law made the settlers mere tenants. The settlers believed they owned the land outright. As a result of this dispute the Temne almost wiped out the colony in 1789. In 1800 when the British soldiers arrived with the Maroons, the Temne began to realise the seriousness of the threat and again tried to uproot the colony.

The settlers had many complaints about company rule. British officials, soldiers and sailors were often racially prejudiced and this enraged the colonists. They had hardly suffered so much for the sake of freedom in America only to allow the British to establish a master-servant relationship in Africa. The company governor was autocratic, failed to provide the land promised to each family and imposed land rents where the settlers had been promised free land.

In 1800 a section of the Nova Scotians rebelled. A larger section, while opposed to force, remained neutral and unwilling to support the company because of their grievances against the administration. The rebels put up a public placard declaring a new code of laws which meant, in effect, the founding of a rival and virtually independent government. The governor and his few supporters were in serious danger of being overthrown when a large shipload of settlers, the Maroons, who came originally from Jamaica, arrived with an escort of soldiers and overpowered the rebels. When the company found that profits were not what it expected, it welcomed the British government's action in taking over Sierra Leone as a Crown colony in 1807. Although 3,000 black settlers had landed in Sierra Leone, only half of them were alive in 1807, the rest having died, the victims of pioneer life.

## The recaptives 1807-50

When the British navy decided to patrol the West African coast to stop the slave trade, the colonists' new settlement of Freetown became its headquarters. The captured slaveships were brought to Sierra Leone and their cargoes of slaves when freed became known as liberated Africans or 'recaptives'.

The little colony began to receive an annual influx of hundreds and occasionally thousands of recaptives. Altogether 40,000 were settled in Sierra Leone and the population grew rapidly from 2,000 in 1807 to 11,000 in 1825, and to 40,000 in 1850. Sierra Leone became one of the great cultural 'melting pots' of the world, its population being a blend of peoples with different customs, religions and languages originating from every people and state in West Africa from Senegal to Angola.

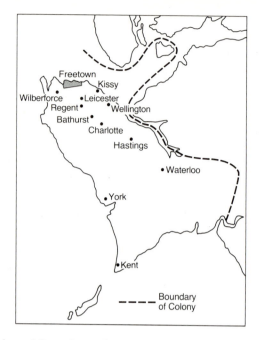

*23    The colony of Sierra Leone during the 1830s.*

Governor Charles Macarthy (1814-24) saw an opportunity to spread Western education and Christianity among the recaptives who were uprooted and cut off from their own societies. The settlers were to be the models of educated Christians which the recaptives were expected to imitate. The missionaries would be the agents of this cultural and religious change. Macarthy began systematically to settle the recaptives in villages in which the school and church were the prominent institutions. Most of the villages were given English names, like Kent, York and Wellington. Two villages founded by discharged West Indian soldiers, Waterloo and Hastings, recalled British military history. Africa, however, was remembered in Kissy (named after the Kissy people), Kru Town and Congo Town. Not all the recaptives were settled in the farming villages. Some were either recruited into the army, the Royal African Corps, or apprenticed (adopted) into the homes of the settlers who educated them and gave them their own surnames.

At first the settlers looked down on the recaptives as crude and illiterate heathens. However, the recaptives took to education and Christianity with zeal, left the village farms, moved into Freetown

114

*Freetown in the mid-nineteenth century.*

and built their mud houses alongside the elegant houses of the settlers. At first they were lowly pedlars, hawkers, tailors, barbers, carpenters or masons, but soon they began trading in the interior, operating respectable shops and buying or building storey houses like the settlers. By 1839 two recaptives were rich enough to purchase auctioned slave ships for their coastal trading operations. The recaptives worked hard, lived cheaply, co-operated in wholesale purchases and were soon outselling both European and settler merchants. Many became wealthy and educated their children in secondary schools in Freetown and even in universities in England. As the children of both groups intermarried the distinction between recaptive and settler slowly disappeared. The recaptives were not assimilated by the settlers. Instead the Creoles, who emerged as a distinct group by 1850, were a blending of settlers and recaptives, the proud inheritors of European, American and numerous African cultures.

The Creole culture which flowered after 1850 was Christian but with an emphasis upon the events of the life-cycle—birth, baptism, circumcision, marriage, death—reflecting the influence of African religions. The Creole social system was built on monogamy like European society but ties of relationship in the extended family were strong, the rich sharing their money with the less fortunate as in African societies. Creole food was a blend of West Indian, French and African cooking. The Creoles developed their own language, Krio, which has been aptly described as the English language Africanised. It is particularly suited to describe African society and life and has a melodious liquid tongue which eliminates the harshness of English. The numerous cultural strands which make up the Creoles are best seen in Krio, which is English and Yoruba enriched by Portuguese, Spanish and French vocabulary and containing elements of Temne, Mandinka, Igbo, Susu and Arabic.

# The height of Creole civilisation 1850-98

By 1860 a greater percentage of children were attending school in Sierra Leone than in England. This magnificent effort was achieved by the co-operation of the government, the missionary societies and the Creoles, many of whom went into debt to educate their children. The school system was completed by the addition of secondary schools for boys (1845) and girls, and a teacher training college, Fourah Bay (1827), which in 1876 achieved University College status. The educational system poured forth a stream of teachers, clergymen, doctors, lawyers and writers producing many of the 'firsts' of the professional class of West Africa; John Thorpe the first African lawyer 1850, J. B. Horton the first Western-medicine doctor 1859, S. A. Crowther the first bishop 1864, Samuel Lewis the first knight 1896, as well as the first newspaper editor and owner and the first to be granted Cambridge and Oxford degrees. In the church and government Creoles pioneered the path which future generations of West Africans would follow. In 1861 the Anglicans withdrew their missionaries from Sierra Leone and turned the entire work over to Creole clergymen under the semi-independent Native Pastorate Church. Creoles had always sat in the Governor's Council but in the 1850s the growing maturity of the society brought forth agitation for increased representation. In 1863 a new constitution introduced

*Sir Samuel Lewis.*

116

executive and legislative councils in both of which Creoles were represented. In 1872 when Creoles held almost half of the senior civil service posts, Governor Pope-Hennessy maintained that there were enough qualified Creoles to replace the entire European staff. In 1893 Freetown was made a municipality with its own mayor. By the end of the century Creoles formed an educated society, proud of their achievements, who voiced their views in a vigorous and flourishing press and took a prominent part in religious and secular government.

Agriculture was an exception to the story of success. The original settlers worked hard growing pepper, cotton and cinnamon on a large scale. The two commodities Europe wanted, however, sugar and cotton, did not grow well, nor could the settlers really compete in the world market without the use of slave labour. The recaptives first turned to farming but, although they understood African agriculture, they could not achieve a respectable standard of living. Like the settlers, the recaptives were ambitious and like them turned from farming to trade. The villages declined as the young people left for Freetown to become shopkeepers or traders.

Necessity made the Creoles an adventurous and exploring race. Their traders first spread out into the northern rivers, the interior and the Sherbro. They purchased condemned slave ships and traded farther down the coast. In about 1839 recaptives began to return to Egbaland in search both of their relatives and work so that by 1851 there were 3,000 Egba recaptives living in Abeokuta. By the 1880s Creoles were operating businesses in Bathurst, Monrovia, Cape Coast, Accra, Lomé, Porto Novo, Lagos, Abeokuta, on the Niger and in the Cameroons. These 'sons abroad' called upon Sierra Leone to send missionaries and teachers. Some Europeans were sent but it was the Creole teachers and clergymen far more than the Europeans who, in responding to these appeals, were the pioneers of education and Christianity along the coast. In the Niger Delta Bishop Crowther led an all-Creole staff which Christianised the city states and created a self-supporting self-governing Delta Church before the end of the century. Creoles were pioneers among the Igbo and Yoruba. In 1875 the Lagos Anglican churches were organised into a pastorate on the Sierra Leone model almost totally operated by Creole clergy. Even as late as 1900 Creole clergy formed the majority of the missionaries among the Yoruba. Everywhere Creoles held the prominent church positions: an Anglican bishop, superintendents in Anglican and Methodist churches, a colonial chaplain in the Gambia, archdeacons on the Niger. It was the Creoles who pioneered the independent African churches among the Yoruba.

*The Sierra Leone senior civil service in 1885, showing its inter-racial composition.*

As the British expanded their empire in West Africa they were dependent upon the Creoles to fill the junior and many of the senior civil service posts. Creoles sat in the executive and legislative councils of Ghana, Gambia and Nigeria. In Ghana Creoles were judges of the supreme court, Colonial Treasurer, Solicitor-General, Postmaster General, Chief Medical Officer, district officers and one acting governor. In Nigeria the Registrar of the Supreme Court, Colonial Treasurer and Postmaster General were Creoles. In the Gambia two successive Chief Justices and in Abeokuta both the President and Secretary-General of the Egba United Board of Management were Creoles. In Liberia one Creole was elected mayor of Monrovia and another, President of the Republic. Under the Niger Company and in Lagos and Dakar they held responsible positions as marine engineers. In Fernando Po a Creole prospered as a cocoa plantation owner. Everywhere along the coast they were the first, or among the first, clergymen, lawyers, doctors and newspaper-owners. As late as 1925, 44 of Nigeria's 56 barristers were of Creole descent.

Freetown became the hub of the West Coast. The Creole 'sons abroad' came and went on leave, and returned to Freetown to marry. Freetown newspapers were read all along the coast, more copies being sold outside than inside Sierra Leone. The 'sons abroad' sent money back to their relatives. The wealthy endowed charities, built schools, churches and public buildings which gave Freetown the appearance of comfort and wealth. Freetown was the centre and the Creoles the agents of a unique fusion of European and African culture which inspired Africans to imitate them. Thus Sierra Leone was the mother of Christianity, Western education and culture, and the English language in British West Africa.

Although the major Creole group was Christian, there were Muslims as well. Muhammed Shitta Bey, born in Waterloo of Yoruba recaptives, was typical, except in his religious conviction, of hundreds of other Creole sons abroad. As a child he emigrated to Badagri with his parents. As a man he traded on the Niger from his business headquarters in Lagos. When he made his money he did not forget Freetown but gave generously towards the rebuilding of Fourah Bay mosque in 1892. In Lagos he spent £4,000 on building a mosque which still bears his name. He was one of the earliest advocates of Western education for Muslims. In recognition of his good works the Sultan of Turkey awarded him a decoration and the title 'Bey'.

Freetown was also an intellectual centre in the nineteenth century. Sierra Leone's 'sons abroad' sent their children back to Freetown for their secondary education. Creole children, along with the children of the rising African educated class along the coast, still returned to Freetown for teacher-training, divinity and university degrees. As a result the largest proportion of the student body of Fourah Bay College was drawn from outside Sierra Leone.

Creole culture was creative. In linguistics J. C. Taylor's work on Igbo, C. Paul's on Nupe and P. J. Williams' on Igbirra are less well known than Bishop Crowther's *Grammar and Vocabulary of the Yoruba Language*, 1843. In medical research, Dr J. B. Horton wrote a number of books on tropical medicine, the most important of which, *The Medical Topography of the West Coast of Africa,* was published in 1860. Dr J. F. Easmon, head of the Ghana Medical Service, researched on blackwater fever and Dr Oguntola Sapara studied the Sopono smallpox society of Lagos. In history, in 1868, A. B. C. Sibthorpe published his *History and Geography of Sierra Leone,* and J. B. Horton his *West African Countries and Peoples.* Samuel Johnson, son of a pioneer Creole missionary, completed his classic *History of the Yoruba* in 1897.

Between 1850 and 1898 the Creoles (called Sierra Leoneans by Africans along the coast), although a very small community, excelled in every field of endeavour open to them, trade, religion, the professions, administration and the creative arts. Freetown in the last fifty years of the nineteenth century shone with a brilliance and held an importance quite out of proportion to its small size. These were the golden years, the height of Creole civilisation.

# Gambia

In 1816 the British established the colony of Bathurst (now Banjul) on St Mary's Island in the mouth of the Gambia River. The Wolofs of Senegal formed the largest group. Later, recaptive ex-slaves settled in Bathurst. In the 1820s when the British disbanded the Royal African Corps and two West Indian regiments which had been largely recruited from recaptives in Sierra Leone, many of the ex-soldiers settled in Bathurst. In the 1830s more recaptive settlers arrived from Sierra Leone—Yoruba, Igbo, Hausa and Popo—and were apprenticed to Europeans or Wolofs. One of the prominent pioneer traders was Thomas Joiner, in his youth a Mandinka griot who had been sold to America, freed there and returned to settle in Bathurst. Here he engaged in trade and shipping and became neighbour of the mulatto merchant who had sold him into slavery and whom he now surpassed in wealth and respectability.

The recaptives organised ethnic societies to assist them in their adjustment to Bathurst life. The Igbos led in 1842 under the leadership of Thomas Reffell. The Yoruba communities—Egba and Oyo—followed. In the 1850s the societies became important in politics, helping to inform public opinion and criticise colonial administration. In the 1860s Joseph Reffell, son of Thomas, who had been educated in Sierra Leone and England, was debarred from practising law by the colonial officials whom he described as 'perfect tyrants to the African inhabitants'. In the 1870s the recaptives (now being referred to as Creoles) complained of the preference given to Sierra Leone Creoles in the civil service. In reply Governor Kennedy called the recaptives 'the rakings of the Gambia', showing that Britain was not concerned with helping the Gambia Creoles to advance.

The Gambia was a neglected colony. It was governed from Sierra Leone for most of the nineteenth century from 1821 to 1843 and from 1866 to 1888. In 1883, long after Sierra Leone, a Creole of Yoruba descent, J. D. Richards, was the first African to be brought into the Legislative Council.

The Bathurst colony continued to expand slowly in the nineteenth century and came into conflict with the Mandinka state of Barra across the river from St Mary's Island and later with marabout or Islamic reformers on the Kombo mainland. The king of Barra controlled and taxed all foreign traders using the Gambia River, and his subjects were trader-middlemen between the interior and European traders on the river. The British gradually intruded on Barra land and sovereignty. In 1826 the king was forced to cede a mile-wide strip of his land along the north bank of the river. The British then built a fort at Barra Point across from Bathurst. The British not only wanted land for settlement of recaptives but also wished to dominate the mouth of the Gambia, control its trade, monopolise customs revenue and suppress the trade in men which interfered with their trade in produce.

The main issue of the war that followed (1827-31) was which middleman, British or Barra, was to share the Gambia River trade with the French at Albreda. The war was part of the movement by which Europeans reduced competition among themselves while at the same time eliminating African middlemen competitors and securing a monopoly of the import-export trade of West Africa. The Barra captured the new British fort and held it for a time, but inevitably British military might was decisive. Henceforth the defeated Barra kingdom, shorn of its revenue and sovereignty, slipped under British influence and ultimately under British control.

Further expansion in the 1850s brought the British into conflict in the Combo with two Moors, Ismail and Omar, the latter having fought for Abdel Kadir against the French in Algeria. These leaders were devout Muslims seeking to overthrow nominally Muslim chiefs who were prepared, in turn, to sacrifice their land for British assistance. The small area the British ultimately seized came to be known as British Combo or Combo rural. The larger part of Combo had come under marabout control by 1875. Relations between the British and Combo Islamic leaders were never cordial. The British were unsympathetic to the cause of Islamic revolution in the Gambia Valley.

The economy of the Gambia was based on the groundnut trade from about 1840. This trade was severely disrupted by the jihadist campaigns of the 1850s and 1860s in the interior. The British came into conflict with Ismail and Omar but most disturbance to trade was caused by the wars of Maba Diakhou Ba (see chapter 3). The British did not clash directly with Maba, but Maba's wars against the traditional rulers of the Senegambia states seriously affected the economy of the Gambia colony. The Creole and English traders at Bathurst suffered from the decline in groundnut production and distribution in the wars. The Bathurst traders followed a con-tradictory policy towards the groundnut-producing states of the interior. On the one hand, they sold guns and gunpowder to the leaders of these states to enable them to fight jihadists. Bathurst traders were active in attempting to persuade the interior chiefs to seek British protection. The traders hoped that by selling arms to the interior rulers and influencing them with pro-British propaganda, British rule would be extended and the wars that dislocated trade would come to an end. On the other hand, the sale of arms to interior rulers made them more capable of resisting jihadists and therefore made them less dependent on British aid. Moreover, the sale of munitions resulted in more wars and continued dislocation of the groundnut trade.

In the 1860s and 1870s the British and French governments discussed an exchange of West African colonies. The British wanted to hand over unprofitable Gambia to the French. This issue overcame the ethnic divisions among the Africans in Bathurst. Joseph Reffell organised the Bathurst Native Association to demand that Britain should give the Gambia self-government rather than transfer it to France. The association enjoyed the support of British merchants, who joined the Bathurst Africans in a common defence of their property and economic interests, which they feared would be put at risk by French rule. Much the same kind of situation in the Gold Coast—a scheme of British and Dutch transfer of colonies—brought similar demands for self-government from the Fante Confederation. In 1876, however, the transfer scheme was dropped, as a result of pressure on the British Government from the Bathurst community and from business and Protestant missionary interests in London.

The Bathurst Native Association next turned its attention to demanding much-needed roads, other public works and municipal government. Reffell proposed the setting-up of a Town Council for Bathurst as a much-needed channel of communication between the government and the people, and as a first step towards ultimate self-government. At the same time Reffell set up a company to create experimental farms which would grow different kinds of tropical produce. The farms would be organised in rural co-operatives. Reffell's company was undercapitalised and failed. But the episode shows Reffell's vision and foresight in attempting to plan a future for the Gambia based on agricultural development as well as carrying trade. Moreover, he envisaged that Gambia's agriculture would be based on various crops instead of relying only on groundnuts. Joseph Reffell died in 1886, without seeing the fulfilment of his hopes for a modernised Gambia freed from racial injustice and progressing towards self-government. As in Sierra Leone, the path towards progress was blocked and even set back in the late nineteenth and early twentieth centuries when the British abandoned their earlier policy of assimilation and took measures to reduce the role of Western-educated Africans in the administration and the economy.

## CHAPTER TWELVE

# Liberia 1822-1914—the love of liberty kept us free

## Foundation and independence

Liberia, like Sierra Leone, was a product of the efforts to abolish slavery and the slave trade. This new country was founded in 1822 when a few free Afro-Americans (people of African descent in America) negotiated for land at Cape Mesurado and began the pioneer settlement later named Monrovia. In the next fourteen years more pioneers settled at Grand Bassa, Sinoe and Cape Palmas. But the idea of a state in Africa peopled by Afro-Americans dated back to the foundation of the American Colonisation Society in 1816. The society was formed by a few white American clergymen, businessmen and slave owners, inspired by a mixture of religion, economics and politics. The return of Afro-Americans to Africa was expected to lead the country to Christianity, begin the expansion of American trade along the West Coast, and rid the United States of the free Afro-Americans, who were considered undesirable citizens because they were not slaves. Therefore, among the early settlers there were clergymen such as the Baptist, Lott Carey, and representatives of American firms.

For free Afro-Americans there were two alternatives: segregation in America or emigration to Africa. The majority opposed emigration. They were determined to fight the battle for equality between white and black in America. They looked upon emigration to Liberia as a white excuse to banish them from the United States. A small minority of Afro-Americans was ready to leave. They had little hope of blacks winning equality with whites in America. They believed emigration offered the only hope of political liberty. Their passionate desire for freedom is reflected in Liberia's national motto: 'The love of Liberty brought us here'.

Liberia was called the Lone Star Republic, not only because its flag carried a single star but because it had few friends, either white or black. White Americans who supported the Colonisation Society were few. They had conflicting aims, quarrels followed and the

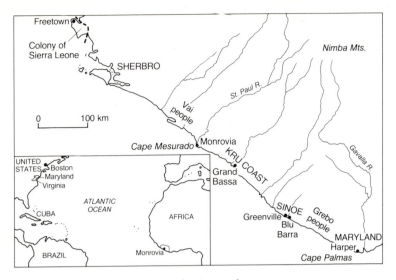

24 *Liberian settlements in the early nineteenth century.*

Society's funds dried up. When Liberia sought independence in the 1840s, many in the Colonisation Society were happy to rid themselves of an unprofitable burden.

Like their Sierra Leonean neighbours, the pioneers faced local African hostility, and did not get the land promised them. The death toll was frightening, especially among mulattoes (those of mixed African and European ancestry) and those from non-malarial areas of of the United States who had no natural immunity. About 12,000 emigrated to Liberia, many more than the 3,000 who pioneered Sierra Leone. But while the British navy freed as many as 40,000 Africans in Freetown, the American navy freed only 2,000 in Monrovia. Therefore, after the pioneers and freed slaves had mixed, the Creoles of Sierra Leone were much more African in culture than were the Americo-Liberians. The Americo-Liberians were the Afro-American settlers from America, not the local Liberians, and their culture was more white American than African.

Almost immediately they landed, as in Sierra Leone, the settlers suffered from the arrogance and despotism of the white officials sent to govern them, and of the constitution forced on them on board the ship while they were crossing the Atlantic. By the constitution they swore an oath of allegiance to the society, whose officers were given power to permit entry or deport anyone from the colony and to appoint and dismiss all officers of government. But the settlers had seen enough of slavery, and from the beginning they resented the society's paternalism and the arrogance of its white officers.

The white governors were not very successful. When they visited America and left the Afro-American, Elijah Johnson, in charge, the colony was quiet and peaceful. A major complaint was that the governors favoured mulattoes in the distribution of land. But petitions of grievance to the society were answered by expressions of shock at the ingratitude of the settlers. The white officials of the Society called the black settlers 'deluded, depraved and deserving banishment' whenever they complained of injustice. While Elijah Johnson sought to be a moderate and tried to compromise, Lott Carey led the agitation for reform. Since the society did not possess a navy it could not prevent reform. A conference of colonists in 1839 drew up a constitution of self-rule. The society rejected it and imposed their own, whereby the governor held a veto over acts of the council and full control over land distribution. But in 1841, to pacify the settlers, the society appointed the first non-white governor, a mulatto, Joseph Roberts.

In order to pay for its administration expenses, Liberia imposed customs duties on ships trading in its ports. Some Europeans refused to pay, because Liberia was neither an independent nation nor a United States colony and held a status unknown in international law. This gave Roberts an excuse to press towards independence. In a referendum the settlers supported him, and at the Monrovia Convention of 1847, a constitution and national flag were adopted and independence was declared. Roberts was elected the first president of the Republic of Liberia in 1848.

*The emblem of the Republic of Liberia.*

## Americo-Liberian achievements

The settlers, or Americo-Liberians, were building up a large foreign trade by the 1830s in palm oil from the Kru coast, camwood, used for dyes, from the St Paul River, and fibres from the raffia palm. By the 1850s plantations of coffee and sugar were flourishing, and Liberian coffee was considered the finest in the world, while sugar and molasses were manufactured in quantity for the export market. Liberian merchants entered the overseas trade, and their merchant ships manned by the skilled Kru sailors carried the Lone Star flag of Liberia into European and American ports. Merchant princes such as R. A. Sherman, Joseph Roberts, Francis Devany and E. J. Roye owned ocean transports, coastal vessels and trading posts along the coast and in the hinterland. They built southern American-style mansions in Monrovia. Roberts left £2,000 in his will to the cause of public education. Newspapers flourished—the first being the *Liberian Herald*, founded in 1826. Liberia College, founded in 1862, became the second institution of higher learning in West Africa, preceded only by Sierra Leone's Fourah Bay College.

Americo-Liberians never shone with the brilliance of the Sierra Leone Creoles in the professional fields but they did produce outstanding men. The traveller, Benjamin Anderson, wrote *Narrative of a Journey to Musardu*. Published in 1870, it ranks with the best of travellers' accounts in its understanding of African society. The missionary writer, Alexander Crummell, wrote *The Future of Africa* (1862). Above all, Liberia produced probably the most outstanding Western-educated West African of the nineteenth century, E. W. Blyden, whose writings influenced later generations of Africans. Of his many published works five major ones were about Liberia, from the first in 1862, *Liberia's offering*, to the last in 1909, *Problems Before Liberia*. In addition, the Liberian Vaughan family were pioneers of the Nigerian Baptist Missions, and the Jackson family's newspaper, *The Lagos Weekly Record* (1890-1930) was a powerful advocate of the right of Africans to self-determination and a bold and influential champion of the African. When the French occupied Abomey and the king of Dahomey fled, the *Record* defended him. Lastly, the famous Liberian evangelist, William Wade Harris, brought about perhaps the largest number of conversions to Christianity ever credited to one man in West Africa in his preaching in the Ivory Coast between 1914 and 1916 (see chapter 20).

Another Liberian, a woman, Emma White, deserves special mention. Born in America of slave parents she emigrated to Liberia and traded along the West Coast. In 1875 she settled in Opobo under King Jaja, changed her name to Emma Jaja, married an Opobo man and became the king's private secretary and chief adviser. Jaja wanted to introduce secular Western education in his kingdom, but he refused entry to Christianity. But secular Western education was almost impossible to secure, for only the Christian missionaries provided this type of education and their price was conversion. Emma Jaja, however, solved Jaja's problem when she established a secular school which in 1885 enrolled sixty students.

## Liberian politics 1839-83

In the pre-independence period the major political division was between the commercial groups of Monrovia, led by Joseph Roberts, and the agricultural groups in the other coastal settlements. The agricultural groups opposed the total break with the Colonisation Society at independence. In some areas they boycotted the referendum and in Grand Bassa they threatened to break away and form a separate state. In the presidential election Roberts of the Republican Party defeated the opposition candidate but immediately named him first Chief Justice of the Supreme Court. This technique of giving opposition leaders government posts became typical of the way the opposition was absorbed into Liberian politics.

The republicans dominated Liberian politics from independence to 1877, but the two-party system continued to function. Roberts was a capable administrator, politician and statesman, who extended the nation's boundaries, maintained fairly peaceful relations with the local Africans, and won international recognition for Liberia. He had the advantage that his presidency coincided with the era of the

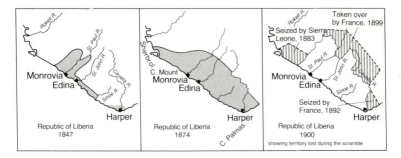

25   The growth of Liberia 1847-1900.

merchant princes and prosperity, before 1880. However, Roberts, a light-skinned mulatto, fostered a caste system based on skin colour. The light-complexioned mulatto governing class kept socially apart. They claimed that since the climate took a greater toll of their numbers than of Americo-Liberians of only African descent, they should be favoured in administrative positions. The Society in America made the situation worse by favouring mulatto emigrants, who supported the Republican Party when they arrived. But after the American Civil War immigration to Liberia sharply declined, and with the high death rate among mulattoes it was only a matter of time before the Republicans fell from power.

In 1869 the victory of E. J. Roye brought the opposition, the True Whigs, to power. Roye was a settler of pure African descent who had arrived in Liberia in 1846, became Speaker of the House of Representatives in 1849, published a newspaper, was a successful merchant, and was nominated Chief Justice in 1865.

Even at this stage the Republicans continued to show their racial arrogance. After retiring from the presidency, Roberts became principal of Liberia College where he made it a policy to admit only mulatto students. The Masonic secret society became an exclusive mulatto club. Opposition grew around Roye and Blyden. Roye gained immense prestige when as chief justice he resigned in protest against the government attempt to bring treason charges against True Whig leaders.

When Roye became president he inherited a civil service which resented his colour and his rapid rise to wealth and power. With advice from Blyden, Roye advocated the opening of the interior. He tried to get American money for a railway, and welcomed foreign investments. To secure money for road building he negotiated a loan from London bankers, who handled it in such a way that only two-thirds of the amount reached Liberia, where most of it was pocketed by government officials, until less than one-tenth of the original sum was available to the Liberian treasury. Aware of his growing unpopularity, Roye unconstitutionally extended the presidential term from two to four years.

Although Roye's aims were enlightened, his lack of control over his officials and his fear of standing for re-election in the normal two years aroused fears among the people. He was accused of planning to sell the country to foreigners and set up a personal dictatorship. In 1871 an angry Republican mob attempted to lynch Blyden, stormed the presidential mansion and imprisoned Roye, who died shortly afterwards in mysterious circumstances. Joseph Roberts came back

*Edward Wilmot Blyden.*

for two more terms as president. In 1877 the True Whigs again won an electoral victory and they have never since lost power, although the Republicans continued strong in the civil service. In 1883 H. R. Johnson, son of the pioneer Elijah Johnson, was supported by both political parties because of his immense popularity. However, on his election he declared for the True Whigs. The emergence of the one-party state in Liberia dates from Johnson's election in 1883.

One-party rule was sustained because all positions were in the patronage of Whig politicians. These positions included the staff of Liberia College, judges, heads of church denominations, and newspaper owners. All of them were bound together in the Masonic secret society, which had passed from Republican to Whig control. The system was not the invention of the Whigs. The Republicans had introduced it between 1848 and 1877. While under the Republicans Liberia College was exclusively mulatto, when Roye came to power Blyden was given the principalship and there were hardly any mulatto students. Following Blyden, principals were either politicians on the rise or politicians being quietly pushed into retirement. The result was that thirty years after its foundation Liberia College had produced only eight graduates. This was why an intellectual class did not arise to challenge the ruling oligarchy.

The civil service existed not so much to benefit the country as to provide jobs for members of powerful families. The Americo-Liberian colonists had arrived in small American-type family groups. Like the Creoles of Sierra Leone, they developed extended families. Government became the art of balancing the number of civil service jobs held by each family, and if a great family became aggrieved it was

129

conciliated by the offer of more positions. Opposition was absorbed by offers of government posts, so the civil service became overburdened with staff. The Justice Department, for example, absorbed nine per cent of Liberian's revenue compared with two per cent in Sierra Leone. Every time government revenue increased, the struggle began among the great families as to how it was to be shared.

## Relations with African peoples

From the arrival of the first pioneers at Cape Mesurado, the competition for land disturbed relations between the settlers and the local Africans. African rulers were forced to sign away their land at gunpoint. At Cape Palmas the Grebo were prepared to exchange land for Western education and welcomed the pioneers on condition that settlers and Grebos be treated alike. But the settlers tried to persuade the Grebos to move inland and leave the coastal strip to them. The Grebos refused, and in 1855 the militia from Monrovia, supported by an American warship, drove 2,000 Grebos out of Cape Palmas.

The period from 1850-80 was one of peace between settlers and local Africans. Merchant princes opened interior trading posts and co-operated with interior rulers. The government sometimes paid subsidies to the chiefs to keep the trade routes open to the coast. The era of peace ended in the 1880s. European encroachments made it necessary for the government to establish effective rule in the interior. However, the economic depression of the 1880s brought a decline in government revenue. But more revenue than ever before was needed to establish rule inland. Therefore, local Africans were taxed, and taxed heavily. This taxation led to revolts by the interior peoples.

The Americo-Liberians had to deal with progressive and ambitious local African people. The commercial ability of the Mandinka has already been noted. The Vai had developed their own system of writing, created by Momolu Daolu in the early nineteenth century, so that by mid-century a majority of adult Vai males could read and write the Vai script. The Kru, and related Grebo, had a passionate desire for education and English was widely spoken along their coast when the pioneers arrived. The Kru and Grebo were also devoted to their country, their institutions and their freedom, which was symbolised by their facial mark, called the 'mark of freedom' because the Kru were never sold as slaves. They enthusiastically embraced Christianity, becoming teachers, catechists and clergy in the missions operated by American churches. The Kru were commercially successful in fostering trade along their coast, and many worked on European merchant ships and were praised for their efficiency as deck hands, stevedores and firemen. In 1884 President Johnson permitted groups which paid more than a specified amount of tax to send members to the House of Representatives, but only the Kru and Grebo had the wealth to qualify.

The Americo-Liberians often mistreated the local African peoples. The settlers showed cultural arrogance to them and restricted their educational opportunities. In order to exclude local Africans from the already overburdened governing class, the settlers proposed technical rather than literary education for the Kru. But there was little chance for the technically-trained in a non-industrial society. The Kru had difficulty in securing employment, and even those who qualified in literary education were discriminated against in government jobs.

Many of the local peoples of Liberia became assimilated into Americo-Liberian settler society through the apprenticeship system. Local African children worked in Americo-Liberian homes, became familiar with the settlers' customs and way of life, adopted their names and later married among them. This system offended the pride of the Kru and they seldom took part in it.

In addition to their grievances over education, the Kru complained of economic discrimination. They were energetic trading people. But when the government declared six Americo-Liberian cities as international trading ports, Kru cities declined into villages. Repeatedly the Kru asked that their city, Setta Kru, should be made an international port of entry. In 1905 the president agreed. However, the Americo-Liberians of the area forcibly prevented customs officials from taking up their duties in Setta Kru, and the government made no attempt to compel obedience to the president's order. The Monrovia government was a settler government enforcing settler policies. The senator of Sinoe county lynched six Kru leaders and imprisoned a number of others, demanding 2,000 dollars apiece for their freedom. He personally pocketed this money, but despite repeated Kru petitions the government did not interfere.

Under these conditions, local Africans frequently revolted against Americo-Liberian rule. There were major revolts among the Grebo and Gola and also the serious Kru revolt of 1915. The Kru hoisted the British flag, believing that advancement and education would be quicker under British than under Liberian rule. There had been a long connection and trading partnership between the Kru and the British, who were the best customers for Kru palm oil exports, while thousands of Kru worked on British ships along the West Coast. Kru colonies had developed in Freetown, Takoradi and Lagos. Although British merchants and the British press were sympathetic to the revolt, the British ambassador in Monrovia was hostile to it. British support was denied to the Kru, who were defeated. The Liberian Government claimed the revolt was provoked by the British as an excuse to bring Liberia into their empire, but the real cause of the revolt was oppressive and intolerant rule.

In 1900 there were about 12,000 settlers and 60,000 local Africans in the counties where Americo-Liberian law, customs institutions and religion were practised. The Monrovia government pursued a policy of assimilating those Africans. In order to become assimilated, Africans had to give up their language for English, give up their traditional religion or Islam for protestant Christianity, give up their rights in communal land for private ownership and their loyalty to local rulers for loyalty to the Monrovia government. No sharing of the two cultures was intended, but instead total assimilation to the foreign culture. The Americo-Liberians were culturally arrogant; they thought their culture was superior to African culture. However, they permitted progress towards assimilation. In the 1920s, of a school population of 9,000, only 600 were Americo-Liberians. A secretary of state married a Grebo in 1881, a chief justice married a Vai in 1910, a Kru had risen to be secretary of state for education in 1915, and in 1925 a Grebo held the second highest position in the Republic, Vice-President.

The Monrovia government's policy was assimilation at the coast but indirect rule in the hinterland. Indirect rule was developed under Presidents Barclay (1904-12) and Howard (1912-20). Local rulers were to govern according to tradition, assisted by district commissioners from the coast and backed by the frontier police. Local law was administered. President Howard, an Americo-Liberian who was fluent in two African languages, had a broad national outlook. He improved the hinterland administration by appointing five travelling superintendents responsible to the president to check and supervise the district commissioners.

## The economic problem 1880-1918

Between 1880 and 1900 Americo-Liberian plantations collapsed and their merchant princes were swept from the oceans. The world-wide depression of the 1880s and 1890s which bankrupted many European

traders hurt the Liberian merchant princes as well. The
European powers partitioned West Africa, they developed t
colonies, and their own trading patterns which ignored Libe
French and British West Africa developed palm oil and ra
production. Liberia's large and important American trade was
abandoned when Americans left West Africa to the Europeans and
turned to exploit Latin America for their tropical requirements.

The Liberian coffee plant was introduced into Brazil, which
quickly monopolised the American market. Prices fell and Liberian
coffee plantations were ruined. Liberia's sugar plantations were
ruined, too, by the expansion of sugar-growing in Cuba and Brazil,
and the discovery of beet sugar in Europe. Then around 1900 the
German synthetic dyes destroyed the camwood industry. Thus
between 1880 and 1900 a series of disasters hit Liberian exports of
palm oil, raffia, coffee, sugar and camwood. British and French
ships passed by Liberia for their own colonies and American traders
stopped coming, so that Liberia sank into economic unimportance.
Americo-Liberians were unable to offset their losses by exploiting the
interior. The major obstacle was the power and domination of
internal trade by the Poro society and Diula Mandinka. In 1856, for
example, when the government had financed an expedition to the
interior, the Mandinka and Poro demonstrated their power by a
trade boycott of Liberian settlements. Liberian rivers were not
navigable, so penetration into the interior was very difficult.

Since Germany's colonial empire was unable to supply her tropical
needs, her merchants moved into Liberia before 1900 and eventually
they monopolised Liberia's trade. By 1914 twenty German firms were
doing business and two out of every three ships calling in Liberian
ports were German. The sons of the Liberian merchant princes
became agents of German firms, and not independent traders as their
fathers had been. The Americo-Liberians were caught between the
Mandinka and Poro in the interior and the Germans on the coast, and
abandoned business in favour of the civil service, teaching and the
priesthood.

Liberia's twentieth-century problems were the direct result of the
economic collapse between 1880 and 1900. This collapse destroyed
Liberia's effective occupation of the interior and resulted in loss of
territory. During the scramble for Africa, European powers decided
that areas claimed must be effectively occupied. Liberian travellers
had 'explored' the interior as far as the Nimba mountains and had
negotiated treaties with the local rulers. However, Liberia was slow to
react during the scramble, and lost Sherbro to the British and the

*Sande society masquerades. Sande is the female equivalent of the Poro society.*

coast east of Cape Palmas and a large section of the interior to the French.

Liberia's economic collapse also increased friction with local Africans as the Americo-Liberians were forced out of the export trade and entered into greater internal competition with local Africans. It slowed the growth of Western education for the traditional African peoples. Economic competition and poor education became the causes of repeated revolts, especially among the progressive and ambitious Kru. The revolts resulted in overstaffing of the civil service in an effort to provide jobs, and government revenues fell below expenditure.

In 1906, with the assistance of a British firm called the Liberian

Rubber Corporation, the government negotiated a loan from the British. The Rubber Corporation began to develop plantations in the interior, but rubber prices fell, the corporation failed to make profits, the Liberian Government was unable to collect enough revenue, and so could not repay the British loan. The corporation then began to work for a British take-over, and the British Government suggested that Europeans be employed to supervise Liberian finances and the army. In 1908 Liberia began to organise a military force under the command of an Englishman, Major Cadell, to establish more effective control of territory in the interior. Cadell helped Liberia extend its territory and save a larger and rich hinterland for future development. But Cadell was almost the instrument of Liberia losing its independence. The intervention of the United States of America helped to maintain Liberia's independence in the early twentieth century.

The French, the Germans and the British all had designs on Liberia. Cadell's troops who were stationed in Monrovia came from Sierra Leone, and Cadell took his orders from the Governor of Sierra Leone rather than from the President of Liberia. Cadell encouraged rebellion among his men because of alleged arrears in salaries and nearly carried out a *coup d'état*.

Fortunately the prominent black American scholar and educator, Booker T. Washington (see chapter 21), raised the alarm in the United States. Washington roused the American President, Theodore Roosevelt, to intervene and save America's foster-state in West Africa. Roosevelt put diplomatic pressure on the governments of Britain, France and Germany and Liberia's formal independence was preserved.

Liberia turned to America for economic as well as political assistance. In 1912 American bankers were approached to pay off a loan to the British. The bankers agreed to pay off the loan, on condition that an American be placed in control of Liberia's customs collection. With Americans in control of its finances and army Liberia had become a semi-colonial state, though formally independent.

In 1914 the British navy cut off German trade with Liberia and refused to allow British goods to be imported by German firms. Since there were no other firms this put a total stop to Liberian trade. In 1917, when the United States entered the war against Germany, Liberia had little choice but to follow and much to its own loss confiscated the German firms and bank. This left the British-controlled Bank of West Africa as Liberia's only financial institution, which attempted through its monopoly to bring about the financial collapse of the government and thus to establish a British take-over. By 1918 Liberia had reached the lowest point in its history, tottering on the verge of collapse and full British or American colonialism.


## Conclusion

Americo-Liberian history is a record of a struggle for survival, and a passionate devotion to independence. The struggle began with the throwing off of the Colonisation Society's control and recognition as a sovereign state. It continued in the efforts to save Liberian territory during the partition of Africa, and then to survive the intrigues of foreign bankers.

Internally it was a struggle to develop a national loyalty and national unity. At first the division was between mulatto settlers and settlers of only African descent. After 1883 the division was between the settlers and the coast peoples, the Kru, Grebo and Vai, and later between the people of the coast, including the settlers, and the people of the hinterland. Credit for survival was largely due to the one-party state, but the development of the country suffered.

Unity had its price. The True Whigs hoped to keep many groups happy by multiplying civil service posts and overburdening an already economically weak nation. When the party brought the courts, press and schools under its control this weakened independent thought and action. Americo-Liberians also sought to keep control over national politics and keep out the local peoples. The settlers also concentrated on politics as the main road to success and wealth, and neglected business and commerce.

Liberia's basic weakness was economic. Its plantations and merchant class, following a brief but brilliant beginning, were destroyed by changes in the world economy over which Liberia had no control. The country's continuous lack of revenue left it exposed to imperialism, widened the gulf between settlers and local Africans, made it impossible to apply assimilation to the whole country, accounted for the abuses of the administration of the hinterland, drove every ambitious man into seeking a government job and left the economy of the country to be exploited by foreigners.

Liberian history is very important for Africa, because modern independent African states face many of the problems faced by Liberia before 1914, and many of them are following similar paths to those followed by Liberia.

## CHAPTER THIRTEEN

# City-states of the Niger Delta

In the eighteenth century the Niger Delta city-states had been the leading West African participants in the slave trade. But their economy was changed because of British naval interference and their proximity to the palm oil belt. In the nineteenth century the city-states quickly converted to the palm oil trade and by the middle of the century had become the leading African exporters. This conversion of the economy led to a social revolution: a weakening of the position of the freeborn traditional rulers and the rise to power of ex-slaves. Thus the change brought about by the suppression of the slave trade was the major factor in the history of the Niger Delta in the first half of the nineteenth century.

The history of the city-states also illustrates how the abolition of the slave trade led to a greater European involvement in African politics, and thus to the partition. The late nineteenth-century trade war between the city-states and the European firms throws much light on the economic background to the partition.

In 1800 the Niger Delta area was dominated by five city-states: the Itsekiri kingdom of the west, the kingdoms of Brass, Elem Kalabari and Grand Bonny to the east and the state of Calabar at the mouths of the Cross and Calabar rivers. Each city-state was composed of three parts: the capital at its heart in the mangrove swamps, its colonies of satellite villages along the creeks and waterways to the interior, and its trading empire in the palm oil belt of the interior. In the trading empire citizens of the city-state enjoyed a monopoly of trade, and hundreds of them lived there during the buying season. The city-state protected the people of its trading empire, advanced credit to them and intermarried with them. King Pepple had an Igbo wife from the Bonny trading empire. Nana of Ebrohimi married a number of Urhobo women from the Itsekiri trading empire.

Grand Bonny was ideally located and organised for trade. It was closer to the palm belt than any other delta state except Calabar. It possessed an excellent river transport system, the Imo, which tapped a densely populated Igbo area. Bonny and to a lesser degree Brass and Calabar had developed a partnership with the Aro who had created a trading system over much of the territory of the Igbo and Ibibio. As a result Grand Bonny was the largest Delta exporter of slaves in 1800 and of palm oil by 1850. Elem Kalabari, the second city-state of the Delta, had its trading empire along the Sombreiro River. The kingdom of Brass, with its capital at Nembe and its port at Twon, was in trading partnership with the Igbo kingdom of Aboh. The Itsekiri kingdom had its capital at Warri and its ports on the Benin River.

## The House system

Originally the city-states, like the Igbo and Ibibio clans, possessed a political system based on lineages. But important changes had taken place in order to enable them to organise their trading more effectively. The lineages developed into Houses each with a head, who once elected became an absolute ruler with the power of life and death over the members of the House. The head also looked after his House's property and finances.

The Houses were like trading corporations and were in fierce competition with each other. The weak were driven into bankruptcy and thus absorbed by the strong. A House was judged by the size and quality of its fleet of trade and war canoes. Every House maintained at least one war canoe mounted with cannon, manned by about 50 paddlers and carrying 80 to 140 soldiers. Most Bonny Houses could boast of ten or more such canoes. A war fleet was a vital necessity because loss of control of the waterways could cut off the capital from its empire and bring immediate ruin. The Houses also established villages and markets where they employed their own trading agents and advanced credit to their interior partners.

There was a continual process of breaking apart and joining up of Houses. A large House, through mismanagement or poor leadership, economic disaster or political quarrels, might split up into a number of small separate Houses. On the other hand a successful House often became the head of a House group, either through alliances or by paying off the debts of weaker Houses and thus getting control of them. As a House prospered it needed more men to man its war and trade canoes and to act as buying and selling agents. Slaves were purchased to increase the population of the House, and often they outnumbered the freeborn. King Amakiri I almost doubled the population of Elem Kalabari by buying slaves.

*Kalabari screen representing a deceased House Head surrounded by the male members of his household. He is depicted wearing the headpiece of the masquerade for which he was well-known during his lifetime.*

Originally only royal princes could found or head Houses, but in the commercial competition of the eighteenth and nineteenth centuries a House either chose its ablest man as leader or collapsed before its rivals. As a result, except in Itsekiri, capable and energetic businessmen among the slaves rose to prominence in the Houses. In Elem Kalabari and occasionally in Calabar they rose to the head of subordinate Houses, and in Bonny and Brass they often became the heads of senior Houses and of House groups, positions which were next in rank to the king.

There was a royal family in each city-state except Calabar, which was a republic. An example is the Pepple royal family in Bonny. By the beginning of the nineteenth century the Bonny monarchy was four hundred years old. The king ruled through a state council of House Heads, was responsible for relations with the European traders, collected the comey (customs dues) and settled inter-House disputes. He was believed to be semi-divine, his person was sacred and he performed rituals to the God who protected the state. Each House head performed similar duties to the ancestor-founder of the House.

House society was organised in layers, with the royal princes at the top, freeborn commoners in the middle, and slaves at the bottom. Slaves were divided into those who had been born in the state and could not be sold outside it, and purchased slaves who could be sold in times of financial difficulty. In the nineteenth century freeborn commoners and slaves were becoming House heads but there remained a strong prejudice against their election as kings. By the mid-nineteenth century House heads who had been born slaves were electing kings and were therefore king-makers although they were never kings.

House organisation was like the segmentary political system of the Igbo, though much altered. The capital city and villages around it were internally organised into Houses and represented the major segments of the lineage in the Igbo village, except that there were House heads instead of lineage elders. The principle of election was kept, but the democracy had been weakened by the concentration of power in the hands of the House heads and the king. Competition and wealth were greater than in the lineage system. Respect for age and blood relationship was less important than among the Igbo, but the king and House heads continued to perform the ritual functions of lineage elders. The idea of a royal family and of a partly divine king were new ideas added on to the segmentary system. Every city-state had its secret society but only in Calabar did it possess political powers as it did among the Igbo clans. Splitting apart and joining up again kept altering the political balance in Igboland between lineages. The division of Grand Bonny into two, and of Elem Kalabari into three, separate states was the same sort of phenomenon that occurred under the Igbo segmentary political system.

## Commercial rivalry 1807-56

After the slave trade had become illegal for British subjects, former British slave-traders began coming to the Delta city-states in search of palm oil for the rapidly expanding factories of Britain. However, other Europeans rushed in to take over the slave trade which the British had abandoned, and to profit from the rising price of slaves on expanding American, Brazilian and Cuban plantations. The palm oil merchants found they could not compete with the slave merchants, because the city-states naturally concentrated principally on the more profitable trade. Therefore, in the late 1830s the Anti-Slave Trade Squadron of the British navy began to prevent the export of slaves by blockading the city-states. Bonny, close to the open sea, was easily watched and had to change her exports rapidly from slaves to oil. Bonny's misfortune brought prosperity to Brass, which became a major slave exporter for the first time as it was surrounded by a maze of creeks where slave ships could slip away unnoticed by the British navy. In Itsekiri slave captains were afraid to be caught inside the dangerous bar of the Benin River and stopped coming. Oil merchants failed to take their place and a long depression followed which ultimately caused the collapse of the Itsekiri monarchy.

The palm oil trade, like the slave trade, operated on the trust (credit) system. European merchants advanced goods on trust to House heads who in turn gave them out on trust to their buying agents in the interior. When a ship arrived the captain expected that the merchants to whom he had given trust would have a cargo of oil ready to load so that there would be little delay in returning to Europe.

Trust was not only a source of friction but also a weapon of commercial rivalry. An African was compelled to sell all his oil to the European whose trust he held. The European never wanted his trust totally repaid by a reliable African merchant because the African would then be free to sell to the European's rivals. Europeans tried every method, honest and dishonest, to keep Africans in debt to them. When a new firm arrived it found that all House heads were under trust to the old firms. To break the monopoly the new firm would offer either higher prices for oil or trust on easier terms which tempted Africans to break their original trusts. If Africans supplied the new merchant with oil the old firms would forcibly seize it. The king would then declare a boycott of all trade until the dispute was settled. The king might also proclaim a trade boycott if the European firms combined to fix prices. In this case one or two of the firms could usually be bribed to buy above the fixed price so that the European combine would collapse.

Between 1830 and 1850, when twelve Liverpool firms were buying in Bonny, the price and demand for palm oil kept rising steadily. In the 1850s two factors combined to cause supply to run ahead of demand and prices to fall. The first was the regular steamship service between West Africa and Europe, started in 1852, which greatly increased the number of European buyers (200 in the Delta in 1856). The other was that Bonny, Kalabari and Calabar, the major exporters, were joined after 1850 by Lagos, Brass and Itsekiri. In addition to these two factors all the city-states were busy extending their trading empires into the interior to increase their oil exports.

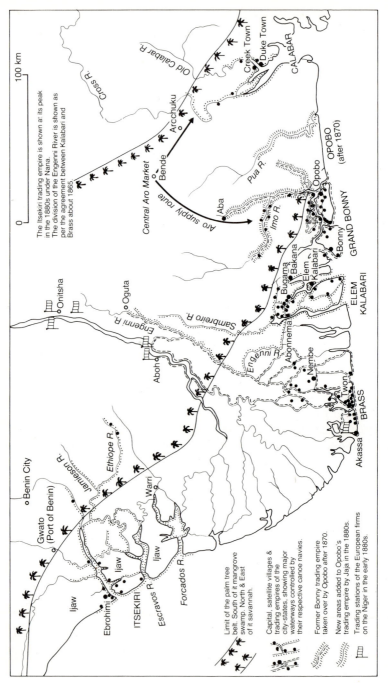

The Itsekiri trading empire is shown at its peak in the 1880s under Nana.
The division of the Engenni River is shown as per the agreement between Kalabari and Brass about 1865.

100 km

0

Cross R.

Old Calabar R.

Creek Town

Duke Town

CALABAR

Arochuku

Bende

Central Aro Market

Aro supply route

Pua R.

OPOBO (after 1870)

Aba

Imo R.

Opobo

Bonny

GRAND BONNY

Bugama

Bakana

Elem Kalabari

ELEM KALABARI

Sambreiro R.

Abonnema

Engenni R.

Nembe

Twon

BRASS

Akassa

Onitsha

Oguta

Oguta

Engenni R.

Aboh

Benin City

Gwato (Port of Benin)

Jamieson R.

Ethiope R.

Warri

Ebrohimi

ITSEKIRI

Escravos R.

Ijaw

Ijaw

Ijaw

Forcados R.

Limit of the palm tree belt. South of it mangrove swamp. North & East of it savannah.

Capital, satellite villages & trading empires of the city-states, showing major waterways controlled by their respective canoe navies.

Former Bonny trading empire taken over by Opobo after 1870.

New areas added to Opobo's trading empire by Jaja in the 1880s.

Trading stations of the European firms on the Niger in the early 1880s.

26  *The Niger Delta in the mid-nineteenth century.*

The 1850s were years of bitter commercial rivalry as the weaker European firms and African Houses were forced into bankruptcy. There was rivalry among African Houses, between city-states as they overlapped each other's trading empires, between African Houses and European firms, and between the European firms themselves. In 1855 and again in 1857 the Efik of Calabar sought to ship their oil direct to Europe by chartered ships, thus by-passing the English middlemen and raising their profits by one hundred per cent. The British had no intention of allowing this kind of trade and the navy threatened to bombard Calabar so that the scheme was dropped. Without British naval support British firms were hardly the commercial equals of the House trading corporations. But once Africans lost political control they lost their economic prosperity as well.

## The rise of the new men—Bonny

Bonny reached the height of its power between 1792 and 1830 under Opubu the Great. At his death the heir to the throne, Prince Dappa Pepple, was still a minor. The headship of Opubu's House, Anna Pepple, passed to Alali, who was one of the first and most capable of the new men—men not of royal or even freeborn ancestry—who were beginning to feature in Delta society. Alali was not a royal prince, not even a freeborn commoner, but an assimilated slave; he was appointed regent in 1833. Had Bonny overcome its remaining prejudices against men of his origin and elected Alali king the state might have avoided some of its later troubles.

In 1836 the British navy, without warning, violated Bonny's policy of allowing all nations to trade with her, and entered her territorial waters to seize a Spanish slave ship in her harbour. In retaliation for this outrage against international law, Alali imprisoned the British merchants. The British navy then threatened to destroy Bonny unless the merchants were released. Prince Dappa, anxious to rid himself of Alali and take over the throne, offered co-operation. In return for a promise never to touch British subjects again, Prince Dappa persuaded the British to force Alali to sign his own deposition. As a result British subjects became an arrogant and often criminal element, a privileged group above the law of Bonny. Alali thus gained the support of those who resented British privilege and felt that Prince Dappa had only sold Bonny's sovereignty to further his own personal ambition.

King Dappa was not wealthy and his power was challenged, both from without by the British who expected his subservience since he owed them his throne, and from within by Alali who was prospering and increasing his political power by absorbing Houses into the Anna Pepple group. To check Alali, the king passed a law forbidding the further absorption of Houses and ruled that Europeans might only give trust to, and Africans hold trust from, the king. These policies were universally unpopular. In 1854 Pepple seized a British merchant ship, in place of the payments they owed him under a treaty. Thereupon Alali and his supporters signed a proclamation for the king's deposition, and the British consul, backed by the navy and the British merchants, deported the king. A civil war followed in which Alali, leading a combination of the new men, who were mainly ex-slaves, destroyed the royalist and freeborn supporters of the ex-king.

Alali was now the real power in Grand Bonny. He might even have overcome the prejudice against his servile origins, but the British were too much aware of his hostility to their privileged position to favour him as a replacement on the throne. They supported instead a Regency Council of four; and although three of these were new men, the British were careful to see that only one was from the Anna Pepple House group. Since this government ignored the realities of political power, chaos and confusion followed, until the British merchants called for the return of King Dappa.

Dappa returned in 1861, now only a shadow of his father Opubu the Great. At British insistence he was forbidden to engage in trade and forced to rely upon comey (the customs due paid by foreign traders). His deportation had undermined his divinity, the civil war had destroyed his fortune and the trade ban prevented the rebuilding of his wealth. The British wanted a king who held absolute power over his subjects and who would do their bidding and be able to command his people to do likewise. This was impractical, for whether there was a king or not real power lay with Anna Pepple House under Alali and Manilla Pepple under Oko Jumbo, both new men of servile origin. King Dappa Pepple died in 1866 and was succeeded by George Pepple who in external affairs did what Oko Jumbo wanted.

When Alali died, Anna Pepple House elected Jaja, a purchased Igbo slave, to succeed him. Jaja had risen to prominence in the House, was popular in the interior markets, had a quick eye for the promotion and advancement of capable men and like Alali continued to build up the Anna Pepple group and absorb other Houses. In 1868 the Manilla Pepple House under Oko Jumbo attacked the Anna Pepple House with the support of the king. Rather than engage in a

*Jaja of Opobo dressed in ceremonial garments.*

civil war Jaja withdrew his House group and established it at Opobo, carefully placed so as to cut off Bonny from its trading empire on the Imo river. Jaja invited British firms to establish themselves in Opobo, but made it clear that they must operate under African law without special privileges.

Bonny and the British firms called upon the British consul to force Jaja to return. The consul advised a boycott of Opobo until Jaja's ammunition was exhausted, when it was believed he would collapse. But Jaja had what everyone wanted, palm oil. A couple of firms moved to Opobo, the boycott failed, and in 1872 the British consul recognised Opobo as an independent city-state. While Grand Bonny and the British firms who remained loyal to her declined, Opobo and her commercial allies prospered as never before. Opobo was fortunate in having control of the Imo and Qua markets and in having good trading relations with the Aro. Within the state Jaja was not threatened by internal divisions and was not much affected by the British break-through into the Niger, which was too far to the west to tap his oil markets. British traders tried to smuggle oil out of the Qua valley, which they refused to recognise as Jaja's trading empire, but Jaja more than made up for this by shipping oil direct to England and by-passing the European middlemen.

As the greatest king of the Delta, Jaja represented the triumph of the new men of servile and common origin. These men had risen with the palm-oil trade at the expense of the nobility who had declined as the trade in slaves came to an end. In all the city-states the pattern was the same, with the lower classes challenging the upper. But in none was the social revolution so complete or dramatic as that led by King Jaja of Opobo.

## The rise of the new men—Calabar

Brass and Elem Kalabari were farther from the sea and thus from the pressure of the British consul and navy, so their royal families—the Mingis and Amakiris—lost neither their power nor their wealth to the same degree as the Pepples of Bonny. Nor in those states did the new men rise beyond headships of subordinate Houses. In Itsekiri, however, the monarchy collapsed after the cessation of the slave trade and, following a period of anarchy, the new men represented by Nana, 'the uncrowned king of the Itsekiri' rose on the profits of the palm oil trade. Nana was not of servile origin but a freeborn commoner who by tradition could not be chosen to rule.

The rise of the lower classes in Calabar took a different form because of the unique political and economic organisation of that state. Calabar was organised in Houses but was divided politically under two kings. Real political power, however, lay neither with the kings nor with the House heads; but with the Ekpe secret society, which was divided into grades, the highest being the Nyampa or governing grade. The Nyampa were the real rulers of Calabar and its supreme judicial authority through which the British merchants collected their debts.

Unlike the other city-states, Calabar's economy was based on palm plantations which, like the plantations in America, bred a new and more oppressive form of slavery. The freeborn and slaves were more segregated than in the eighteenth century, the former living in Calabar town, and the latter on the plantations along the Cross and Calabar rivers. There was less opportunity for assimilation, promotion or inter-marriage. Except for those privileged to be employed in the House trading activities in Calabar, the slaves were looked upon as no more than a source of cheap labour by their absentee freeborn masters.

It was Efik custom that upon the death of a king or prominent person the House concerned displayed its wealth by the number of slaves it sacrificed to accompany and render service to the dead in the next world. Competition among Houses in sacrificing greater and greater numbers became a terrifying abuse of the slave class. Ultimately runaway slaves established their own community on the Qua River where they founded the Order of Blood Men, which was organised in grades like the Ekpe, and formed as a protection against their oppression. Slaves from the plantations as well as from Calabar town joined the Order for protection. It undertook its first defensive action in 1851. When the Ekpe arrested some slaves, thousands of Blood Men poured into Calabar threatening to destroy the town utterly if their brethren were harmed. Although the British consul and merchants tended to favour their trading partners in the Ekpe, without an army they were helpless against the slaves. In 1852 when King Archibong I died the Blood Men again poured into Calabar, standing around the town, watchful but non-violent. No funeral sacrifices took place either then or later as the Order repeated these tactics upon the death of every prominent freeborn man in Calabar. In 1857 when a freeborn man killed his slave, the Blood Men demanded and got the offender delivered up to justice. Many of the poorer freeborn began to join the Order as a protection against Ekpe oppression.

The Order of the Blood Men, through non-violent methods, secured a measure of equality for the new men (both freeborn and slaves) so that by 1863 they were able to win court cases against the nobility and Nyampa. The Order sought justice and equality but not domination. It neither attempted to set up its own king nor to destroy the Ekpe. The social revolution it created did not replace one class by another. Rather it compelled the nobility to govern in the general interest rather than for the advantage of one class. This revolution in Calabar was perhaps the most remarkable non-violent revolution in nineteenth-century West Africa.

## Commercial war 1856-86

The commercial rivalry of the earlier period changed after 1856 to commercial war. Three new competitors entered the palm oil trade: Brass, Opobo and the Royal Niger Company. Until the Anglo-Brass treaty of 1856, by which Brass promised to stop shipping slaves, Brass had continued slave smuggling in co-operation with the Brazilians

*A nineteenth-century drawing of war canoes from the kingdom of Brass accompanying members of Richard Lander's expeditionary party through the Delta.*

and the Portuguese. Following the treaty Brass began to exploit the oil markets up the Engenni river to Oguta and at Aboh and Onitsha.

Opobo, having taken over the Imo River market from Bonny in 1870, began to develop the Qua river. Bonny, squeezed out of its traditional markets, invaded Kalabari markets to the west and the Kalabari were thus compelled to push up the Engenni and began to fight Brass for control of Oguta. The resulting wars put a heavy strain on the finances of the city-states, especially at a time when they were attempting to increase their exports of oil to make up for lower prices.

It was in these circumstances that British firms broke through the Delta and established themselves on the middle Niger at Aboh, Onitsha and Lokoja. The beginning of this process was the discovery in 1830 by the Lander brothers that the Delta was the mouth of a large river. Early efforts to establish trade on the Niger failed due to the hostility of the city-states and the death toll from malaria. In 1854, however, Baikie, a medical doctor with a British expedition to the Niger, kept everyone alive by the use of quinine, a discovery of momentous importance to the subsequent history of tropical Africa.

Immediately a British merchant, Macgregor Laird, with the aid of a British Government subsidy, opened trading posts in and behind the Brass trading empire, at Aboh, Onitsha and Lokoja. Brass in reply fortified the river and encouraged the destruction of Laird's factories at Aboh and Onitsha. Again it was the British navy which decided the issue. Laird's ships were given naval escorts through the Delta, and

Aboh and Onitsha were bombarded to punish them for their attacks on Laird's factories. By 1878 four British firms were trading on the Niger. British merchants in the Delta, who had originally opposed Laird, began to transfer to the Niger where oil could be bought more cheaply.

The British effort to take over the middleman's position and increase their profits was a serious threat to the very existence of the city-states. On the Niger a price war raged between British and French firms, African merchants from Lagos and Freetown, and Brass and Kalabari traders. In 1879 an Englishman, George Goldie, aiming 'to paint the map red', united the British firms on the Niger into the United Africa Company, established up to a hundred trading posts supported by twenty gunboats, and offered very high prices for oil until the French firms were made bankrupt. The only effective competition that continued to stand in Goldie's way now came from the Lagos and Brass traders.

In 1886 Goldie secured a royal charter for his company, now renamed the Royal Niger Company, by which the company became the government of the Niger. Immediately it eliminated its last opposition by imposing heavy licences and taxes on the Lagosians and Creoles, by refusing to allow Brass or Kalabari traders to enter its area, and by confiscating the trade canoes of those caught smuggling. The company went so far as to threaten Igbo traders who tried to pay their debts to Brass merchants. The kingdom of Brass was thus economically strangled by the most severe and rigid monopoly of middlemen that the Niger had ever witnessed.


## The Christian revolution in the Niger Delta

Christian mission work in West Africa before the European conquest was nowhere more successful than in the Niger Delta, except in the humanitarian colony of Sierra Leone, where nearly all the Delta missionaries came from.

Calabar was the first of the city-states to come under missionary influence. A Presbyterian mission began work in 1846 when the earliest missionaries were first entering Yorubaland. The most prominent pioneer missionary was Hope Waddell who laboured from 1846 to 1857 and whose name is as closely linked with Calabar as Crowther's with Bonny, Townsend's with Abeokuta or Hinderer's with Ibadan. The Presbyterian mission in Calabar did not develop the same highly Western-educated elite that the Anglicans produced in

Yorubaland. The Efik and the missionaries had a prolonged quarrel over the type of education desirable. Throughout the nineteenth century the Efik wanted a strong commercial bias in their education: arithmetic, book-keeping, accountancy and business management. They were, after all, a nation of merchants and wanted their sons fitted to compete with the Europeans and succeed in business. The mission was not geared to provide this. Rather it concentrated upon biblical knowledge and technical or manual training. The emphasis was on bare literacy to make the converts, according to a Nigerian author, 'to live literally as the "unlearned and ignorant" apostles of old, according to the tenets of the new faith'. In 1895 the Hope Waddell Institute was founded; this stressed carpentry, masonry, blacksmithing for boys and domestic science for girls. By this time, in contrast, the Yoruba country was producing professionals—doctors, lawyers, and graduate clergymen—in an ever increasing stream.

Since the Presbyterian mission pursued this type of education it failed to produce the indigenous evangelists whom the Anglicans produced among the Egba, for example. It was slow to train African teachers, clergy and catechists and found itself handicapped in spreading into the interior once the opportunity came.

The beginning of missionary work in the other city-states was delayed until Bishop Ajayi Crowther of the Anglicans responded to the invitation of King William Pepple of Bonny in 1864. Thereafter Brass received missionaries in 1868, Elem Kalabari in 1874 and Okrika in 1880. Crowther's mission was financed from England, but his personnel was drawn entirely from Sierra Leone. The Niger Mission became the particular pride of Sierra Leone and the Creole community of Lagos. Under the bishop's supervision the pioneer missionaries were Dandeson Crowther, the bishop's son, and James Boyle. The Delta mission became Christianity's greatest success in nineteenth-century West Africa and for this Crowther and his all-black staff must receive great credit. The missionaries stepped into a situation ripe for Christian expansion. Not only were the city-states eager for education, they were also in the midst of a social revolution which the Christian philosophy literally set on fire.

Christianity first triumphed in Brass. Religious tolerance was extended to Christians almost from the beginning. King Ockiya, who became a Christian and was baptised under the name 'Constantine', maintained that Christians were the most law-abiding and trust-worthy of his subjects. Upon his death in 1879 the Christian converts took up arms to forestall a bid by the traditional religionists to seize political power. In Bonny the struggle was more difficult. In 1864

King Dappa Pepple invited Bishop Crowther to establish a mission, despite the objections of the Anna Pepples led by Jaja. George Pepple, who became king in 1867, had lived in England for eight years and was an ardent Christian. The Manilla Pepples, supporters of the monarchy, embraced Christianity zealously, Oko Jumbo being the first to learn to read and write. Oko Jumbo became an ardent reformer decreeing the end of twin murder in 1868, supervising the slaughter of the big lizards, the totem animal of Bonny, and financing thirteen children in the mission school. Jaja, on the other hand, rebuilt the *Ikuba*, the traditionalist temple, to make it more impressive than the church. Thereafter in the struggle for political and economic dominance between the Manilla and Anna Pepples (1869-73), religious ideology widened the rift between the two parties.

When Jaja withdrew and set up the kingdom of Opobo, he forbade Christian proselytising. Jaja was a priest of the traditional religion and the only Delta monarch to combine both secular and religious power in the kingship. He believed that traditional religion was the cement of African society, that Christianity would ultimately lead to social chaos and foreign political subversion. He was determined that under his hand things would not fall apart. He also became a staunch

*Bishop Samuel Ajayi Crowther with a group of converts. The 'idols' seen in the photograph were given up to Crowther by King Ockiya of Brass.*

151

supporter of the political forces of traditional religion elsewhere in the Delta. He influenced the civil strife in 1879 in Elem Kalabari in which the missionary was expelled and the traditionalist party wiped the schoolchildren's faces with a lotion to cleanse them of all the nonsense they had learned. Between 1882 and 1886 he intrigued with a faction in Bonny promising that he would open the Opobo markets to Bonny traders if Bonny expelled the missionaries.

European hostility to Jaja was not only because he blocked their access to the interior oil markets but also because of his anti-Christian policy. One British consul said that the missions taught their converts 'a desire for political incorporation within the British Empire'. This was why Jaja opposed the missions. He was a nationalist whose prime concern was the preservation of African independence. It was ironic that Jaja, the finest example of the 'new men', the most successful product of the social revolution, became the prime defender of the old religion against the new. Elsewhere it was 'new men' who led the Christian crusaders.

Following the Christian coup in Brass there was a mass movement of slaves and the lower classes of Bonny into the church. The new converts were determined to assert their independence within the Houses and openly flouted the orders of the House heads. They refused to work on Sunday, abandoned their excess wives to the charity of the Houses and insisted on their right to wages in order to support the church. Under circumstances which amounted to a break-up of the social structure, Oko Jumbo, early patron of the church, intrigued with Jaja to expel the missionaries. In 1883 the House heads deposed King George, deported Dandeson Crowther and let loose a reign of terror on the Christian converts. This produced a number of martyrs who refused to abandon their faith under the most severe torture. With this kind of devotion it was unlikely that Christianity could have been suppressed for long even if the British had not interfered. However, the conquest of Africa had begun, and in 1884 the British consul forced the chiefs to sign a treaty of protection which guaranteed religious freedom, In 1886 the consul removed Oko Jumbo from all authority, reinstated King George at the head of a constitution which made him an autocrat and allowed Crowther to return to Bonny. In 1888 the *ikuba* was destroyed and the Christian revolution was complete.

## CHAPTER FOURTEEN

# The fall of southern Ghana

The development of British power and jurisdiction culminating in the annexation of southern Ghana in 1874 forms the theme of this chapter.

When the nineteenth century began, the British were by no means the only European traders on the coast of Ghana. The Dutch and the Danes were also quite active. The British and the Danes supported the coastal and southern states, while the Dutch were very friendly with the Asante. The British, for reasons already discussed, came out openly in support of the southern states from 1821 onwards, when the Colonial Office assumed direct responsibility for the administration of the forts. But the British government decided to hand over the administration of the forts to British traders and grant them an annual subsidy of £4,000. They were asked to exercise their authority and jurisdiction only over the people living within the British forts, and not in any way to interfere in local politics. The forts were to be administered by a council in Cape Coast elected by British merchants who had been resident at Cape Coast and Accra for more than a year. The council was to be under a president elected by its members.

## Administration of George Maclean

The company administration, which began in 1828, continued until 1843, and instead of British jurisdiction being confined to the forts, it had by the end of the period been extended over all the states along the coast, with the exception of Elmina, and for about forty miles inland. This great extension of British power and influence was mainly the result of the work of George Maclean, who was appointed as President of the Council in October 1829. He arrived in Cape Coast in February 1830 and remained in Ghana until his death in 1847. How did he accomplish this?

Maclean realised that unless peace and order were established in Ghana, neither legitimate trade nor missionary activities would flourish. Therefore he deliberately ignored the British government's instructions and actively interfered in local politics. Indeed, no sooner had he arrived than he began to negotiate with the Asante. These negotiations were successfully concluded and a peace treaty was signed by the Asante and the British and their allies in April 1831. According to the terms of this treaty, the Asantehene recognised the independence of his former vassal states to the south—Denkyira, Assin, Twifu, Wassa, Fante, Cape Coast, Nzima, etc.—and agreed to refer all disputes between himself and the southern states to the British for peaceful settlement. He also agreed to deposit 600 ounces of gold in Cape Coast Castle, and to hand over two young men of the royal family to the British Government for six years, as security that he would keep peace with the British and their allies. The allied states, for their part, undertook to keep the paths open and free to all persons engaged in lawful traffic, not to force them to trade in any particular market, and not to insult their former master. Finally, all parties to the treaty agreed to stop 'panyarring', that is, forcibly seizing debtors or relatives and imprisoning them or selling them. This treaty was a very clever piece of work, since it satisfied both principal parties. The allied states at long last regained their independence, while the Asante gained the direct access to the forts that they had been fighting for since the eighteenth century.

Maclean also sought to maintain peace and order among the chiefs of the southern states, to stop human sacrifice, panyarring, attacks or raids on peaceful traders, and slave trading. He did this mainly by peaceful means, though he did not hesitate to use force when necessary. Thus in 1833, he stepped in when war broke out between Wassa and Denkyira, and fined the chief of the Denkyira, Kwadwo Tsibu, whom he blamed for the fight. In the same year or the next, he arbitrated between Akwapem and Krobo; in 1836 and 1838 he tried to settle the long-standing dispute between Upper and Lower Wassa, that is Wassa Amenfi and Wassa Fiasi. In 1835, on the other hand, he sent an army to Nzima against Kwaku Ackah, the famous chief who was accused of slave trading, human sacrifice, panyarring and attacks on peaceful Wassa traders.

The other method by which he established order and peace was by administering justice impartially among the peoples of southern Ghana. At first Maclean and the council left the local authorities to deal with all their criminal cases. But from 1836 onwards, Maclean attended the courts in person or sent a member of the council to watch the actual process of the trial and to see that justice was really done. Later on Maclean also allowed the chiefs, as well as their

*The burial register of the Garrison Church at Cape Coast showing the burial entries of Governor Maclean and his wife.*

subjects, to bring cases of all kinds to his court, and he tried the cases and imposed sentences of fines or imprisonment on the guilty. He also stationed magistrates in Dixcove, Anomabo and Accra. Furthermore, he used the soldiers of the forts as police, to see that order was maintained.

As a result of Maclean's work in the political and judicial fields, order was established in southern Ghana. Peace also existed between Asante and its former allies throughout the 1830s and 1840s and the external slave trade was effectively suppressed. The inevitable result was that traders and farmers were able to go about their activities, and trade therefore boomed. The growth of trade that occurred during Maclean's administration is borne out by the trade at Cape Coast. The value of exports from Cape Coast increased from £90,000 in 1830 to £325,000 in 1840, and that of imports from £131,000 to £422,000. The main exports from Ghana at this time were palm oil, gold, ivory, pepper and corn. The production of palm oil, coffee and corn greatly increased, particularly due to the extinction of the external slave trade, and to the encouragement of British traders.

Besides traders, missionaries also received encouragement from Maclean's administration. Although the Basel Missionary Society had started operations in Ghana in 1828, not much had been accomplished when Maclean began his term of office. But, taking advantage of the peace and order, the Basel missionary, Riis, was able to abandon the coast, which was considered to be unhealthy, and settle inland at Akropong in 1835; from that time the work of that mission began to take root, and to spread northwards and southwards. By 1843 Riis had established a school at Akropong, and soon opened others in Accra and Aburi. In 1848 a catechists' training college was established at Akropong, and another at Osu in 1850. Six years later, the latter was amalgamated with the one at Akropong. The Wesleyan Missionary Society also began operations in Ghana in 1835, and the work made rapid strides with the arrival in Ghana of the mulatto missionary, Thomas Birch Freeman, in 1838. He not only established churches in the coastal areas, but also began the missionary drive into Asante with a visit to Kumasi in 1839. By 1843 twenty-one missionary stations had been established in Ghana by the Wesleyans, and there were 360 children attending their schools. The Methodists expanded their missionary and educational activities during the second half of the nineteenth century, and even founded a secondary school, the now famous Mfantsipim school, in 1876. Maclean did not establish any schools himself, for want of funds, but he gave the missionaries every encouragement.

## Britain assumes direct responsibility

By the early 1840s peace had been established in Ghana, and British power and jurisdiction had completely replaced that of the Asante. A British protectorate had in practice come into existence. But however successful Maclean's jurisdiction was, it had no legal basis whatsoever. Moreover, reports reached England that Maclean was not preventing ships which took part in the slave trade from buying goods at Cape Coast. It was mainly for these reasons that, on the recommendation of the Parliamentary Select Committee of 1842, the British Government once more assumed direct responsibility for the administration of the forts, and appointed Captain Hill as governor and Maclean as judicial assessor.

Hill arrived in Cape Coast in 1844. He got a delegation of Fante chiefs to sign a document now known as the Bond of 1844. The document contained three clauses. The first clause set down that the signatory chiefs recognised the power and jurisdiction that had been exercised in their states, and declared that 'the first objects of law are the protection of individuals and property'. The second clause stated that human sacrifice and 'other barbarous customs, such as panyarring, are abominable and contrary to law'. The third clause stated that murders, robberies and other crimes were to be tried before British judicial officers and the signatory chiefs, and that the customs of the country were to be 'moulded in accordance with the general principles of British law'. This document was originally signed by eight Fante chiefs, but Hill got eleven more rulers to sign it. The Bond is not as important as has been supposed. First, it merely recognised Maclean's former administration of justice, and did not create it. Secondly, the new jurisdiction that it granted to the British was limited only to criminal cases, and even this limited power was to be exercised in co-operation with the chiefs themselves. In other words, the sovereignty of the signatory chiefs was fully recognised.

Since Maclean was appointed as the judicial assessor, the exercise of British jurisdiction continued very much as before; that is, in close co-operation with the chiefs. In August 1846, for instance, a murder case was tried before him and four chiefs. However, after his death in 1847, the system of administration of justice began to change to the disadvantage of the African rulers. By the 1860s English law, and English law courts with attorneys, had in many cases entirely replaced customary law and the courts of the chiefs, especially in the coastal states.

The problem of administration, however, was not satisfactorily solved until 1850. In that year the Ghana forts were again separated from Sierra Leone and given their own executive and legislative councils, consisting of the governor, British officials and merchants.

The other task that Hill and his successors tackled between 1843 and 1865 was that of promoting Western civilisation and trade. They had in view the construction of roads, hospitals and schools. These measures, as well as the great extension of British power and jurisdiction already mentioned, were costly. It was partly with a view to raising revenue to meet these costs that in 1850 the Danish forts were bought by the British Government, and two years later the Poll Tax Ordinance was passed. With the acquisition of the Danish forts it was hoped that increased customs duties could be imposed. But these hopes were frustrated because the Dutch authorities refused to co-operate. The Poll Tax Ordinance was passed by the Assembly of Chiefs which met in Cape Coast in April 1852 and was ratified by a similar body of chiefs that assembled in Accra. The ordinance imposed a tax of one shilling per year per head on every man, woman and child in the 'Protectorate'. This attempt at raising revenue through direct taxation also failed. Instead of the estimated annual revenue of £20,000 from this tax, only £7,567 was collected in the first year, and even this yield fell steadily to £1,552 in 1861 when, for reasons to be discussed, the tax was abandoned (see the next section on the Fante Confederation).

In spite of the work of Maclean and Hill, British power and jurisdiction in the southern states of Ghana was threatened by the Asante invasion of 1863 (see Chapter 9). The mishandling of the war by British officials at the coast led to the setting up of the Parliamentary Select Committee of 1865 to go into the affairs of the British West Africa settlements. One of the major recommendations of this committee was that there should be no further extension of British power and jurisdiction, nor any more treaties offering protection to African states, and that the objects of British policy in West Africa should be 'to encourage in the natives the exercise of those qualities which may render it possible for us more and more to transfer to them the administration of all the governments, with a view to our ultimate withdrawal from all except probably Sierra Leone'. Had this recommendation been fully carried out in Ghana, all would have certainly been different. But it was not. On the contrary, far from preparing to withdraw, the British began to entrench themselves even further. In 1866 they deposed and exiled Aggrey, the king of Cape Coast, and they revived their negotiations with the Dutch; this led first to an agreement in 1867 to exchange their forts, and four years later (February 1871) to the purchase of all Dutch forts on the coast of Ghana. Three years later the British went on to annex the whole of southern Ghana as a crown colony.

## The Fante Confederation

We must now examine the reaction of the traditional authorities to this steady growth of British power and jurisdiction, and the reasons for the Colonial Office's final decision to annex southern Ghana, a demand that they had been resisting since the 1840s.

The answer of the Ghanaian rulers to the steady growth of British power and jurisdiction was the formation of the Fante Confederation based at Mankessim. This movement began in 1868, after the report of the Select Committee of 1865 and the Anglo-Dutch exchange of forts. But its roots go much deeper into the past, as far back as the period of Maclean's administration. The first of these roots was political. It seems clear that the southern states were not prepared to see their newly won independence from Asante being encroached upon by any other power, African or European. Therefore, right from the time of the company administration, they protested against this. Owing to the enlightened way in which Maclean exercised his power, and the respect he showed to the local rulers and their customary law, there were not many instances of resistance to his rule. But a few did in fact occur.

As early as 1834, the king of Denkyira sent a petition to the Secretary of State for the Colonies, protesting against the treatment he had received at the hands of Maclean. Kwaku Ackah, the notorious Nzima king, also steadily resisted any attempt to lessen his power, and Maclean's influence was never really effective in Nzima. In 1846, the people of Tantum released their chief, who had been arrested on the orders of Maclean, and assaulted the policemen. In the same year, the king of Gomoa also refused to obey the summons for repeated extortion served on him by a policeman sent by Maclean.

In the 1850s and 1860s, as British judicial power became wider, Assin rebelled and began to negotiate with the Asantehene to return to former allegiance. But even more significant was the reaction in the 1850s to the poll tax that was proposed in 1852. Resistance to it broke into the open in the eastern districts in January 1854, when protest meetings occurred and the chiefs and people refused to pay. Though this protest was suppressed, it broke out even more violently later in the year, when an army of more than 4,000 men, not only from Accra but also from Akyem, Akwapem and Krobo, attacked the Christiansborg Castle after a British bombardment of Labadi, Teshi and Osu. This movement was again crushed, but in Krobo a fierce civil war broke out four years later between pro- and anti-British parties over the tax. The latter were defeated with the help of a British force, and a fine was imposed on them to meet the cost of the expedition, but they refused to pay it. Similar protests also broke out in the western districts, centring on Cape Coast, and only the threat of the use of force compelled the chiefs and people to continue to pay. But even here, so reluctant were the people and so strong was the spirit of resistance that the money from the tax continued to get smaller until 1861 when it was so little that the collection was stopped.

It should be noted that the main reason for the failure of the tax was that the chiefs had no say either in its collection or in its expenditure. In fact the assembly of chiefs which passed the tax ordinance was not summoned again. In other words, the British officials did not follow the principle which the chiefs and people of the southern states were insisting upon, the well-known principle of no taxation without representation. But the end of the poll tax did not mean the end of British jurisdiction in the country. In 1864 the new governor, Richard Pine, even passed an ordinance making it compulsory for all traders in wine and spirits to obtain a licence of £2 per annum; this was to be enforced not only in the British forts, but 'over the whole of the British possession and to a distance of two miles inland'. The chiefs of Cape Coast protested strongly against this, mainly on the grounds that since they and their people were not British subjects, they could not be taxed without first being consulted.

This steadily growing protest against the extension of British power and jurisdiction came to a head in 1865 when John Aggrey was elected king of Cape Coast. Two months after he became king he clashed with the government when he objected to appeals against the decisions of his court being sent to the British court. He went on to criticise Maclean who had, he said, 'in a very peculiar, imperceptible and unheard-of manner, wrested from the hands of our kings, chiefs and headmen their power to govern their own subjects'. And, to strengthen his claims, he sent a delegation of two (Martin and Carr) to England, who gave evidence before the Select Committee of 1865. His opposition to British jurisdiction became even fiercer after the recommendation of the Select Committee, and finally, in December 1866, he sent a letter to Governor Conran in which he expressed this opposition in very strong terms. 'The time has now come for me,' he wrote, 'to record a solemn protest against the perpetual annoyance and insults that you persistently and perseveringly continue to practise on me in my capacity as legally constituted king of Cape Coast.' And he reminded the governor that, 'the government in England has expressed its desire that we, kings and chiefs of the Gold Coast, are to prepare ourselves for self government and no protection'. He followed this letter up with a petition to the Colonial Secretary. The governor felt so angry about his power being challenged that, a day or two after receiving this letter, he arrested Aggrey, declared him deposed, and deported him to Sierra Leone. He was not allowed to return to Cape Coast even as a private citizen until March 1869, and he died later in the same year. But neither Aggrey's deportation nor death ended the demand for self-government.

The growth of British jurisdiction and the reactions to it were not the only deeper causes of the rise of the Fante Confederation. The other equally important force pulling the southern states together, particularly in the 1850s and the 1860s, was the old Asante problem. Just as the Asante never abandoned the hope of reconquering their former subject states to the south, so the coastal and southern states never gave up their desire to regain their middleman position and safeguard their independence. Politically, too, the Asante neither surrendered their traditional hold on Elmina in the west, nor their strong alliance with Akwamu and the Anlo in the east. Thus relations between the Asante and their former subjects never became smooth. With his reputation and tact, Maclean was able to maintain peace between them, and settle all disputes that arose in a friendly way. But after 1843, when he ceased to be in sole control of affairs, the old abuses, insults and attacks on traders began again.

With the death of Maclean, relations between the two sides worsened, and in 1853 only a last-minute change of heart by the Asantehene prevented an invasion of the protectorate. But this eventually did occur in 1863 for reasons already discussed. The early victories won by the Asante once more showed the southern states the need for a strong united front for the preservation of their independence. Indeed in 1863 the wealthy Fante gentleman, Hutchinson, formed a Rifle Volunteer Corps for defence purposes, and though the British broke up the corps, the formation of a national army was one of the programmes of King Aggrey.

What finally led to the formation of the Fante Confederation was the agreement between the Dutch and the British for an exchange of forts which was drawn up in March 1867, and was to come into force in January 1868. According to the convention, all the Dutch forts and settlements and 'rights of sovereignty and jurisdiction', east of the mouth of the Sweet River, near Elmina, were to be taken over by the British, while the Dutch were to take over those of the British to the west. The news of this agreement infuriated the Fante because they had not been consulted. It also alarmed the rulers of the western districts because they knew that the Dutch were the traditional friends of the Asante, and they expected their states would soon be overrun by the Asante. In fact it was the Denkyira who hurriedly sent ambassadors to the Fante kings to ask about their response to the news and followed this with another delegation to Mankessim where all the Fante chiefs, as well as the other delegations from the western districts, assembled. And it was at this meeting at Mankessim in January 1868 that the delegates present refused to accept the Anglo-Dutch agreement, and significantly decided to form a government which would 'be to ourselves a head, having no king under the British'.

The Fante Confederation continued to be active until 1871, and from then on it began to decline until 1873 when it ended altogether. What did it achieve during its brief spell of life and why did it fail?

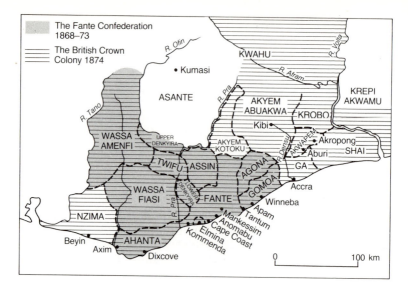

*27   The Fante Confederation 1868-73 and British Crown Colony 1874.*

First and foremost, it succeeded in establishing an administrative machinery. At the first meeting in January 1868, a council was set up in which each state was to be represented by seven elected members. Three joint-presidents to head the council were elected and also a magistrate and a secretary. Then in 1869 Ghartey of Winneba was elected as president. Finally, in November 1871, after discussions among the educated Africans, the Confederation successfully worked out a written constitution and adopted it. The discussions were led by the Sierra Leonean scholar and nationalist leader, J. (Africanus) B. Horton. In 1868, Horton had published a book entitled *West African Countries and Peoples*, in which he proposed a plan for self-government for Britain's West African territories. The constitution was advanced. There was to be an executive council of *ex-officio* members and others appointed by the Confederation. A representative assembly was to be established consisting of two delegates from each state, one of whom must be a chief, and the other an educated man. There was to be a national assembly of kings and principal chiefs which would meet annually to confirm the proceedings of the legislative assembly, to elect the *ex-officio* members of the executive, and also to elect the president, the constitutional head of the confederation. And the Confederation did in fact elect officers to the executive. J. F. Amissah was elected as secretary, J. H. Brew as under-secretary, F. C. Grant as treasurer, and

*J. (Africanus) B. Horton.*

J. M. Abadoo as assistant treasurer. However, because of the rivalry between the kings of Abora and Mankessim, it was not until a year later that the latter was elected as president (July 1872). The confederation also adopted a national seal which consisted of the now familiar elephant standing against an oil palm tree, encircled with the words 'The Government of the Fante Confederacy, Mankessim'.

Secondly, the Confederation set up a national army which was able to send military assistance to the Kommenda and the people of Dixcove, who were resisting an attempt to take them over by the Dutch. The army also besieged Elmina and the Dutch headquarters. Indeed, it was mainly the strong action taken by the Confederation which made things so difficult for the Dutch that they finally decided to leave Ghana altogether.

Thirdly, the Confederation did impose and collect a poll tax as well as export duties, though it is clear that the money from these began to decline in 1871. Fourthly, it set up a confederate court in December 1868 at Mankessim under the presidency of King Ghartey, and many cases were referred to this court by some of the chiefs.

It should be clear from the above that the Fante Confederation was not just a paper scheme, but a movement that did come into existence, that did draw up plans, and did attempt to execute them. However, by 1872, it had lost its real drive and it had ceased to exist by the early

163

months of 1873. One of the main reasons for its failure was undoubtedly the rivalry among the chiefs, especially the rivalry between Edu, the king of Mankessim, and Otu, the king of Abora. This rivalry did not allow for sincere and complete co-operation between these two kings, who were by then the most powerful of the kings of the western district. But the second and more decisive cause was the hostile attitude of the British officials on the coast. Both Ussher and Salmon, who acted as administrators during the period, saw the Confederation as a real challenge to British power and jurisdiction in southern Ghana, and did everything possible to crush it. And they did this first of all by playing off the chiefs against the educated Africans and then, as Ussher himself confessed in 1872, by detaching the chiefs one by one from the Confederation.

The British determination to crush the movement became greater in 1871 when the Confederation adopted a full constitution. The Acting Administrator, Salmon, had all the members of the executive arrested early in December 1871 on the ridiculous charge of treason. Though the Colonial Office condemned the action and ordered the immediate release of the officials, the Confederation never recovered from it. And, indeed, so successful had the British become in spreading disunity among the states of the western districts by the end of 1871, that not even the possible invasion of the Asante could bring them to act together. Had the confederation movement received the blessing and support of the British officials, it would most probably have succeeded.

## The establishment of British rule

Having killed off the Confederation, the British went on to annex not only its constituent states but all the states of southern Ghana as well in July 1874. Why did the British take a step that they had been refusing to take, in spite of the demands of the traders and some local officials, since the 1840s? The final annexation of southern Ghana was due to three main factors. The first was the withdrawal of the Dutch from the coast of Ghana in 1872; the second was the beginning of the 'new imperialism' in England; and the third was the decisive defeat of the Asante in 1874. One of the main reasons why the Colonial Office constantly objected to any great extension of British power in Ghana was the fear of increased administrative costs. But with the final departure of the Dutch from the Ghanaian scene in 1872, the British were in a position to raise greater revenue than before from increased customs duties, and they could therefore extend their power.

The second factor was the changing attitude in England towards the acquisition of colonies. Until about 1860, the attitude in Britain had on the whole been anti-imperialist and anti-colonial. Preference had been given to informal empires and protectorates, while formal empires and increased responsibilities were frowned upon. But in the 1870s opinion began to change in favour of the acquisition of colonies. This change was caused mainly by the need for markets and raw materials, as international trade became more and more competitive. Indeed, in 1873, when the Colonial Office considered the question of whether the British were to withdraw from Ghana, one of the under-secretaries cautioned against withdrawal on the grounds that British public opinion would be against it. 'In the present tone and temper of the British mind,' he wrote in February 1873, 'no abandonment of territory would be permitted by the Parliament or sanctioned by public opinion.' Nevertheless, the Colonial Office would most certainly not have annexed southern Ghana at the time it did, but for the Asante war of 1874.

The decisive defeat of the Asante by the British in 1874 put them in a position to do whatever they liked with Ghana. With the recent victories and prospects of increased revenue, and the changing mood in England, and since the Fante Confederation was by that time destroyed, annexation was the obvious choice. In July 1874, therefore, the British issued an edict formally annexing southern Ghana as a British crown colony.

*A nineteenth-century drawing showing a scene from the British campaign against the Asante in 1874.*

165

## CHAPTER FIFTEEN

# Partition and conquest

'A forcible possession of our land has taken the place of a forcible possession of our person'

For most West Africans the partition marks the end of political independence and the beginning of subjection to foreign rule. Like the Islamic and abolitionist movements, it was revolutionary in its effects upon West Africa. Like these earlier movements it affected people unequally, some being only slightly touched and others being affected greatly. Just as the abolition of the slave trade led the way to the conquest, so the conquest and partition in turn stimulated the rise of modern nationalism, the fourth great theme of West Africa's two revolutionary centuries.

European powers for a long time showed little interest in creating colonies in West Africa. But during the nineteenth century a gradual increase in foreign authority took place until by the 1880s the entire coast was dominated by European nations. In some places the Europeans governed long stretches of coast, as the French did in Senegal, the British in Sierra Leone and Ghana, and the Black

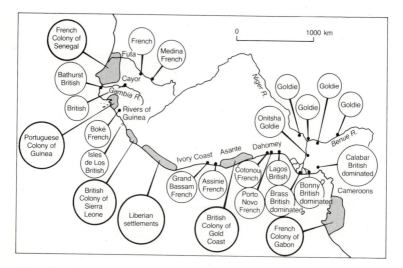

28  Alien domination of the import-export trade of West Africa in 1880.

American settlers in Liberia. In other places the Europeans possessed a few strategic points, such as Banjul in Gambia, Grand Bassam and Assinie on the Ivory Coast and Lagos on the Yoruba Coast, through which they controlled the trade of African states.

Even in African-ruled areas European merchant firms supported by European navies were dominating the coastal states almost as if they were the rulers. In Bonny, Onitsha, Brass and Calabar they possessed their own courts, which placed them above African law. The British in Calabar and the Cameroons and the French in Cayor and Futa Toro decided the succession to the throne.

In the seventies and early eighties European positions were strengthened. The Dutch sold out in Ghana, and the French sold out on the Niger-Benue, leaving both entirely to the British. The French took over the Dahomey coast and squeezed the Sierra Leone Creoles out of the rivers of Guinea. The position of African kingdoms weakened, for they were no longer able, in their own interests, to play off one European group against another. European merchants of one nationality found it easier to combine together and pay lower prices or to control or ban the importation of firearms and ammunition.

In the 1850s Europeans began to penetrate the interior via West Africa's great water highway, the Niger. While the British entered from the Delta, the French came from the Senegal. A new phase of expansion began in the interior in the late 1870s with French activity on the Senegal in 1878 and Goldie's amalgamation of British firms on the Niger-Benue in 1879. European expansion before 1880 was slow and steady, though with a quickening of pace in the seventies. But after 1880 it developed into a feverish rush or 'Scramble'. The causes of this change in the pace of European expansion were due to important developments in the internal politics of Europe, to new economic conditions, and to an alteration in European attitudes to non-European people.

## The European balance of power

The scramble was partly the result of European rivalries resulting from the rise of Germany. Before 1870 the German people were split up into numerous small states dominated by France and Austria. The German states were united by Bismarck in a series of wars in which Austria and France were defeated. Bismarck dictated terms to the French whereby two French provinces, rich in coal and iron, became part of the new German nation. Bismarck constantly feared France

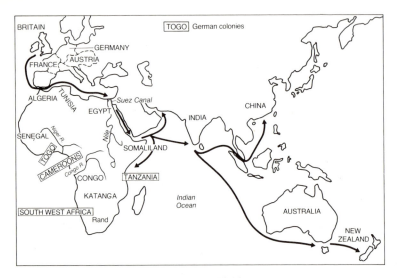

*29    The Suez Canal: a British commercial lifeline.*

would try to win back the lost provinces from Germany, and make an alliance with England against her. Bismarck's policy was to seek friendship with Britain and France, but encourage disagreement between them in Africa so that they could not co-operate together in Europe. An opportunity arose in Egypt.

In 1882 Egypt was on the edge of bankruptcy with debts owing to a combination of French, German and English bankers. French bankers held the largest bloc of Egyptian debts and French teachers, technicians, merchants and military officers far outnumbered other Europeans in Egypt. Egypt was considered to be in France's sphere of influence. However, Britain moved first, and occupied Egypt in 1882.

Once the Suez Canal opened in 1869 it became a most important link in Britain's trading connections with British India. Britain was happy if Suez was in the hands of a weak Egypt but not if it was in the hands of a strong France. Germany supported British occupation because it made France angry with Britain. British occupation of Egypt was one of the factors which led to the scramble and partition because Germany encouraged the French to make up for their two lost provinces in Europe, and for Egypt, by seeking empire elsewhere in Africa.

Quite unexpectedly both Bismarck of Germany and King Leopold of Belgium showed their imperial ambitions in Africa. Bismarck personally disapproved of an overseas empire but he began to see that

168

*A procession of ships sailing through the Suez Canal at its opening in 1869.*

if Germany was to play off England against France it would help to possess territory in Africa for bargaining purposes. In a surprise move in 1884 he sent warships to declare German sovereignty over the coasts of German Togoland, Cameroons, South West Africa and Tanganyika. These were areas of British influence where their missionaries and traders were at work. This was designed to make the French feel that Germany was on their side in Africa. Leopold of Belgium, described as a big-minded king in an insignificant kingdom, created an International Association. This was supposed to promote scientific knowledge about Africa, but was in fact established to carry out his secret territorial ambitions in the Congo.

The French wanted to enlarge their African empire. They might yet strike a blow at Britain in Egypt by linking up their existing colonies: Senegal on the west, Somaliland on the east, and Algeria and Tunisia on the north. If the French could get control of the upper Nile they would be in a position to turn Egypt into a desert and force the British out. Furthermore, Germany possessed a larger and younger population with a higher birth-rate than France. In an age when battles were decided by foot soldiers, every year the balance of manpower in Europe was turning against France. One way of reversing this was to create an empire from which to recruit soldiers.

Britain, unlike France, was quite content to leave the African situation alone, except for Egypt. Its traders dominated African trade because their cheaper prices assured them of an advantage over any rivals. However, German, French and Belgian manoeuvres were a challenge to British supremacy. If Britain did nothing Africa would go behind the customs barriers erected by other nations in their colonies and its own traders would be excluded.

The British occupation of Egypt was vital in starting the scramble elsewhere on the continent. Its importance for West Africa was much less. Long before the British occupation of Egypt there were many signs in West Africa that a new imperial advance could be expected. There was the British defeat of Asante in 1874, renewed French activity on the Senegal in the late 1870s, British and French manoeuvring on the Niger and French and Belgian activity on the Congo. It was the rivalry on the Niger and Congo which prompted the Berlin conference.

Once it became evident that the carving up of Africa was to begin, the European powers met in 1884 at the Berlin West Africa Conference, 'a memorably absurd gathering', because it achieved nothing except to proclaim what was quite obvious: certain powers had imperial ambitions in Africa. It resolved that the Niger and Congo should be open to the trade of all nations, but Goldie and Leopold promptly created monopolies which excluded other traders on these rivers. It declared that a coastline must be 'effectively occupied' before it could be declared a colony, but by the time the conference met most of the West African coast was already occupied by European powers.

*The Berlin West Africa Conference, 1884.*

The Berlin conference did ensure that the occupation of Africa was to be a co-operative European effort. European rivalries were controlled to ensure they did not lead to open conflict between European powers. Whenever African rulers signed away their sovereignty in treaties with European powers, all other powers accepted these treaties as valid claims for colonies. It did not matter that these treaties were fraudulent, misunderstood, deliberately mistranslated or even repudiated by the African rulers afterwards. Africans were kept out of the scramble which was to be a strictly European affair. No European power allied with an African state against a rival European power. Such an alliance might have enabled an African state to obtain modern firearms and save its independence. There were jealousies and divisions among Europeans, but the striking feature for Africans was the unity of Europeans in their assault upon the continent.

## Economic imperialism

The diplomatic manoeuvring of nations is often based on economic interest. Merchant groups were among the most powerful pressures upon European governments. For example, in the late 1870s and early 1880s German trade with West Africa had been growing rapidly and the merchants engaged in it had been clamouring for colonies. Bismarck's surprise move in 1884 therefore was not purely diplomatic. As a politician needing support he won the merchants' favour with an African empire. Similarly, Britain's occupation of Egypt may have made strategic sense, but it was Britain's economic interests in Asia that led to it.

Until the 1870s Britain, the first industrialised nation, held a virtual monopoly of the manufactured goods of the world. But by the 1880s France and Germany were industrialising, and they resented dependence on British sources for their tropical products. They found it difficult to compete with British merchants in the credit they could offer, in the quality and cheapness of their products or in the price offered for raw materials. Their merchants therefore wanted colonies from which they could exclude British and other traders. These colonies would also provide raw materials for their factories and markets for their goods.

Many Europeans believed in the theory of economic imperialism: the object of having empires is to make commercial profit from them. Traders, travellers and missionaries stressed the value of Africa's raw materials and markets, and put pressure on politicians, through the press, to obtain colonies.

Between 1873 and 1896 the world passed through a severe economic depression. Trade was slow, prices low and profits small. European firms looked to their governments to cut out the African middlemen, for if they could be brushed aside, European traders could deal direct with the producers, and prices could be driven lower and profits thereby maintained. By the 1880s West Coast firms were loudly calling for the help of their governments in crushing coastal states and middlemen. As one colonial governor said, 'The commercial world are insatiable; they say "we want territorial expansion, open roads and interior markets for our wares and for the overflow of the produce in return". They seem no longer satisfied with the sandbeach policy of past years....'

Compared to Europe's trade with America or Asia, her trade with Africa was small. It has been argued it was hardly worth the expense of conquest. However, it was often not present trade but future prospects which lured Europeans forward. Africa was believed to possess great potential wealth. In 1886 the largest gold deposits in the world were discovered on the Rand in South Africa and there were already rumours of vast copper deposits in Katanga. Few nations felt they could sit idly by and see undiscovered riches fall to their rivals. Even if a nation had no immediate need for African products and markets, it was believed to be good insurance to take as large a slice as possible for future use.

## Racialism and nationalism

Early in the nineteenth century Europeans believed that Africans were inferior to them but only because of the effects of centuries of the slave trade. Europeans believed Africans could be raised to the European level by cultivation and selling of export crops, by Christianity and by European-style education. They also believed in a partnership between Europeans and an educated Christian African middle class of merchants, farmers, clergymen and teachers to raise up the other Africans. Originally these partners were the Creoles of Sierra Leone, the 'Habitants' of Senegal and the Americo-Liberians. Eventually educated Yoruba, Efik, Fante, Ga and Wolof people joined the small but growing middle class.

The flourishing churches of Freetown, Cape Coast, Lagos and the Delta showed African initiative in religion. Liberia, the Fante

Confederation and the Egba United Board of Management showed that educated Africans could take political leadership. In commerce a number of Anglo-African partnerships were created such as Christie and Davies. Christie, the Englishman, ran the business in England and the African, Davies, handled it in Lagos and on the Niger.

European attitudes towards Africans changed for the worse after quinine was discovered as a cure for malaria and the industrial revolution gave Europeans vast technical, scientific and military superiority over all other peoples of the world. Writers such as Richard Burton and Winwood Reade argued absurdly that the races of the world were at different stages of evolution. The white had evolved the furthest and the black the least. Neither Christianity nor a university degree could overcome inborn African inferiority. Europeans were born to rule and dominate commerce, religion and government. Some Europeans fought against this new racialist doctrine but in the end it was widely accepted. Europeans believed that it was a privilege for Africans to be ruled by them, and that the conquest and partition was a blessing to Africa.

Nationalism had also been growing in Europe. Towards the end of the nineteenth century each nationality claimed superiority over others. The possession of an empire became a test and a proof of a nation's superiority. This extreme nationalism easily led to the slogan 'my country right or wrong' which was used to justify any action against foreigners. Flags and national anthems became sacred symbols. The churches promised a life after death in paradise for those who died for king and country. Service to one's country and the defence of its honour were believed to be the greatest of virtues. Poets, composers and novelists glorified the empire-builder far out on the frontiers, bringing the so-called 'savages', 'heathen' and the 'lesser breeds' within the sway of their European 'benefactors'.

'Painting the map red' became the driving force behind men like Goldie and Lugard, who tramped, sweated and fought across Africa in what they thought was a noble cause. Nationalistic imperialism was often intense among the lower classes, the industrial workers. They were at the bottom of European society but they liked to think that, as Europeans, they were superior to the rest of mankind. They took pride in 'our empire' even though they might not quite know where it was. They had the vote, so they could take out their anger on any politician who appeared ready to barter away any part of the empire.

The causes of the partition were various and complicated. The long, steady process of European expansion in West Africa seemed likely to increase in speed in the late 1870s even before a host of new factors appeared in the next decade. The French and German challenge to British industrial supremacy, together with the economic depression, drove the European nations to political and commercial rivalry in Africa. These rivalries were further inflamed by the excessive growth of nationalism in European nations. The growth of racialism among Europeans also helped to propel them into Africa. In addition the British occupation of Egypt in 1882, the personal ambitions of Leopold, and the discovery of the Rand goldfields in 1886 all contributed to the haste and hurry.

## The pattern of partition

Some historians argue that the pattern of the partition was caused by the British occupation of Egypt. France decided to strike a blow at the British in Egypt by creating a west-east empire from Dakar to the Red Sea. This led Britain to block French aims and protect Egypt by securing the entire Nile Valley and occupying Uganda and Sudan. Britain concentrated on the Nile and neglected its West African empire, allowing it to be cut into four separate colonies surrounded by French territory.

Other historians reject the idea of the importance of Egypt in determining the pattern of partition in Africa. They suggest that Britain took those parts of West Africa which were paying profits to its traders and ignored the rest. They argue that Britain deliberately built its colonies around the rivers—the Niger, Volta and Gambia— which gave access to the products of the interior.

Britain left the governors of the colonies in West Africa to enlarge their territories as best they could with their own soldiers and finance. The poverty-stricken Gambia received almost no more territory. Governor Cardew of Sierra Leone had to fight his war of 1898 with money borrowed from Britain, paying it back over the following years. The Gold Coast colony was bigger and financially stronger and so was able to carve out a larger area inland. Governor Carter of Lagos was fortunate when he brought the Yoruba states under protection after only one short war against the Ijebu. On the Niger Goldie's Royal Niger Company defeated Nupe and Ilorin and laid the basis of Northern Nigeria. Otherwise the lands north of the joining of the Niger and Benue would probably have fallen to the French.

Almost every colonial border absurdly separated kindred people.

The geographical and cultural area of the Lake Chad region was split up. The related Kanuri and Kanembu were divided. The Nigeria-Dahomey border separated Ketu from the other Yoruba kingdoms and split the people of Borgu. The Nigeria-Niger border split the kingdom of Kebbi in half. The Nigeria-Cameroon border split the emirate of Adamawa, putting Yola, the capital, in Nigeria and most of the emirate in Cameroon. The ruler of Adamawa exclaimed in despair, 'They have left me the latrines of my kingdom... they have left us the head but they have cut off the body'. The borders of Ghana split the Ewe with Togoland, the Akan with Ivory Coast and the Mossi with Upper Volta. Probably the most absurd colonial boundary in all West Africa was the boundary between French Guinea and its two neighbours, Liberia and Sierra Leone. It divided in half at least six ethnic groups: the Susu, Yalunka, Koranko, Kissi, Loma and Kpelle.

None of the imperial powers established a colony of sufficient area or population to enable it to become a major or first-class power by the standards of the late nineteenth century. Educated Africans like E. W. Blyden repeatedly urged upon Britain the necessity of creating a mighty empire in West Africa. He was not thinking of its value to the British. He was convinced that European empires would be temporary, and he looked forward to the day when African colonies would emerge as independent states. British imperialism in the past had created large states such as Canada, Australia and India. Blyden wanted the British to repeat this process in West Africa.

## The views of educated Africans

What was the reaction of educated Africans to the conquest and partition of Africa? Most of them, like Blyden, supported imperialism, but at the same time disapproved of many of the beliefs and actions of white men.

Many of the educated merchant princes of the coastal cities, like their European counterparts, were suffering from the economic depression and hoped to benefit from colonisation of the interior. Yet men like G. W. Johnson, a Sierra Leonean who re-settled in Egbaland, condemned merchants 'who in this our world of haste to be rich' were willing to sacrifice African national interests.

Devout Christian Africans cautiously welcomed British colonialism as a substitution of Christian for non-Christian government. They believed that Christianity was Europe's greatest gift to

Africa. Others did not have the same faith in the virtues of Christianity and were angered by those who supported political subjection as a step to conversion. Missionaries probably suffered the greatest abuse, because Africans expected them to be better than traders and consuls. This is indicated in the following parody of a Christian hymn in a Gold Coast newspaper:

> Onward Christian Soldiers unto heathen lands;
> Prayer books in your pockets, rifles in your hands;
> Take the happy tidings where trade can be done;
> Spread the peaceful gospel with the gatling gun.

As the partition advanced, educated Africans discovered they were absolutely helpless to stop it. Furthermore, as the French appeared to be advancing more rapidly than Britain, English-educated Africans felt Africa must fall to Europeans they understood and whose language they spoke. Therefore they reluctantly supported British imperialism as the lesser of two evils. Lagos feared French encirclement. The *Lagos Weekly Times* moaned, 'We now find ourselves on the threshold of the fate which has befallen Sierra Leone and the Gambia—a colonial failure and a political ruin.' In other words, Lagos feared its Nigerian hinterland would become French. English-educated Africans felt their cultural ties to be with the British against French and Germans. 'We "Black Englishmen", who have been so large benefited by English benevolence and justice cannot sit still and see her [England] robbed of the well-earned fruits of her sagacity, enterprise and goodwill.'

At the same time, European claims to racial superiority were deeply offensive to educated Africans. Blyden pointed out that the European brought to Africa 'his prejudice, his faith in a natural inequality and his profound disbelief in any race but his own'. The hypocrisy of Europeans in claiming that it was in the best interest of Africans to be subjugated aroused the greatest resentment. Herbert Macaulay, the early Nigerian nationalist, pointed out in 1905 that, 'The dimensions of "the true interests of the natives at heart" are algebraically equal to the length, breadth and depth of the whiteman's pocket.'

It was a natural reaction for Africans to feel sorrow at the passing of African independence, and inevitably they made the comparison between the slave trade and the scramble. A Lagos editor in 1891 summed up the scramble, partition and subjugation of Africa as: 'a forcible possession of our land has taken the place of a forcible possession of our person'.

176

## CHAPTER SIXTEEN

# Collapse of independence

'The Maxim-gun inspires the most profound respect' (Lagos journalist in the 1890s)

## Military weakness

The European conquest of Africa was generally carried out with ease. Frequently African armies of 20,000 were defeated by European-led armies of 2,000 or less, and this was primarily because of the vast superiority of the weapons used by the Europeans, in particular the Maxim-gun (a late nineteenth-century invention). A European poet wrote:

'Whatever happens we have got
The Maxim-gun and they have not.'

By 1885 Europeans had banned the importation of guns and ammunition to West Africa. The firearms which African armies already possessed were not modern. Few Africans possessed fast-action repeater rifles. Even fewer had cannon. Few, if any, possessed the destructive repeater-action Gatling or Maxim-gun which almost every European-led army in Africa was equipped with. The Europeans also experimented with other new weapons in the subjugation of Africa. Goldie's army against Nupe employed such experimental devices as flares, searchlights, incendiary shells to set thatch roofs alight and Maxim-guns which could be dismantled for easy porterage.

Against these military products of the industrial revolution, the walls of West African cities and traditional massing of troops provided ideal targets. The French destruction of the walls of Sikasso and the slaughter of Nupe cavalry by Goldie's modern guns showed the hopelessness of traditional methods of warfare.

Africans had some success against the Europeans only when they abandoned traditional tactics. Samori avoided walled cities and massed cavalry. The Baoule of the Ivory Coast adopted guerrilla warfare, which was especially suitable in a forest region. West Africa lacked natural defensive barriers such as the rugged mountains which the Ethiopians used to advantage in saving their homeland in East

Africa. The Sahara provided a limited barrier in which the Tuareg and Sanusiyya resisted until as late as the 1920s. However, the vast majority of West Africa was gently rolling open savannah, and was ideally suited for European military methods.

West African states were agricultural not industrial. Therefore, they were unable to manufacture modern weapons. Moreover, they could not remove too many men from the land to serve as soldiers without causing famine.

The coastal states had small populations. The 'powerful' state of Dahomey had less than half a million people. The Aro were probably no more than 10,000-strong. When Brass was fully mobilised it produced an army of 1,000 men.

## Political weakness

The military weakness of African states was caused partly by their political character. Many African states had no clearly defined rules of succession to the throne. Prominent members of the royal lineage were often leaders of opposition factions. Power struggles were intense. There was lack of national feeling. Neither the contestants nor their followers would submerge their personal or material interests in the national cause. Candidates might even accept foreign assistance to gain power. The advancing European powers often found African allies. In the Tokolor empire Ahmadu was fighting a number of pretenders to the throne while trying to control French advances.

The large empires of the western Sudan—Sokoto, Rabeh, Tokolor and Mandinka—were relatively recent creations. Their subject people were either not totally subdued, like the Bambara under the Tokolors, or resentful, like the Kanuri under Rabeh.

No African state had developed the powerful nationalism common to European states in the nineteenth century. Asante and Dahomey came closest to it. In Asante the concept of the national soul, symbolised in the Golden Stool, was akin to the idea of nationalism. The national spirit of Dahomey was likened to water in a calabash punctured with holes plugged by the fingers of the citizens. But hardly anywhere did people have absolute loyalty to the state.

In the western Sudan, Islam played a unifying role in place of nationalism. However, once the European invaders convinced the people that they did not aim to subvert their religion, the will to resist and unity of the state were undermined.

There were few cases of inter-African alliance against the European invaders. An alliance of the Futa Jalon, Mandinka and Tokolor empires against the French was prevented by jealousy and religious disputes. It was often easy for the European power to secure the alliance of one group of people against another. The British had the assistance of Ibadan against Ijebu, of the Fante against Asante, and so on, while the French found allies everywhere in their march from Senegal to Lake Chad. In addition, the European armies were made up of African soldiers, led by a few European officers. Lugard, for example, conquered the Sokoto caliphate with troops who had been born in Hausaland. In the late nineteenth century the ties of race and colour were strong among Europeans. Race meant little to Africans. There was little feeling that two African states should ally merely because they were African. Many African states looked upon a European alliance as an instrument of gaining ascendancy over or equality with a neighbouring rival. In contrast, the European nations prevented their rivalries from disrupting a unified assault upon the African continent.

## The French conquest—from Senegal to Lake Chad

French interest in expansion from Senegal into the interior was renewed with the appointment of J. S. Gallieni as political director of St Louis in 1878. He began work on a railway, a road and a telegraph system to connect St Louis with the French forts as far as Medina on the Senegal river. In 1881 he travelled to Segu to sign a commercial treaty with Ahmad. The terms of the treaty were:
1  The French were to be given the monopoly of all trade within the empire. They were to build roads (for trade purposes only) to increase Tokolor prosperity.
2  The French were to give Ahmad 4 cannon and 1,000 rifles at once and 200 rifles every year.
3  The French were not to build forts nor in any way infringe Tokolor sovereignty.
   However, the French Government in Paris wanted more than just trade. Although Gallieni had signed a treaty in which he promised to respect Tokolor sovereignty, a French general was sent to build a fort at Kita and liberate the 'oppressed' Bambara. The Tokolor knew the French were not to be trusted. 'We like the French but do not trust them, they on the other hand trust us, but do not like us.'
   The French built forts in Tokolor territory: Fort Kita 1881, Fort

Bamako 1883. They also clashed with Samori, the Almami of the Mandinka empire to the south. Samori proposed an alliance with Ahmad against the French. This would have been a great opportunity to defeat the French, especially as there were already revolts against the French in Cayor (led by Lat-Dior Diop) and near Medina (where people resented forced labour and seizure of food for railway workers). Ahmad, however, rejected the alliance. By 1886 the French had crushed the revolts in Senegal and negotiated a treaty of friendship with Samori and Futa Jalon. The Tokolor were isolated and the empire was doomed.

In 1890 the French, using artillery against cavalry and mud walls, captured Segu and placed a member of the old Bambara dynasty on the throne under the watchful eye of a French Resident. Ahmad fled to Nioro in Kaarta. The French captured Nioro and Ahmad fled to Macina. In Kaarta the French ironically met their strongest opposition not from the Tokolor but from the Bambara whom they were supposed to be liberating. The following year they gave up this pretence and executed their newly-created Bambara king in Segu. In 1893 Jenne and all Macina fell to the French, and Ahmad fled once again, this time to Sokoto, the home of his mother. It was here that Ahmad died in 1898.

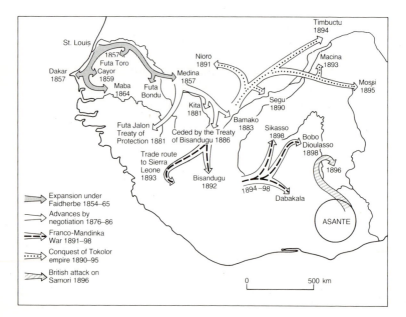

30   *The French conquest of the western Sudan.*

The French armies went south against Samori and east towards Lake Chad. One column captured Timbuctu in 1894. Another under Voulet and Chanoine burnt villages and executed friends and enemies alike as they advanced. They placed a puppet on the Mossi throne, but their advance to Lake Chad was slowed by water shortage, the vast quantity of booty they carried, and slaves. The French Government sent a political officer to report on Voulet and Chanoine, who so resented this action that they killed the political officer and declared their independence from France. However, their soldiers mutinied and killed both officers.

In 1900 three French forces, one from Macina, one from Algeria and one from Gabon converged upon Rabeh at Lake Chad. Rabeh had conquered Borno in 1893. He was born in the eastern Sudan of slave parents, served in the Egyptian army, and later commanded the private troops of Zubair Pasha, an Arab slave trader in the Nile Valley. When the Mahdi, a religious leader in the Sudan who drove the Europeans out of the country, expanded his state along the Nile, Rabeh marched his army to the west. He defeated Wadai, conquered Bagirmi and Borno, burnt Kukawa and made Dikwa his capital.

Rabeh's first aim was to organise a united opposition to the Europeans who were advancing to conquer Africa. He had supported the Mahdist opposition to Europeans along the Nile and dressed his troops in Mahdist style. He now called for a jihad against the Europeans. However, neither the caliphate nor the Sanusiyya, who controlled his supply of firearms, wanted to join his jihad. The caliphate refused because he had seized Bagirmi from Wadai. The Bagirmi allied with the French, and in 1900 Rabeh was defeated and killed by a French army. Finally the British took Borno and placed a descendant of al-Kanami on the throne, whose descendant reigns today as Shehu of Borno.

## Samori's confrontation with the French

Between 1881 and 1889 Samori thought that the French were busy with the Tokolor empire and would leave him alone. When he realised the full strength of the French and their ambition to conquer the whole Sudan, he began to try to ally with the British.

Both the Creoles of Freetown and the British in Sierra Leone wanted to ally with Samori. In 1886 Samori made a boundary settlement with the French. They signed the Treaty of Bisandugu which said:

1 Samori would give up all of his territory north of the River Niger to France.

2 The French would respect Samori's empire south of the Niger.

Samori thought the treaty could remove the causes of war or at least delay war long enough to strengthen his own position. He wanted to gain time to make an alliance with the British and get a stock of arms from Freetown to build up his military strength. The French signed the treaty because they also wanted to gain time in order to destroy the Tokolor empire before challenging Samori. To stop a possible Anglo-Mandinka alliance, the French officially stated that by the treaty of Bisandugu Samori had given up his empire to France.

Samori thought the British were willing to ally and this gave him a false sense of security. He then made one of his greatest blunders. In 1887-8 he besieged Sikasso for eighteen months, probably the best fortified city in the western Sudan. He lost 10,000 men and all his horses. Until then Tieba Traore, king of Sikasso, had been undecided about policy. Samori's siege of Sikasso made Tieba sign a treaty of protection with the French. The French then secretly urged Tieba to attack Samori and also made their own plans for advance. When Samori discovered this treachery he sent the treaty of friendship back to the French. The seven-year Franco-Mandinka war began in 1891.

Samori realised the French were much stronger than he was and in a last effort to form an alliance with the British he told the Sierra Leoneans he was willing to give up his empire to the British, and warned that if Britain did not send troops to occupy his empire, France would. But the British had accepted the French version of the Treaty of Bisandugu and felt it was dangerous to approve Samori's version in case it should encourage African kings in British spheres of influence to rebel against Britain, and Samori was abandoned to the French. Even the Freetown market was closed to him in 1893.

Samori's professional standing army even in peace-time was 2,000-strong made up of the 200 and 300 sofas in each province plus Samori's special guard. There was also a regular call up of a different set of men from the villages for military training every six months. It has been estimated that this gave a total military strength of 100,000. However, these men could not all be taken from the land at the same time as it would have harmed farm production and caused a famine. Only about 20,000 were ever armed at one time and of these only half were actually fighting. Those not fighting were used in the carrier corps or the supply division, which transported food, baggage and ammunition or tended the horses.

Since he lacked enough guns (which caused his failure at Sikasso),

Samori avoided being caught in fortified cities and with his troops all massed together, where the French artillery could be especially effective. Samori seldom used more than 1,000 soldiers against the French at one time, and the French occasionally outnumbered the Mandinka. Samori realised that in modern war numbers did not count as much as quality, discipline, organisation behind the lines, adequate arms and food.

The war was financed by (1) the ten per cent tax on the gold miners (used to buy arms from Freetown), (2) the sale of produce from the Almami's field in each village, and (3) the sale of slaves to buy horses (an estimated yearly requirement of 2,000) from the north. At the height of the struggle the state completely took over all markets and agriculture in order to regulate prices and keep a steady food supply. There were also state-controlled workshops where blacksmiths repaired and copied all makes of guns and manufactured gunpowder. Samori was almost totally dependent upon the state workshops for five years after the Freetown market was closed in 1893.

Lacking artillery, Samori avoided pitched battles, preferring small engagements, followed by a slow retreat to the east. At this stage he divided the army into three divisions. One, armed with repeater rifles, attacked the French and retreated. A second organised the population, evacuating them, leading and protecting their retreat. A third conquered and organised the new area in preparation to receive the people. As they retreated they carried out a 'scorched-earth' policy, burning villages, crops and everything of value, leaving the French not a grain of maize nor a single man, woman or child to work for them. The French took over dead and deserted country. There was little food and supplies had to be brought from farther and farther away. This slowed the French advance as much as did the actual fighting.

Most West African opposition to European aggression consisted of one sharp encounter followed by collapse. This happened in Ijebu-Ode, Dahomey and Borno under Rabeh. But although Samori lost almost every battle, his forces remained intact, ready to fight again.

By 1896 the Mandinka empire had moved from its first area far to the east until further retreat was impossible. Samori rebuilt his state in the new area which is called the second Mandinka empire. Samori made his new capital at Dabakala, the centre of the second empire. His new position was not as good as the old one. He had lost the goldfields and the wealth they provided. He was cut off from Freetown and had to depend entirely upon his workshops for his military supplies. The southern frontier of his old empire had been protected by Sierra Leone and Liberia, but the new one was open to attack from French forts on the Ivory Coast.

In the centre of the new empire was the city of Kong which felt secure because it had signed a treaty of protection with the French. The religious leaders of Kong disliked Samori; they were Qadiriyya, and they looked down upon Samori as an uneducated Tijaniyya. In 1895 Samori destroyed Kong. This shocked Muslims generally because Kong had been the respected centre of Islamic learning among the Mandinka. However, Kong had allied with a non-Muslim against fellow Muslims, so Samori's attack could be justified in the same way as Umar's on Macina or Bello's on Borno.

Samori now shared a common frontier with the Asante who were eager for an alliance against the British. But Samori did not want to add the British to his enemies. In 1896, having taken over Asante, a British force left for the north, invaded the Mandinka empire and took a number of towns. Samori's commander wanted to avoid battle and asked the British lieutenant to withdraw. When the lieutenant refused he was taken prisoner, his force scattered and Samori's army captured the first two cannon it had ever possessed. However, Samori did not want to arouse British hostility, so he set the lieutenant free with gifts for the British governor of the Gold Coast. In 1898, French

*Samori Touré in French captivity.*

184

armies advanced from the north, west and south and the British in Asante were blocking further retreat to the east, so Samori evacuated Dabakala. When the French offered him safe conduct and a quiet retirement in his home village, he accepted and gave himself up. In spite of this promise, Samori Touré was deported to Gabon where he died in 1900.

The Mandinka might have maintained their independence during the period of European conquest. They offered the strongest opposition to the Europeans in West Africa and tried to do for the west what Ethiopia did for the east of Africa. The main reason they failed was because West African leaders did not want to make a formal alliance or even a joint attack upon the French. Few realised how far the French planned to expand until it was too late. The African leaders of Futa Jalon and Sikasso were jealous and suspicious of Samori. The Tokolor and Mandinka disliked one another. Minority groups such as Kong allied themselves with the French. The French used these divisions to stop an African alliance and then struck down the African states one by one.

In 1896 the French invaded Futa Jalon, killed the Almami, installed a puppet and then deposed him on the charge of being sympathetic towards Samori.

Tieba of Sikasso died in 1893 and his brother Ba Bemba succeeded him. The French demanded that Sikasso accept French soldiers and a Resident. Ba Bemba refused, and so on 18 April 1898 French cannon began the destruction of the walls. The Sikasso cavalry failed to drive the French away, and after twelve days of cannon fire, French forces entered the walls. The fighting continued inside the walls until finally Ba Bemba and the captain of his bodyguard retired into the palace. Minutes later French soldiers entered the throne room to find Ba Bemba slumped over the throne, his captain sprawled at his feet. They had committed suicide.

The Franco-Mandinka war was the first 'modern' or total war in Africa. Samori used the whole population for war. His tactics were modern: ambush, surprise, scorched earth and the mass movement of people. The results too were similar to results of twentieth-century wars. Thousands died (the population may have been reduced to one-third of its original size), and the land was ruined and depopulated.

Some people blame Samori for depopulation. Others say that he was so ruthless and so indifferent to human suffering and many feared him so much that they turned to the French as the lesser of two evils.

This is true, but the French also share blame for the ruin and depopulation of the country. They were the attackers and they also were harsh and brutal. They suspected everyone of sympathy for Samori, and they mercilessly destroyed villages and people, many of whom were really their friends. Even their own soldiers deserted. Gallieni, certainly no friend of Samori's, wrote: 'In pursuing the war by these methods the French army will leave only desolate solitude for our merchants.'

Not everyone blames Touré. He has been called 'the greatest West African of the nineteenth century', 'Napoleon of the Sudan', and the finest example of the African personality in its struggle to retain independence. The areas Samori converted to Islam remained mainly Muslim, and people do not usually adopt the religion of those that they hate. Even in the second empire, which existed for only five years, about 40 per cent of the people accepted Islam as a result of his rule.

## Dahomey

France occupied Porto Novo in 1883, and from that moment Dahomey declined in prosperity and began to lose its independence. French firms moved from Ouidah to Porto Novo, and Dahomey lost revenue from customs duties at Ouidah. In 1887 Dahomey's exports through Ouidah fell to less than £100,000-worth. This loss of wealth made it very difficult for King Glele to buy enough guns and

*Fon wooden figure of Behanzin, represented with the head and fins of a shark.*

ammunition to defend Dahomey against France. He said, 'He who makes the powder must win the battle.' He allowed France to strengthen its position at the coast unchallenged. In 1889 he even conceded the Dahomeyan claims to the port of Cotonou and acknowledged French claims to it after the French sent a threatening mission to Abomey. Glele was so ashamed that he committed suicide rather than live to watch the ruin of his kingdom.

Factions arose in the court about whether to surrender or resist. Behanzin, the son of Glele, favouring a policy of resistance, was enthroned and crushed a revolt of those who wished to surrender. In 1892-3 a French army advanced from the coast, commanded by General Dodds, a Senegalese mulatto. Dahomey's army far outnumbered the French, France having only 2,000 men against Dahomey's 16,000 soldiers. However, the French had far more modern weapons than the Dahomeyans and were much more experienced in using them. The French also had African allies like the coastal Popo kingdoms. Moreover, the thousands of Yoruba slaves on Dahomey palm oil plantations rose in revolt in the rear of Dahomey's army when it went to fight the French. Behanzin's army was defeated by Dodds and the king was captured, deposed and deported to the West Indies.


## Wars of independence in the Ivory Coast

The coastal-forest people of the Ivory Coast fought for twenty-seven years (1891-1918) to preserve their independence. This was the most prolonged war of independence and, along with Samori's, the fiercest struggle against subjugation anywhere in West Africa.

The Africans rose in revolt because the French broke the protectorate treaties of 1887-9 by demanding slave porters, by meddling in the election of chiefs, and by sending two military expeditions to strike at Samori in the north. In 1900 the French tried to levy a head tax on the entire population, and three years later began the construction of a railway which required the seizing of African lands, and increased demands for forced (slave) labour. The measures brought home to each individual the real intention of the French, which was not to treat the people as allies but to rule them as subjects. The result was a supreme effort to try to throw the French out of the Ivory Coast. A general war of independence, led by the Baoule people, forced the French to abandon the interior. By 1908 they were clinging to a small coastal strip.

There were no centralised kingdoms but the small chieftaincies achieved exceptional co-operation. While the French were busy suppressing one, two or three others arose to harass them. There were no large armies against which the French could use their artillery and the forest proved ideal for guerrilla 'strike and retire' tactics.

In 1908 the French sent Governor Angoulvant to the Ivory Coast. He was a man who was prepared to be tough and who blamed French defeats on the softness of his predecessors. Angoulvant began a methodical and brutal military occupation. Hundreds of villages were destroyed and their people herded into larger settlements which the French army could guard and thus prevent the people giving support to the guerrillas. One group formerly living in 247 villages were forced into 17; another originally in 147 were herded into 10.

By 1915 the country was under the iron discipline of military rule. The French had seized 100,000 guns, imposed £50,000 in fines and deported 220 African leaders. The administration was poor and its finances exhausted by the military effort of holding down a resentful people. To maintain itself slave labour was recruited on a scale larger than ever. In addition, the French, facing collapse before the Germans in the First World War, began to recruit African soldiers for the battlefields of Europe. The people of the savannah in the north responded to the recruitment campaign, but to the coastal-forest people it was just another intolerable burden. In 1916 the Baoule led another uprising which came almost as close as that of 1908 to expelling the French. In 1917 in hopeless despair of victory the Agni (a people closely related to the Asante) migrated as a body to the less harsh colonialism of the British in neighbouring Ghana.

## British tactics—Nigeria

In general, the British used less force than the French in occupying their West African territories. Sometimes they did use much force, as in Asante and Benin, where they were determined to destroy local institutions and impose direct rule. Often, however, they used a mixture of force and diplomacy. British diplomacy was at its best in Yorubaland and close to its best in the Sokoto caliphate. Where an officer held only limited military means (Carter in Yorubaland and Lugard in Hausaland), greater diplomacy was essential.

In 1892 Governor Carter of Lagos created an incident with the Ijebu which led to war. British machine-gun and cannon fire led to a crushing and spectacular military victory. The object of this violence was to overcome tough Ijebu defence of their sovereignty and independence, as well as to show how futile it would be for other Yoruba kingdoms to do the same. Carter wanted one small war with Ijebu that would make a large-scale war with all Yorubaland unnecessary. He wanted a protectorate which would change little in the indigenous political system, but would merely set up British paramountcy. When the Awujale (Oba of Ijebu) claimed he had advocated peace but had been overruled by his chiefs in council, Carter confirmed him in his position. This was a hint to other obas that co-operation with Britain would not go unrewarded. Immediately after the conquest of Ijebu, Carter opened treaty discussions with the Egba and Ibadan. He negotiated with them and did not impose his terms. The Egba secured internal autonomy. The Ibadans rejected the first treaty draft and a new one was drawn up to meet their objections. Not one oba was deposed. Little force was used but Carter dragged his Maxim-gun around the country so that it might impress and inspire respect. If the British had kept to the letter of these treaties their position would have been little more than that of an 'influence', and not one of colonial subjugation. Some years later, after the people were disarmed, the chiefs discovered that they were powerless to prevent the British from ignoring the terms of treaties and behaving as outright conquerors.

In the Sokoto caliphate Lugard's tactics were similar to Governor Carter's. Lugard demonstrated his military strength by conquering Nupe and Kontagora. He deposed the Etsu Nupe and replaced him with a rival Fulani candidate. He then wrote to the Amir al-Muminin at Sokoto informing him that he had taken this action because of the oppressive rule in these two emirates, and requested that he nominate someone for the vacant throne of Kontagora.

Through these tactics Lugard sought to show two things: first, that opposition was futile, and secondly, that he was not hostile to Islam or the Fulani if they co-operated. On the other hand Lugard posed as the 'liberator' of the subject people from Fulani 'oppression' (though there is little evidence of Hausa dissatisfaction with their Fulani rulers). Thus the Fulani were warned that if they opposed the British, they might be replaced by the pre-jihad Hausa ruling families.

Lugard's mixture of force and persuasion brought confusion into Fulani councils. There was no strong lead from Sokoto. Zaria decided to accept, and Kano to reject British overtures. The Amir al-Muminin had just died and Attahiru, the new caliph, hesitated too long before he decided to defy the British. While Attahiru hesitated the British occupied Sokoto city in 1903 after defeating a Fulani-

Hausa army. Six hundred British soldiers, well equipped with the latest guns and well trained in the use of them, routed Attahiru's army of 30,000. Attahiru fled and later the same year was defeated and killed at the Battle of Burmi.

There is little doubt that if the caliph had called upon his people to fight the British at the right moment, Lugard's supply lines could have been cut and he and his forces utterly destroyed. However, the Fulani estimate of the overall situation was correct. They could not in the end defeat the military might of the British empire which would be sent against them if Lugard was destroyed. Furthermore, French forces were advancing all around the northern frontier of the caliphate. Lugard was offering less severe terms of surrender than the French were likely to impose, judging by reports from the former Tokolor empire.

The approach of the British to Benin was entirely different. In Benin the British mixture of force and persuasion caused a serious rift in the Oba's council. Oba Ovonramwen preferred to negotiate, but a majority of his chiefs desired to fight the British. The dispute almost brought about a civil war. To provoke a crisis the British advised Urhobo traders to refuse to pay Benin customs dues and sent a negotiating party to Benin City under Acting Consul Phillips. The party ignored repeated Bini warnings to halt. The Oba wished to receive Phillips in friendly fashion, but to prevent this some chiefs ambushed and destroyed the advancing party. This action precipitated war, against the Oba's wishes.

In 1897, a British army advanced into Benin, burnt the capital and looted it of nearly 2,500 of its famous bronze treasures. Ovonramwen was deported and the British offered positions of importance to chiefs who were willing to co-operate. Few chiefs responded. The British left the throne vacant and made little effort to recreate the Bini political system. Instead, they ruled directly through African agents in the manner of the French.

In the Niger Delta, the British took control first by diplomacy (treaties) and later by force. In 1884 when the partition of Africa was under way, Jaja of Opobo signed a treaty of protection with the British but refused to include a free trade clause. He also refused to allow Christian missionaries into Opobo. From 1884 to 1887 he came into increasing conflict with the British over his attitude to missionaries, and over trade. The British palm oil firms wanted to fix the price of oil bought from Opobo traders, but Jaja refused. He also refused the demand by the British Consul, Harry Johnston, to allow British traders access to any part of his kingdom. Johnston then invited Jaja to a meeting, promising that after it he 'would be free to go'. At the meeting, however, Jaja was informed that if he left British naval guns would destroy Opobo. To save his capital and people, Jaja stayed, and was taken by Johnston as a prisoner to Accra. There Jaja was tried and deported to the West Indies. He died in 1891, his corpse being brought back to Opobo for a royal funeral and burial within the palace walls. Johnston's duplicity and treachery gave the British a bad name for a long time in the eastern Delta. But even if the British had been honourable and met Jaja in open war, the result would have been the same. The British were determined to take over the middleman position of the palm oil trade.

In 1885 Nana, 'governor' of the Itsekiri of the western Delta, signed a treaty of protection with the British. Like Jaja, Nana rejected a clause which would have allowed British traders to operate anywhere in his trading empire on the Benin River. He also refused to admit missionaries. In 1894 Consul Moor demanded revision of the 1884 treaty to include free trade and permission for missions to enter Itsekiriland. Nana refused to attend a meeting with Moor, fearing he would be arrested and deported like Jaja. A British naval expedition, using Maxim-guns, cannon, incendiary rockets and dynamite, was sent and destroyed Nana's capital, Ebrohimi. Nana escaped and reached Lagos where, after some time in hiding, he surrendered to the

*Nana of Itsekiri, whose capital, Ebrohimi, was destroyed by a British naval expedition in 1894. Nana subsequently surrendered to the British in Lagos and was deported to the Gold Coast.*

British. He was deported to Accra, and was not allowed to return home until 1906.

In 1893 Goldie tightened the Royal Niger Company's customs controls on the Niger so severely that the Brass smuggling trade was stopped. In 1895 King Koko of Brass led his people in a desperate bid for survival. With about 1,000 soldiers in thirty war canoes he destroyed the company's headquarters and port at Akassa. Brass had no quarrel with the British Government, but the British navy assisted the company troops in retaliation. The British blew up Nembe and Twon, the capital and the port of Brass, confiscated all Brass war canoes, fined the king £500 and drove the people into the swamps, where starvation and a smallpox epidemic killed more people than did British bullets. Brass was broken.

In contrast to the fall of large states like Benin and Asante, which fell at a single blow, the Igbo of eastern Nigeria were conquered piecemeal and they opposed and later resisted piecemeal. The British found it very difficult to take control of very small states. It took nineteen years, from 1898 to 1917. The Igbo chose armed confrontation from the beginning, when in 1898 the Ika Igbo west of the Niger attacked the Royal Niger Company's depots. A secret society, the Ekumeku, rose up among the Ika. Ekumeku was an underground resistance movement dominated by the young men, and using guerrilla tactics. Its members came from many clans, and there was no single leader. It opposed all forms of foreign rule and influence, whether political, economic or religious. The British Government took over from the company in 1900, but had no more success than the company in combating Ekumeku. As soon as one group was defeated, another rose up elsewhere. Ekumeku fought the British until 1911. In eastern Igboland, the Aro traders at first tried to keep the British away by 'palaver', long and tedious negotiations. This worked from 1896 until 1901, but an Aro raid on Igbo under British protection led to the 1901-2 British armed expedition against the Aro. Arochukwu, the Aro capital, was captured, and the famous oracle was destroyed. The Afikpo Igbo of the Cross River Valley supported the British against their Aro rivals, but they resorted to arms (1902-3) when they realised they would be the next victims of the British. The Ezza Igbo in north-east Igboland could offer only their machetes and their courage when they were heavily defeated by British machine guns in 1905. Finally, isolated Igbo villages held out against accepting British rule until administration was effectively established throughout Igboland by 1917. The Igbo nicknamed the white man 'Otikpo', 'the Destroyer'.

## British tactics in Asante

The British occupied Asante for two main reasons. Firstly, they wanted to forestall the French and the Germans who were closing in on Asante from the Ivory Coast and Togo respectively. Secondly, they wanted to stop Prempe forming an alliance with Samori against European imperialism. In 1895 the British began to prepare to invade Asante from Gold Coast Colony. Prempe decided to resort to a strategy of diplomacy rather than armed confrontation. As soon as he heard the British invasion was being planned, he resolved to negotiate not fight, and sent a strongly-powered diplomatic mission to England. He also gave way to Britain's demands that he accept a British Resident in Kumasi, and hoped for a protectorate treaty that would leave him in power. However, Prempe had miscalculated. The British went ahead with their invasion, determined to crush Asante once and for all. In March 1896 a powerful British force occupied Kumasi, and arrested, deposed and exiled Asantehene Prempe, along with his mother, his father and his uncles, together with a number of local kings and Kumasi divisional chiefs. The captives were detained first in Elmina Castle and then transferred to Sierra Leone where they arrived in January 1897.

As soon as Prempe was out of the way a British protectorate was declared. No new Asantehene was appointed. Britain planned to destroy Asante institutions and rule the state directly. Above all, the British were determined to prevent any revival of Asante imperialism which might threaten their own imperialism in Ghana.

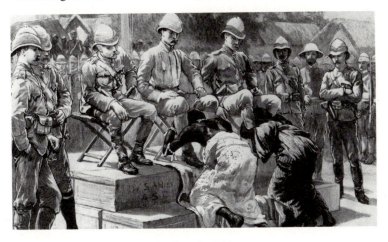

*The submission of Prempe to the British, 1896.*

Though deprived of their leader, the Asante were still confident of his restoration in the very near future. They would not have reacted very quickly if Governor Hodgson had not added insult to injury by demanding the surrender of the Golden Stool in March 1900. The Golden Stool was the one sacred object that the Asante could not part with. Their answer to the governor's demand was an armed rebellion in April 1900 under the leadership of Yaa Asantewaa, the Queen Mother of Edweso, and the siege of the governor in the Kumasi fort. The Asante war of independence was crushed but only after the British sent four expeditions, the first three having been defeated. Even then, the Asante soldiers, using skilful guerrilla tactics under their general Kofi Kofia, were only defeated because they ran out of ammunition. Asante was now formally annexed as a crown colony, but the British removed Prempe and his party of fifty-five away from Freetown to the far-away Seychelles Islands. The object of this was to quench the last embers of hope of restoration of Prempe and of opposition in Asante. Prempe did not return to Ghana until 1924.

## Sierra Leone

In Sierra Leone, Governor Cardew (1894-1900) in 1896 proclaimed a protectorate over what remained of the colony's hinterland, the French having taken most of it. Sierra Leone had to bear the full expense of the new administration because the British Government gave no subsidy for it. Cardew set up indirect rule in the interior. The chiefs continued to govern, supervised by district commissioners and financed by an annual five-shilling tax on every house in the interior. This house tax caused war.

To the Temne and Mende peoples it was a war of independence. They had grievances against Cardew's police, occasionally recruited from runaway slaves who took revenge on their former masters. Chiefs were installed who had no traditional right. Even the chiefs were mistreated by the government, and some were publicly flogged. The people suspected the merchants of price-fixing. They resented missionary teaching, which undermined respect for their institutions. Above all, they saw the tax as tribute which meant the surrender of their independence.

In 1898 Bai Bureh, ruler of the small Temne state of Kassah, refused to pay the hut tax and the police opened fire on his people. An experienced professional warrior, who had hired out his military

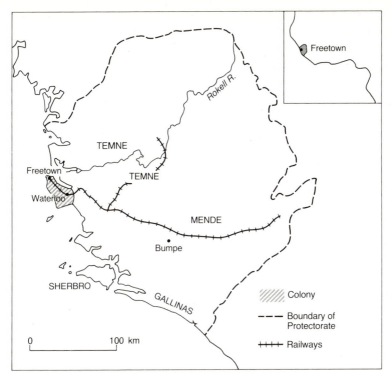

31  *Sierra Leone: colony and protectorate after 1896.*

*Bai Bureh, the Temne ruler of Kassah, after his capture.*

services for over thirty years, Bai Bureh organised a skilful guerrilla war against the British in the thickly-wooded Temne country. Well-armed from the coast, he tied down several British expeditions by ambushes and bush-fires. Bai Bureh also fought a 'gentleman's war', attacking the police and army but not molesting European or Creole civilians.

The Mende military effort was directed by the Poro, a secret religious, educational and trading society with headquarters at Bumpe. The Poro waged 'total war', killing anyone connected with the Freetown government, Creoles, whites or Mende who wore European-style dress. The Creoles suffered most. Over 1,000 men, women and children were slaughtered until the Poro ordered that women be spared.

The Temne-Mende War weakened the position of the Creoles in the Sierra Leone Government. The Creoles lost many lives in the war, but they blamed the war on misgovernment and called it Cardew's war. The Creole-owned Freetown press had repeatedly warned Cardew about his interior policy and tax before the war broke out. When Bai Bureh gave himself up and was brought as a prisoner to Freetown he was welcomed by the Creoles as a conquering hero. The Creoles, as Africans, tried to be spokesmen for the grievances of the Temne-Mende people, even though they were their main victims. Cardew, however, interpreted Creole actions as disloyalty. In the interior the Creoles were killed because they tried to explain European actions to Africans, while in Freetown they were despised because they tried to explain African feelings to Europeans.

The war of 1898 became an excuse for the British to begin discrimination against Creoles in all fields. As we shall see in Chapters 17 and 18, Creoles were forced out of the Sierra Leone civil service. They were also forced out of responsible positions in the church (Chapter 20) and out of the economy (Chapter 19).

The conquest not only subjugated vast areas of West Africa to European rule, it also led to the end of the Anglo-Creole partnership in the exploitation and development of West Africa. There was no place for Creole civilisation in colonial Africa, dominated by a new and vicious type of European racial arrogance.

# PART FOUR

# Response and resistance to foreign rule 1900-45

## CHAPTER SEVENTEEN

# Colonial government (1): indirect rule and the chiefs

'The last administration has made the very name of the white man stink in the nostrils of the native' (*Lagos Weekly Record*, 1920)

The European partition of the continent added large areas to the British and French West African empires, and brought major problems of administration, personnel and finance to the colonial powers. Nineteenth-century British policy towards West Africa had sought the creation of a Westernised class of Black Englishmen who would be British partners in religion, trade and administration. This was a policy of *assimilation*, whereby Africans would be assimilated to European civilisation and culture (and abandon African civilisation and culture). As a result Africans rose in colonies around Freetown, Bathurst (Banjul), southern Ghana and Lagos to important positions in the church, in commercial firms and in colonial government. The French, too, followed a policy of turning Africans into Black Frenchmen in the four communes of Senegal, where Africans even had the right to elect a deputy to the French National Assembly in Paris. However, in the newly-expanded empires Western-educated Africans were heavily discriminated against in the administration, due to the growth of European racialism noted in Chapters 15 and 16. The British brought in European administrators as fast as the growth in finances would allow instead of speeding up the training of African administrators. Western-educated Africans like the Creoles were even forced out of the senior civil service. In 1910 the Colonial Office expressed the opinion that Englishmen naturally expected to enjoy the fruits of their conquests and therefore they should be preferred over Africans in senior positions.

## The dual mandate and indirect rule

However, a major difficulty Britain faced was that there were simply not enough Englishmen prepared to serve as colonial administrators in West Africa. In response to this, Lugard in Northern Nigeria adopted the policy of *indirect rule*: ruling through the aristocracy of conquered people. This had been a popular policy of imperialists throughout history and was extensively used in African empires of the nineteenth century. Indirect rule had the additional great advantage of being cheap: traditional rulers were less expensive than European officers. In 1914 Lugard was appointed to join together the various colonies which later made up Nigeria. In his years as Governor General of Nigeria, 1914-19, he began to extend his theories to the peoples of Southern Nigeria. After he left Nigeria he described his theory of indirect rule in a book, *The Dual Mandate in Tropical Africa* (1922). *The Dual Mandate* became the handbook of British officers everywhere in the empire. Noted examples of colonial governors who adopted Lugard's methods were Cameron in Tanganyika, Guggisberg in Ghana and Palmer in the Gambia.

Indirect rule formed the basis of local government in British West Africa. It did not apply to the central government of colonies. The central government was controlled entirely by white men. The executive and legislative councils of the four separate British colonies were composed mainly of white British colonial officials, with perhaps one appointed Western-educated African in the legislative council, to maintain a pretence of African political progress. In local government, however, the African chief was the key figure. He appointed all officials who were responsible to him. He or his officials presided over the law courts which as far as possible applied African law. His agents levied taxes for the local treasury. Part of the revenue was sent to the central government and the remainder kept for local improvements such as roads, sanitation, markets and schools, and to pay the salaries of local officials.

The chief was responsible to a British official, a Resident or district officer, who in turn was responsible to the central government. The Resident also oversaw the operation of taxation, the treasury and courts, but always operated through the chief. British officials were expected to remain in the background, making changes appear as if they came from the chief.

If the indirect rule system was to work successfully, a chief's authority had to be accepted by the people. But, many African leaders did not have such authority (see Chapter 10, and later parts of

*A government-appointed chief in Benin. Indirect rule only stood any chance of success if the authority of the nominee was accepted by the people. Too often the African leaders appointed by the colonial power possessed little or no such authority.*

this chapter), and indirect rule could not operate properly. In Northern Nigeria the caliphate was 'successful' mainly because of the authority of the emirs. Moreover, Lugard had specially designed indirect rule for the caliphate where he had some understanding of the society. When he and others began to apply it elsewhere its unsuitability became more apparent.

The British assumed that African society had been static for centuries, that their political institutions were fixed and that the population was very conservative and disliked change. On the contrary, many African societies passed through important political, economic and social upheavals in the nineteenth century. Many of these upheavals were led by ordinary people in society—for example, peasant palm oil farmers, and traders of commoner or even slave origins. The British, however, assumed that change could only come from the top, through chiefs, emirs and kings. Emirs of the caliphate and the Oba of Benin had centralised a good deal of power in their hands. But in Yorubaland, Asante and Borno, although the monarchy appeared powerful, this power was actually divided in a complicated way in the society. Among other peoples, the Mende, Temne, Fante, Kru, Igbo and Tiv, either the chiefs were under popular control or there were no chiefs at all. Among the Igbo, Tiv and Kru, chiefs or elders were spokesmen, powerless to act without popular consent. More West Africans lived under this system then under ones which placed power in the hands of a single ruler. Therefore, indirect rule through chiefs was an unsuitable form of administration for most West African communities.

Another weakness of indirect rule was that it allowed no place for the Western-educated Africans, whose numbers increased steadily with the spread of missionary education. The Western-educated Africans looked upon Lugard as the symbol of the worst aspects of British imperialism. They accepted Lugard's theory of the double duty (dual mandate) of the imperial power to govern in the interests of Britain and the colonial people. This required that each colony must finance its own administration, not become a burden on British taxpayers, and provide ideal conditions for the expansion of British trade. But the Western-educated Africans disagreed with Lugard and the British over two assumptions which underlay the dual mandate. The British assumed, first, that colonialism would last indefinitely, and secondly, that traditional African government was autocratic. Therefore, the British made no attempt before the Second World War to prepare any of their West African colonies for self-government, and did very little to introduce democratic institutions in West Africa. Unlike some Europeans, who doubted African ability to develop at all, Lugard felt African society could be changed. However, he believed only Europeans could reshape African society. He also believed that Europeans should lead Africans not towards a European pattern of society but towards a distinctly African one. Educated Africans could not accept Lugard's views. They wanted to be free to choose by themselves whatever aspects of European life they wanted, and to reject whatever they wanted, and not to have this vital decision taken for them by Lugard or by any other European, or by any African traditional ruler imposed on them under the system of indirect rule.


**Indirect rule in Northern Nigeria**

Following the conquest of the caliphate Lugard confirmed the co-operative emirs in their positions, enthroned a new Amir al-Muminin at Sokoto and permitted the alkali courts and bureaucracy to function as before. British Residents were to advise and, if necessary, force the emirs to follow policy approved by the conquerors. The caliphate had always been run by local governments and the British

*Lord Lugard, the architect of indirect rule.*

took over Sokoto's former position of supervising these local rulers. They also confined the authority of the Amir al-Muminin to strictly religious matters. The Residents increased the independent powers of the emirs at the expense of the Amir al-Muminin. In that way the Residents were able to boost their own importance as 'the power behind the throne', until they appeared to be working towards separate states and thus undoing the unification brought about by dan Fodio a century earlier.

Indirect rule in Northern Nigeria was regarded by the British as a success because it produced peace, order and tranquillity. There was little trouble and few arguments or disputes. But while trouble could indicate rapid social change, tranquillity might mean nothing more than stagnation. A number of factors combined to isolate the caliphate from the great twentieth-century world movements, Westernisation and anti-European nationalism. By the middle of the nineteenth century the trans-Saharan routes began to decline as a result of the trade contacts opened up on the Niger River by British merchants (see Chapters 5 and 13). Thus, when the Muslim world was beginning its modern transformation, the caliphate began to lose contact with it. Colonial boundaries completed this isolation.

In the surrender terms the British promised not to interfere with the Muslim religion. This was interpreted by both parties to mean that Christian missionaries should not be encouraged. Thus the isolation of Northern Nigeria was increased, for it thereby missed an influence which was, in Southern Nigeria, the main agent for Westernisation.

201

The British had not foreseen that shielding the people from the stimulating influence of Christianity would slow down the process of change. The British did allow mission activities in non-Muslim areas, many of which had not been brought within the caliphate in the nineteenth century. Relatively backward areas during the nineteenth century, through their acceptance of the Western education brought by missionaries, became some of the most progressive areas in the twentieth century. The British did set up a few non-religious schools for the Hausa-Fulani aristocracy, but they were never popular because they were in competition with the already existing Islamic system. Therefore, the Hausa-Fulani Western-educated group was very small. Not surprisingly, when the British needed to recruit clerical staff in the north—for the junior civil service, the railway system, the postal services and in commercial firms—they recruited from the south. In Southern Nigeria a surplus of school leavers was developing even before the first World War.

The British never saw the problem this was creating for the day of eventual self-government. Their main concern was that northern Muslim society should be protected from the radical ideas of the southerners. It was a cheap way of staffing, but it did not lead to the ultimate goal of self-government. Northern Nigeria, cut off from the Maghreb and the Middle East, and protected from Southern Nigerian ideas and movements, presented a picture of tranquillity strangely out of place in the upheavals of the twentieth century.

## Indirect rule among the Yoruba

Lugard believed his system could be adapted and modified to work anywhere. When in 1914 he was sent to achieve Nigerian amalgamation, he began to introduce to the Yoruba his own ideas of ruling through traditional institutions. The Yoruba states possessed a centralised government headed by obas who held a certain respect for the Alafin of Oyo and the Oni of Ife. Lugard mistakenly saw the Yoruba family of states as an arrangement similar to the caliphate. His task as he saw it was thus to establish British rule through the traditional obas, as if the obas were emirs in the north. Yet the Yoruba oba did not, like the Fulani emir, possess a considerable degree of autocratic power. In fact, power was shared among a number of chiefs, representing lineages over which the oba had limited power. When the British tried to control the oba's selection of chiefs they discovered that his power was much less than they had believed. Titles were often the property of lineages who selected the title holders to represent them. The British, unable to control this selection, resorted to doubtful methods, such as threatening to take land from unco-operative lineages and giving it to those who more readily accepted British aims.

Another mistake the British made in Yorubaland was to try to return to the conditions of the eighteenth century and to make Oyo the chief power. The refusal of many Yoruba to accept this had been a major cause of the nineteenth-century Yoruba wars. In the 1890s the British had recognised their ally Ibadan as the most powerful of the Yoruba states, yet now they sought to make it subordinate to Oyo. The Bale of Ibadan, after surrendering to British orders, took his own life because he knew he had acted against his people's wishes.

One reason the British tried to elevate Oyo above the other Yoruba states was that Oyo was one of the least affected by Western education. In contrast to Oyo, in Abeokuta the Western-educated had taken over control, in Ibadan they were advisers to the chiefs, and in Ilesha one had even become oba. Lugard ignored this vital development and tried to introduce the system which existed before the rise of the Western-educated men. In Abeokuta he overthrew their semi-independent government, recognised by Carter in 1893, and reverted to chiefly government. It was not surprising therefore that the Yoruba Western-educated class were suspicious of Lugard and ready to lead opposition to British rule. In any case, few Yoruba were willing to see their obas' powers increased.

How West African artists portrayed their colonial masters. On the left is a sculptured representation of a Divisional Officer being towed in a canoe; the piece was carved by Thomas Ona of Ijebu. On the right is a wooden carving of Queen Victoria.

Probably no governor in the history of Nigeria was so intensely hated by the Western-educated Yoruba elite as Lugard. For his part he made it very plain that he sought to undermine their influence in Yorubaland. In 1914 he wrote, 'a strong Native government is in the process of being built up under its own rulers which will be able to resist the sinister influence of more or less alien influence which was rapidly destroying it'. The *Times of Nigeria* hit back, '... his legislative measures, his political administration, his educational methods ...'. are so entirely un-British-like that one could hardly conceive where to draw the line of distinction between the system of our governor-general and the system of German colonial rule in Africa'. Then it asked, 'Is it that the Anglo-Saxon fears the rapid intellectual and industrial strides the darker races have made?'

The *Lagos Weekly Record* claimed Lugard 'was obsessed with the maintenance of white prestige' and that indirect rule fostered the idea that, 'The advanced and progressive African is the Nigger; the naked specimen in the forest, or on the river in his canoe is nature's gentleman'. When Lugard's book was published the *Record* wrote, '*The Dual Mandate in Tropical Africa*, which they are advertising as a classic in imperial administration, is nothing but a tissue of misrepresentation'. The *Record* never tired of publishing the comment about indirect rule made by an English judge, that it was 'a setback to a condition of things resembling the barbarous ages'. So poisoned was the atmosphere in Lagos that Lugard's successor, Clifford, admitted that 'the government and the intelligent sections of the public are almost completely divorced from one another'. When Lugard left, the *Record* heaved a mighty sigh of relief.

> For six long years we have had the sword of Damocles dangling over our heads; for six long years we have lived under the cramped condition of a military dictatorship when the law from being a means of protection had become an instrument of crime and oppression in the hands of unscrupulous officials ... The last administration has made the very name of the whiteman stink in the nostrils of the Native.

## Indirect rule among the Igbo

A system of indirect rule could never work among the Igbo. There were few chiefs whom the British could control. Even if they could control the Ama-ala, the elders could not control the ward meeting, the basic institution of Igbo government. However, Lugard's theories, developed in *The Dual Mandate*, became widely accepted among colonial servants, and these men refused to put a practical approach before theory.

If the British had approached the Igbo free from the theories of *The Dual Mandate*, they might have attempted to introduce their own forms of local government, which would have been much closer to nineteenth-century Igbo political theory. British and Igbo democracy were far from being the same, but they possessed the common quality that authority came directly from the people. The units of Igbo society were possibly too small for meeting the increased demands of modern government. But it would have been better to have introduced elected representatives who came from the village meetings and were responsible to them, rather than to give a lineage elder an authority which made him a chief and gave him powers unknown in Igbo society. A jury system would also have been a better replacement for the Ama-ala in court cases than were the judicial powers given to these artificially-created chiefs.

However, the idea of election by Africans in a British colony was distasteful to Lugard and his disciples. If the British had shown an open mind and imagination, they might have created a system which harnessed Igbo ambitions. They could have developed a system of rule in Igboland which could have become as much admired as that of Northern Nigeria. Then the Igbo might have been considered the most co-operative rather than most troublesome West African people.

In Igboland the British had to deal with a society which was undergoing rapid change in the twentieth century. The Igbo used the co-operative strength of their clans to build schools, educate their promising sons and play off one mission against the other to get the greatest benefits. The Roman Catholics under Bishop Shanahan in the 1920s caught the spirit of the Igbo movement, making many converts and educating thousands. Within thirty years the Igbo were emerging into Nigerian public life in a way which was quite unexpected by other ethnic communities. This advance was largely brought about within nineteenth-century social and political institutions, and not within the newly-imposed British system.

Igbo ambition, Igbo search for status and wealth, Igbo in-individualism and a firm belief in change were all readily adapted to the colonial situation. Igbo individualism was rooted in group solidarity and the group an Igbo desired to push forward was his village. Progress became not only an individual's desire to better himself but also an obsession to help his town 'to get up'. The prestige of the individual was very much tied to the prestige of the town and vice versa. In the colonial period the symbols of 'getting up' were educational, religious and medical facilities plus the size and activity of the town's market. Thus Onitsha was a model town because it possessed all these things and as a result produced the greatest number of educated men and women. Onitsha had 'got up'. In addition prominent educated individuals were a pride to their town. An Igbo writer pointed out that a constant cry of town-based Progressive Unions was, 'It is a matter of shame that we have educated nobody abroad. Other towns are ahead of us and we shall soon be their slaves. We can no longer content ourselves with "equal heads". We must have "educated heads"—"the mouths that can speak for us".'

British administration in Igboland was a series of failures followed by attempted reorganisations. When the British conquered eastern Nigeria they set up a system of indirect rule. Although in the Delta the autocratic House heads served this purpose well, the lineage elders of the interior did not respond happily so that the political officers turned to more direct administration. When Lugard took over in 1914 he was disturbed by this development of policy. He therefore sent a northern officer, Palmer, to 'find' the chiefly system, over the protests of officers who had been working for years among the Igbo. Palmer 'found' the chiefs, who were given warrants to increase their authority. These warrant chiefs, with their unrestrained authority and control of the courts, were seen by the people as miniature tyrants. When in 1929 the British tried to impose direct taxation, and the famous Women's Riots followed, the main targets of attack were the warrant chiefs.

Following the riots a number of anthropologists were sent to 'discover' Igbo traditional government. But Lugard's prestige was still too strong, and although adjustments were made there was no one of sufficient influence among the British to challenge the whole system. So the search for chiefs continued.

Donald Cameron, governor of Nigeria from 1931 to 1935, has been considered a reformer of indirect rule. He checked the growing independence of the emirs in the north as well as the efforts to elevate the Alafin in Yorubaland. He was hailed because he put emphasis on developing the institutions rather than preserving them. Thus he introduced selected Western-educated men into certain chiefly councils in southern Nigeria. But his 'reforms' were merely adjustments, and were not nearly sweeping enough to meet the needs of a rapidly changing society.

## Indirect rule in Ghana

By the early twentieth century the Fante-Ga coastal area of Ghana possessed the largest Western-educated class in West Africa. Ghanaian contacts with Europe dated back for centuries, and as early as 1844 the Fante chiefs had voluntarily handed over certain powers to the British. Many of the chiefs were also Western-educated men and the division between chiefs and Western-educated was less distinct than in Nigeria. When it appeared in the 1860s as if the British might withdraw from the Ghanaian coast, the Fante Confederation, a body including chiefs but in fact the creation of the Western-educated elite, prepared a constitution to take over and rule an independent Fante state. This was a definite pointer to the way in which Fante society was moving.

In Asante we have seen how the British tried to destroy the nation and set up direct administration. In fact, by making the Asantehene a martyr in exile, they forced Asante nationalism and opposition to centre upon him. Governor Gordon Guggisberg, who introduced the Lugardian theories to Ghana, brought Prempe back to the Asante stool in 1924. This was a popular measure and encouraged the Asante to continue to work towards the reconstruction of their nation.

*Sir Gordon Guggisberg (in the felt hat in the centre of the picture) leaves London for Ghana in 1925.*

Guggisberg merely recognised Prempe as Kumasihene (chief of Kumasi) but to the Asante people he was Asantehene (king of all the Asante), and the British finally accepted this fact in 1935. In 1943 the British gave back all stool lands which they had confiscated when Asante was conquered. A major concern of the Asante throughout the colonial period was to reconstruct what the British had destroyed at the conquest.

Guggisberg, a Canadian, was governor of Ghana from 1919 to 1929. In the coastal regions the Western-educated elite were far too strong to be ignored. In order to secure their support for his scheme of indirect rule he combined it with a number of projects very close to the hearts of the Western-educated class. He began a rapid acceleration of Ghana's economic development, founded Achimota College for higher education in 1927, introduced three elected members into the legislative council and drew up plans which would increase the twenty-five Ghanaian civil servants in 1925 to 151 ten years later.

As noted above, Ghanaian leadership, both chiefs and those who had received a Western education, had long co-operated. In 1897 the two groups had come firmly together against British efforts to confiscate land in Ghana and organised the Aborigines' Rights' Protection Society which upheld Ghanaian rights against any imperial attempt to reduce them. Guggisberg's introduction of indirect rule caused serious divisions in Ghanaian leadership. The chiefs, led by Nana Ofori Atta, a capable and Western-educated chief, were enthusiastic. The Western-educated elite feared the revival of chiefly power and also that the chiefs would become agents of British rule. Certain individuals were, however, ready to try the system and Ghanaian leadership was broken into conflicting factions over the issue.

After Guggisberg left in 1929 Nana Ofori Atta and Casely Hayford, a prominent leader of the Western-educated elite, settled their differences. Then in 1934 the seditious ordinance introduced by the colonial government united Ghanaians once again. Nana Ofori Atta continued to uphold the interests of the Western-educated by pressing for Africanisation of the civil service, which had fallen far behind Guggisberg's suggestions.

As elsewhere, but more prominently in Ghana because of its large Western-educated class, the greatest complaint against the British version of indirect rule was that it emphasised the conservative and illiterate in society. In 1945, for example, out of 2,471 members of local government, only 614 were educated. This was a sad fact in West

Africa's most literate colony. In 1948 a commission of enquiry condemned this state of affairs, but the colonial government, backed by the Colonial Office, said that the commission had listened too much to city politicians and not enough to the 'solid good sense of the countrymen' who were much attached to tradition. Another commission followed and on the whole confirmed the opinion of the first commission. Few Ghanaians wanted chieftaincy abolished but few also approved of the bias in the system against Western-educated men. Rural Ghanaians wanted both their chiefs and their educated men.

## Indirect rule in Sierra Leone and Gambia

In Sierra Leone it was the policy of Governor Cardew (1894-1900) both to destroy assimilation at the coast by replacing Creole senior civil servants by Europeans (see Chapter 18), and to introduce indirect rule in the interior. He rejected the plan of J. C. Parkes, the Creole head of the Department of Native Affairs, for a scheme of indirect rule to be supervised by Creole officers. Supported by the London government he laid down the policy that only Englishmen should administer the interior. Creole influence was to be kept out, the Mende and Temne were to remain uncreolised, and unspoilt. Indeed, for the first forty years of British rule the interior communities peacefully stagnated. There was little commercial activity or development of natural resources, and as a result there was little social change. As late as 1931 there was not even a road connecting Freetown with the interior over which modern ideas might pass. There were very few schools. The little education that was given was unprogressive. It was designed to train the Mende and Temne for 'tribal' life, not for senior posts nor as modern leaders of protest or nationalist movements. Indirect rule in the interior, instead of narrowing the gulf which history had already created between the Creole and interior people, sought to make it wider and deeper, and delay the time when Sierra Leone could emerge as a nation.

In the Gambia the protectorate in the interior which was ruled indirectly was kept carefully separate from the directly-ruled colony area around Bathurst (Banjul). In the protectorate, the British looked for chiefs to rule but seldom found them. The old royal families of the Gambia kingdom had been destroyed in the Marabout wars of Maba and the Fulani incursions under Musa Mollah. Therefore men of little or no traditional authority were made chiefs. The British then found it necessary to appoint five of themselves as travelling commissioners to act as 'paramount' chiefs, in the absence of Africans with claims to such positions.

The Gambian interior was hardly developed at all in the colonial period. Education was almost completely ignored. Between 1900 and 1940 the colonial government averaged about £2,000 annual expenditure on education. The excuse was always the lack of revenue, but this was an *excuse*, not a *reason*, for in 1920 when the government spent £3,000 on education it had a reserve fund in London of almost £329,000. What education was given was provided by the Christian missions and because the protectorate was Muslim it was woefully neglected. In 1938, for example, there were six mission schools in Bathurst (Banjul) and six in the protectorate, four secondary schools in Bathurst and none in the protectorate. Under indirect rule, the lack of schools and the absence of roads and railways combined to produce economic and social stagnation.

## Indirect rule—French-style

When the Mandinka and Tokolor empires as well as the Aladaxonu dynasty of Dahomey were overthrown, their centralised political systems were destroyed and direct European colonial rule was imposed on their peoples, in much the same way as the British initially treated Benin and Asante. Since no Lugard emerged to dominate French colonial philosophy these states were not, like Benin and Asante, reconstituted at a later date. Where the French entrenched themselves without force such as among the Hausa of Niger, the Fulani of Macina, northern Dahomey and among the Mossi, they confirmed the chiefs in their position as long as they continued to co-operate. Chief-inspired revolts occasionally led to a reduction in chiefly status and powers. For example, in the Futa Jalon following revolts in 1900, 1905 and 1911, the French re-drew the boundaries of the administrative units and cut down on the power and influence of the chiefs, but they continued to nominate them from the leading families and maintain the Almami. Zinder in Niger was even more severely punished. After its sultan had plotted against the French in 1906 he was deposed and no successor was chosen until 1923.

The outstanding examples of French indirect rule were among the Hausa of Niger and the Mossi of Upper Volta, whose king, the Moro Naba, represented a dynasty going back to the eleventh century. The

Moro Naba's government had eight provinces subject to it, five ruled directly and three as vassals. The French interfered relatively little with the Mossi system and it proved as adaptable to the French as it had to the African invaders of previous centuries. The important role of the Moro Naba and his chiefs after the Second World War indicated their continuing influence among the people. In Niger the French tampered very little with the established Hausa emirates. Territorial divisions were not artificial and the autocratic chieftaincies preserved their traditions. It was significant that in similar and neighbouring societies—Niger and Northern Nigeria—the French and British pursued similar policies.

Indirect rule required not only the preservation of traditional chieftaincy but also its adaptation to modern conditions. The British tended to be preservers, the French adapters. Particularly in the early years of French rule, chiefs who could not adapt were not preserved merely to conform to tradition, as in British colonies. They were swept away if the French believed they stood in the way of modernisation. In dealing with chiefs the French were much more pragmatic—where the chiefs were useful they were maintained, where they were not they were ignored—than the British who held a 'superstitious' feeling for chieftaincy and monarchy, so much so that they went about finding chiefs where they had never existed. Chieftaincy became a British 'fetish' with Lugard as its high priest. As the colonial period advanced a number of prominent officials from the governor-general of French West Africa, William Ponty in 1909, to the governor-general of French Equatorial Africa, Felix Eboué in 1942, stressed the value of chiefs who held traditional positions of authority. Thus dynasties which 'survived' the period of French imperial establishment and consolidation before 1914 normally maintained their positions throughout the colonial period.

The French employed agencies other than the chiefs as instruments of indirect rule. In Guinea, Soudan (Mali) and Senegal they refused to reconstruct the Tokolor and Mandinka empires which they had overthrown, but they nevertheless co-operated closely with the Tijaniyya brotherhood, supporting it in numerous ways and persecuting opposition brotherhoods such as the Hamalliyya. In return the Tijaniyya gave its blessing to French imperial rule. This was a kind of indirect rule, through the brotherhoods rather than through the chiefs as in British practice.

## CHAPTER EIGHTEEN

# Colonial government (2): the Western-educated elite

## The British abandon assimilation

Assimilation, whether of the British or French variety in West Africa, meant a colonial policy of transferring to the colonies the institutions, culture and economic organisation of the imperial country, of moulding the colony in the image of the imperial country and of turning its people into Europeans in all aspects except colour. In the nineteenth century in the four British West African colonies around Bathurst, Freetown, Lagos and the Fante-Ga areas of the Gold Coast, the British policy of assimilation had given Africans the status of British subjects, introduced a British judiciary, a British educational system, the British religion and British political institutions such as municipal and legislative councils. Assimilated Africans, or Black Englishmen, held office at all levels in the judiciary, the school system and the civil service up to and including the position of acting-governor.

Following the successful demand of the Canadian colonies in the 1840s for internal self-government, British policy came to accept that most other colonies would follow suit. However, foreign affairs, defence, currency, international trade, citizenship and final decisions in judicial matters remained under the control of the government in London. The British empire appeared to be evolving as a gigantic federation, with the colonies as the states and the federal capital in London, with the major exception that the colonies were never offered representation in the central government. Black Englishmen like the Creoles in Sierra Leone hoped that the four West African colonies would move towards a federation or union and internal self-government as the Canadian and Australian colonies had done. Readiness for self-government appeared to depend upon the degree and extent of assimilation, and Black Englishmen were eager to demonstrate their thorough anglicisation.

Black Englishmen were not unique. In the same period brown and yellow Englishmen were being produced in Asia and prominent French Canadians and some Dutch Boers were proud to be known as

British. They all studied English history, English literature, the geography of the British Isles, British political theory, British morals and codes of etiquette and the British god. They all gloried in 'one fleet, one throne, one God' and many fully believed that they lived under the most enlightened and beneficial political system in the world. To foreigners, the British, whatever shade of white, black or brown, were insufferably arrogant, as well they might be, for the fleet was quick to send its gunboats to protect their interests against foreigners, whether in defence of White or Black English in Liberian or French West African territory.

Between 1880 and 1900 this situation changed out of all recognition. White Englishmen began to proclaim an inborn superiority over all others and claim a position of dominance in the empire and right by conquest to exploit it. The extensive enlargement of the empire during the scramble for Africa and the addition of many lands in Asia bred white arrogance and a caste system based mainly on colour which discriminated against such non-Anglo-Saxons as the West African Creoles. The imperial policy of devolution of power to the colonies was abandoned in West Africa.

In West Africa the colonies and policy of assimilation for which they stood were not extended. Instead the vast new territories brought under British rule were called protectorates and their people British-protected persons. In the protectorates British law, land tenure and governmental forms were not to be extended. Black Englishmen were looked down upon, and were gradually removed from the positions of responsibility which they held.

Governor Cardew of Sierra Leone began the destruction of *assimilation* in Sierra Leone at the coast and introduced *indirect rule* in the interior. It was Cardew's policy that every government department in Sierra Leone must be headed by a European assisted by a European. Creoles were replaced upon death or retirement. Whereas in 1892 50 per cent of the senior civil service posts were held by Creoles, by 1917 the percentage had dropped to ten. Now that malaria was controlled the 'white man's grave' which had earlier killed 109 Anglican missionaries in twenty-five years, became rather pleasant, especially with a pension after only twenty years' service. Sitting high and cool on their reservation on the mountain above Freetown, the British began to talk of their imperial mission, shunned social mixing with the Creoles and were placed above the law by being exempted from trial by Creole juries. The European population rose steadily, and although many office holders were capable men, others got jobs because they were unemployable at home.

*Governor Cardew, seated centre with hat in hands, and members of his administration at a garden party in Freetown. Cardew introduced indirect rule in the interior of Sierra Leone and gradually replaced Creoles in his administration.*

Cardew's policy became general practice throughout British West Africa. By 1911 there was not one Creole left in the judiciary or executive council of any British colony. In 1902 African doctors were excluded from the government medical services, but by then up to twenty Creoles had qualified in medicine. When the military forces of British West Africa were united it was policy that the men were to be illiterate, the officers European. There was no place for the Creoles. By 1914 the majority of Europeans in West Africa viewed the Creoles with disfavour, jealousy and hidden fear. The Europeans were extremely irrational. Some despised the Creoles because they were not completely English but practised certain African customs. Others advised them to 'go back to the bush' and become 'real' Africans.

In place of assimilation the British substituted the policy of indirect rule through traditional rulers in which there was no place for the assimilated African.

## French policies—assimilation and association

The French in the ninteenth century, like the British, pursued a policy of assimilation which sought to transfer the civilisation of France to its West African colony, Senegal. Inhabitants of the four Senegalese communes, the towns of St Louis, Gorée, Rufisque and Dakar, were given French citizenship, governed under French law and through French political institutions, municipal councils and a general council. They studied French history, French literature and French morals and etiquette. They became as thoroughly and proudly Black Frenchmen as their neighbours down the coast had become Black Englishmen. In two respects France carried the assimilation process further than Britain. First, the elective principle had been far more extensively introduced, and secondly the Senegalese elected a representative to the French parliament in Paris. While the British conceived of their empire as a kind of federation the French saw theirs as a unitary state with the Paris parliament containing representatives from all over the empire. The British were decentralising, the French centralising. Many overstress this difference between the British and the French and fail to see the striking similarity in their goals. Both were assimilationist, determined to turn Africans into their own brand of European.

Following the conquest of vast areas in West Africa during the scramble, the French did not extend the commune system to the enlarged areas. While the British at the same time abandoned assimilation for indirect rule, the French abandoned it for a policy called *association*. However, the French did not as thoroughly abandon the ideals of assimilation as did the British. Thus association for many Frenchmen meant a stage in the process of the assimilation of the peoples of the newly conquered lands. Under association all Africans outside the communes were classified as subjects who were not protected by French law nor had any say in government through municipal or general councils. Subjects were totally subjected to the autocracy of colonial officials who could demand their labour without pay and jail them without trial. This was the hated *indigénat* which was intimately linked with the colonial policy of association. Those who held to the ideals of assimilation expected that with the spread of French education a growing number of subjects would become citizens and enjoy the rights of French political and judicial institutions. A process was legalised whereby subjects might become citizens. But when only slightly over 2,000 had become citizens out of 15,000,000 people by the late 1930s, it was obvious that association as a step to assimilation was not working. Nevertheless, association remained official French policy from around 1900 to the Loi Lamine Gueye of 1946 by which all Africans were proclaimed citizens of France. This signalled the collapse of the policy of association and a return to the nineteenth-century policy of assimilation.

In those areas where the paramount chiefs had been swept away during the conquest, French officials became the new chiefs, issuing orders to a hierarchy of African officials below them. For example, in the Mandinka area when Samori and his centralised hierarchy had been overthrown, the political units left were the villages under headmen or chiefs. The French, like Samori before them, more or less allowed the villages to continue to choose their chiefs. A number of villages were grouped into a canton which did not coincide with Samori's cantons, nor did they always follow ethnic lines. The French purposely ignored these things to which the British gave a great deal of attention. African officials, called canton chiefs, were placed in charge of the cantons but they were not chiefs in any traditional sense. They were French-appointed officials. They were not hereditary but chosen for their efficiency. The French favoured African officials who were literate in French with experience in the French army or civil service. If they also came from respected leading families in the canton this was all to the good but by no means necessary. Among the Fon of Dahomey canton 'chiefs' were often members of the Aladaxonu dynasty not because of their royal blood but because they proved the most efficient. Their efficiency arose not only from the habits inculcated by the Aladaxonus in the nineteenth century but because they commanded respect and obedience from the people.

A number of cantons were grouped in a *cercle* under a French officer called a *commandant*. The cercle commandant was much more a chief than the African canton head, not because he possessed traditional status but because he did possess real power. Canton heads lobbied him at his 'court' where the commandant issued orders, bestowed favours and punished those out of favour since he possessed judicial as well as executive power under the provisions of the indigénat. At almost any time a number of canton heads might be seen waiting outside the commandant's office to be ushered into his presence. Occasionally, as in some nineteenth-century African governments, the canton heads maintained representatives at court whose duty it was to communicate the big chief's will to the sub-chiefs, the canton heads. The canton head was, in turn, responsible for seeing that the village-chiefs carried out the commandant's orders. The more efficiently he did this, the more he was able to secure the co-operation of the villages and their chiefs, the more he assured his own position. This was the system of administration most closely identified with the policy of association. It has often been called direct rule, in contrast to indirect rule which was practised by the British generally and by the French among the Mossi, Hausa and Fulani.

## Contrasts between British and French policies

British indirect rulers were frequently alarmed at the lack of concern among the French for nineteenth-century political divisions or even ethnic differences among the people they ruled. British respect for ethnic history and tradition often led them into becoming 'traditionalists' themselves and reinforcing ethnicism in those they ruled. British officers in Hausaland were not normally transferred to Igboland, for example, because they were steeped in Hausa lore and prejudice and ignorant of Igbo lore and prejudice, and it was felt they would not make good administrators of the Igbo. The French, in contrast, freely transferred their officers all over West Africa regardless of African ethnic groupings. In referring to Africans they tended to talk of Senegalese and Dahomeans, not Wolof or Fon. On the other hand British officers seldom referred to Nigerians. They did not know Nigerians, they only knew Hausa or Yoruba or Igbo. Every British official form had a space asking for tribe and British officers frequently ridiculed Africans who referred to themselves as Nigerians or Gambians. When a black man was not called a native he was designated by his tribe and in flattery occasionally he became an African. All of this had some importance for the future in the degree and intensity of ethnic enmities. If educated French West Africans carried a heavy load of French culture, educated British West Africans carried a double burden, one of English culture and the other of ethnic consciousness. If the French-speaking elite was too French and not sufficiently African, the English-speaking elite was too ethnic and not sufficiently African.

Neither the British nor the French in the twentieth century were prepared to face the consequences of their nineteenth-century policies. The British white colonies had moved steadily toward independence, but if the old policy was applied to Africa and Asia it would lead to the disintegration of the empire. If representation in Paris was granted to the much enlarged French empire, overseas representation would exceed that of the imperial power and France would become a colony of its own colonies! Therefore, nineteenth-century policies of assimilation were abandoned by the British for the policy of indirect rule, and by the French for the policy of association. However, the policies of assimilation had been intensely popular with Western-educated French and British West Africans since they saw in them the hope of their eventual emancipation and liberation. Both imperial powers, therefore, pretended that their long-term goal remained to prepare the African colonies for self-government.

This led to imperial inconsistency which was particularly glaring among the British. The British claimed that their policy was the preparation of Africans for eventual self-government but quickly added that Africans were 'not ready'. When pressed to explain what was meant by 'not ready' they said that Africans had not assimilated enough of the British way of doing things. On the other hand they refused to pursue a policy whereby Africans might become 'ready'. They refused to give them experience in the senior civil service or push higher education. They actually condemned highly educated Africans, arguing that because of the totally Europeanised education they had received they were unfit to understand and hence govern the African masses. At the same time they did nothing to change the complete European bias in the education they provided, nor explain how European administrators with an identical education learnt how to understand and govern Africans. In truth the British turned against the African elite which their own nineteenth-century policy had created. They imposed a colour bar in hotels, churches and residential areas.

Among the French, despite the new policy of association, the ideals of assimilation were not as totally abandoned so far as the black elite was concerned. French colonial civil servants preferred the French-educated Africans to others. They took them into the civil service, preferred them as chiefs and mixed with them socially. As far as the French were concerned the more French an African was, the better treatment he deserved. Not all Frenchmen lived up to these ideals, just as not all Englishmen despised the assimilated African, but on the whole life was much more pleasant for the African with European education in the French than in the British empire. Very few modern leaders of former French West Africa have experienced the evils of racism which their counterparts in English-speaking West Africa came to expect as normal practice under colonial rule.

## British and French educational policies

Strange as it may seem, the British, who did not want an elite, produced a far larger one in their colonies than the French, who wanted an elite and were prepared to treat it decently. The English-speaking West African elite after 1900 was produced not by the British administration but in spite of it. The British African elite was produced largely by the labours of the Creoles and the missionary societies and the economic development of British West Africa, plus the reluctance of colonial governments to interfere with the system of education which was operating.

British West Africa possessed a higher percentage of religious traditionalists relative to Muslims than did French West Africa, and traditionalist peoples embraced Western education first and in greater numbers than Muslims. Furthermore, thanks to the production of export crops, British West Africans had a higher per capita income than French West Africans and were thus able to pay for education for their children without government aid. In West Africa the new elite emerged where the money was, among the Asante and Yoruba on cocoa revenue, among the Igbo and Mende on palm oil and among the Senegalese on groundnuts. In the British colonies, in the nineteenth-century age of assimilation, the missionary societies had built up a complete educational system topped by a university college at Fourah Bay. This success was largely due to the labour and enthusiasm of the Creole and Creolised population in all the British colonies. Mission schools were maintained by school fees, communal labour and by money raised by Africans and missionaries in the churches of West Africa and overseas. In addition the colonial governments of the nineteenth century which looked on these efforts with sympathy provided grants to the missions for educational work.

When the British abandoned assimilation after 1900 they found it difficult to alter the educational system to force it into line with their new political policy. Given a free hand they would have replaced academic studies for Africans with the attainment of bare literacy combined with manual training. But the missions had influential supporters within the London government, and Africans in Lagos, Accra, Cape Coast and Freetown could finance schools unassisted. The first grammar school in Lagos, for example, had been founded without assistance from mission or government. Colonial governments had few funds and they were not prepared to intervene, but continued the policy of small subsidies to the missions. The smallness of the educational grants in relation to other expenditure showed both the colonial dislike for the academic educational system and the lack of enthusiasm for education for Africans generally. Much of the subsequent trouble in British West Africa was that it had an educational system designed to promote assimilation and a political policy completely opposed to it.

Occasionally, as in the Gold Coast, a governor pursued both assimilation and indirect rule at the same time. Governor Guggisberg introduced indirect rule to the southern Gold Coast after 1919. The black elite along the coast opposed it as likely to delay the devolution

*Achimota College, conceived of as an institution for the production of Black Englishmen.*

of power into African hands. On the other hand Guggisberg also introduced a limited franchise for the legislative council and promised a more rapid Africanisation of the civil service via the graduates of the proposed new Achimota College. Achimota was planned as an institution more thoroughly geared to produce Black Englishmen than any other institution in British West Africa at that time. It was originally designed to place African students in European hands at the kindergarten stage and keep them there until graduation at university level. Strong emphasis was to be placed on the mixing of staff and students at study, at work and at play. In other words, during the most impressionable and formative stage Africans were to be immersed in British culture and then emerge from the assimilating process English in everything but colour. Successors to Guggisberg were less favourable to Achimota and it did not grow as fast as originally planned, nor did Guggisberg's programme of Africanisation even approach the goals he set for it. Guggisberg was an unusual type of twentieth-century British governor. Few others were as enthusiastic about African education as he, the whole idea of Achimota was his, and the colonial civil service was unenthusiastic.

The French were considerably handicapped in their attempts to advance assimilation by spreading Western education. Their empire was much poorer and largely Muslim, among whom missionaries had no success under the French or British. Furthermore, while they were prepared to permit missionary societies to operate, they were not inclined to support them. Among many French administrators there was an ingrained belief that the mission of France in Africa was not to destroy one set of superstitions (those of traditional religion) merely to replace them with another set (those of Christianity). In their view the finest example of French culture was the rational man and they aimed in Africa to produce him. Secondly, education was the universal inheritance of mankind and the French did not believe in charging for it. The French set up free state schools, although not many could be provided out of the restricted resources at hand. Only Senegal had a school system comparable to that of the British colonies. Only Senegal had secondary schools which were designed to serve all French West Africa. Of these the William Ponty School was the oldest and most famous but a school of medicine was created in 1918, the Lycée Faidherbe in 1920 and another secondary school in Dakar in 1940. Secondary education facilities did not spread outside Senegal until after the war. A lycée was opened in Bamako in 1945 and one in Abidjan in 1953. Dahomey was an exception. The Fon and the Yoruba worked closely with the Catholic Church in British-African fashion to create a large number of mission schools. Thus in the secondary institutions in Senegal, Dahomeans formed the second largest group after the Senegalese themselves.

A good deal of criticism from British sources over the years has been levelled at the kind of education provided by the French. Attacks have been made upon the use of the French language as the medium of instruction from the earliest grade, whereas the British system employed the vernacular initially. Again this was the result of mission influence in British areas; the missions being primarily interested in spreading the gospel, the quickest way to do so was in the vernacular. Although Lugard and many of his successors opposed the vernacular and wanted to eliminate it, they decided not to, and thereby avoided a clash with the missions. In addition vernacular education was effective mostly where it had been firmly established by 1900 in Yorubaland. Elsewhere, as in Igboland, the small amount of vernacular education given in the infant section did not create a people who wrote and read their first language as fluently as English. Finally where the vernacular was stressed over English, as in Hausaland, it was believed it was designed to prevent school leavers from seeking positions in the English-language civil service.

Another criticism of French education was its heavy 'Frenchness'. The textbook which taught Africans about their 'ancestors the Gauls' has rightly been the object of British humour, but it was hardly more humorous than British West Africans who were at the same time memorising the British king-lists. To Englishmen, French Africans might appear ludicrously French, but hardly more ludicrous than British Africans who to the French seemed distastefully English. Diagne and Senghor were black Frenchmen but J. K. Aggrey and Henry Carr were just as thoroughly English.

After the Second World War indirect rule and association were abandoned under African pressure which by then was prepared for violence if constitutional agitation failed. Both the British and French reverted to their nineteenth-century policies; the British of devolving power, the French of extending the rights of citizenship. Both initiated a crash programme of assimilation to produce elites in their respective cultures. Money was poured into schools. Universities (or European culture mills) were founded and were tied as colleges to universities in the imperial country, following identical courses and in many cases insisting upon the same dress and even eating habits to produce Black Frenchmen and Black Englishmen to take over the colonial structure built by the Europeans. It was ironic that imperial apologists claimed that this had been their country's consistent policy throughout the colonial period. Just enough shreds of their nineteenth-century policies survived into the twentieth century to make the claims of the apologists appear plausible.

An excerpt from a poem by the President of Angola, Agostinho Neto, is a fitting epitaph to the colonial period.

> I live
> In the dark quarters of the world
> ... where the will is watered down
> and men
> are confused with things.

## CHAPTER NINETEEN

# The colonial economy

'The native in this country ... will soon find himself ground to powder between the stones of European and Asiatic intensive economic aggression.' (*African Messenger*, Lagos, 1924)

## Colonial economic ideas

The main features of the colonial economy were:
1   Economic exploitation of the agricultural and mineral resources of colonies by the imperial powers.
2   Direction of the trade of the colonies in the interests of the imperial power not the colonies.
3   An almost total absence of modern manufacturing industrial development until the Second World War.
4   A policy of financing piecemeal development in the colonies out of the colonies' limited revenues.
5   The development of new forms of transport based especially on railways and motor vehicles.
6   Considerable initiative by African farmers and traders in the continued development of export crops.
7   Domination of the export trade by great European monopoly combines at the expense of African farmers and traders.

Both France and Britain believed the economies of the colonies should be tied to those of the imperial power, in such a way that the imperial power benefited. For example, according to a theory called the Colonial Pact by the French, the colonies must provide agricultural export crops for the imperial country, and buy its manufactured goods in return. This led to economic exploitation of the colonies by the imperial powers.

The countries of French West Africa were forced to buy and sell in French markets even when they could do so more profitably elsewhere. On the other hand the Colonial Pact did not oblige France to buy from her colonies. If Ghanaian cocoa was cheaper, the French could buy it to the loss of their own colony, the Ivory Coast. Thus the Colonial Pact was binding on the colonies but not on the imperial country. When France agreed to purchase Senegalese groundnuts at above the world price in 1931, instead of buying more cheaply from British colonies, it was the first break in the Colonial Pact, the first acceptance by France of economic responsibility to her colonies.

Britain was more liberal, usually allowing her colonies to buy and sell in the best markets. However, after the First World War the British placed special taxes on palm oil going to Germany, and in the 1930s excluded Japanese cotton cloth from colonies where it was underselling her own. The Nigerian press was quick to point out that while Africans were now forced to buy high-priced English cloth, Britain continued to buy cheaper Norwegian whale-oil, in preference to Nigerian palm oil. When there was a burden to bear it was the colonies that bore it.

There was hardly any modern manufacturing industrial development in West Africa before the Second World War. Industrialisation would compete with the industries of the imperial country and would upset the Colonial Pact. For example, when groundnut oil mills in Senegal began exports to France in 1927 French oil millers complained of the competition, so the French Government limited the amount of Senegalese oil that could be imported to France. Moreover, local West African industries were allowed to die in competition with European manufactured goods. The development of railways allowed European cotton goods and iron tools to be sold in the interior much more cheaply than those of African manufacture. Only in Mossi country in French Upper Volta were local iron industries able to compete in price with European imports. Generally, African craftsmen, especially weavers and blacksmiths, were hardest hit.

Another idea in the Colonial Pact was that colonies must be financially self-supporting. Therefore, development projects such as harbours, railways and roads had to be built entirely out of local funds. Obviously, this limited the amount of development that could take place. Finance was not lacking in the imperial capitals, but it was invested in the British and French economies rather than in the colonies. The British treasury even deliberately held back development funds by a policy of creating reserve funds for the colonies. Reserve funds kept losing their real value through inflation. The Gambia suffered most from this policy. In the early 1920s the British treasury had to demonetise the French five-franc piece which had been legal tender in the Gambia since 1843. However, the treasury made a gross fiscal error in its handling of the demonetisation, and as a result the Gambia Government lost £200,000 of its reserves. This was one of the worst examples of the lack of imperial responsibility towards the welfare of the colonies. The British Government insisted on colonial self-sufficiency, but it was going too far to saddle its colonial subjects with the burden of its own fiscal incompetence.

# Transport

Freetown possessed the only good natural harbour in West Africa, and elsewhere enormous sums had to be spent to create artificial harbours. The French colonies' taxes went into turning Dakar into the best harbour in West Africa. The Ivory Coast did not get an ocean port until the development of Abidjan in the 1930s. Guinea, Gambia and Liberia had no modern ports until after the First World War. Togo and Dahomey had none when the French left in 1960. Nigerian tax money was swallowed up in creating deep water ports at Lagos, which was opened in 1913, and at Apapa, opened in 1926. Guggisberg created Ghana's first modern port at Takoradi.

Most colonies struggled to finance a cheap one-track railway from the coast into the interior. Railways were begun from Dakar in 1880, Lagos and Freetown in 1896, Sekondi in 1898 and from Conakry, Abidjan and Cotonou in 1900. Many of these railways were not completed until the Second World War and all were quite inadequate. Only Nigeria had enough money, due to the discovery of coal at Enugu and tin at Jos, to create a railway system of two major and three branch lines. None of the railways of one colony linked up with those of any other so that there was no West African railway system similar to the one in Europe. In Ghana the railway still does not connect the north with the south, and by far the largest part of French West Africa has no railway services at all. The imperial powers built these railways only from cash crop and mining areas to the coast to make it easier to export vital foodstuffs and raw materials for Europe. Yet the burden of financing even these inadequate railways fell upon African tax-payers.

With the coming of motor cars and lorries, colonial governments began to build roads to link up with and feed the railway, but not trunk roads to the seaports. New areas could now cultivate export crops which were sent on lorries to the railway. Cocoa farmers in Nigeria and Ghana ran fleets of lorries for this purpose. Colonial governments tried to prevent lorries, which were popular because they were faster and cheaper, from competing with the railways by refusing to build trunk roads and by charging high licence fees. Since lorries were usually African-owned, this discriminated against African businessmen.

Africans pioneered not only the widespread use of lorries but also the development of commercial passenger motor services. The most successful of these early motor transport entrepreneurs was a Nigerian, W. A. Dawodu.

Railways and roads produced a transport revolution that was one of the important results of colonialism. A head load from the coast to Kumasi, which had cost 26s 6d, cost only 4s by rail. However, as we have seen, if the railway helped agricultural exports, it also harmed local industry.

An important result of harbour, railway and road building was the growth in population of port cities such as Dakar, Takoradi and Lagos. People from all ethnic groups travelled to the big cities looking for jobs and education. The colonial governments were financially unable to undertake low cost housing and as a result vast sprawling slums developed. Discontent fanned by the press became widespread, and new associations were formed, including churches, trade unions, ethnic and progress unions, and parties agitating for political change.

## Export crops and food crops

The major export crops of West Africa were palm oil, groundnuts, coffee, cocoa and rubber. Igboland and Dahomey remained, as in the nineteenth century, the leading exporters of palm oil, although the French failed to keep up the volume of oil exported by the kings of Dahomey before the conquest. At the conquest there were forty million palm trees in Dahomey. In the 1950s there were only thirty-two and a half million, most of which were old, having been planted before the conquest. The prices offered by the French middlemen firms were often so low that the people preferred to grow food crops and use the palms for production of wine rather than oil. In 1946, for example, the firms were buying oil for a little over 3,500 francs per

*Groundnuts stacked for export in Kano, Nigeria.*

226

tonne and selling it in France for 38,000 francs, thus receiving ten times more than they had paid the producers.

Groundnuts, first planted in Senegal in about 1820 as a domestic food crop, later became the main export of that country, the area of production expanding with the expansion of the railway. Groundnuts also became the major export crop of Hausaland, centred on Kano, after the railway reached that city from Lagos in 1911. Coffee was originally cultivated by Europeans in the Ivory Coast, but it requires more labour than most crops. Eventually African farmers took over from the Europeans because they were more successful in securing and holding labourers. Ivory Coast became the world's third largest coffee exporter.

Cocoa was West Africa's most important export crop. Ghana became the world's largest producer followed by Yorubaland and the Ivory Coast. Cocoa was first introduced to the mainland from Fernando Po in 1879 by two Ghanaians, the Tetteh Quashie brothers. Its production grew and Ghana's thirteen tonnes of cocoa exports in 1895 reached 4,000 tonnes in 1911 and brought an economic revolution to the whole country. From Ghana, cocoa was introduced into Yorubaland in the 1880s, first at Agege, later spreading inland to Ibadan with the railway, and to Ondo along the feeder roads. Aware of the 'cocoa miracle' in Ghana, Governor Angoulvant in 1912 introduced it into the Indenie area of Ivory Coast from where it spread rapidly.

In 1925 Liberia began to pull out of its economic slump when a million acres of land were leased to the Firestone Company (USA) for rubber plantations. Americo-Liberians also developed plantations of their own and soon rubber made up ninety per cent of Liberia's exports.

*A very early photograph of cocoa packing in Lagos which was taken in the 1880s.*

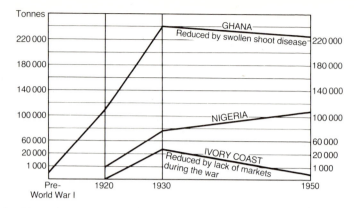

32　West African cocoa production in the 1950s.

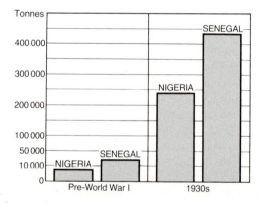

33　Groundnut production in Nigeria and Senegal before 1939.

In colonies which developed export crops—Nigeria, Ghana, Ivory Coast, and Senegal—there was a rise in both living standards and in government revenue for the development of ports, railways, roads and education. In Senegal groundnut prosperity contributed to small scale industrialisation, which included oil and lumber mills, soap, beverage and brick factories, lime works, salt works and fisheries. In Nigeria and Ghana profits went into education, better housing and transport lorries.

Everywhere in West Africa, except Nigeria, the rise in the value of export crops was partly counterbalanced by the decline of food crops and the rise of food prices. This was due to the scarcity of land, the neglect of food crops because of the greater value of export crops, and to the lack of a labour force. Sierra Leone, Liberia and most of French West Africa imported rice even though they could grow their own. Food crops were also neglected by the colonial governments because they did not directly contribute to the welfare of the imperial country. Mali—called the granary of French West Africa— produced surplus millet which it sold in the groundnut-producing areas of Senegal, but because of the lack of railways and roads, Mali was unable to transport any of this surplus to other surrounding areas. In 1932 the French began the Niger project in Mali to irrigate an area of the Niger Bend for the growing of cotton as an export crop, but African farmers found that rice was more profitable. This emphasis on cash crops was typical of colonial policy, and if food crops were encouraged this was often accidental.

Only in Nigeria was the development of cash crops not balanced by a decline in food crops. In Igboland food crops were grown along with the palm trees. In Yorubaland, around the edges of the cocoa belt, in Oyo and Ekiti, food crop production was increased to feed the cocoa areas. There was also a lively trade in kola nuts going north and cattle moving south. Ghana, however, was more typical of West Africa generally. With its cocoa revenue it was the wealthiest West African state but more of its money than Nigeria's was spent abroad on rice and other foods brought in by sea, and on cattle coming mainly from Hausaland in the north-east.

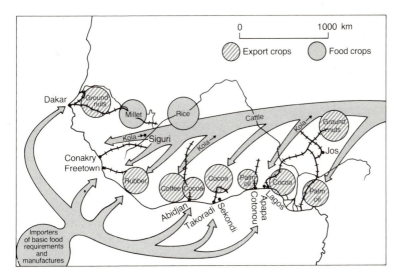

34   *West African trade patterns 1900-39.*

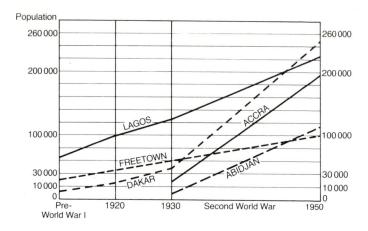

*35    The growth of West African cities before 1950.*

Many colonies developed no important crop and had therefore no money for railways, roads or education. Economic conditions in some were worse than in the nineteenth century and their people fell far behind those in export crop areas. Poverty drove the young men of Mali to the groundnut areas of Senegal in search of work, and thousands of young Mossi left home to work on the coffee and cocoa plantations of Ivory Coast and Ghana. While Mali and Mossi exported 'manpower', Dahomey exported 'brainpower'. Poor as it was, Dahomey struggled to educate its sons who found employment with French firms and in the civil service in other parts of West Africa. Money sent home by all these migrant workers helped to lessen the poverty of the homelands.

## The *grands comptoirs* and African merchants

Three great monopoly enterprises dominated the economic life of British and French West Africa. They controlled the wholesale and retail trading, the buying of export crops, banking, and transportation systems on land. These *grands comptoirs*, or combines, were the Compagnie Française de l'Afrique Occidentale (CFAO) founded in 1887, the Société Commerciale de l'Ouest Africain (SCOA) founded in 1906, and Unilever, a world-wide organisation whose African branch was the United Africa Company (UAC).

The *comptoirs* were usually formed as a result of a long process of amalgamation. For example, in 1880, the African Association was formed out of the union of a number of small companies, and after the First World War it joined with Swanzy and with Miller Brothers, two other West Coast firms, to form the African and Eastern Trading Corporation. In 1920 Unilever purchased the Niger Company and in 1929 joined it with the African and Eastern Trading Corporation to form the UAC.

The *grands comptoirs* were involved in almost every aspect of West African commerce. In 1927 CFAO had 33 branches and 154 trading centres and was making a profit of 90 per cent in good years and 25 per cent in poor. SCOA at the same time had 21 branches and 122 trading centres, while the UAC was the dominant company in all British West Africa besides having subsidiary companies in Senegal, Mali, Guinea and Ivory Coast. CFAO controlled most of French West African river transport, was involved in a number of banks, and dominated the steamship lines serving French West Africa, just as UAC was heavily involved with shipping to British West Africa. SCOA had palm oil and banana plantations in Ivory Coast, while UAC held the mineral rights to practically all of Northern Nigeria. So widespread was the *grands comptoirs'* influence that a Ghanaian remarked, 'The earth is Lord Leverhulme's [head of UAC] and the fulness thereof.'

The *grands comptoirs* agreed to fix prices so as not to compete with each other and were therefore under no compulsion to give good service, to cater for African tastes or to modernise their businesses. They sent most of their profits to the home country, and colonial governments were too subservient to imperial interests to force them to invest in West Africa by taxation of profits sent abroad.

In Ghana and Nigeria the *grand comptoirs* repeatedly sought to fix cocoa prices paid to farmers. To protect themselves against the 'combine clique', farmers' unions grew up from 1914.

Another merchant group, the Syrians and Lebanese, began to move into West Africa in the 1890s. Their numbers grew until in 1935 there were 6,000 of them in French West Africa and even more in British colonies. Organised in close-knit family groups, the wealthy members brought in poor relations and helped them set up in business. They pushed into the small retail trade—beads, cloth, kola nuts, and road transport—until then dominated by Africans. Syrians and Lebanese received much of the blame for the colonial economic system, for African anger against exploitation was often directed against them while Europeans—who wanted to direct attention away from themselves—encouraged the idea that the Syrians and Lebanese were the major obstacle to African commerce.

One of the most lucrative nineteenth-century trades was the exchange of kola nuts from the forest for cattle from the savannah. Where the railway, as in Guinea, Ivory Coast and Nigeria, went from the coastal forests to the savannah, this trade expanded. Since kola required less labour and brought more revenue than cocoa, many early cocoa areas in Nigeria, such as Agege and Abeokuta, changed to kola planting. Asante, however, probably the greatest kola exporter of the nineteenth century, lost some of its markets because there was no railway running north to the savannah.

In the nineteenth century, before the development of the *grands comptoirs*, a number of African merchant princes—Creoles, Brazilians, Ghanaians and Senegalese—made large commercial fortunes. Although they had less capital than European firms, they were more trusted, had greater influence and more access to African kingdoms. As a result a number of Afro-European business partnerships developed which combined European money and African influence to the benefit of both.

After the partition there was a steady decline in the prosperity of these merchants. The political advantages they had enjoyed under African kings became disadvantages under colonial rule, and the old partnerships were no longer necessary to Europeans. Often the merchant princes were crushed between the developing *comptoirs* and the incoming Syrians and Lebanese. Furthermore, while European firms were building up capital reserves, an African merchant's estate was usually broken up at his death among children and relatives, so that while Europeans built one generation upon the other, Africans began afresh in each generation. European firms established branches inland, following first the railway, and later the roads, which cut out African middlemen, especially produce buyers.

Colonial governments seldom stepped in to protect Africans against European competition, though they did occasionally do the reverse. Nothing was done in 1895, for example, when the shipping companies gave lower freight rates to larger than to smaller firms, and so made it impossible for African firms to sell as cheaply as the larger European ones. In the Ivory Coast government action between 1912 and 1925 intentionally cut out Ghanaians from the mahogany industry to make way for European firms.

A contrast is provided by the development of the goldfields of Asante with those of Siguri in Guinea. A gold boom followed the conquest of Asante when 400 European companies wanted to mine, and ultimately employed 10,000 Africans. The Asante goldfields, for centuries in African hands, passed to Europeans, and except for the wages paid to labourers Africans got little benefit from them, for there was not even an income tax, or a tax on company profits through which the colonial government might secure revenue for development purposes. In Guinea the French also tried to come in with big companies, but since the deposits were not as rich as in Asante, they failed and gave up the venture. At Siguri every dry season about 100,000 Africans mine for gold which is sold as in the nineteenth century through Diula traders. Thus it appears likely that the poorer Guinea goldfields have contributed more to African living standards than the richer fields of Asante.

## Land and labour

The French assumed that they owned the land in their colonies by right of conquest, and in 1904 they declared all vacant land state property. It was difficult to define vacant land because in a system of shifting cultivation land which may appear vacant is in fact merely resting in preparation for a crop in three to seven years' time. The French desired to attract French planters and to encourage Africans to take out individual titles to their land. Considerable land was given to settlers, especially in Ivory Coast and Guinea, but frequently European farmers were unable, as noted previously, to compete with African farmers and much land was later abandoned.

In British West Africa, with its much heavier population, the giving of land to settlers would have created hardship. The educated elite— Creole, Fante and Yoruba—conscious of what settlers were doing in British colonies in South and Central Africa, were determined to prevent the same thing happening in West Africa. In Ghana, the British tried in 1894 and 1897 to follow French policy by lands bills, which proclaimed unoccupied lands, forest lands and minerals the property of the state. The successful Ghanaian opposition to these bills is described in Chapter 20.

Colonies had to be self-sufficient, and yet large sums were required for harbours, railways and roads to get export crops out, and European goods into the continent. Therefore, costs were reduced by the use of forced and unpaid labour. France relied upon forced labour more than the British because her empire was larger in area and smaller in population. Her colonies also had smaller revenues because cash crops developed more slowly and on a smaller scale and also because French merchants invested less in their colonies than British merchants. By 1936 British merchants had invested £117

233

in West Africa, but French merchants had invested only £30
With all these disadvantages the French required more ports
re miles of railway and roads than the British because of the
greater size of their empire.

Under French colonial laws every male between 18 and 60 years of age was compelled to contribute a certain number of days' labour to the state. Between 1927 and 1936 15,000 men were forced to labour on the Niger project and on railway construction, and probably as many again were employed on road building and other projects. Forced labour was not abolished until 1946 and was one of the most hated aspects of French colonialism. African chiefs were used as recruiting agents, greatly lowering their position in people's eyes.

Conditions under which the forced labourers worked were often very bad, the food was inadequate, the housing poor, disease frequent and the death-rate high. Especially cruel were the conditions in the Cameroons under German rule, where men recruited in the high plateau free of the malarial mosquito were forced to work in the mosquito infested plantations of the lowlands. Lacking the natural immunity of people born in malarial areas, only about ten per cent of them ever saw their homes again.

Africans under British rule suffered less because wages were offered, but occasionally the pay was too low to attract labourers and the government then recruited labour through the chiefs. The result was very similar to the French system. The chiefs forced their people to work. In Ghana the government used the chiefs to assist the gold mines to recruit labour in the Northern Territories. The chiefs were often reluctant to do this, especially after the influenza epidemic of 1918-19 had killed 25,000 people, thus reducing the farming labour force in the north. Investigations after the Asante goldfields strike in 1924 showed that most of the evils of forced labour, including an unusually high death-rate, were present in the mines.

Forced labour was used because colonialists believed that Africans would not work without compulsion. Low wages were paid on the false argument that African labour, regardless of its wages, was unproductive. Africans who travelled long distances to find work desired to return home for visits and to marry. Many young workers did not look forward to a life of daily paid labour, and indeed most hoped to settle down and farm. In fact, ample evidence showed that high wages attracted labourers. One of the problems of the Asante mines was that labourers preferred to work on the Asante cocoa farms where the money and living conditions were better. Europeans were slow to see that they had to pay more than a subsistence wage to

*African women breaking open cocoa pods to extract the beans. Large numbers of men also worked on the cocoa farms in Asante, where money and living conditions were better than on the goldfields.*

attract workers since all Africans could get that on farms, and those in export crop areas could earn much more. In any case forced labour is always inefficient labour, and low-paid labour only slightly less so.

Wage levels were tied neither to supply and demand, nor adjusted to prosperity and depression or rising and falling costs. They remained static over long periods of time, and because of the rising cost of living, became worth less and less. In 1896 in Ghana the lowest paid government employee earned £36 per year. In 1919, although the cost of living had risen one hundred per cent (so that £36 would only buy what £18 had bought in 1896) the basic wage remained the same. The wage was then raised to £48, although the cost of living continued to rise in the 1920s so that low wages were actually becoming lower in real terms.

## Economic slump

While the 1920s had been a period of general economic prosperity the 1930s witnessed the most severe economic depression in modern times. No part of the world escaped. Nor could any colonial government do much about it for even the greater powers suffered almost helplessly. Prices of raw materials fell disastrously, and government customs dues were therefore reduced with a consequent reduction in revenues, and in government services. Many civil servants were discharged from their posts and others had their

235

salaries reduced. For the common man money became so scarce as to become almost a curiosity.

The depression produced widespread loss of faith in colonialism. It intensified the struggle between the *grands comptoirs* and African farmers. The co-operative movement was born to market export crops and thus bypass the European firms. Countries with a one-crop economy, which meant almost all African colonies, were particularly hard hit, African demands became louder for a wider economic base, for more emphasis upon food crops, and above all for industrialisation, especially to produce locally consumed items such as soap and building materials. The depression led to political dissatisfaction, and hostility towards colonialism resulted in the birth of modern nationalism.

## The Second World War

The war brought revolutionary changes to West Africa. It provided a great stimulus to modern nationalism and the movement towards self-government. It also led to a rapid revival of the economy, and to the beginnings of modern industrialisation. Raw materials were in much greater demand to supply the needs of British and French armies with equipment and food. Japanese conquests of European colonies in Asia led the Allies, Britain and France, to seek substitutes for Malayan tin and rubber and Indonesian palm oil in West Africa. Imports were severely reduced by German air attacks on British industrial towns, German submarine attacks on Allied shipping, and Allied use of all available shipping for war purposes. Therefore, new import-substitution industries grew up in West Africa. Senegal's oil mills greatly expanded production, and new mills sprang up in Mali, Upper Volta and Niger. Cement, household goods, cigarette and sugar processing factories were built. Public works of military value, such as ports and airports, were constructed.

The economic revival brought many new jobs, but it also added fuel to the growing nationalist discontent. Firstly, many farmers were forced to grow crops for Allied war needs, at the expense of their own food crops. Secondly, forced labour was used in mines, public works schemes, and even in factories, on the grounds that it was a form of conscription to help win the war. Thirdly, in spite of industrialisation, there was a scarcity of imported goods, and prices of imports rose rapidly. The economic revival caused by the war did not revive the faith in colonialism that had been lost in the pre-war depression.

## CHAPTER TWENTY

# Responses to colonialism (1) : the early period

The imposition of colonial rule or foreign domination on Africans did not go unchallenged. At different times and in different places, in the religious, economic and political fields, Africans responded to the loss of their sovereignty and independence. The earliest reaction against colonialism manifested itself in the religious field, as is signified by the rise of independent African churches.

## Independent African churches

In the mid-nineteenth century the Creoles had played the leading part in Christianising not only Sierra Leone colony but Lagos and Abeokuta in Yorubaland and the Niger Delta. Bishop Samuel Ajayi Crowther's Delta Pastorate was the great success story in nineteenth-century Christian mission work in West Africa. However, towards the end of the century the Creoles in the missions began to meet the same troubles from British racial arrogance as their brothers in the colonial civil service. The British Europeanised the leadership of the churches as well as the administration and abandoned assimilation. Anglicans and Methodists replaced their Creole archdeacons and superintendents by Europeans. A European succeeded Bishop Crowther and no Creole or African was consecrated to this high office again for sixty years. The result of this new policy was that many African Christians broke with the European churches and formed new churches, independent of foreign control. Important major independent churches were, in Nigeria, the African Baptists (founded 1888), the United Native African Church (1891), the African Church (1901) and the United African Methodists (1917); in the Cameroons the United Native Church (1885); and William Harris's church in the Ivory Coast. The major cause of the earliest breaks from the missions was the leadership issue. The independent churches have sometimes been classified as Ethiopian, after an independent church in South

Africa, and also because Ethiopia was a symbol of ancient Christianity and independence from foreign control. In West Africa the term 'African' has been more popular. The Ethiopian or African churches had little quarrel with the doctrine, practice or ritual of mission Christianity. Their main complaint was the control of leadership by Europeans.

Were the independent churches nationalist? The vast majority did not involve themselves in politics. To many independent African Christians, religion provided a retreat from the political and secular world. They failed to see that religion cannot be divorced from economics and politics and the affairs of this world, that religion is not merely a question of personal morals and personal worship. On the other hand, the African churches were an assertion of nationalism simply by their creation and existence. Their refusal to submit to European leadership in religion indirectly encouraged other Africans to question European leadership in politics as well. Certainly, colonial governments were alarmed by the new African Churches which they regarded as anti-European and therefore dangerous to colonialism. The founders of two of West Africa's leading independent churches, William Harris and Garrick Braid, suffered from persecution by the colonialists (and so did many more independent church leaders throughout the continent, notably Simon Kimbangu in Zaire and Elliot Kamwana in Malawi). Independence in the churches was an early step on the path to political independence.

The racial and leadership crisis in the Niger Mission triggered off the independence movement in the church. Between 1887 and 1890 a group of European missionaries arrived in Nigeria and soon began labelling Bishop Crowther's mission a total failure and saying that he was not fit to be a bishop. They steadily worked to take the Niger Mission, including the Delta area, out of his hands. Leadership, so they argued, could only be effective in the hands of the 'superior' white race. They sacked most of the Sierra Leone missionaries in the Niger Mission. Lagos and Freetown became storm centres loud in their defence of African capabilities in general and Crowther's all-black Church Mission in particular. The Niger Delta churches broke away from the Church Missionary Society (CMS)—one of the mission societies of the Anglican Church and the one responsible for Anglican work in Sierra Leone, Yorubaland and the Niger—and formed the Niger Delta Pastorate in 1892 on a guarantee of financial support from Sierra Leone. In the middle of the crisis Bishop Crowther died, and the Delta Pastorate, which still claimed to be

Anglican but no longer under the CMS, asked the Archbishop of Canterbury to consecrate the Sierra Leonean James Johnson as bishop of their church. The CMS was offering a white bishop free of charge, but the Delta Christians claimed this would be admitting that Crowther had been a failure. Considering the tremendous success of his work in the Delta, they said 'this will be the greatest piece of injustice and ingratitude'.

Crowther was succeeded by a white bishop and the CMS offered to make James Johnson his assistant over the Delta Pastorate. This compromise nevertheless fulfilled the aim of keeping ultimate control in alien hands. The Pastorate took over entirely its own financing but towards 1900 the Delta economy was collapsing, and the Creoles of Sierra Leone, as indicated earlier, were also in economic difficulties. The declining economic position of the Delta was reflected in the devaluation of its currency by 67 per cent. In 1900 the Pastorate was unable to bear the cost of an independent bishop, and accepted James Johnson as 'half bishop', as he was dubbed by critics.

The Niger crisis had a double significance for the future. First, the succession of a white man to Crowther's position was the signal for the inauguration of the colonial policy in church, state and commerce of eliminating and excluding Africans from positions of authority. Second, a number of Africans in Lagos refused to accept the new policy. Two groups broke away from the missions and established independent churches, the United Native African Church in 1891 and the African Church in 1901, to defend the dignity of African Christians and demonstrate their ability to manage their own religious affairs. The founding resolution of the United Native African Church in 1891 set forth what was to become the philosophy of all the African independent churches:

> That this meeting in humble dependence upon almighty God is of opinion that Africa is to be evangelised and that the foreign agencies at work at the present moment taking into consideration climatic and other influences cannot grasp the situation; resolved that a purely Native African Church be founded for the evangelisation and amelioration of our race to be governed by Africans.

## The Braid movement 1915-18

Between 1900 and 1914 the city-states of the Delta declined rapidly, surpassed by inland cities such as Onitsha which became entrepots of the palm oil trade. Young men from the Delta were forced to leave home and seek work or opportunities in trade, in wage labour or in the civil service. In 1914 Nigeria's most important palm oil market—Germany—was cut off by the First World War and this greatly increased the economic misery in the area. In 1915 a devout Christian, Garrick Sokari Braid, began a spectacular evangelising mission in Bakana, one of the successor towns to Elem Kalabari. His reputation as a prophet spread over the Delta. Thousands of people thronged to hear him speak and discarded their secret or open practices of traditional religion. Bakana and Bonny were particularly strong centres of the movement and Delta Pastorate clergy from both towns became Braid's supporters.

Gradually the forces of colonialism ranged themselves against Braid and his followers. The European traders were annoyed because he preached against gin, the mainstay of their trade, and gin ceased to sell. The Delta Pastorate, originally sympathetic, became jealous of Braid's success and placed petty obstacles in the path of his converts so that a new church—the Christ Army—emerged in competition to the Pastorate. Finally the British administrator, P. A. Talbot, interpreted Braid's movement as 'essentially one of Ethiopianism, of blacks against whites', which opened the way for judicial persecution. Between 1915, when he first became famous, and his death in 1918, Braid was before the British courts of 'justice' four times and spent over half of the time in jail where he died. The trials were rigged, the defence not even calling witnesses to support Braid's testimony. It was claimed that Braid prayed for the Germans to kill off the English. The English provided him with good reasons for a prayer of this kind, but he was too sincere a Christian to practise such spite.

The Braid movement was important in a number of ways. It represented a continuation of the Christianisation process which had begun when Bishop Crowther accepted the invitation to Bonny in 1864. Before Braid, Christianity had been making its converts from traditional religion. Braid's revival marked a second phase in the Christian revolution where Christianity began to bring deeper spiritual conviction among its followers. It was first and foremost a religious revival. This does not alter the fact, however, that Braid's success was born out of the economic and political misery of the people of the Niger Delta whose great past was behind them and whose future appeared bleak. The people took refuge in Christianity in the same way that the Christian Church became a refuge for Africans in the United States and Southern Africa. If a people see no hope of a future in this world, Christianity promises at least a future in the next. In addition the Sierra Leone missionaries had done little to advance Delta Christians in the Pastorate leadership. There appeared no hope even within the church for Delta people of ambition to exercise their powers of leadership for which they had been justly noted in the nineteenth century. Thus the Christ Army was born, like the African churches of Lagos, from a desire for independence in order to provide an opportunity for leadership.

Finally it should be noted that the acid test of religious freedom in colonial Africa was the tolerance extended to African-inspired and African-led religious movements, in opposition to the European-controlled missions which were frequently the spiritual arm of colonialism. The colonial government and the European missions might dispute details of method but their assumptions and general aims normally coincided. The missions often sought to reduce the harsher aspects of colonial rule, but both they and the administration were foreign to the societies in which they worked. A man like Braid appeared as a threat to both to them.

## The Harris Movement 1914-16

By 1914 Africans of the forest zone of the Ivory Coast were an exhausted, humbled and leaderless people. Killings and deportations over the past twenty-seven years had almost wiped out the chiefly class. When the chiefs were destroyed the priests of the traditional religion attempted to lead the resistance. They, like the chiefs, failed. The people lost faith in the religion and gods they represented. Military failure led to the collapse of political institutions and a weakening of faith in African religious beliefs and principles. For the Ivory Coast people things had fallen apart. It was in this political, religious and social chaos that a remarkable mass conversion to Christianity took place under a Liberian Christian preacher by the name of William Wade Harris.

The right to self-determination is one of the strongest instincts in any community. When a people make a supreme effort to uphold this right and fail hopelessly, they may lose their self-respect and their faith in their institutions and beliefs. A society is one whole and cannot easily be separated into its political, social, religious and economic parts. To interfere with one aspect of a society is to interfere with all. To destroy one is to damage the society so badly that an entire reconstruction may be necessary. In the chaos which accompanies reconstruction the society gropes for survival. Large elements of the conqueror's culture and techniques may be adopted,

*William Wade Harris, the Grebo preacher from Liberia, who in one year, 1914, converted about 120,000 people to Christianity in the Ivory Coast.*

for it is only with the instruments of the conqueror that groups are likely to overcome their difficulties and reassert their self-determination. In non-Muslim Africa where religion ran through and bound together the social, political and economic aspects of society, the European's religion was often looked upon as the key to his power and success.

It was not, therefore, unusual in non-Muslim Africa for the European conquest to result in a general turning to Christianity. The spread of this movement varied. Sometimes it was gradual, gaining momentum as the colonial situation bore more heavily upon the people. Elsewhere it was so rapid that mission societies could not cope with it. Occasionally, as in the Ivory Coast, it took the form of a spontaneous mass movement of the population.

In the Ivory Coast the Roman Catholic missionaries, who arrived with the French imperial forces in the 1890s, were too closely allied to the conquerors to be trusted by the people.

In 1914 Harris, preaching in English through an interpreter, began to attract attention near Grand Lahou. Harris denounced the old religion, challenged the traditional priests and even converted some of them to the new faith. Thousands followed his advice. Villages cut down their sacred groves, destroyed symbols of the old religion, built churches and elected their own leaders to conduct Christian worship. About 120,000 people were converted in one year. Harris thus inspired the greatest Christian mass movement in West African history.

The wars of independence were not over. A few young men educated in Catholic schools and employed as clerks in the administration and commercial firms became Harris converts and, because of their literacy, rose to positions of importance in the new churches. These men were anxious to influence the movement to support the cause of African independence and to achieve the expulsion of the French from the Ivory Coast.

Originally the French favoured Harris because he was striking at the power of the traditional priests who were encouraging resistance to French rule. In 1916 when they saw that the new Christian leaders were seeking to take over the political as well as religious role of the traditional priests the French deported Harris to Liberia. Although these educated youths failed to turn the movement into political channels, it survived and without foreign aid produced the largest Protestant population in any French West African colony.

## The elite

British colonies in West Africa were divided into two parts, colony and protectorate. In Gambia, Sierra Leone and Nigeria the colony was confined to a small area around Bathurst, Freetown and Lagos. The colony area of Ghana was larger, and included the coastal area of the Fante, Ga and others. Only in the colony areas was modern political agitation possible. Political associations could be formed without permission from the British, and newspapers could operate, on the whole, free of interference. English law was enforced and lawyers were available to check the worst abuses of colonial rule. In the protectorates, however, lawyers were forbidden to practise and associations for political discussion had to conceal themselves as cultural or social organisations.

The colony areas had come under British rule in the early or mid-nineteenth century, while the protectorates were the areas added during the partition of Africa at the end of the century. Because of the longer tradition of Western education in the colonies there was by

1900 a sizeable number of Western-educated people—called the elite—who through their newspapers and associations acted as watchdogs of colonial rule, protesting against its abuses. Members of this elite were well known to each other all along the coast from Bathurst to Lagos, partly because the core of them were Creoles with ties to Freetown, partly because they were intermarried and had interlocking trading relations, and partly because many were old boys of the same schools at Freetown, Cape Coast or Lagos. Many moved freely from one colony to the other in the course of their work.

Isaac Wallace Johnson, for example, had been acting editor of the *Nigerian Daily Telegraph* and general secretary of the African Workers' Union which he organised in Lagos in 1931. He moved to Ghana where he worked with the Nigerian, Nnamdi Azikiwe, on the *African Morning Post*. He then returned to Sierra Leone where he organised a political party, the West African Youth League. Thus the elite formed a West African community and thought of themselves as West Africans rather than Ghanaians or Nigerians.

In French West Africa only the four communes—Dakar, St Louis, Gorée, Rufisque—enjoyed a similar position to English-speaking Africans in the colony areas. Those born in the communes enjoyed the status of French citizens and could form political associations and run newspapers. Since the communes also had a long tradition of education, the elite of French West Africa were at first entirely Senegalese but later others—especially Dahomeans—began to take advantage of the secondary schools of the communes.

Like their English-speaking counterparts, the elite were well known to each other, being old boys of the same schools, especially the famous William Ponty School of Senegal which has been called 'the nerve centre, the most solid link which joined the elite' of French West Africa. The French-speaking elite mostly served in the colonial civil service, had worked in many of the colonies, looked upon themselves as West Africans rather than Senegalese and performed the function of watchdogs of French rule.

The millions of Africans who were not citizens were classed as subjects and they suffered under many more disabilities (such as forced labour and the indigénat) than people in British protectorates. Naturally they could not establish newspapers or form associations without the permission of the French authorities. They could, however, belong to a branch of a French society. Often such branches were set up to conceal discussion of purely African political topics, but, as will be noted later in relation to Dahomey, this could be dangerous.

## The press

The West African press was an important element in keeping the elite united. A West African newspaper was seldom profitable. The reading public was small and the habit of many people reading the same copy reduced the numbers of copies sold. European firms whose advertising was urgently needed were quick to withdraw this if a paper was critical of European rule or wanted to promote ideas of nationalism. The best papers, and therefore the poorest, were those in which there were few European advertisements.

The life of many papers was short. By 1937 fifty papers at one time or another had been registered in Nigeria. There were, however, a number of good newspapers which lasted between thirty and forty years and left behind a solid impression on African thinking. Some of the most famous were the *Lagos Weekly Record* begun in 1890, the *Sierra Leone Weekly News* begun in 1884, and the *Gold Coast Independent* founded in 1895.

In French West Africa newspaper problems were multiplied, because the readership was smaller and the censorship was strict. In Senegal in the nineteenth century newspapers were owned and edited by Frenchmen. Even in the 1950s the widely-read newspaper, *Paris-Dakar*, begun in 1933, was owned and edited by a European. Dahomey's first regular newspaper was *Le Guide du Dahomey* (1920), while *L'Eclaireur de la Côte d'Ivoire* (1935) was the first African-owned paper in Ivory Coast.

In British West Africa the press was the most important single element in the birth and development of nationalism. The press kept African claims before British officials, was quick to point out oppression, kept African claims to advancement and dignity alive, stimulated creative writing, and never allowed the British to forget that their ultimate aim was to develop self-governing modern states. The press brought before West Africans the issues of the larger world, especially the black world extending from Africa to America and the West Indies.

## Defence of land rights

The press played an important part in defeating the British attempt in the 1890s to take over land in Ghana for European settlement. The British introduced a land bill in 1894 which proclaimed unoccupied lands, forest lands and minerals the property of the state. Protest meetings, petitions, demonstrations and a newspaper outcry brought the chiefs and educated elite together in opposition. The *Methodist Times* called the bill 'civilised robbery and British brigandism'. The chiefs demanded that the bill be 'abandoned, dropped and thrown overboard'. Three years later a similar bill was introduced. To mobilise opposition the elite and chiefs organised the Aborigines' Rights' Protection Society (ARPS), and again a storm of protest arose. Since the church forced the *Methodist Times* to keep out of politics, the society established its own paper, the *Gold Coast Aborigines*, as its mouthpiece. The chiefs paid for a deputation from the society to go to England where the government was persuaded to drop the bill.

The victory of the ARPS was a landmark in West African history. The society brought both groups of Ghanaian leaders together to watch carefully the actions of the colonial government. All along the West Coast it made educated Africans suspect British intentions regarding land. British West Africans were frightened that a Kenya, Congo or even Ivory Coast type of settler-dominated colony would result. Although for centuries the malarial mosquito had protected African lands, now that Europeans had discovered artificial immunity to malaria through the use of quinine, there was little but African anger to stop the coming of white settlers.

In 1912, a land law in Nigeria brought about the formation of an African society of opposition. The effort of the governor to get all 'waste' lands under his direct control inspired the setting up of the Anti-Slavery and Aborigines' Protection Society, as a branch of the English society of the same name. The advantage of this was that the parent society in London could bring complaints from Lagos before the British House of Commons and the British public. The new society was more active than the older Peoples' Union which had originally come into being in Lagos to protect land in the colony and to protest against taxation policy and efforts to control the press. But by 1912 the Peoples' Union had become a conservative wealthy man's club defending the colonial government.

Unfortunately both the ARPS in Ghana and the Anti-Slavery and Aborigines' Protection Society in Nigeria soon ceased to be effective organisations of political protest against colonialism. After its victory over the land issue in 1897 the ARPS, composed of the Fante chiefs and their educated advisers, lost much of its original impetus. As the years passed the society failed to organise branches and so lost contact with public opinion. The society was centred and controlled in Cape Coast, and other cities such as Accra denied that the society spoke for the nation. The society became conservative, and British governors saw to it that its leading members monopolised the nominated seats for Africans on the legislative council.

In Nigeria the Anti-Slavery and Aborigines' Protection Society soon declined. The disadvantage was that the parent society had the right to decide which issues could be raised and which could not. When a delegation of chiefs and elite members set out for London to protest against the proposed land changes, the society broke into radical and conservative wings in Lagos, and discredited its own delegation. Thus before the First World War no Nigerian political organisation was able to function as a forum of African opinion in the same way that the ARPS had done for a time in Ghana.

## Blaise Diagne and Senegal 1914-34

The communes of Senegal from 1848 had the right to elect a member to the French Chamber of Deputies (parliament) in Paris. The communes also elected their own municipal councils like the cities of France. During the nineteenth century those who ran and were elected for office were Europeans, even though the electorate was largely African. French firms usually supported different candidates and by massive bribery and corruption controlled political appointments in their own interest. In the early twentieth century the firms combined to stop both the economic and political competition which had previously existed between them. They became known as the 'Bordeaux clique' because most of them had their headquarters at Bordeaux (pronounced Bordo) in France. The clique began co-operation by fixing the price of groundnuts, and then followed this up by joint support of a candidate for election.

Just as the Creoles of Sierra Leone by 1900 had begun to suffer from changing European ideals, so the citizens of the four communes began to discover that colonial governors were seeking to restrict both their privileges of citizenship and their access to higher posts in the colonial civil service.

In order to break the Bordeaux clique and defend their rights the communes in 1914 voted for Blaise Diagne, an educated Senegalese who became the first African to sit in the French Chamber of Deputies. In 1916 he was responsible for the passing in the French Chamber of the Loi Diagne, which confirmed French citizenship on the people of the communes while allowing them to retain traditional law in family matters. In 1919 Diagne was re-elected and all the municipal seats were won by members of his Republican Socialist Party.

*Blaise Diagne, the first African to sit in the French Chamber of Deputies, and who in 1916 was responsible for the Loi Diagne which gave French citizenship to the people of the Senegalese communes.*

The Bordeaux firms, the French settlers and the administration were alarmed by Diagne's popularity and election victories. A tough governor was sent to Senegal and all Diagne's efforts for progressive reforms were blocked by united European opposition. Diagne sought a compromise and, like the ARPS and Nigerian Peoples' Union, drifted into conservatism and outright support for the colonial system. The compromise was sealed in the Bordeaux agreements of 1923 in which, in return for Bordeaux support, Diagne dropped his radical demands. The Senegalese elite called this a 'sell-out', and Diagne only won the 1928 elections with the help of French rigging and the falsification of election results.

While Diagne was elected by the four communes and was therefore only responsible to them, all French West Africa expected him to speak for them as Africans. Those outside the communes of Senegal, however, came to feel that he took no notice of their condition and that he was actually ready to sacrifice them for the sake of the citizens. This suspicion made it difficult for any future Senegalese leader to get the support of Africans outside Senegal. This suspicion was based on Diagne's wartime recruitment campaign and his defence of forced labour.

During the First World War Diagne agreed to tour West Africa recruiting men to fight in the French army in Europe. The vast number of men who volunteered, fought and died for France were subjects, not citizens. Those who returned were annoyed to discover that they had achieved little and were still subject to the humiliations of French colonialism, trials without jury or lawyers, arbitrary taxation and worst of all, forced labour. Then in the 1930s Diagne was called upon by the French Government to represent it at international labour conferences. Here he found himself, an African, defending forced labour in the French empire in Africa. Little wonder many of the subjects saw Diagne as a 'stooge'.

However, in the rigid world of colonialism before the Second World War, Diagne had little choice. The alternatives involved following the path he chose or being thrown out. He felt that there were advantages to be gained from working within the French Government. For example, in 1931 when the depression began, he was able to negotiate a special price for groundnuts which was higher than usual and which helped Senegal over the worst years of the depression. This was the first break in the colonial pact under which Africans got most of the disadvantages and few of the advantages of the colonial economic system. Furthermore, Diagne was hailed and admired all over the black world—America, the West Indies and Africa—as someone who had reached the highest position ever held by an African in the white world, a symbol of black ability and a rebuke to all those who were writing about the inferiority of the African race.

## Dahomey and Hunkanrin

In French West Africa, outside the four communes of Senegal, politics was a dangerous occupation, as the fate of the Dahomean elite indicates. It was King Tofa of Porto Novo, of the De Lokpon lineage, who invited French protection for his city. At first the French ruled indirectly but gradually, as was their normal colonial custom, they cut down the monarch's powers so much that after Tofa's death in 1908 his son was reduced to the position of a head chief. Traditionally the monarchy had alternated between two 'royal' lineages but the French confined it to De Lokpon because they were 'loyal'. This policy threw the rival lineage led by Sognigbe into opposition to the French regime.

In addition the Muslims of Porto Novo were disunited. Jose Paraiso, a Brazilian Muslim and chief adviser to the De Lokpon lineage, controlled Muslim affairs and in this had full French support. A number of Yoruba Muslims returned from the hajj (pilgrimage) determined to purify Islam in the city. They were particularly disturbed because Muslim affairs were being run by a non-Muslim dynasty and Christian overlord. Thus the Yoruba Muslims' opposition to the colonial government came to be expressed in support for Sognigbe's claim to the throne.

Charles Noufflard's governorship (1912-17) was particularly burdensome; the humiliation of the indigénat, heavy taxation and arrogant officials were combined with flagrant corruption. In 1917 the efforts of a wealthy Dahomean merchant, Tovalou Quenum, of a Senegalese lawyer, Germain Crispin, and of Louis Hunkanrin (son of Tofa's chief blacksmith), aided by the support of Blaise Diagne and contacts in Paris, led to the recall and investigation of Governor Noufflard. This was a notable victory and from it Hunkanrin emerged as the leader of the opposition to the colonial administration.

Hunkanrin, who had lived in Paris and made contact with anti-imperialist groups there, returned to Dahomey and organised a branch of the *Ligue des Droits de l'Homme* (League for the Rights of Man). While it was illegal to form political associations, this could be evaded by forming a branch of a French society. The Ligue gave publicity in France to maladministration in Dahomey and to demands for reform. In addition Hunkanrin received anti-colonial literature from Paris, including Garvey's *Negro World*.

In 1923 the occasion arose for a showdown when Governor Fourn raised taxes by 500 per cent just as Dahomey's main export of palm oil fell in price. Mass meetings were organised by the Ligue, and the opposition royal lineage led by Sognigbe and the Yoruba Muslim faction all co-operated in protesting against the new tax. The Ligue organised a campaign of passive resistance which led to a refusal to pay taxes, a boycott of markets and a general strike which included the port workers of Cotonou. As passive resistance spread in the countryside around Porto Novo, Fourn called for troops from Togo and Ivory Coast, and declared a three-month state of emergency during which the army collected the taxes, seized firearms, burnt some villages and compelled others to move.

Fourn treated the affair as a revolt against French rule rather than an effort to bring reform to a colonial administration. There was not even an inquiry into the causes of discontent and as a result Fourn was able to get all the leaders of the rival royal lineage, of the Yoruba Muslim faction, and also Sognigbe and Hunkanrin, exiled and imprisoned in Mauritania for ten years. There all of them except Hunkanrin died under detention. In one blow the colonial administration had managed to rid itself of all its opposition.

The Dahomean efforts for reform indicated the impossible difficulties under which African leaders had to work in the French colonies, and partly explain why the colonial empire appeared so peaceful. Restrictions on protest were equally strict in the protectorate areas of British colonies, but British officials could seldom behave as Fourn did. In the nearby colony area educated Africans controlled newspapers and had access to lawyers, who could have demanded and secured at least a commission of inquiry into such an affair. The communes of Senegal had similar weapons but they were thousands of miles away and could be just as ignorant of conditions in Dahomey as the Paris government itself.

Protest in the French empire had to be in the vernacular, in the songs of the griots and troubadours such as the following excerpts translated from poems composed in the Futa Jalon.

> Destroy the European throughout all Futa; cast him
>     out Futa,
> O Thou our help ... They put down the men of worth and
> exalt the worthless; and if even our chiefs tremble
> before them, what of the poor peasants?

## CHAPTER TWENTY-ONE

# Responses to colonialism (2): the inter-war years

## The black world

Between the two world wars, from 1918 to 1939, the various sections of the world inhabited by black people became more conscious of each other than ever before. Events among blacks in America and the West Indies were influencing their brothers in Africa, and African events were being closely watched by a growing number of New World blacks. The elites of Africa and the New World began to feel that the elevation of the race must be an international effort, that a victory of black men over segregation in America was as important as a victory over colonialism in Africa. Many felt that a black man could not carry himself with dignity, no matter what his degree of freedom, as long as brother members of his race were being humiliated elsewhere in the world.

During and after the First World War the United States and Europe talked of self-determination as the basis of the peace settlement. They meant the ethnic groups of eastern Europe under the Austro-Hungarian empire, who were to be allowed to choose their independence and form of government. The idea was picked up by British colonies such as Canada, Australia, South Africa and India, who had sacrificed much to help win the war and who demanded greater powers of self-government and a seat on the British empire peace delegation. Colonial nationalism in Canada and white South Africa after the war continued to press the British, and eventually resulted in their virtual independence in the Statute of Westminster in 1931. The Congress Party in India was agitating in the same direction. The Irish, after a bloody war of independence, cut themselves away completely from English domination in 1921, and Egypt secured partial independence in 1922. These last two events prompted a West African chief to say, 'This is the beginning of the end of the British empire'.

These many triumphs for self-determination had a powerful influence in West Africa. The Ghanaian press asked for West African representation on the empire peace delegation, and it also raised the question of self-determination for Africa. It came therefore as a considerable shock when the German colonies of Togo and Cameroon were split between Britain and France, in absolute contradiction of the doctrine of self-determination. The considerable opposition of the Ewe people of Togoland was ignored. The result of all these world war influences was the Ewe Union Movement and the National Congress of British West Africa, which will be discussed later.

## Washington and Aggrey

In the meantime events in black America were also holding West African attention. The first black American to achieve real prominence in the United States was an educator, Booker T. Washington, who advanced his doctrine of race relations in Atlanta, Georgia, in 1895. In what came to be called the 'Atlanta compromise' Washington supported racial segregation and the submission of blacks to the dominant white group. He claimed that the best way to

*Booker T. Washington, the black American educator.*

253

rise in American society was for blacks to equip themselves with agricultural and manual skills.

In so many ways Washington was like the elite of his day in West Africa, the ARPS, Nigerian Peoples' Union, J. K. Aggrey and the conservative Blaise Diagne. He accepted white dominance and because of it could be friendly with American presidents, just as his counterparts in Africa might be friendly with British and French governors. Washington's emphasis upon technical training was also echoed in West Africa. Some West Africans went to train at his technical institute at Tuskegee, and in Nigeria an effort was made to create an institution like it. Achimota College in Ghana was also influenced by similar ideas. Particularly in Liberia, where a number of black American missionary societies were working, there was a strong feeling in favour of technical education. The Booker T. Washington Institute became Liberia's major industrial training centre.

Kodwo K. Aggrey, baptised James (1875-1927), was probably the best known West African in the black world in the early 1920s, holding ideas similar to Washington's about race relations. Aggrey was born at Anamabu of Fante parents, his father being a linguist, or one who carries a gold-headed staff and reports the king's words to the people. Educated in Cape Coast, he became a teacher in 1890 and acted as interpreter to the British forces marching against Asante in 1896. Two years later he went to the United States for higher education under the influence of an independent American Negro Methodist Church of which Aggrey became an enthusiastic member. He went to their college, secured three higher degrees and became a member of staff. He later became a clergyman and remained in the United States until 1924.

Aggrey served on both the Phelps Stokes Commissions on education in Africa, the first in 1920, the second in 1923 during which the members visited West, Central, South and East Africa. Aggrey received a tumultuous welcome everywhere in the Gold Coast and in Cape Coast was installed as a linguist in the room of his father. In 1924 he accepted a post in the proposed new college—Achimota— near Accra. Achimota, which opened its doors in 1927 a few months before Aggrey died, was designed to evolve as a complete institution of learning from kindergarten to university level. It aimed to take its students early and mould them into the best possible finished result. While all Africans wanted high quality education the more thoughtful criticised Achimota. They feared its products were likely to become too highly anglicised. Aggrey defended Achimota against its critics and was largely responsible for its eventual acceptance by the people of the Gold Coast. His own position as third in charge on the staff reduced fears that it would be a stronghold of British imperialism. However, Achimota became probably the most powerful instrument for the spread of British culture in West Africa in the inter-war years.

Among Europeans Aggrey was the most popular West African of his day. A racist white settler of East Africa said of him, 'the man's a saint: damn his colour'. European praise caused Africans to criticise him, then and possibly even more so now. He promoted, one of his European admirers wrote, 'harmonious co-operation between the African and the European races', significantly adding, 'which is so essential to progress'. Aggrey's philosophy of black-white partnership has always been linked with his use of the symbol of the piano keys. 'You can play a tune of sorts on the white keys, and you can play a tune of sorts on the black keys, but for harmony you must use both the black and the white.' Piano keys fitted into a shield became the badge of Achimota College. In his day this philosophy could be interpreted as favouring the colonial partnership, the partnership of the white rider and the black horse. When Aggrey visited South Africa he was severely criticised by African nationalists on his racial attitudes. This criticism was justified. He was travelling through Africa at the pleasure of colonial regimes at the very time that Marcus Garvey was stirring the black world by a militant philosophy which included 'Africa for the Africans', not Africa for a black-white partnership of whatever nature. There was never a possibility of black-white partnership in Aggrey's day, nor throughout the colonial period. Only after independence, when Africans became the 'riders', was anything like a partnership of the black and white piano keys achieved in West Africa. However, racial harmony in modern West Africa owes much to Aggrey and many lesser black men who clung to his ideals, despite white racial prejudice during the colonial period.

European writers have been at pains to stress Aggrey's philosophy of racial harmony, but he knew the other side of the coin as well. He suffered institutionalised racism in the United States. He was a victim of colour prejudice by the government of the Belgian Congo, as well as by Governor Guggisberg of the Gold Coast. He was shocked at Portuguese colonialism in Angola, saying, 'It was the first time in my life that I had smiled at my brother, my sister, and he, she smiled not back.' He welcomed the new self-discovery and self-realisation in young Africa. After his continental tour he said, 'We found a lot of restlessness. It was vocal in the British colonies, subdued in the other colonies. I thank God for that restlessness. Some people are afraid of it. You talk about youth movements in other countries. There is a youth movement coming in Africa that some day may startle the world.'

## DuBois and Garvey

Washington's opponent, and after his death the foremost American coloured leader, was William DuBois, who believed that white Americans must be forced to grant full equality to black Americans. He felt that if the people did not resist segregation and agitate for equality they would gradually come to accept the American caste system as normal and inevitable. DuBois was a founder of the National Association for the Advancement of Coloured People and the editor for many years of its magazine, *Crisis*. DuBois in his ideas and leadership was very like the West African elite which emerged in the National Congress in 1919.

Before DuBois could establish his leadership among black Americans, a man by the name of Marcus Garvey stirred the black

*W. E. B. DuBois.*

*Marcus Garvey, founder of the Universal Negro Improvement Association. It was Garvey who first made famous the slogan 'Africa for the Africans'.*

# The
# Lagos Weekly Record

The OLDEST ESTABLISHED NEWSPAPER, and BEST ADVERTISING MEDIUM in the COLONY of NIGERIA representing ADVANCED NATIVE OPINION.

Vol. XXXI No 96 [New series].     LAGOS, WEST AFRICA, APRIL 23—30, 1921.     Price Numerous.

*An advertisement for shares in Garvey's Black Star Shipping Line, from the* Lagos Weekly Record, *April 1921.*

world as no one before or since until the rise of Kwame Nkrumah. Garvey was a Jamaican, one of the most stirring orators of his race, who organised the biggest mass protest movement in American history around his Universal Negro Improvement Association (UNIA), which by 1923 claimed six million members. Garvey preached racial purity, glorified the colour black, upheld a black Christ and a black Madonna and called upon his followers to 'forget the white gods'. His slogans were 'Africa for the Africans', 'the renaissance of the black race', 'Ethiopia awake', and he demanded that Africa be freed from colonial oppression.

Garvey began the recruitment of a black army for the liberation of Africa and set up the Black Star Shipping Line which, however small in comparison, was an attempt to invade the white monopoly of world commerce. In 1920 he sent a mission to Liberia to negotiate for the settlement of between 20,000 and 30,000 black American families, who would be helped to emigrate to Liberia and presumably represent the spearhead for the liberation of Africa. In 1925, with the help of 'moderate' American black leaders, the United States Government jailed Garvey. It later deported him, and while the influence of Garvey's thought remained strong, the movement itself soon collapsed. The Liberian scheme also failed. But Garvey's ideas have pervaded black American and West African thinking ever since.

Regardless of how impractical and impossible Garvey's schemes may have been, his words echoed the feelings of millions of blacks: black redemption not as humble beggars but as proud soldiers demanding and forcing concessions; equality in America, freedom in Africa, dignity everywhere; a share in the world economy and a black Christ overseeing all. Mainly in intellectual circles, Garvey's journal *Negro World* was eagerly read throughout West Africa.

In Ibadan a group of about a dozen men met quietly to read the *Negro World*. After reading the journal one member wrote in his diary, 'the most inspiring message of Marcus Garvey to the Negro people of the world nearly maddens me. I feel as if I am in America as one of the hearers of his golden speech.' Although the same writer was quite aware of Garvey's impractical plans he believed that his prophecy about Africa's freedom would be fulfilled. On 3 March 1921 he wrote in his diary, 'Garvey though a great champion of the race does not know the aims and aspirations of Africans' but 'my conviction is that Africa *will be free*'.

The colonial powers were certainly worried about Garveyism. In Lagos every mission church refused to permit their meeting halls to be used for UNIA rallies. *Negro World* was banned in French West

Africa, and confiscated in the post in Nigeria. To be caught with a copy of it in Dahomey could bring life imprisonment.

Garvey's rise indicated the growing unity of feeling in the black world. With the fall of Garvey, DuBois attempted to assert his leadership among the American coloured elite, and he sought, as Garvey had done, to approach the problem from the point of view of the black world. He believed that blacks who were suffering under the caste system in America and the West Indies, and blacks who were suffering under colonialism in Africa must get to know each other better, and realise that the struggles of black people for equality were all part of one movement, that black Americans and Africans could inspire and encourage each other, and that a gain for one was likely to bring a gain for the other. In pursuit of this ideal he was the leading spirit of five pan-African congresses held between 1919 and 1945.

The first pan-African congress had been held in London in 1900 under the inspiration of a Trinidad lawyer, H. Sylvester Williams, to protest against the inhumanities practised during the partition of Africa. It was not repeated until DuBois, inspired by the ideas following the First World War and assisted by Blaise Diagne, organised the second congress in Paris in 1919 to draw up a Charter of Human Rights for Peoples of African Descent. The conference was mainly attended by Africans living in Paris because the United States, although the main supporter of self-determination for Europeans, was not anxious to see this applied to its own black population, and therefore refused to grant travel permits to black people who wished to attend the Paris conference.

The third pan-African conference was held in three sessions in 1921, in London, Brussels and Paris where Diagne presided. The fourth in 1922 was held in London and Lisbon; and the fifth in New York. These congresses helped to keep the demands of the black world before the public of the world and brought together leaders of the black world. In the 1921 London session there were 41 Africans, 35 American blacks, seven West Indians and 24 Africans living in Europe. DuBois, a university professor and prodigious writer (his first book appeared in 1896, his fifteenth in 1952), helped to keep the pan-African unity of the black world alive.

## Negritude

Black men brought up under British colonialism in Africa and the West Indies or in the caste system of America talked, wrote and agitated for their rights as men. They were spurred on by the discrimination and prejudice which everywhere faced them. The 1923 pan-African congress manifesto summed up this preoccupation: 'We ask in all the world that black folk be treated as men'.

In the French world this was much less the case. While the illiterate blacks were treated with more harshness in French colonies than in the English ones, the black French-speaking elite in Paris were nevertheless basically accepted as men in French society in a way which Englishmen and Americans found impossible to understand. But although in France Africans were accepted as men, African culture was branded as inferior. Frenchmen believed that their own culture and way of life was superior to all others, and that it was their mission to export it to their African empire.

Most of the African elite accepted the superiority of French culture, but a few Africans and West Indians turned their attention to seeking out the values in African culture. This movement was known as Negritude, a philosophy which sought a combination of French and African culture and values, as against the French policy of assimilation, which required the complete abandonment of the African heritage and adoption of the French. Originally Negritude developed in Paris among West Indians, a West Indian, Aimé Cesaire, being considered its father. Negritude was similar to pan-Africanism in that it saw a oneness and basic similarity among Africans everywhere in the world. But while the English-speaking pan-Africanists spoke in political terms, Negritude was expressed in poems, novels, drama and even dance. The greatest African contributor to Negritude has been Léopold Senghor of Senegal. Others included the novelist Bernard Dadie, the dramatist Cofi Gadeau of Ivory Coast, and the Guinean ballet producer, Keita Fodeba.

After the Second World War, while political developments in British West Africa began to affect French-speaking Africans, the influence of Negritude began to affect English-speaking West Africans. A few English-speaking Africans have been critical of Negritude. For example, Wole Soyinka, the Nigerian playwright, has said that 'a tiger does not proclaim its tigritude'. Yet many of them have written novels, plays and poetry which, had they been produced in the French rather than English language, would have been considered within the tradition of Negritude. Negritude was partly designed to convince the non-black world that Africans had made a contribution to universal civilisation. It also aimed to prove to the assimilated black, be he of French, English or American education, that he belonged to a culture of which he might be proud. This was necessary in order to combat the colonial mentality which often afflicted Africans with foreign education. Thus the first World Festival of Negro Arts was held in 1966 in Senegal to demonstrate the Negro contribution to world music in the Negro spiritual and jazz, of the influence of Negritude on the white French novelist, Jean-Paul Sartre, and the contribution of African carvings to European painting and sculpture in modern times.

Negritude has also been attacked as being a doctrine of racialism, an attempt to glorify black at the expense of white. Except for a very few writers this has not been so: it does not propound the superiority of black as a colour or black people as a race. Negritude does argue that African thought and African life can be effectively expressed within the vehicle of European languages. This may in fact prove doubtful unless European languages are enriched by vocabulary and expressions from African languages.


## WASU and Solanke

The hub of the black world, the centre through which American, West Indian and African ideas passed back and forth, was the student organisations in London. The first such organisation began in 1917, but the West African Student Union (WASU) organised by the Nigerian, Ladipo Solanke, became the centre of social and political activities in which modern militant nationalism was born. In 1921 WASU had 21 members, in 1924 it had 120. In 1928 Marcus Garvey gave WASU its first hostel and it published a journal which offered an outlet for nationalist writings. Many of West Africa's leading modern statesmen at one time or another held executive positions in WASU. Two of its leading members produced books setting forth West Africa's claim: Solanke's *United West Africa at the Bar of the Family of Nations* (1927) and the Ghanaian J. W. de Graft Johnson's *Towards Nationhood in West Africa* (1928). Between 1929 and 1932 Solanke visited the major cities of British West Africa to collect funds for the WASU hostel, to organise branches of the society and to get support from the chiefs. Nana Ofori Atta of Ghana, the Alake of Abeokuta, and the Emir of Kano became patrons of the union.

African students were much slower to go to America for education, but after the return of Azikiwe and Nkrumah from the United States many began to follow their example. In 1941 an African Students' Association with its own magazine, and closely linked with WASU, was formed. Few things stimulated nationalism more than student life in Britain or America. There were contacts with white liberals, socialists, communists (all anti-imperialists), West Indians and black Americans. There was the powerful nationalism of Englishmen and Americans which made people nationalist in defence. There was open prejudice and discrimination, polite and informal in Britain, crude and institutionalised in America.


## Ethiopia

Then in 1935 came the Italian attack upon Ethiopia, a country that represented 'the sole remaining pride of Africans and Negroes in all parts of the world'. Ever since Ethiopia's survival at the time of partition, when Menelik defeated the Italian army at Adowa in 1896, Africans and New World blacks had looked upon that country as a proud symbol of African independence and achievement.

When the world was shocked at Italy's action, Mussolini hit back with the language of racism and white supremacy, which all Europeans had used during the partition but which by 1935 had become somewhat embarrassing. Italy felt it was bringing 'civilisation' and 'Christianity' to a 'barbarous, primitive and backward' people who were accused of slave raiding and slave holding. Italy was a great and expanding nation. It had come late to the partition of Africa and got very little. According to the doctrine of the survival of the fittest, it must expand at the expense of the weaker races. When the League of Nations sought to restrain him, Mussolini scoffed, 'Has the League of Nations become the tribunal before which all the Negroes and uncivilised peoples, all the world's savages, can bring the great nations which have revolutionised and transformed humanity?'

The protest of the black world was more prolonged and widespread than ever before in history. There was hardly a black organisation or black city that did not organise a protest. In New York 20,000 black Americans demonstrated in support of Ethiopia. Demonstrations followed in South and West Africa, London and the West Indies, in which young men offered themselves to fight for Ethiopia. WASU organised an Ethiopian Defence Committee, and an African Friends of Abyssinia Committee in London was probably the most pan-African committee ever organised. Those connected with it were three Ghanaians, including J. B. Danquah, five West Indians, a Somali and Jomo Kenyatta of Kenya. The committee organised a reception for Haile Selassie, Emperor of Ethiopia, when he arrived in London to begin his exile after Italian forces had defeated and occupied Ethiopia.

In Nigeria mass meetings in Lagos continued to draw over 2,000 people to demand 'hands off Abyssinia'. Committees were formed in Nigerian cities which had never before engaged in modern political protest. Money poured in for an Ethiopian Defence Fund, young Nigerians offered to fight, and Italian firms were victimised and boycotted. The invasion of Ethiopia brought forward the most national response Nigeria had ever witnessed. So deep was the emotion that even the elite were surprised. The ultimate deal by which England and France 'sold' Ethiopia to Italy convinced many that the white world would stick together regardless of moral or other issues. Ethiopia, and Garvey's fall a decade before, demonstrated that power lay with the white and not the black world. But the Italian defeat of Ethiopia nevertheless marked another vital step in the growing unity and determination of Africans to change world realities. Political movements in West Africa from 1918 to 1939 must always be seen against this larger black world background.

## West African reforms and self-determination

During the partition of Africa the Ewe people had been divided between British Gold Coast and German Togoland. During World War I British and French forces overran Togo and, since the British occupied Lomé and the south, the Ewe were reunited. In 1919, without reference to the people, Togo was divided between Britain and France in such a way that the Ewe were more seriously split apart than ever. The Ewe under the leadership of O. Olympio repeatedly appealed to the British and Americans on the basis of the doctrine of self-determination. So illogical was the division that Ewe on one side of the border had their cocoa farms on the other, and this could result in double taxation for some and none for others. The *Gold Coast Independent* gave wide publicity to Ewe grievances until it was banned by the French in Togo. One of the first points raised by the National Congress of British West Africa was the bartering around of African peoples by the European nations.

The National Congress of British West Africa, formed in 1919, held its first conference in Accra the following year, and was in its West African outlook the natural expression of the unity of the elite of English-speaking West Africa. The moving spirit behind the congress was Casely Hayford of Ghana, who consulted with his compatriot Nana Ofori Atta and R. A. Savage of Nigeria; the congress had the almost unanimous support of the English language

West Coast press. The Accra conference was attended by six Nigerians, three Sierra Leoneans, one Gambian and 40 Ghanaians. Resolutions were passed requesting the introduction of the franchise, equal opportunities for white and black in the civil service, opportunities for higher education, and a clearer separation of the judiciary from the colonial administration. The conference decided to send a deputation to press its claims in London.

The West African governors were annoyed because the congress went over their heads. They warned the Colonial Office that the deputation represented no one in West Africa. Governor Clifford of Nigeria was particularly scornful that West Africans could ever consider themselves one nationality, and even laughed at the idea that Nigeria could ever be a nation. All the governors insisted that only the chiefs could speak for the people. Because of the attitude of the governors, the deputation achieved nothing in London. However, the congress continued to exist, holding conferences in Freetown (1923), in Bathurst (1925) and in Lagos (1930).

*Members of the National Congress of British West Africa who visited London in 1920. From left to right seated: Dr H. C. Bankole-Bright (Sierra Leone), T. Hutton Mills (President of the Congress), Chief Oluwa (Nigeria), J. E. Casely Hayford (Ghana), H. Van Hein (Ghana). Standing: J. Egerton Shyngle (Nigeria), H. M. Jones (Gambia), Herbert Macaulay (Chief Oluwa's Secretary), T. M. Oluwa (son of the chief), F. W. Dove (Sierra Leone), and E. F. Small (Gambia).*

Changes took place in West Africa in the direction the congress desired even though the British (anxious to discourage political agitation) claimed that these reforms were presented to the West Africans by the British and not forced upon them by congress pressure. By 1925 a limited franchise had been extended to Calabar, Lagos, Accra, Cape Coast and Freetown. Achimota College was set up in Ghana in 1927 for higher education, and the West African Court of Appeal made the judiciary less subject to the control of the governors. However, the elected Africans had no power in the legislative council and past pupils of Achimota were discriminated against in the civil service, so that the gains were minor.

Meanwhile the congress, like earlier political organisations in West Africa, became conservative. In 1930, when Hayford died, the congress passed away with him. The common people were never stirred and little effort was made to bring them into the congress, so that the governors' contention that the elite of the congress represented no one was at least partly true. People from the interior were dismissed as 'bush'. A party of Ibadan leaders approached the congress to take up certain local grievances. They were treated with such snobbery that the Ibadan branch of the congress melted away and could never be reformed. The lack of interest and even fear of elite leadership was shown by the few who turned out to vote. Seldom did more than 40 per cent of eligible voters do so, and the figure was often as low as 20 per cent.

In Ghana the congress members were soon entertaining the governor, a sure sign that their political enthusiasm was declining. In Nigeria big wealthy men, on the whole quite satisfied with colonialism, fought over congress positions to gather a large following for prestige purposes. Some were interested in removing a few colour bar restrictions but at heart they would have feared major reform. Common men were interested in real reforms but money was a problem. No one, whether British or Yoruba, was likely to pay attention to a society of commoners. Many branches which were led by commoners were much more lively than the Lagos headquarters, where the big names fought over positions.

In all the colonies the elite leadership won seats in the elections to the legislative council. Those who did not were nominated to sit by the British governors. In a way the British bought them over by offering position and a salary. In Ibadan the British nominated the president of the local congress branch to the legislative council. Thereafter, fearing that he was the eyes and ears of the British administration, the local branch elevated him from president to patron, in which capacity he did not attend executive meetings and so was excluded from hearing political discussions.

Hayford had stressed that the congress was a movement of the elite. He thereby broke with the old ARPS tradition of representing both the elite and the chiefs. Some chiefs were ready to accept this, but others rallied under the leadership of Nana Ofori Atta in Ghana and attacked the congress for jumping over the heads of the chiefs. These divisions, deliberately encouraged by the British, gave them every political chance to kill the congress. Just before he died in 1930 Hayford expressed his disillusionment with elite leadership:

> The African God is weary of your wranglings, weary of your vain disputations, weary of your everlasting quarrels which are a drag upon progress and which keep from you, as a people, the good that is intended for you.

## Macaulay and the Democratic Party

Herbert Macaulay, grandson of Bishop Crowther and son of the founder of the first secondary school in Nigeria, first came to public attention by his exposure of European corruption in the handling of railway finances in 1908. Thereafter he engaged in defending the royal lineage of Lagos, which the British normally treated with little respect unless they had some unpopular policy to enforce, when the Eleko (king) was requested to use his influence on the government's behalf. In 1919 the government took over land in Lagos, and Macaulay, acting on behalf of the chiefs, carried the case to the Privy Council in London. He won and forced the government to pay £22,500 compensation for the land. In 1920, in a mood of nasty retaliation, the colonial government deposed and deported the Eleko and appointed another. Macaulay kept up a ten-year fight against the government during which time he was jailed twice, until, again by a Privy Council decision, the Eleko was restored to his throne in 1931.

The formation of the National Congress and its later activities received less attention in Nigeria than it might otherwise have done. Macaulay was a bitter critic of other educated leaders, and he lashed out in the press against his rivals and one-time friends, setting loose anger, bitterness, and division among Lagos politicians. This prevented the emergence of a united reform movement in Nigeria. Indeed it may well have been the Lagos leaders whom Hayford had in mind when he spoke of 'your wranglings', 'your vain disputations' and 'your everlasting quarrels'. In addition, although Macaulay paid

266

lip-service to the ideals of the National Congress, he did nothing to assist its work in Nigeria.

However, regardless of the division which he created among the elite, Macaulay, like no other politician of his age, could keep in touch with the common people. This was all the more unusual when many potential leaders felt it was below their dignity and status to appear too 'common'. But Macaulay was different. Market women sang his praises, Muslims admired him, and he was always ready to address socially unimportant groups. This, together with his repeated victories in the Privy Council over the colonial governors, earned him the reputation of being the father of Nigerian nationalism.

In 1922 the Nigerian constitution was altered to permit three elected representatives (one from Calabar and two from Lagos) to sit on the legislative council, and at the same time a municipal government was set up in Lagos. Macaulay's Nigerian National Democratic Party swept all seats in the elections of 1923, 1928 and 1933. However, after the restoration of the Eleko in 1931, relations between Macaulay and the British governor gradually improved. As they did so he and his party drifted into conservatism and support for the colonial government. So bitter was the British governor in 1920 that he refused to attend any social function to which any member of the Macaulay family had been invited. But after 1931 the governor actually held conferences with the Democratic Party, and regularly invited Macaulay to Government House parties.

The rebels of the 1920s had become the conservatives of the 1930s. Desire for reform had so far disappeared that Macaulay and his chief supporters were almost the only members of the Lagos elite who did not support the 'Hands off Abyssinia' campaign in 1934. The Democratic Party had fallen into the self-satisfied conservatism which had crept over the ARPS by 1918 and the National Congress by the late twenties. When the reformers achieved elected positions, when the governor asked their advice and they mixed with Europeans and received invitations to Government House parties they ignored the continuing abuses of colonialism. It was the way clever colonial governors 'bought off' their critics. It was little surprise that the people lost interest in such parties. In Lagos in 1933, of the 3,000 people eligible to vote, only 700 bothered to do so.

### The youth movements

In the 1930s in Nigeria, Ghana and Sierra Leone there was a reaction against the older politicians which developed through the organisation of youth leagues. Partly the leagues opposed the conservatism of the old parties and partly they sought to interest many more people than before in politics. They tried to get away from the idea that political protest should be the monopoly of a top elite and confined to the cities of Lagos, Cape Coast and Freetown. There had always been a feeling that the older politicians wanted improvements in their own personal position or at best in the interests of a small elite at the top. The youth leagues attempted to study the problems of their countries from a broader view.

In Calabar in 1932, Eyo Ita organised the Nigerian Youth League mainly to support reform in education. Eyo Ita managed an industrial school, the West African Peoples' Institute, which aimed at preparing youths to be self-supporting rather than to spend their time looking for civil service jobs.

In 1934 in Lagos the Nigerian Youth Movement (NYM) was formed and put forward a charter which sought to encourage national feeling in Nigeria, and demanded self-determination and Africanisation. The NYM also opposed the setting up of Yaba College (Lagos) because it was proposing a standard of education below that which was common in Britain. Later it took up the cause of lorry owners, against whom the colonial government was discriminating, because it feared the competition with the railway. In addition, the party established branches throughout the country in order to be truly Nigerian rather than just a Lagos party. In 1937 Azikiwe returned to Nigeria and established his *West African Pilot*. He supported the NYM, which overthrew the Democratic Party in the elections to the legislative council in 1938. Some writers would date the birth of modern nationalism in Nigeria from the organisation of the NYM in 1934, because the movement was the first to possess a Nigerian image, and because of its concern for a wide range of national interests, including Africanisation, education and transport.

In the new constitution of 1925 in Ghana nine Africans had been elected to the legislative council, but of these only three were elected by the people, and the other six were chiefs selected by chiefs. Many of the elite opposed this emphasis on chiefs, since they were considered to be supporters of the colonial government. Because the National Congress had ignored the chiefs, and attempted to assert the claim of the elite as leaders of the people, there had been bitterness between the two groups and a personal quarrel between Hayford and Nana Ofori Atta.

The National Congress originally boycotted the elections, but Hayford then decided that a boycott could achieve nothing and he ran for election; he won a seat in the legislative council. As a result the Ghanaian leadership was split and no unified pressure for reform was possible. The chiefs were divided, those led by Nana Ofori Atta remaining in close co-operation with the government, and those following the elite boycotting the elections. The elite was also split between those centred in Cape Coast, who continued to boycott, and those led by Hayford who were prepared to enter into limited co-operation. During the 1930s these divisions were gradually healed and greater unity restored among the African leaders. Nana Ofori Atta, to win the support of the elite, pressed the government for more rapid Africanisation of the civil service. In 1934 the government introduced a sedition ordinance which gave it wide powers to control the press and, departing from the major principle of British law, made it the responsibility of an accused person to prove his innocence. Then the cocoa hold-up of 1937 brought the admiration of the elite and proved that the chiefs still had a claim to popular leadership.

In 1938 J. B. Danquah organised the Gold Coast Youth Conference. Like its Nigerian counterpart it indicated a turning away from the older politicians and its interests centred on the economic and social needs of the country. Again like the NYM it attempted to involve more people in national interests. However, unlike the NYM it was not organised as a political party. Its aims were rather to bring Ghanaian youth together for the discussion of national problems.

The most lively and purposeful of all the youth movements was organised in 1938 by Isaac Wallace Johnson. In Sierra Leone, politics and political protest had been confined to the Creole elite in Freetown, although the city now had thousands of citizens drawn from the protectorate in the interior. The Creole elite was removed from the common people of the interior to a much greater extent than in Ghana or Nigeria. In Lagos, for example, the elite was Yoruba, and bound to the Yoruba of the interior by ties of culture, language and tradition, so that it never lost complete touch with the people. Members of the Nigerian and Ghanaian elite belonged to extended families of whom the majority belonged to the common class. In contrast the Creoles in Sierra Leone had few such ties with the people of the interior. It was a common Creole attitude to look down upon those from the interior as 'bush', and unimportant in political issues.

Wallace Johnson strove to change this state of affairs and to combine the Creoles with the Temne and Mende of the protectorate, hoping to involve all groups in his West African Youth League. The league was the first indication in Sierra Leone of thinking in national terms rather than in terms of Freetown and its surrounding colony. As a result it could be said of the league, as of the NYM in Nigeria, that it signalled the birth of modern nationalism in Sierra Leone. Through its newspaper the *African Standard* the league was the first in West Africa to preach outright socialism and show concern for the 'toiling masses'. But Wallace Johnson was ahead of his time. He was deported from Freetown for the duration of the war, which at least indicated the impact he was having upon thinking in Sierra Leone.

## The response of African farmers and businessmen

The rise of elite-based political associations was not the only form of African reaction to colonial rule in the inter-war period. Sometimes African opposition to colonialism took the form of economic enterprise, like farmers' unions, co-operative societies and banks.

We have seen in Chapter 19 how the European *grands comptoirs* (great combines) tried to fix cocoa prices paid to African farmers. To protect themselves against the combines farmers' unions grew up in Ghana and Nigeria. The earliest farmers' unions were at Larteh and Dodowah in Ghana, and Agege and Abeokuta in Nigeria. In 1914, 1916 and 1921 some Ghanaian farmers held back their cocoa crop, demanding higher prices. The pioneers in organising farmers' unions were John Ayew of Mampong in Ghana and J. K. Coker at Agege in Nigeria. They sought to ship cocoa direct to Europe and thus bypass the foreign firms. In 1920 the National Congress of British West Africa suggested the formation of a co-operative association in which Africans might 'harness and control the economic resources of their own continent, and so ensure that they would enjoy the fruits of development and not merely export them'.

The man who sought to carry out this resolution and challenge the dominance of the *grands comptoirs* was Winifred (later Musa) Tete-Ansa, a Ghanaian businessman from the state of Manya Krobo who had studied banking and commerce in Britain. Between 1924 and 1930 Tete-Ansa set up three companies: (1) the West African Co-operative Producers, to consist of farmers' unions through which they would sell all their cocoa; (2) the Industrial and Commercial Bank, to finance the purchase of the crop, and (3) the West African American Corporation, with a black American directorate, to sell the cocoa in the United States and ship back manufactured goods. The aims of these interlocking companies were first, to secure a higher price for the farmers, secondly, to bypass all the British middlemen by selling directly to the United States, the world's largest cocoa market, and finally, by keeping the companies under black control, to secure for West African businessmen a position in the import-export trade—the commanding heights of the economy—a position from which they had been excluded by the *grands comptoirs*. The expatriate firms had secured their dominance through amalgamation and co-operation. If they were to be challenged Africans must employ the same methods. This was why Casely Hayford had said that co-operation was 'the greatest word of the century'. Tete-Ansa sought this co-operation through a racial appeal; for example, his advertisement in the *Lagos Daily News* ran, 'If you are proud of your race and expect civility, come into your own bank.'

Tete-Ansa, dubbed the 'Napoleon of West African Commerce' received a good deal of support. Forty-five farmers' unions including Ayew's and Coker's supported him and these unions produced almost 60 per cent of West Africa's cocoa. A number of prominent businessmen and professionals became company directors, such as Dr C. C. Adeniyi-Jones, T. A. Doherty, C. da Rocha and A. A. Oshodi in Nigeria and A. J. Ocansey, J. B. Danquah and Dr F. V. Nanka-Bruce in Ghana. However, despite the enthusiasm, the companies went bankrupt through lack of capital and dishonesty among the directors.

In 1928 Ayew helped to organise the Gold Coast Federation of Cocoa Farmers which in 1930 unsuccessfully attempted a boycott of the *grands comptoirs* to force up prices. Tete-Ansa had predicted the boycott would fail without the backing of African companies and a bank. He then sought to establish another set of companies in 1934 which again failed in spite of the support of Ayew, his farmers' federation and some of the chiefs including the Asantehene.

In Nigeria the colonial government, fearing the militancy of the farmers, especially the Ibadan Planters' Union, began to organise official co-operatives. The co-operatives spent a good deal of time diverting the farmers' grievances away from the *grands comptoirs* and on to the African buyers. They were careful not to allow discussion of efforts proposed to sell direct to Liverpool.

In 1937 fourteen firms led by the United Africa Company agreed on a fixed cocoa price. But Ghanaians, led by the farmers' unions and latterly supported by the chiefs, not only refused to sell their cocoa but also boycotted all the retail shops of the firms involved. The Lagos press fully supported the boycott, but Yoruba cocoa farmers had few unions outside the officially-sponsored ones and were ill-organised to assist the Ghanaians. The colonial government in the

Gold Coast obviously sympathised with the *comptoirs* and their secret agreement, but could hardly force the people to buy and sell. At the cost of great suffering the farmers brought a complete halt for months to the economic life of Ghana until colonial government revenues were seriously affected. Ultimately the price-fixing agreement was broken. The 1937 cocoa hold-up has been described as the largest demonstration of rural discontent in West African colonial history.

Tete-Ansa died in obscurity in 1941. His economic theory had been sound but he failed in its execution. Since the *comptoirs* operated throughout West Africa they had to be challenged on that basis. His was the only attempt to do so. He was an economic pan-Africanist. Following Tete-Ansa the Western-educated elite concentrated upon the individual colonial unit, Nigeria, Ghana, Sierra Leone and Gambia. This tactic won political freedom but no economic independence. The most positive and immediate achievement of Tete-Ansa's ideas was the founding in 1933 of the National Bank of Nigeria, the first successful indigenous bank in West Africa, by T. A. Doherty, A. Maja and H. A. Subair, all of whom had been directors of Tete-Ansa's Mercantile Bank. The National Bank made slow and unspectacular progress in the early years but has grown with Nigeria to become one of its major financial institutions. Nnamdi Azikiwe followed Tete-Ansa's career sympathetically, became a shareholder in the National Bank in 1937 and later established Nigeria's second successful indigenous financial institution, the African Continental Bank. Very indirectly the Napoleon of West African Commerce has left his mark in modern West Africa.

## The response of African labour

It was not only the Western-educated elite which opposed aspects of colonialism. The African labouring class frequently resisted attempts to impose the colonial economy on them. Few revolts against French rule were unconnected with the hated forced labour system, and many young men travelled from home to escape it and to earn wages. About 250,000 went annually to the cocoa farms of Ghana for this reason, and another 70,000 went from Mali and Guinea to the groundnut farms of Senegal. One of the most important revolts against forced labour under British rule was in Enugu in Nigeria in 1914. Originally the Enugu coal mines paid certain chiefs so much for every labourer supplied. The chiefs did not recruit workers but conscripted them by force. In 1914 some of the chiefs around Enugu were so hated for this conscription for the coal mines that they were driven out of their towns. The British army arrested those responsible and a court fined the towns concerned by forcing them to supply 2,000 labourers for railway construction.

Labour strikes became more common in West Africa after the First World War. Until the 1930s neither the British nor French colonial governments recognised the right of Africans to form trade unions or to strike as a legitimate way of forcing employers to improve conditions. Most governments took the attitude of the governor of Sierra Leone, who in 1926 called the railway strike 'a revolt against the government'. The first serious post-war strikes were on the railways and in the mines, notable among which were the Sierra Leone railway strikes of 1919 and 1926, the Senegal railway strike of 1925, the Asante goldfields strike of 1924 and the Enugu coal mines strike of 1925.

The employers' usual method of dealing with strikes was to sack all workers concerned. After the Enugu coalminers' strike of 1925 the men were sacked, and for the next twenty-five years the mines refused to hire labourers from the clans from which the strkers came. To strike, therefore, might hurt not only the men involved, but their relatives, and even their children yet unborn.


## Conclusion

The period of 1897-1939 saw not only the establishment of colonial rule in Africa but also the reactions and responses to it of the Africans. It is evident from the above that Africans did not passively sit down unconcerned and watch their land, their labours and their rights being taken away from them. Their common experiences under the oppressive colonial yoke generated in them a shared consciousness of their plight as the oppressed and the exploited, and it is from this that we should date the rise of modern African nationalism. This feeling itself grew in strength and became more radical and militant as the years passed by. While the objectives by and large remained the same—the reform rather than the abolition of colonialism—the way it was expressed varied from period to period. In the 1890s and 1900s the nationalist aspirations and protests were expressed mainly in the religious field, though the formation and activities of the ARPS show that political instruments were not ignored. In the inter-war period the main instruments used were various elitist organisations such as the National Congress and the youth movements and the press.

One interesting feature of the nationalist activities of the period under review is the steady increase in their appeal. The National Congress had a wider support than the ARPS or the Peoples' Union of Nigeria, and the youth movements appealed still more widely. Possibly this expanding popular support was due to the larger numbers of literates being produced by the schools, and consequently the larger readership of the press. Possibly it also had something to do with the worsening economic conditions in the 1930s.

The period under review was notable not only for the birth of nationalism but also for the growth of pan-Africanism, and the increasing recognition throughout the black world of shared disadvantages. In these years pan-Africanism was initiated and advocated mostly by American and West Indian blacks, but West Africans were drawn more and more into it, and through it to an understanding of black problems in the New World. Garvey, in particular, DuBois and, to a lesser extent, Washington, had extensive contacts, either directly through correspondence or through journals like the *Negro World*. Other contacts were through student organisations in Paris, London and in America. Indeed, so strong was the impact of the activities of people like Garvey and DuBois on the educated elite of West Africa that, especially during the inter-war years their pan-Africanist sentiments were even stronger than their nationalist sentiments, as is shown in such names as West African Students' Union, National Congress of British West Africa, and West Africa Youth League.

In its entirety the period 1897 to 1939 is an important one because it was the time when many of those things which have come to play such a vital role in present-day West Africa were born and first flourished. These included the leadership of the elite and the eclipse of the chiefs, the rise of nationalism, the rise of Negritude, and the spread of pan-Africanism and with it the growing awareness of black peoples throughout the world of their common identity and destiny.

# PART FIVE

# Independence regained 1945-60

## CHAPTER TWENTY-TWO

# The independence movement

## Effects of the Second World War

West Africans had numerous reasons for seeking independence from European control, but they succeeded in achieving it after the Second World War partly because the European powers had been weakened by the war. Before 1939 it had been Britain and France who ordered and policed the world. The war changed all that. France was defeated in Europe, Britain was defeated in Asia by the Japanese, a 'coloured race', and Europe was dependent for her salvation upon America. During the war two new super powers emerged to dominate the world, the Soviet Union and the United States of America. Both of them opposed the old-fashioned imperialism of Western Europe, on ideological grounds. Both wished to see their own influence spread in Africa and Asia as that of Western Europe waned.

The Second World War exposed the myth of white superiority built up by the segregation of Europeans on their reservations where their frailties were concealed from African view. West Africans were recruited in large numbers for military service. The pre-war British West African army of about 7,000 was increased to 176,000 men. African soldiers overseas saw the dirty, the illiterate, the drunken, the stupid and the poor of Europe. Many European troops served in West Africa. Some white servicemen indulged in habits which revolted Africa's sense of morality. The behaviour of Australian seamen in Freetown became a part of Creole oral tradition. Furthermore the soldiers introduced some of the crudest forms of racial discrimination ever seen in West Africa.

275

On the other hand some European soldiers were shocked at colonial conditions in West Africa. They made African friends and took some part in secret political discussions which condemned British and French rule. The outcome was that Africans developed a more realistic picture of European life, of both its weaknesses and its strengths, its immorality and its higher instincts.

The war forced European colonial powers to make promises to their African subjects. The Germans under Adolf Hitler were outspoken in their belief in white racial supremacy, especially of the German branch of the white race, and their proclaimed aim was to replace the French and the British as the dominant European power. To combat this propaganda and rally the world to their side, the Allies (Britain and France, and later America) expressed their belief in equality and the fundamental rights of all peoples to self-determination. To win West African loyalty the British made specific promises, such as to give an African majority on the legislative councils, and to make money available from British sources—for the first time in British imperial history—for colonial development. Thus British West Africans contributed loyally to the Allied cause. Azikiwe cheerfully wrote 'Nigerians are shouldering the white man's burden with equanimity'.

*Men of the Royal West Africa Frontier Force unloading ammunition cases on their arrival in India, 1944.*

West African soldiers did not, however, fight to defend imperialism. They fought for a new world, and when they were demobilised after the war they were impatient of anything less. Having fought for a free world they wanted a free Africa and were among the most militant followers of the nationalist leaders when the final struggle against colonialism began. Many of them had fought in Burma and India against the Japanese, had been impressed by the defeats inflicted on white men by yellow men, and had been influenced by the ideas of the Indian nationalist movement led by Mahatma Gandhi, struggling for India's independence. Obafemi Awolowo commented, 'India is the hero of the subject countries. Her struggles for self-government are keenly and sympathetically watched by the colonial peoples.'

Britain and America had proclaimed their belief in the equality of man and his right to self-determination in the Atlantic Charter of 1941. The wartime British Prime Minister, Winston Churchill, wanted to apply the charter only to the German-occupied countries in Europe, such as Poland and Belgium. He declared he would neither preside over the liquidation of the British empire nor cast away India, 'the brightest jewel in the British crown'. But the American President, Franklin D. Roosevelt, and the British Labour Party leader, Clement Attlee, insisted that the charter applied equally to the peoples of Asia and Africa. Attlee was reported by the West African press as saying, 'If Britain wanted to persuade others that it wished for a world free from imperialism and imperialist domination then it must rid itself of any taint of imperialism.' Had the Labour Party been seeking votes in West Africa in the early 1940s, it would have won a landslide victory. The *Nigerian Daily Service* in 1945 exclaimed, 'If we are in a position to say so we shall cast our vote solidly for Labour.' When the Labour Party won a handsome victory in the British general election of 1945, and Attlee became Prime Minister, British West Africans naturally expected revolutionary political change in Africa. Attlee's government immediately began to prepare for the granting of independence to India (which was achieved in 1947). The new British Government played a major role in the formation of the United Nations Organisation (UNO) in 1945-6. The new UN Charter went further tha the Atlantic Charter by calling for the evolution of all subject peoples towards self-government. This led a British colonial governor in the 1940s to complain bitterly that of the United Nations' 80 member-countries, 57 were anti-colonialist. The new British Government was also anti-colonialist, but it disappointed the hopes of West Africans and created growing impatience and frustration.

During the war, slight reforms had been carried out. Africans were appointed to the executive council in the Gold Coast and Nigeria in 1942, and in Sierra Leone in 1943. Attlee's government failed to satisfy West African nationalists who were demanding 'self-government now'. The Burns Constitution of 1946 gave the Gold Coast an elected African majority in the legislative council, but most of the elected members were chiefs, and real power was in the hands of the executive, heavily dominated by the British. Similarly, the Richards Constitution in Nigeria in 1946 provided for an unofficial majority in the legislative council, but with advisory powers and largely under the influence of conservative chiefs. Likewise, Sierra Leone's constitution of 1945 led to the creation of a legislature dominated by chiefs.

France and Britain raised and then shattered the hopes of their West African subjects. When Germany defeated France in Europe, two French governments emerged: the Vichy regime, a puppet of Germany, and the Free French under General de Gaulle, operating in exile from London. French African sympathies lay with de Gaulle. French Equatorial Africa, led by the black governor of Chad, the Guyanese Felix Eboué, declared for the Free French but the colonial regime of French West Africa declared for Vichy.

In protest against this action one Ivory Coast chief in 1941 led 10,000 of his subjects into Ghana and placed them at the service of the Free French. French West Africa under Vichy extended the system of forced labour, introduced forced cultivation, and kept wages and the prices of export crops low while the cost of living doubled. In addition, for the first time racial segregation was practised in French West Africa in line with the race theories of Vichy's German masters. Hotels, clubs and cafés marked 'whites only' appeared and African customers were served separately in shops. However, the Free French victory over the Vichy regime brought hope to French West Africans. The Brazzaville Conference of governors of the French empire in 1944, organised by the Free French, advised upon a sweeping programme of reforms away from the policy of association and towards the nineteenth-century policy of assimilation and promised development of French Africa with funds from Paris. The *Southern Nigeria Defender* hailed Brazzaville as laying down a charter for colonial emancipation. In the new French constitution of 1946 the status of 'subject' was abolished, and all French West Africans became 'citizens' of France. Forced labour was ended, and so was the indigénat, whereby an African could be arrested and imprisoned without trial. Each colony was to have a representative assembly and to be represented in the National Assembly in Paris, and political parties were allowed.

In many ways, however, the 1946 constitution disappointed the hopes of French West African nationalists. Territorial governors had far stronger powers than the territorial assemblies. Very few Africans were allowed to vote, only about 1,000,000 out of a population of 16,000,000. White voters elected their own representatives to the territorial assemblies, which they dominated. French West Africa was given only 13 out of 622 seats in the Assembly in Paris.

## Post-war protests

Britain and France were aware that changes must come after the war, but they both underestimated the strength and urgency of African feelings. As a result the first constitutional proposals were fiercely resented as totally inadequate. In addition, Britain and France had promised economic development, but once the development began in the late 1940s it became clear that the Europeans did not plan a fundamental change in economic policy.

Economic policy changed in three ways. First, the imperial powers abandoned the doctrine of economic self-sufficiency of the colonies (see Chapter 19), and began to inject substantial funds from Europe into West Africa. Secondly, the colonial governments began to play a major role in planning the economy. Thirdly, the industrialisation that had begun during the war (see Chapter 21) was continued afterwards.

However, certain undesirable features of the pre-war colonial economy remained. Industrialisation proceeded, but slowly, so reliance on export crops remained the mainstay of the economy. The European *grands comptoirs* continued to dominate the import and export trade and make massive profits at the expense of Africans. Part of the earnings of producers continued to be kept back by official marketing boards, which fixed prices at levels lower than world market prices. The inflation of prices of essential imports during the war (see Chapter 21) was not immediately checked when the war ended. In the late 1940s farmers were paid higher prices for their cash crops, and state employees were paid higher wages, but these increases were below the increases in the cost of living. Living standards for West Africans did not rise above the levels of the 1930s until the 1950s.

Not surprisingly, therefore, the growing African political protest of the 1940s was caused to a large extent by economic discontent (as well as by dissatisfaction with the slow pace of political advance). Among the notable events of these years were the Nigerian national strike of 1945, the Dakar railway strike in 1947-8, the 1948 Gold Coast boycott of European firms, and the miners' demonstration at the Enugu coal mines in 1949, when twenty-one miners were shot dead.

The formation of new and militant political parties at the end of the war and after it was closely linked with protest at unsatisfactory economic conditions. The Rassemblement Démocratique Africain (RDA), founded in French West Africa in 1946, gained most of its support from discontented trade unionists, export-crop producers and traders. The Diula long-distance traders were active members of the RDA, and hoped to use it to safeguard their commercial interests. The Ivory Coast section of the RDA, led by Félix Houphouët-Boigny, gained much of its following from coffee and cocoa farmers. The Senegalese section under Léopold Senghor relied on support from groundnut farmers, and factory-workers in Dakar. The National Council of Nigeria and the Cameroons (NCNC), formed by Nnamdi Azikiwe in 1944, was based at first on urban trade union backing. The Action Group, formed in 1951, began as a pressure group for the cocoa farmers of Yorubaland. In Ghana, the United Gold Coast Convention (UGCC), founded by J. B. Danquah in 1947, and Kwame Nkrumah's Convention People's Party (CPP) of 1949, were composed of cocoa farmers, traders and trade unionists. In addition, the CPP gained massive support from the poorer urban migrants.

These militant new political groupings wanted political self-government in the near future. But they wanted economic reforms immediately, such as changes in the marketing boards that would give farmers better prices for their products; restrictions on European commercial firms to give more opportunities for African traders; more industrialisation, to provide more jobs in the towns; and higher wages for industrial workers.

**Towards independence**

In the 1950s West African opposition to colonialism became less bitter, and nationalist leaders became moderate in dealing with their British and French overlords. There were several reasons for this change of mood. Firstly, the economy improved. Farmers secured higher prices for their export crops, and also gained by selling foodstuffs to the rapidly expanding towns. Government aid to agriculture led to increased use of higher yielding seeds, of fertilisers for oil palms and pesticides for cocoa trees. Production expanded in all branches of agriculture. African traders benefited from an expanding domestic commerce, and from gaining a share in the import and export trades (from 5 per cent in 1949 to 20 per cent in 1963). Secondly, the imperial powers bowed to African political demands by taking positive steps towards granting self-government, particularly after the 1951 elections in Ghana. Once West Africans felt that self-government was inevitable, they became much more co-operative towards the imperial powers. Thirdly, there was a justifiable fear that the old imperialism might well be replaced by a new imperialism of one of the new super-powers. During the independence agitation, the nationalist leaders expressed their support for foreign policies of non-alignment, but with a few exceptions the new West African independent states that arose under the nationalist leaders displayed a definite bias in favour of their former masters, especially in French-speaking West Africa. This was not necessarily the product of a colonial mentality; it was following the principle that the devil you know is preferable to the devil you do not know.

A fourth reason why some nationalist movements became more co-operative with the colonial powers in the 1950s was the redirection of animosities away from Europeans and towards ethnic opponents. Once independence became merely a matter of time, some ethnically-based nationalist movements devoted much of their energy to seeking political advantages over their ethnic rivals. The internal power struggles of Nigeria in the first decade of independence in the 1960s, were a continuation of the battles within the Nigerian independence movement of the 1950s.

There were, in fact, two kinds of nationalism in West Africa during the struggle for independence after 1945. Firstly, there was the ethnic nationalism of a community speaking one language. National feeling of this kind plagued the newly-independent states of Sierra Leone and Nigeria. Secondly, there was multi-ethnic nationalism, where men and women of different ethnic nations strove together to develop a feeling of patriotism, or love for one's country, and to build one nation out of many ethnic groups. In certain West African countries this task was much easier, notably Ghana and Senegal, than in others, such as Sierra Leone and Nigeria. In Ghana the Akan-speaking people comprise the majority of the population. The Akan (who include the Fante and the Asante) lived in all the three administrative regions into which the colonialists divided Ghana. They never formed a political bloc against the non-Akan. There was no Akan nationalism to become a barrier to the growth of Ghanaian patriotism. In Senegal the long historical interaction between Wolof, Tokolor and Serer, plus the influence of assimilation agencies like Islam and French culture, have blurred ethnic consciousness. In neither Ghana nor Senegal did ethnicity (ethnic nationalism) become a serious obstacle to the growth of a true country-wide patriotism. Particularly in Nigeria, Sierra Leone and Ivory Coast, a common patriotism is ardently sought as the ultimate goal of these states, but at the time of writing it has not been completely achieved, though it is in the process of creation. Nigeria, for example, is one of the most complex multi-ethnic states in the world. It is almost impossible to define what a Nigerian is or what he should be. The best that can be said, considering the complexity of the state, is that to be a Nigerian a citizen of Nigeria must be broadminded and tolerant of a wide range of attitudes, customs and ideologies.

Next to ethnic tension the most serious problem of West African states was the lack of probity among political leaders. In certain states the extent of nepotism and corruption gave the man-in-the-street the impression that the new Western-educated elite had gained power merely to plunder the resources of the country. In this regard there appeared little distinction between states like Nigeria and Ivory Coast which professed to favour capitalism and those like Ghana and Senegal which proclaimed their adherence to socialism.

Some states, however, such as Guinea and Mali, escaped the widespread financial corruption in West Africa, largely due to a combination of historical and ideological factors. Historically, the people of these states had been strongly influenced by Islamic reforming movements under the Qadiriyya and Tijaniyya brother-hoods. Both the Parti Démocratique de Guinée (Guinea) and the Union Soudanaise (Mali) stressed puritanism and egalitarianism as the Islamic reformers had done. The Union Soudanaise argued that 'poverty is the best proof of honesty'. An example of austerity had been set by the party's first president, Momadou Konate, who died in 1956 and whose poverty and honesty were legendary. The organisers of the Parti Démocratique de Guinée, led by Sékou Touré and others of a trade union background, possessed poor houses and clothes and few cars. They gloried in being dubbed 'vagrants', 'illiterates' and 'badly dressed'. Yet one must also remember that Sékou, being a great-grandson of Samori Touré, was identifying himself and his party not only with the poor but with the Islamic purifying zeal displayed by his great-grandfather.

One major difference between English-speaking and French-speaking West Africans was whether or not to seek independence. Until the emergence of Sékou Touré in the late 1950s French-speaking Africans struggled less for independence and more to become assimilated to France. They appear to have been converted at the last moment, and only reluctantly, to independence. To them, the independence movement was first and foremost a movement for emancipation, its aims being to secure dignity and equality for Africans. They agitated for those things that would show European acceptance of African dignity and equality: Africanisation, a voice in government, equal pay for equal work, equality before the law, the elective principle, education and modernisation. French Africans were aiming at equality of black and white within the French empire. Leaders such as Senghor and Houphouët achieved ministerial posts in French governments in Paris. Such an option was never available to British West Africans, who could only hope for full racial equality after political independence.

Most French-speaking nationalist leaders, however, were not at all eager for independence. They were too painfully aware that, given their weak economic circumstances, independence could only be nominal and would place their countries in a greater inferiority to France. This would be especially so after a balkanised independence, if French West Africa was broken up into many small states. For many of them the issue of an African federation was a first priority and took precedence over independence. However, if French West Africa's nationalist leaders were conservative, their followers were much more enthusiastic about independence. This became obvious at the 1958 Cotonou Conference. Sékou Touré's successful bid to lead this enthusiasm forced the other territorial leaders in the same direction, if they were to retain the support of their followers.

Sékou Touré in Guinea, like Nkrumah in Ghana, represented the desire of the masses to end colonialism unconditionally. Independence did not come from on high, granted by the good grace of the colonialists or achieved solely by the efforts of the elite. The demand for independence came strongly from below. Men like Nkrumah and Touré were led by the people as much as they led them. They reflected popular opinion.

## CHAPTER TWENTY-THREE

# From Gold Coast to Ghana

## The pioneer of the independence struggle

The period after the Second World War was dominated throughout the African continent by the struggle for independence. The pioneer of this movement was the Gold Coast which, on the attainment of independence, was renamed Ghana after the medieval empire that had arisen and developed in the area of modern Mali and Mauritania between the fifth and thirteenth centuries. Ghana was not only the first sub-Saharan colony to throw off the colonial yoke but throughout the late 1950s and the early 1960s she was the pace-setter for the liberation movement throughout the continent. Among the very first conferences independent Ghana organised in Accra were the First Conference of Independent African States in April 1958 and the All-African Peoples' Conference in December of the same year, at which the artificial colony frontiers were denounced and support for all African freedom fighters declared. The question we will attempt to answer here is why Ghana was the first black colony in Africa to achieve independence.

In the first place, ethnic disputes hardly existed. A single group, the Akan, constitutes as much as 45 per cent of the entire population. Furthermore, their language and other cultural institutions, such as chieftaincy and the system of naming children, had also been adopted by many of the non-Akan peoples, including the Ewe and Ga of the south. Ghana therefore has been saved some of the worst features of ethnic animosity, whose conflicts and rivalries have dominated the struggles for independence of some African states and have subsequently bedevilled their politics since independence.

The second factor is that, by the end of the Second World War, Ghana was more advanced economically and socially than most other African countries. By 1945 Ghana had the best road system, a railway and a deep water harbour and had one of the highest per capita incomes of all the countries on the continent. Ghana then had a sizeable educated elite and a rising middle class of teachers, contractors and private businessmen, and was therefore in a much stronger position to spearhead the attack on the colonial system than the other West African countries.

Thirdly, Ghana had a longer tradition of political agitation than any of the other West African colonies, from the anti-poll tax movement of the 1860s to the youth movements of the 1930s, which were stronger in Ghana than elsewhere in West Africa.

However, what ensured Ghana's lead was undoubtedly the nature, leadership and activities of the political parties that emerged in the country immediately after the Second World War. Between 1947 and 1949 as happened in many of the colonies in West Africa, two parties emerged, namely the United Gold Coast Convention (UGCC) and the Convention Peoples' Party (CPP), and it was the latter that was to lead the country to independence about a decade later. Unlike those of Nigeria, such as the Action Group or the Northern People's Congress, they were not regionally or ethnically based political groups but national parties which enjoyed support throughout the length and breadth of the country. These Ghanaian parties, therefore, could and did speak on behalf of the whole country. It is true that in the early 1950s, as we shall see, a number of parties emerged that were regionalist and ethnic in approach. But most of them were short-lived and they never really affected the struggle for independence.

## The formation of the United Gold Coast Convention and the Convention People's Party

The general discontent that had been generated in West Africa by the end of the Second World War has already been discussed. Instead of conditions improving after the war, they got rather worse. Imported goods became more scarce and prices rose steeply while the expatriate firms and mining companies continued to dominate the economy of the country. Unemployment rose sharply with the demobilisation of 65,000 Ghanaian soldiers after the war and an increase in the number of school-leavers. The educated Ghanaians continued to be denied positions in the Civil Service or on the Bench. And what angered them even more was the Burns Constitution which was introduced after the war. This constitution was indeed an important landmark since, for the first time in any British colony in Africa, it provided for an African majority in the legislative council. However, it fell far short of the hopes of most Ghanaians for a number of reasons. The first was that the then Northern Territories of Ghana was left out of the legislative council and that region was not brought in until 1951. Secondly, out of the 18 elected members of the 31 members of the council, only five were to be directly elected by the municipalities of Cape Coast, Sekondi-Takoradi, Kumasi and Accra. Of the rest nine were to be elected by the Joint Provincial Council of Chiefs and four by the Asanteman Council. This constitution thus strengthened the indirect rule system and the supremacy of the traditional rulers in national affairs.

The Burns Constitution was completely intolerable in the light of the current liberal ideas and the political aspirations of the educated elite and the ex-servicemen. The Watson Commission concluded that the Burns Constitution was 'outmoded at birth' and went on to point out that 'With the spread of liberal ideas, increasing literacy and a closer contact with political developments in other parts of the world, the star of rule through the chiefs was on the wane'.

In August 1947, less than a year after the promulgation of the Burns Constitution, a new political party was inaugurated. This was the United Gold Coast Convention (UGCC). Its aims were to ensure 'that by all legitimate and constitutional means the direction and control of government should pass into the hands of the people and their chiefs in the shortest possible time' and, more immediately, to oppose the Burns Constitution.

The founders of this party were all members of the upper elite—the intelligentsia and businessmen whose fortunes were seriously declining. The foremost of them was George A. Grant, a once very prosperous businessman and timber magnate whose business had been seriously affected by the competition of European and Syrian companies. Closely associated with him were J. B. Danquah, Francis Awooner Williams, R. S. Blay, Edward Akuffo Addo, Ako Adjei, all of whom were lawyers, and William Ofori Atta, a graduate in economics and secretary to the Akyem Abuakwa State Council.

The United Gold Coast Convention would most probably have remained an essentially upper-class elite party but for two events; the appointment of Kwame Nkrumah as Secretary General in December 1947, and the riots of February 1948. Nkrumah arrived from London in December 1947. He was only 39 years old on his return. Tall, very handsome and with a broad smile, youthful, with a captivating personality, considerable organising ability and oratorical powers, he became an immediate success with the workers, the jobless elementary school-leavers who were found in their hundreds in the towns, and with members of the lower-level elite such as junior civil servants, teachers and small traders. His oratory drew hundreds of people to the political rallies that he soon began to organise throughout the country. Before his arrival, the UGCC's popularity had been largely confined to the colony, but he soon extended its activities into Asante as well as the northern regions of the country.

Besides Nkrumah's charm, oratorical powers and organising ability, the other factor which greatly accelerated the spread of the UGCC were the riots of February 1948. This event was touched off when on 28 February a British police officer fired on a group of ex-servicemen who were marching to the castle to present a petition containing their grievances to the governor. This resulted in the death of two men, the first martyrs of the struggle for independence. A month before this incident, tension in Accra had been built up to a high pitch by the boycott of European goods organised by the formerly prosperous businessman Nii Kwabena Bone III, with a view to forcing the prices of imported goods down, and this boycott spread to Kumasi and some of the other towns. The shooting incident touched off the explosive situation and led to widespread rioting and looting of European and Syrian stores. These activities spread to the other main urban centres of the country, and resulted in the end in a casualty list of 29 killed, 237 injured and property worth £2,000,000 damaged.

The effects of the events of February 1948 on the independence movement were far-reaching indeed. In the first place, they converted the leaders of the UGCC in general and Nkrumah in particular into national heroes and the UGCC into a real nationwide movement overnight. Though the leaders of the UGCC were not responsible for organising either the boycott or the riots, they were held responsible for both and branded as communists by the colonial government, and were therefore arrested and detained for about eight weeks. Far from suppressing the movement, the arrest of its leaders, soon affectionately called the 'Big Six', speeded up its spread in the country. The membership of the UGCC increased by about twenty-five fold between March and May 1948.

The second effect was that the February events brought about the first constitutional victory of the nationalist movement, namely, the new constitution of 1951. The Watson Commission, appointed to go into the disturbances, recommended that far-reaching political changes should be introduced into Ghana. Therefore, an all-African committee under the chairmanship of Sir Henley Coussey, a 55-year-old Ghanaian judge, was appointed in January 1949 to prepare a new constitution for the country. Unfortunately, all the carefully hand-picked thirty-eight members of the committee were either chiefs or

*Kwame Nkrumah, who on 12 June 1949 announced the formation of the Convention People's Party.*

members of the upper elite of intellectuals, lawyers, and businessmen, among whom were all the six leaders of the UGCC with the sole exception of Nkrumah. Though by then he was the most popular leader in the country, he was not made a member of the commission because he was considered too radical.

While the committee deliberated, Nkrumah was free to continue his organising activities and succeeded in building up a large following within the UGCC called the Committee on Youth Organisation whose loyalty was personal to himself. The committee consisted mainly of members of the lower-elite of the workers, storekeepers, teachers, petty traders, clerks, cocoa-brokers, junior civil servants, primary school-leavers, and independent artisans. He also established a newspaper, the *Accra Evening News*, and a secondary school—Ghana National Secondary School—for those students who had been dismissed from their schools for participating in the 1948 strikes. The UGCC leaders decided to remove him as secretary of the party, partly because the groups he was forming were loyal to himself, and partly because of the fears of his radicalism. His radical young followers of the Committee on Youth Organisation, led by K. A. Gbedemah and K. Botsio, urged him to resign altogether from that party and to form a party of his own. Faced with a choice between siding with what he himself had already described as 'reactionary middle-class lawyers and merchants' and the young men

288

and workers, Nkrumah naturally chose the latter. Hence on 12 June 1949 he announced the formation of the Convention People's Party (CPP) before a huge audience.

The programme of the new party was to fight relentlessly by all constitutional means for the achievement of full 'self-government now' for the Gold Coast, to remove all forms of oppression and establish a democratic government, to secure and maintain the complete unity of the chiefs and people of Ghana, to work in the interests of the trade union movement in the country for better conditions of employment, and finally to assist in any way possible the realisation of a united and self-governing West Africa.

Four months after the formation of the CPP the report of the Coussey Committee was published. The committee recommended an enlarged legislature, a responsible executive council with a majority of Africans and also drastic changes in the local government set-up. The British Government accepted most of the recommendations of the committee and the constitution drawn up for the country was based on them and came into force on 1 January 1951. There was to be an executive council consisting of three *ex-officio* members and eight Ghanaian MPs. However, the executive was made responsible to the governor as well as the assembly, but not to the latter alone as recommended by the committee, and the governor was also given reserved powers. But even so, this was a most significant step in the march towards independence and gave Ghana a mainly African cabinet government. There was also to be a single chamber legislature with 75 elected members (37 from the colony, 19 from Ashanti and 19 from the Northern Territories). Of the 75, only five were to be selected directly; 37 of the remaining were to be chosen by the chiefs, while 33 were to be elected indirectly by the people. The constitution was clearly once again a return to the indirect system of administration with the chiefs and their conservative nominees, usually from the upper-level elite, being in a predominant position. Thus, while it was welcomed by moderate and conservative opinion, it was roundly condemned by the CPP. When the constitution was promulgated, Nkrumah described it as 'bogus and fraudulent'. The battle was joined between the CPP on the one hand and the UGCC and the colonial government on the other.

The colonial government assumed the offensive by beginning a series of prosecutions against CPP editors, hoping to suppress the criticism of the constitutional proposals. After the imprisonment of three CPP journalists on charges of writing seditious articles, Nkrumah declared positive action on 8 January 1950, two days after a general strike had been declared by the Trade Union Congress, then an integral part of the CPP. The government struck back by declaring a state of emergency, raiding CPP offices and completely muzzling the pro-CPP press by imprisoning J. G. Markham and Kofi Baako, the editors of the *Accra Evening News* and the *Cape Coast Daily Mail* respectively. Nkrumah himself was tried and sentenced to three one-year terms of imprisonment to be served concurrently.

The imprisonment of Nkrumah and the other leaders of the party, however, only made them and their party even more popular. The brilliant work of K. A. Gbedemah and A. Y. K. Djin during the absence of Nkrumah also strengthened the position of the party. The CPP consolidated its hold on the country during this period. Not only did it win all the seven seats in the Accra Municipal Council elections held in April but it also won all the seats in the Kumasi Town Council elections held in November 1950. Above all, in the February 1951 elections, the CPP swept the polls, winning 34 out of the 38 popularly elected seats. Among those elected was Nkrumah, who was still in gaol. A sign of the changing times was the defeat in his own state of Sir Tsibu Darku IX, one of the most powerful chiefs of the day and the leader of the Joint Provincial Council of Chiefs, by Pobee Biney, a mere engine driver!

Faced with this decisive verdict of the electorate, Governor Sir Charles Arden-Clarke ordered the release of Nkrumah and asked him to be head of the government with the title of the Leader of Government Business.

## The CPP government 1951-4

The CPP government's first term of office which lasted from 1951 to 1954 was, of all their long terms of office, the most constructive, the most successful and the most beneficial to the country. It was easily Nkrumah's finest hour. That period was marked by social, economic and political development that has never been paralleled. The CPP government took advantage of the large surplus revenue accumulated during the war, and of the high price of cocoa in the world market, which continued to rise during the period under review — increasing from £211 per tonne in 1951 to £306 and to the record figure of £474 in 1954. Full of dynamism generated by the spirit of nationalism and prospects of independence, the CPP government took bold and highly practical and imaginative steps calculated to accelerate development on all fronts. Thus in place of the timid colonial Ten Year Development Plan of 1946, with a ridiculous sum of £11½ million, the CPP government produced a Five Year Development Plan together with an Accelerated Plan for Education which was to cost £100 million.

Within the three years from 1951 to 1954, the achievements on all fronts were certainly very impressive, and in the field of communications really spectacular. By the end of 1952, the roads that were bituminous-surfaced had increased from 1,440 kilometres to 1,700 kilometres, a number of new roads had also been completed and work had started on the long-projected coastal road between Accra and Takoradi. The extension of the Takoradi harbour was also continued and the construction of a completely new harbour at Tema, 22 kilometres east of Accra, was begun. A number of railway lines were also projected and one, the Akyease-Kotoku railway which would reduce the journey between Accra and Takoradi by 250 kilometres, was also commenced. This road building activity was continued with great vigour. As Gbedemah, then Minister of Finance, pointed out in his budget speech of 1956, 'of all the economic developments undertaken the most spectacular has been perhaps the expansion of our communications'. Achievements included the completion of the important Accra-Kumasi-Tamale-Bolgatanga route, and the Akyease-Kotoku railway.

Another task which the CPP government pursued with as much vigour was that of agricultural development and in particular the cocoa industry. When the CPP came to power, the cocoa industry, the economic life blood of the country, was faced with the threat of extinction by the swollen shoot disease. Though during the election campaign the CPP had opposed the cutting out of diseased trees, the government drew up a new deal for cocoa in January 1952 under which it promised an amount of 10s for every cocoa tree cut down (4s for every tree cut down and 2s a year for three years towards the cost of replanting). By this reward and also as a result of very effective propaganda in which the need for cutting out was urged on the farmers, the government was not only able to win the co-operation of the farmers but even resume compulsory cutting in October 1952 without any serious protest. The government also set up the Cocoa Purchasing Company in 1952 to buy cocoa directly from the farmers, partly with the view of breaking the monopoly being enjoyed by the expatriate firms, and partly to relieve the age-long indebtedness of the farmers through the granting of loans. The new deal for cocoa and the setting up of the Cocoa Purchasing Company certainly went a long way to revitalising the cocoa industry.

During the period, too, the government attempted to diversify agriculture and increase production, and for this purpose large sums were earmarked for agricultural education, animal husbandry, tsetse fly control, and forest conservation. About twenty-one agricultural stations were set up throughout the country to demonstrate better methods of husbandry, control of pests and diseases, test new crops, experiment with irrigation and mechanised farming and give general advice and assistance to farmers.

Attention was paid to the Northern Territories where the Gonja Development Company was set up to start an experiment in large-scale mechanised farming at Damongo. Encouragement was also given during this period to production on a co-operative basis and the Co-operative Marketing Association was set up.

A great deal was also accomplished in the social field. First on the list was the provision of housing especially for the urban dwellers. The government completed the municipal housing projects already begun in the towns of Accra, Cape Coast, Sekondi-Takoradi and Kumasi at a cost of £2,500,000. The government also brought in the Dutch firm of A. V. Shokbeton to build modern prefabricated houses suitable for people with lower incomes.

Attention was also given to the development of health services, with the construction of the new hospital in Kumasi at a cost of £1,500,000. With a view to encouraging social development in the rural areas, the government also established a very active and large social welfare department whose community development team promoted self-help projects throughout the country.

In the field of education the achievements were no less impressive. As we have seen, such was the importance the government attached to this that a special plan, the Accelerated Plan for Education, was drawn up. In the first place, free compulsory primary education for children between the ages of six and twelve was introduced. Government expenditure on primary education alone increased from £207,500 in 1950-1 to more than £900,000 in 1952. To provide for the necessary staff, the government set up sixteen new Teacher Training Colleges between 1952 and 1954, thereby increasing the annual output of teachers from 791 in 1951 to 1,680 in 1955. Attention was also given to secondary education and the number of government-assisted secondary schools rose from thirteen in 1951 to thirty-one in 1955. University education was also given a big boost. Not only did the government contribute £1,500,000 out of its development fund to the University of Ghana, but it also established the College of Arts, Science and Technology, now the University of Science and

Technology, at Kumasi in 1952 at a cost of another £1,500,000.

Besides expanding educational facilities, the government awarded a large number of scholarships to students to study various applied sciences, law and medicine abroad, mainly in the United Kingdom, with a view to producing the necessary managerial class and the skilled labour force for further development. It was also during this period that negotiations and various feasibility studies for the Volta River Project were commenced.

Some notable achievements were also made in the political field. In the first place Africanisation of the civil service was pushed with great vigour. The number of Africans holding senior or 'European' posts increased from 171 in 1949 to 916 in 1954 and to 3,000 in 1957.

However, it is in the fields of both local and central government that the greatest changes were effected. In 1951, the government introduced a new local government system which abolished the old Native Authorities, though the chiefs retained judicial functions and the right of determining local customary law. In the place of these Native Authorities were established thirty district councils and about 250 local and urban councils. Two-thirds of council members were to be elected by popular vote and one-third to be appointed by the chiefs of the area. These councils were to govern the local areas and to provide such local needs as minor and feeder roads, water supply, markets and some educational services. These were to be financed through rates and direct taxes as well as grants from the central government and from stool revenues.

Changes also occurred in the central government set-up which moved the country a step nearer the goal of independence. The first was the change in Nkrumah's title from Leader of Government Business to Prime Minister, making him the first African in any British colony to bear that title. The second was the promulgation of the constitution of 1954. In response to the great pressure brought to bear on him by the radical members of his party who pressed for immediate self-government without any period of transition, Nkrumah published new constitutional proposals in April 1953. In these the party did not ask for full independence but rather for internal self-government and for a legislative assembly that 'shall be composed of members directly elected by secret ballot, and that all members of the cabinet shall be members of the assembly and directly responsible to it'. The British Government, impressed by Nkrumah's co-operation with the colonial government, readily accepted these proposals and embodied them in a constitution which was to be promulgated in April 1954. There was to be a legislative assembly of

*The CPP cabinet, 1954. Sitting (left to right): A. E. Inksumah, Kojo Botsio, Kwame Nkrumah, K. A. Gbedemah, A. Casely-Hayford. Standing (left to right): A. E. A. Ofori-Atta, N. A. Welbeck, B. Yeboah-Afari, J. H. Allassani, J. B. Erzuah, L. R. Abavana, Ako Adjei, Krobo Edusei.*

104 members, all of whom were to be elected directly, and a cabinet which was to be responsible to the parliament. This constitution was regarded even by the British Government as the last stage before the Gold Coast assumed full responsibility for its own affairs.

From this brief review, the impressiveness of the achievements of Nkrumah and his government during their first tenure of office cannot be doubted. Almost every member of the community, urban and rural area dwellers, the literate and the illiterate, the young as well as the old, benefited from the measures introduced by the new government in the social, economic and even political fields during the period 1951-4. There were, however, some unpleasant, even dangerous, tendencies and also mistakes which became apparent and should have been nipped in the bud.

First was the phenomenal increase in the misuse of public funds and corrupt practices and its accompanying ostentatious mode of living of the newly appointed ministers and the MPs. Secondly, certain dictatorial tendencies and intolerance became apparent on the part of Nkrumah and the other party leaders. This explains the expulsion of so many formerly influential and even foundation members of the party between 1951 and 1952. A growing adulation of Nkrumah also became evident and Kwesi Lamptey, at least, resigned from the party in August 1951 on that score. As he stated, 'Kwame is our leader, admitted. [But] we cannot make him a tin god impervious to criticism.' And in March 1953, Busia, then leader of the GCP, also drew attention to these 'tendencies, even actual practices, which if allowed to continue unchecked might lead to the establishment of a dictatorial or totalitarian system of government'.

However, in spite of all this, there is no doubt that Nkrumah and his party had proved their ability to cope with the complex problems of administration and development, and it is not surprising therefore that they continued to enjoy the backing of the governor, Arden-Clarke, and the British Government.

## The defeat of regionalism 1954-6

The General Election under the new 1954 constitution took place on 15 June 1954. The Convention People's Party was opposed at these elections by as many as eight other parties. These were: United Gold Coast Convention, the Ghana Congress Party, the Northern People's Party (NPP), the Muslim Association Party (MAP), the Togoland Congress, the Anlo Youth Organisation (AYO), the Ghana National Party (GNP) and the Ghana Action Party. All of them except the United Gold Coast Convention (UGCC) were regional and ethnically-based parties, and the strongest was the Northern People's Party which was founded in April 1954. It drew its support mainly from the Northern chiefs and its main battle cries were 'the white imperialists must not be replaced by black' and 'the North for northerners'. Although this opposition looked quite strong, the CPP in fact swept the polls, winning 71 out of the 104 seats.

However, the strong position of the CPP, which appeared to ensure independence sooner rather than later, was effectively challenged soon after the 1954 elections by the rise of the National Liberation Movement (NLM). This was a regional party based mainly on local Asante grievances. Firstly, the Asante were upset when the 1953 Electoral Commission recommended that the number of parliamentary seats be increased in the North from 19 to 26, in the colony from 37 to 44, in the Trans Volta from eight to 13, but in Asante by only two from 19 to 21. The Asante MPs demanded 30 seats for their region, but parliament approved the commission's report and rejected the Asante demand. Secondly, a group of Asante Youth Association members who were not nominated as CPP candidates in the 1954 election hoped to achieve their personal ambitions in a new regional party. Supported by Asante chiefs who were disgusted at the loss of most of their local government powers, the CPP rebels in Asante formed the NLM. They won much popular support from discontented Asante cocoa farmers. The government had fixed the price to be paid at £7 10s per load. The chairman of the NLM was Bafuor Akoto, a chief. The general secretary and national secretary were two ex-CPP rebels, Kusi Ampofo and E. Y. Baffoe.

The spread of the new movement was greatly helped by two events shortly after its inauguration. The first was the murder of E. Y. Baffoe by K. A. Twumasi Ankrah, then regional propaganda secretary of the CPP on 9 October 1954. The second was the official backing that the NLM received from both the Kumasi state council and the Asanteman Council. Not only did this murder give the new movement its first martyr but it stirred up great emotion throughout Asante. Indeed it was two days after this murder that the Kumasi Council swore the Great Oath to give the movement its full support. Since the influence of the chiefs was still very great in the rural areas in Asante, the support that the NLM received from them greatly accelerated its spread and by the end of the year, the NLM had virtually captured the initiative from the CPP in metropolitan Asante. The NLM began to press more vociferously not only for a federal constitution but also for fresh elections before independence in view of the new political developments in the country. The spread of the NLM was marked by very violent clashes between supporters of the NLM and the CPP in which some people were killed and many houses were burnt down or blown up. This violence reigned in Kumasi and its vicinity from 1954 to 1956, during which neither Nkrumah nor any of his ministers could even set foot in Kumasi.

In view of the political crisis caused by the rise of the NLM the Secretary of State for Colonies insisted on fresh elections in 1956 before accepting the CPP's demand for independence. The NLM, having allied with all the opposition parties—the NPP, GCP, the Togo Congress and the MAP, was confident of success. Busia was chosen as the parliamentary leader of the NLM and its allies. But the elections, held on 12 July 1956, resulted in a much larger majority for the CPP than had been expected. The party won all 44 seats in the Colony, eight of the 13 in Trans-Volta Togoland, 11 of the 26 in the Northern Territories and even in Asante eight out of 21, thus gaining 71 out of 104 seats, a clear majority of 38. The CPP won so convincingly partly because Nkrumah's charismatic appeal was still very strong, and partly because the CPP had a lot to show, as they proclaimed in their election campaign—Africanisation, free education, new hospitals, clinics, roads, bridges, harbours, Akyease-Kotoku railway, the formation of IDC, ADC, CPC, the Bank of the Gold Coast, the Volta River Project and Tema Development Corporation.

*Kwame Nkrumah, standing, puts forward the motion for independence in the legislative assembly on 3 August 1956. Independence was achieved on 5 March 1957.*

There was no doubt that the CPP still enjoyed the support of the majority of the people of Ghana. It was not surprising therefore that in August the new parliament passed a motion calling for independence, and the British Government accepted it. In Western Togo—a United Nations Mandate administered by the British as a part of Ghana—a referendum was held in 1956 to decide on its future course. The majority of the people voted for union with Ghana. But the majority of the Ewe people, as they had from as far back as 1919, continued to desire reunion with their brethren in French Togo and rejected union with Ghana. The British and United Nations accepted the wish of the overall majority and the union of Western Togo with Ghana was carried out. This settlement removed the last stumbling block in the way of Ghana's independence.

On 5 March 1957 at midnight, at a mammoth gathering on the polo grounds opposite the legislative assembly building, the Union Jack was lowered and the flag of the new nation state of Ghana, a red, green and gold flag overprinted with a black 'lodestar of African freedom' was hoisted. The independence struggle was over. The British colony of the Gold Coast had been converted into the independent nation-state of Ghana under the banner of Nkrumah and his Convention People's Party.

297

## CHAPTER TWENTY-FOUR

# Nigeria—the path to independence

The political history of Nigeria between 1945 and 1966 (when the military took over control of the government of the country) was dominated by the problem of national unity. While Nigerians thought of themselves as Nigerians when they were abroad meeting Ghanaians or Senegalese, at home they thought of themselves as Northerners or Southerners, Easterners or Westerners, Igbo or Yoruba, Hausa or Tiv, Egba or Ijebu, Onitsha Igbo or non-Onitsha Igbo. Over and above these regional or ethnic loyalties, Nigerians were also divided between educated and non-educated, aristocrat and commoner, rich and poor. Nearly all countries have such divisions among their peoples, but in the case of Nigeria these divisions played a much more important part in politics than almost anywhere else. Understanding this is vital for an understanding of the course of Nigerian nationalism since the Second World War. We must not forget too that the British in their sixty-year long administration of Nigeria did little to emphasise national identity. Despite the amalgamation of Northern and Southern Nigeria in 1914 the two continued to be administered as though they were still separate protectorates. The policy of indirect rule emphasised ethnic and local loyalties rather than loyalty to Nigeria as a whole.

## The patriotic front 1944–51

Modern Nigerian politics is often dated from the return of Nnamdi Azikiwe to Nigeria in 1937 and his establishment of the *West African Pilot*. Azikiwe had been born of Onitsha parents among the Igbo 'sons abroad' in Northern Nigeria. He went to the United States for higher education where he became familiar with the writings of Washington, DuBois and Garvey. He returned to Ghana to edit the *Accra Morning Post* but left when that paper angered the colonial authorities. On his arrival in Lagos—the first of the new Igbo elite—

he was a novelty to the established Yoruba dominated elite and an inspiration to the Igbo, who in growing numbers emulated him by seeking higher education overseas.

During the Second World War Azikiwe's *Pilot* was loyal to the British, 'God grant us that the mother country comes through this fiery ordeal victorious. Let us put our shoulder to the wheel. *Our Empire is in need*' (author's italics). But in 1943 Azikiwe published his 'Political Blueprint' which envisaged Nigerian independence in eighteen years. The colonial administration was little more than amused but, in fact, Nigerian independence was achieved almost exactly eighteen years later.

In 1944 Azikiwe and Herbert Macaulay formed the National Council of Nigeria and the Cameroons (NCNC) which adopted the 'Political Blueprint'. The NCNC was open to affiliation to any type of society and in 1947 some eighty societies had affiliated. Northerners were not as yet in the habit of forming political societies and Northern Nigeria was represented by Southern cultural organisations in the North. The NCNC was not a political party; it was a patriotic organisation designed to bring all Nigerians together to demand independence, to hold the Nigerian communities in alliance against the divisive tendencies of colonialism.

'*H. E. Sir Arthur Richards, Governor of Nigeria, proclaims a new Nigerian constitutional reform. The native intelligentsia in welcoming this however sincerely criticised some of its ordinances, which they feared would not work in the best interests of the people.*' The Richards Constitution as seen by the cartoonist Akinola Lashekan.

In 1946 Governor Richards introduced a new constitution which provided for an enlarged Legislative Council at the centre and which established assemblies for the Northern, Eastern and Western Provinces which now became known as regions. Although in all four bodies there were African majorities, the new constitution did not suit the nationalists. The elective principle was not extended, and the Nigerians sitting in the various bodies were largely powerless. The introduction of regions was interpreted by the nationalists as the old imperial policy of divide and rule. Most of all, Nigerians resented the paternalism of Governor Richards, in handing down a constitution without consulting those who had to live under it.

By extending its competence to Northern Nigeria the Richards Constitution marked the first time that all of the country was brought under one legislative body. However, at the same time it proved divisive by its establishment of regional assemblies. These were to be the basis of what was later known as the 'three Nigerias'. The resultant competition between them was to lead eventually to civil war. Possibly because of its size and diversity Nigeria required a federal type system, and although they resisted it at first, the majority of Nigerians eventually came to support it. But many were later to feel that the British would have been wiser to have built the federal system on the basis of the provinces by which the British themselves had governed the country at the local level rather than these three big but unbalanced regions. For the Nigerian federal system violated an important principle of federalism, in that one region was larger in size and population than the other two combined, and could therefore govern the country alone if it wished to.

The NCNC undertook a tour of Nigeria to demonstrate the unpopularity of the Richards Constitution and to raise funds for a delegation to London to demand its abolition. The touring group included Macaulay, Azikiwe, A. Olorun-Nimbe and O. Imoudu, President of the Nigerian Railway Union. In Kano, Macaulay fell ill, and died later in Lagos. Azikiwe succeeded to the leadership of the NCNC, Macaulay having publicly called him 'my son Zik' and left his mantle of leadership to him. But under Azikiwe the NCNC became increasingly plagued by rivalry between members of different ethnic groups, particularly between the Yoruba and the Igbo.

In 1949 the sense of national unity briefly revived during the strike in the Enugu coal mines when the police killed seventeen workers. There were sympathy disturbances in major cities in Eastern Nigeria. The British governor imposed censorship on all Eastern newspapers and a curfew at Calabar. Those concerned with the future of the nation sought to use this issue to bring the NCNC, which was being increasingly looked on as a party of the East, and the NYM whose membership was largely Western-based, together. A joint committee sent H. O. Davies (a Westerner) and K. O. Mbadiwe (an Easterner) to investigate the strike. But cooperation collapsed as soon as the crisis passed.

The new governor, Macpherson, determined not to be a paternalist, stated that before constitutional change it was 'of the utmost importance to allow adequate time for the expression of public opinion'. This was done thoroughly in a series of village, divisional, and provincial conferences, and finally a fully Nigerian conference at Ibadan in 1950. The Macpherson Constitution of the following year embodied many of the recommendations of the Ibadan Conference. The elective principle was applied throughout the country for the three regional houses of assembly and for the central House of Representatives in Lagos which replaced the old Legislative Council. Regional executives and a central council of ministers were created, the majority of whose members were Nigerians. The regions were to control revenues of their own and have increased autonomy. The Macpherson Constitution made two things clear: the British were now serious in moving towards independence, and Nigerians as well as British had decided on a federal system of three regions which operated in favour of the major ethnic groups in those regions. Both factors worked in favour of regionalist parties and against the formation of a genuine countrywide patriotic party such as the NCNC had sought to be. 'They gave us ropes to hang ourselves and we did so' was a typical comment of a patriot.

The Macpherson Constitution catered for the already strong trend of growing regional nationalisms. This had probably gone too far for a unitary constitution to have been practical in 1951 as suggested by the NCNC. On the other hand, linguist states, that is states built on the ethnic groups, recommended in a minority report by M. Ojike and Eyo Ita at the Ibadan Conference and supported by Obafemi Awolowo, would have encouraged rather than retarded the growth of the various regional nationalisms. No influential group proposed a federation built on the old administrative divisions, the provinces. These would have broken up the three major ethnic groups—the Hausa, Igbo and Yoruba—into several states each, as in the case under the present state structure of Nigeria, and at the same time given states to important smaller ethnic groups or minorities such as the Edo and the Tiv.

## The rise of ethnic nationalism

Before 1951 in Igboland there was a remarkable increase in the Western-educated elite and a large outflow of population from the homeland to other parts of Nigeria. Thus Igbo material interests became Nigeria-wide, demanding a broad Nigerian patriotism best expressed in the NCNC patriotic front after 1944. The same factors contributed to the growth of an Igbo State Union. The conflict between the demands of a broad patriotism and narrow regional nationalism made Igbo political behaviour very confusing during the independence movement. In the fifties and sixties, the NCNC within the Igbo homeland might pursue narrow national interests, accepting the idea of 'three Nigerias' as enthusiastically as the Yoruba or Hausa, while at the same time seeking to project a patriotic 'one Nigeria' image to the country as a whole. The Igbo as much as any other group in Nigeria exemplify the conflicting loyalties to which all were subject during the march to independence.

In 1950 the *Eastern Guardian* noted: 'The farm workers of Igboland are engaged in a mass exodus from the soil and this mass movement has been much more noticeable since the war years.' Igboland was one of the most densely populated parts of Africa outside the Nile Valley. This, together with soil erosion, the building of primary schools and a traditional social and political system which encouraged ambition, led the Igbo to spread out for wage labour. The mobility of the people between Igboland and elsewhere in Nigeria assisted Igbo entrepreneurs to dominate the road transport business. The area of Igbo farming also gradually expanded into the less heavily populated neighbouring minority areas of Calabar and Ogoja. All sections of the population—professionals, businessmen, labourers and farmers—were represented among the 'sons abroad'. Between 1931 and 1952 the Igbo population of Lagos, a Yoruba city, rose from 5,000 to 26,000. The Igbo population of Northern Nigeria grew from 12,000 in 1931 to 167,000 in 1952. Fernando Po possessed 35,000 Igbo labourers against 16,000 local inhabitants. The exodus in the fifties and sixties exceeded these figures. By 1966 it was estimated that there were 2,000,000 Igbo sons abroad.

Much like settlers elsewhere in the world, for example the Creoles of Sierra Leone, the Chinese of South-East Asia or North America or the Asians of East Africa, the Igbo possessed a business acumen and devotion to hard work which aroused unease and resentment among the people among whom they settled. Since it was the educated Igbo—and this was true of many other ethnic groups in Nigeria—

who tended to move out more than the uneducated, the advantages of the settlers over the local people were striking. It was among the Muslim Northerners who, as a result of colonial education policies, were the least equipped to compete in Western education and English, that the greatest unease developed about the presence of immigrants from the South, the majority of whom were Igbo and Christians. The *Gaskiya Ta Fi Gwabo* stated in 1950:

> ... undoubtedly it is the Southerner who has the power in the North. They have control of the railway stations; of the post office; of government hospitals; of the canteens; the majority employed in the Kaduna secretariat and in the public works department are all Southerners.

Throughout West Africa, migrants from the countryside to the towns grouped themselves in cultural and self-help associations. In this the Igbo were no exception. As early as the 1920s sons abroad organised cultural unions or societies in their cities of residence of all those people from the same village group in Igboland. In 1935 the Igbo unions of Lagos federated and in 1948–9 the Igbo unions of Nigeria federated to form the Ibo State Union. Forty-nine unions joined in 1948 but two years later this had risen to 89. The Ibo State Union even adopted a national anthem.

The Ibo State Union seemed to many non-Igbo to be advancing Igbo nationalism rather than Nigerian patriotism and to be at odds with the wider aims of the NCNC. Where did Nnamdi Azikiwe, the outstanding Igbo politician, stand on these issues of regional nationalism and a countrywide patriotism? Azikiwe's newspapers and his bank were Nigerian-wide enterprises. He was like so many of the Igbo sons abroad whose economic interests were dependent upon a peaceful and prosperous Nigeria free of national antagonisms. Azikiwe's problem was how to contain the swelling tide of Igbo nationalism and channel it towards partnership with other Nigerian communities. To some extent he had to go along with Igbo nationalism if he was to retain a strong measure of influence over Igbo politics. This helps us to understand the declaration by this leading nationalist in 1948 to the Ibo State Union: 'the God of Africa has especially created the Ibo nation to lead the children of Africa from the bondage of the ages.' It also helps explain why there were fears among other politicians about Azikwe's real intentions and a growing fear of competition from the Igbo, particularly among the Yoruba. Nevertheless, it remains true that under Zik's leadership the

*Nnamdi Azikiwe, photographed in 1958 standing on the steps of 10 Downing Street, the official residence of the British Prime Minister.*

NCNC gained many votes outside the East and when forces of disintegration were at their most intense it was Azikiwe, the press and the NCNC which stood out most strongly against the 'pakistanisation' of Nigeria (referring to the splitting of India into two separate states). In 1956, when some were condemning the NCNC as an instrument of Igbo domination, the party's executive consisted of seventeen Yoruba, twelve Igbo, nine representatives of minorities in the South, one Fulani, and one from the minorities in the North. The NCNC may have given the appearance of being a Southern party but not an Igbo party.

The Yoruba, like the Igbo, organised unions based on their major sub-divisions Ijebu, Ilesha, Egba. Among the Yoruba, especially the Egba, were a number of families who could boast three or four generations of university-educated ancestors. The NYM represented these Yoruba professional elite families. Unable to compete with the NCNC, and fearing Igbo domination, its leaders organised a cultural society in 1947, the Egbe Omo Oduduwa (Association of the Children of Oduduwa, the famous ancestor of the Yoruba). The Egbe was founded to foster, in its own words, 'the creation of a single nationalism throughout Yorubaland'. Since the Richards Constitution had ignored the Yoruba chiefs, the Egbe also aimed to preserve the monarchical form of Yoruba governments. The Egbe, in the words of a hostile Yoruba critic, was designed to safeguard 'Yoruba superiority', protect 'the Yoruba way of life', consolidate 'Yoruba hegemony, supremacy and paramountcy' and 'revive the ancient glory that once belonged to the Yorubas'.

The Egbe set up a political committee which evolved in 1951 into the Action Group, at first a predominantly Yoruba nationalist political party which was a direct heir to the NYM, whose members were founders of both the Egbe and the Action Group. The *Daily Service*, the NYM paper, became the official organ of the new Action Group. Awolowo emerged as leader. He favoured the British policy of regionalisation as developed in the Richards and Macpherson Constitutions. He believed in linguistic states in a Nigerian federation. He believed such states would allow the Yoruba to advance at their own speed.

> I still feel that the Yoruba people are more advanced politically and culturally, than other ethnic groups, and that owing to the anomalous system of our gonernment, they have been held up to mark time while other peoples make haste to develop and catch up.

## Three Nigerias

The Northern Region, was not only the largest but also the most complex in Nigeria. The most Islamised area of the region roughly represents the nineteenth-century boundaries of the two great Islamic states, Borno and the Sokoto caliphate. The predominant groups of the Sokoto caliphate were the Hausa-Fulani, followed by the Nupe and Yoruba of Ilorin and Kabba. The Kanori predominated in Borno. Islamic brotherhood was directly opposed to ethnic feeling and with the introduction of politics to Northern Nigeria as a result of the Macpherson Constitution its leaders sought to continue the tradition of ignoring ethnic peculiarities by creating a multi-ethnic political party. In 1949 delegates from all over the North met to form the Jami'yyar Mutanen Arewa—the Congress of People from the North—a cultural organisation in which members of the ruling classes of the former Sokoto caliphate and Borno were prominent. During 1950-1, in response to the need for political organisation resulting from the Macpherson Constitution, the organisation broke up and developed into two political parties. The first to form was the Northern Elements Progressive Union (NEPU) which called for the emancipation of the talakawa (common people) from the oppression of the emirs, spoke of the 'shocking state of social order' in the North due to 'the Family Compact rule of the so-called Native Administrations in their present autocratic form' and claimed that the talakawa must 'organise consciously and politically for the conquest of the powers of government'. The leader of NEPU was Aminu Kano, an aristocrat with democratic views. The political philosophy ran counter to 150 years of tradition in the caliphate, but it was representing the egalitarian theme within Islam often associated in the western Sudan with the Tijaniyya brotherhood. It has been often suggested that there was a distinct tie between NEPU and the minority Tijaniyya in Northern Nigeria.

The other political party to emerge from the Jami'yyar was the Northern Peoples Congress (NPC) which was much more within the caliphate tradition. In its programme the NPC urged reform of the colonial system, local government reform, an increased rate of Western education and the elimination of bribery and corruption. Its most radical statement was that the voice of the people should be heard in all the councils of the North and that Nigeria should be eventually self-governing. Finally it sought to extend the assimilating principles of the caliphate to all the Northern Region—its slogan, 'One North, one people irrespective of religion, tribe or rank'.

Ahmadu Bello, the Sardauna of Sokoto (a traditional title), cousin of the reigning Amir al-Muminin and a direct descendant of Uthman dan Fodio, linked by blood and marriage ties with many of the ruling emirs, became the party leader. He was almost the supreme representative of what NEPU called the aristocratic Family Compact. The NPC represented the elitest tendency in Islam, that the intellectual elite should rule, an idea rightly or wrongly associated with the Qadiriyya brotherhood. Despite their tendency to talk of the will of the people, however, the politicians who ultimately came into control of Southern affairs also behaved in practice as if the educated elite had an inborn right to rule. The wishes and desires of the Southern talakawa were often as thoroughly ignored as were those in the North.

Within the NPC the talakawa were represented by Abubakar Tafawa Balewa, a schoolteacher and farmer from Bauchi. He was, unfortunately for subsequent Nigerian history, subordinate in influence to the Sardauna within the NPC.

The future struggle between North and South for dominance in Nigeria became obvious at the Ibadan Conference of 1950 to discuss Governor Macpherson's new constitution. On the basis of its larger population the North would control the federal parliament and, as one Southerner said, 'The West and East will have to accept every legislative proposal from the North.' The South proposed equal representation for each region and naturally, since there were *two* Southern regions, a Northerner remarked, 'If equal representation is

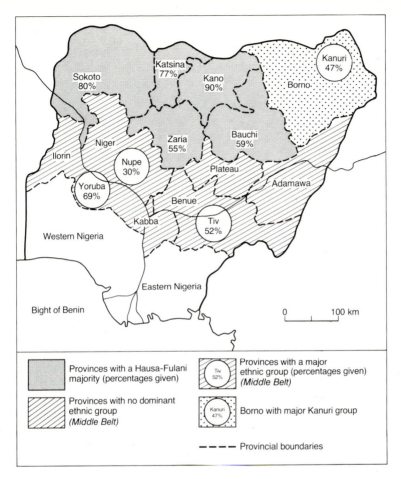

36 *Peoples of Northern Nigeria in 1952.*

given to each region, it seems that the South is to dictate to the North.' Balewa added, 'Now if it is democracy, gentlemen, which we are trying in this country, and which we hope to try in the future, there is no way out, since on democratic principles the North should receive a preponderant voice.' The democratic principle was applied in the Macpherson Constitution and in the elections of 1951–2, the NCNC won the East, the NPC the North and the Action Group the West though the NCNC won well over a third of the seats there. Dr Azikiwe was even elected to the Western House of Assembly as one of its five members for Lagos. The constitution proved unworkable, as

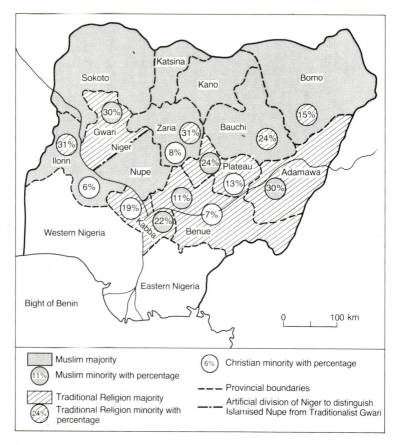

Legend:
- [shaded] Muslim majority
- (11%) Muslim minority with percentage
- [hatched] Traditional Religion majority
- (24%) Traditional Religion minority with percentage
- (6%) Christian minority with percentage
- – – – Provincial boundaries
- –·–·– Artificial division of Niger to distinguish Islamised Nupe from Traditionalist Gwari

*37   Religious conviction in Northern Nigeria in 1952.*

those experienced constitution-makers, the British, ought to have foreseen, and caused one crisis after another. Finally the Action Group, supported by the NCNC, broke the constitution in such a way that it almost broke up Nigeria as well. In 1953 Anthony Enahoro, an Action Group backbencher from the Mid-West introduced a private motion into the federal parliament demanding self-government for Nigeria in 1956. The Federal council, consisting of four ministers each from the North, West and East and six European officials could not agree on a common attitude to this motion and agreed not to take part in the debate. The Action Group ministers resigned and eventually the Action Group and NCNC members walked out of the house. The old rivals, Awolowo and

*Sir Abubakar Tafawa Balewa, a schoolteacher and farmer from Bauchi and representative of talakawa interests within the Northern Peoples Congress, who became Prime Minister of Nigeria on 1 October 1960.*

Azikiwe, symbolised the newly-forged Southern alliance by an embrace on the steps of the House of Representatives while the Southern crowds roared their approval and then turned on the Northern delegates shouting 'His Master's Voice', 'Kolanut chief' and 'slaves of whitemen'. Awolowo and Azikiwe decided to tour the North, convinced that the common people in the North were only too anxious to repudiate their representatives.

Resentment rose fast in the North as a result of insults to Northern leaders in Lagos and the hostile Southern press. As Awolowo arrived in Kano the Southerners of the Sabon Gari (strangers' quarters) prepared to give him a tumultuous welcome. Rioting began which developed into pitched battles between Northerners of the old city and Southerners of the Sabon Gari, in which 36 were killed and about 300 injured. The South learned few lessons from the Kano riots. The *Daily Service* reported, 'the disturbances were clearly the result of a clash between the forces of liberation and those of imperial stooges'.

The Kano riots left a deep wound on the emerging Nigerian state. Much later Igbo leaders of 'Biafra' were to look back upon the Kano riots as part of a continuing pattern which ultimately led to the massacres of 1966. Following the riots Ahmadu Bello reported 'at the moment, all the people I have spoken to say "divide the country". I explain the hardships, but they still say "divide the country".'

The immediate result of the riots was the North's Eight Point Plan of May 1953, which demanded a customs union, complete legislative and executive autonomy for the regions and a central non-political agency to operate the common services. Later in 1953 at a conference

309

in London the one thing which united the big three leaders was the demand for strong regions and a weak federal government. The unexpected harmony at the London Conference was due to the fact that it gave each of the three major ethnic nations an exclusive empire. As one Nigerian put it: 'And so Awolowo can keep the West, Sardauna the North, Azikiwe the East and Lyttleton (the Colonial Secretary) the centre.' The minorities who collectively constituted half of the country's population were particularly disappointed, as expressed by an Ijo from the Rivers area:

> The partition of Nigeria is complete and the regional boundary lines have now been drawn so thickly that the idea of one Nigeria which many of us cherish has been completely destroyed.

The 'National Cake' was shared out on a percentage basis. The marketing boards were regionalised and their assets distributed; mining and income taxes distributed on the basis of derivation, tobacco duties and excise on the basis of regional consumption, and the civil service and judiciary were regionalised, though provisions were made for appeals to a Federal Supreme Court and there were of course still Federal Ministers. Even federal elections were to be conducted under regional rules. With few amendments the constitution of 1954 was the one under which Nigeria would receive its independence. In the federal elections of 1954 the NPC won the North, the NCNC the East and to many people's surprise, the West as well with 23 seats to the Action Group's 18. True, many of the NCNC's seats had been won in the non-Yoruba areas. But it also gained a great deal of support in the Yoruba areas showing that Nigerian politics were not completely dominated by ethnic factors. Even though the NPC had the largest number of seats in the House of Representatives, the NCNC having won both East and West had the right to choose six federal ministers to the North's three. Thus coalition was inevitable between these two parties, whose political views made them strange bedfellows.

## The problem of the 'minorities'

Following the 1954 election the major parties settled down to consolidate their hold over their respective regions for the Action Group still controlled the Western House of Assembly though it had lost the federal election in the West. As new African governments full of enthusiasm to modernise, they often achieved miracles which the old colonial regime would never have dreamed of attempting. They were greatly assisted by the economic boom. Magnificent public buildings were constructed, the educational system dramatically expanded, manufacturing and processing industries developed and the road network greatly improved. Despite mistakes of over-enthusiasm and inexperience, the achievements of the three competing regions of Nigeria could not be denied.

However, the minorities in each region felt neglected, frequently with good reason with the bulk of government expenditure being made in the homeland of the ruling majority. The minorities had hoped for a powerful federal government where the antagonisms among the big three would be a guarantee of a strong bargaining position for themselves. But far from this happening, in 1957 when Sir Abubukar Tafawa Balewa became Prime Minister he brought the Action Group into his coalition government with the NCNC.

After 1954 then the minorities found themselves in powerful regions dominated by one often united ethnic group. Agitation for more states increased. The British Government set up a commission to investigate the fears of the minorities. In 1958 it reported that although these fears existed, the creation of more states was unwise, and the best guarantee for minorities was the competition among the big three to secure their support at the centre. In the pre-independence 1959 election this theory was tested. The Action Group decided to make a definite bid to upset the NPC–NCNC coalition at the centre by launching forth from its base in the West to appeal to the minorities, and thus create Nigeria's first countrywide party and gain control of the federal government. Obafemi Awolowo was the spearhead of this effort to break away from the pattern of largely regional/ethnic based parties. In the result the Action Group emerged the smallest of the three parties but with a more 'national' image than either of the other two. Of its 73 seats, 25 were in the North and 14 in the East. Thus, from being largely Yoruba-dominated, the party emerged after the election with the West in the minority position. This appeared a most hopeful sign for the future of the Nigerian political system. Following the election the NPC and NCNC formed a coalition, both partners having been angered by the successful Action Group invasion of their respective regions and Sir Abubukar did not include Action Group ministers in his cabinet.

On 1 October 1960, Nigeria became independent with Sir Abubukar Tafawa Balewa as Prime Minister and Obafemi Awolowo as leader of the Opposition. Dr Azikiwe, the veteran nationalist took

*Obafemi Awolowo addressing a meeting in Ijebu.*

the honorific role of Governor-General. There was much optimism about the future of the country, but the regional and ethnic interests that had dogged the pursuit of national unity since 1945, were sadly to lead to civil war.

## CHAPTER TWENTY-FIVE

# French West Africa—the path to independence

## Rassemblement Démocratique Africain (RDA)

At the end of the Second World War there was much gratitude in France for the loyalty of the colonies in the gloomy days when France had been prostrate under German domination. France was in a mood to make generous political concessions to her colonies. In the French constitution of 1946 the status of citizen was extended to all Africans, which meant the end of the indigénat and forced labour and gave some of the newly created citizens the right to elect representatives to the territorial assembly, the federal assembly in Dakar and the French Chamber of Deputies (parliament) in Paris.

In the same year, at a conference in Bamako which drew 800 delegates from French West and Equatorial Africa, Félix Houphouët-Boigny of the Ivory Coast formed a federation of parties called the Rassemblement Démocratique Africain (RDA). The RDA allied with the French Communist Party because it took a strong anti-colonial line and copied its excellent organisational methods. However, the RDA rejected Communist doctrines which it considered could not be applied to African society. By 1950 the RDA had 700,000 members and was the largest political organisation anywhere in Africa. It was the dominant party of Ivory Coast, Mali, Guinea, and Chad, and the leading party of Volta, Niger, Congo (Brazzaville), and, after 1956, Gabon.

In almost every colony the colonial administration was bitterly opposed to the RDA, fearing its links with Communists, its refusal to compromise with imperialism, and its wide popularity. Its leaders were arrested, supporters persecuted, demonstrators shot, newspapers closed and chiefs with RDA sympathies deposed. At the same time the administration encouraged and even financed rival political parties and occasionally falsified election returns so that its favourites would win.

The worst oppression was in the Ivory Coast. At first the RDA made rapid progress there, in the home territory of Houphouët-

Boigny, a wealthy Baoule planter. The progressive post-war governor of the Ivory Coast, Latrille, allowed Houphouët so much power that he was dubbed 'the real governor of the Ivory Coast'. But the swing of public opinion in France away from the left (the progressive position) to the right (conservatism) led to the replacement of Latrille in 1948 by Pechoux, who was given orders to crush Houphouët and his party. Pechoux's reign of terror in the Ivory Coast was part of the general French colonial policy during these years, based upon the belief that the desire for freedom in the colonies could be forcibly suppressed. It was part of the larger colonial oppression, not only in French West and Equatorial Africa as a whole, but in Madagascar and Indo-China.

The repression in the Ivory Coast between 1949 and 1951 was surprisingly like the French conquest between 1891 and 1918. In both cases opposition was led by the Baoule and the major issues were the same, taxation and chieftaincy. Taxes were raised on pro-Houphouët villages. Villages were deserted when tax collectors or other French officials arrived. Three hundred pro-democratic chiefs lost their chieftaincies. Around 1900 a chief had been executed by the French in Korhogo for failing to pay his tax. In 1948, Sikaly, a chief from exactly the same area told the French 'I will pay only to Houphouët'. Thereafter ten lorry-loads of French-led Syrian mercenaries attacked his village, killed Sikaly, and arrested as many of his subjects as they could catch. The Catholic Church refused the last sacrament and Christian burial to the martyrs. When a Catholic father said mass for the thirteen of Houphouët's supporters killed by the French at Dimbokro, he was hurried off to France before he could pack. As a result there was a revival of anti-French Harris-ism, like the original Harris movement of the conquest period.

Northern Muslims whose fathers had supported Samori, now supported Houphouët. The leader of the Muslims of Odienne (Samori's most faithful ally), when told to abandon Houphouët because he was not a Muslim, replied to the Frenchman, 'And are you?' The Diula community of Bondoukou which had once supported Samori now backed Houphouët, while the anti-Samori Brong went over to the French. Pechoux sponsored a Northern Muslim party which resembled the French alliance with Kong in the 1890s. Comparison with the conquest was heightened by the French army celebrations near Man on the fiftieth anniversary of the defeat and capture of Samori. Among the settlers who were urging Pechoux to increase the rate of the repression, the arrogant imperial ideas of the 1890s had not changed. One said, 'This matter cannot be settled here without 10,000 deaths.' The settler paper *Climats* rejoiced: 'thus the Africans learned that the sorcerer (Houphouët) and the RDA (Houphouët's party) lied when they said the teeth of the French are broken'.

There were also contrasts between the repression and the conquest. Unlike during the period of the conquest, Africans possessed a single leader in Houphouët who constantly urged the new technique of passive resistance. When the French attempted to arrest him, the people blocked the roads for miles around marching to his assistance. There were hunger strikes in the prisons, women keeping vigil in front of the governor's palace and a railway strike. Domestic servants to Europeans quit their jobs. There was a boycott of European firms, whose profits fell by 90 per cent, and the markets patronised by Europeans were closed. Fishing boats on the lagoon carried banners 'We Resist Aggression' and 'We Defend Liberty'. The French sponsored ethnic parties in the tradition of divide and rule, a Northern Muslim Party, an Agni-Brong alliance, and a Kru Party, and encouraged these parties to cable to Paris asking for the dissolution of Houphouët's party (the RDA) and for troops to be despatched from Dakar. In the election of 1951 Houphouët's supporters were struck off the voting register which was packed with the collaborators, RDA meetings were forbidden, its supporters frightened from the polling booths and ballot papers openly distributed in the market place. Thus the French produced a fake victory for their ethnic parties. But there was little question that the people of the Ivory Coast won the moral victory when Houphouët was able to report, 'No Colon (settler), no trader, no European civilian was disturbed and yet their dispersal in the forest made them very vulnerable'.

The French changed their policy towards the RDA when they realised that repression was more likely to stimulate African demands and drive them into more radical channels. Pechoux was transferred in 1950 (to Togo where he repressed the Ewe in their desire to unite with their brethren in the Gold Coast). The French decided that their best long-term interests lay in conciliating Houphouët and, they hoped, turning him into a collaborator. In this they were successful. The RDA split in 1950, Houphouët leading the moderate wing of the party. He repudiated the radicals and severed his communist affiliations. In return, the colonial administration first tolerated the RDA and finally openly supported it. The RDA emerged victorious in the elections of 1956 in every colony except Senegal and Mauritania. Ultimately Houphouët became a minister in the French cabinet in Paris. He even supported the use of West African troops on the French side in the Algerian War of Liberation.

During the 1950s there was rapid economic and educational development in the Ivory Coast. In 1942 Europeans had produced 55 per cent of Ivory Coast coffee, but in 1952 they produced only 6 per cent. Africans were also producing over 90 per cent of cocoa exports. In 1925 Ivory Coast produced 15 per cent of the exports of French West Africa, in 1951 it surpassed Senegal and by 1956 it produced 45 per cent of all the exports and was the major contributor to federal revenues. By the early 1960s the average Ivoirean income was 35,000 francs against 20,000 in 1945. By 1965 it had risen to 330,000. In the fifties and sixties there was a massive inrush of French capital into manufacturing industries, and in the seventies the Ivory Coast had almost become a self-sustaining economy. Education followed the same trend. Nine per cent of school-age children were in classes in 1947, 30 per cent (equal to Senegal) in the early 1960s. At the same time 1,000 Ivoireans were enrolled in universities in France and 200 in Dakar. A centre of higher studies in Abidjan opened in 1958 and became a university in 1963.

Houphouët himself was an example of a chief who became a planter. Coffee and cocoa produced in the Ivory Coast an African capitalist planter class which depended upon hired labour and the renting of land to tenant farmers. These were the men who led the independence movement, and they were understandably devoted to

*Felix Houphouët-Boigny, photographed with President de Gaulle and their wives on the steps of the Elysée Palace, the official residence of the French President, in 1961.*

free enterprise and opposed to socialism. Houphouët wanted to make the Ivory Coast safe for capitalism in order to please his Baoule planter supporters. The French Government helped Houphouët to break the French settler planters by withdrawing settlers' economic privileges and forcing them to compete (unsuccessfully) with African farmers. However, Houphouët welcomed European financiers and industrialists while the settlers were leaving. In 1954 and 1956 he even sponsored ten Europeans and twenty Africans for election to the Abidjan City Council, and in 1957 and 1960 he sponsored ten Europeans to the state assembly.

The economic boom in the Ivory Coast was to have a vital effect on Houphouët's policy towards a possible self-governing federation of French West Africa.

## Senegal versus Ivory Coast

Before the rise of the RDA, which had its headquarters and main stronghold in Ivory Coast, the Senegalese had been used to thinking of themselves as the natural leaders of French West Africa. This was partly due to the long tradition of education, the large Westernised elite, and the economic dominance of Senegal. Throughout the colonial period, over half of French West Africa's revenues had come from Senegal. But after the war Ivory Coast's development was, as we have seen, very rapid, and by the 1950s it was challenging Senegal's dominance both economically and politically.

The major political party in Senegal immediately after the war was the Socialists led by Lamine Gueye, a Wolof and a 'citizen' and his lieutenant Léopold Senghor, the brilliant poet-philosopher son of a Serer shopkeeper 'subject' from the groundnut belt. Gueye's nepotism and despotism earned him the title of 'the divine right chief of African democracy', and also led Senghor to break away and form a new party, the Bloc Démocratique Sénégalais (1948). In 1952 the Bloc dominated the state assembly and in 1956 swept everything before it except the municipal governments of Dakar and St Louis. Generally it represented the farmers of the countryside while the Socialists remained strong only in the towns and among the Western-educated elite.

From about 1950 in the politics of French West Africa the competition for leadership was between Ivory Coast and Senegal and their respective leaders Houphouët and Senghor. During the repression of 1949-51 the RDA had been suppressed throughout

*Léopold Senghor as a young Senegalese politician in France, 1949.*

West Africa and a number of ethnic parties had risen to prominence with French encouragement. Taking advantage of the eclipse of the RDA, Senghor in 1951 formed an alliance of these ethnic parties, which he hoped would be the basis of a Western Africa-wide political movement under his leadership. But after French rapprochement with Houphouët, the RDA regained its ascendancy and Houphouët his leadership, leaving Senghor and Senegal isolated.

In 1956 the French and Houphouët introduced the *Loi Cadre* reforms which provided wholly elected territorial assemblies with an executive and chief minister and extended a large measure of internal self-government. The federal council in Dakar remained advisory and under the control of the French governor-general. This was the major step in the break-up of the federation. From the French point of view, it was designed to prevent the demand for independence, since the eight small states were economically weak and dependent. From Houphouët's point of view, they were a step towards the preservation of the revenues of the rich Ivory Coast from being shared through the federal council with the poorer states.

Significantly enough Houphouët's views were shared by Leon Mba, vice-president of Gabon, the richest territory of French Equatorial Africa. Gabon and Ivory Coast played similar roles in the dismantling of the federations to which they respectively belonged.

This showed the strength of economics in the determination of political policy. Houphouët envisaged a French community where the ties were strong between each of the states and France, but where the constitutional links among the African states were weak or non-existent. Senghor, on the other hand, desired a strong West African federation linked with France. He said, 'Within the framework of a French federal republic, a French West Africa of twenty million inhabitants can, side by side with the metropolis, form a stable element and develop its own personality.' Each leader thought first and foremost of the narrow interests of his own state: Houphouët of preserving the revenue of the Ivory Coast for Ivoireans, Senghor of maintaining Senegal as the capital colony of a West African federation. Houphouët's policy was more acceptable to France and Senghor accused him 'of being the instrument of France in balkanising Africa'. Senghor's only chance of reversing this policy was to organise the unquestionably strong forces of federalism in West Africa against Houphouët. An opportunity arose at the time of the Cotonou Congress and De Gaulle's proposed constitutional referendum in 1958.

## The 1958 referendum

When De Gaulle came to power in France he sought ratification for a new constitution in a referendum in 1958. The main concern of Africans in the new constitution was the future relations between France and her colonies. In Africa there was growing support for a French Community of states but much disagreement on the constitutional relationships which should prevail within the Community. The majority of the RDA plus Senghor and his followers favoured federations of French West Africa and French Equatorial Africa linked in a super-federation (the Community) with France. Senghor's aim was a strong federation to make the Community as far as possible a federation of equals. Houphouët wanted a loose federation of the individual colonies with France. Sékou Touré of Guinea favoured African federations but wanted few constitutional links with France. He would apparently have supported a French Community based on the principles of the British Commonwealth. Despite the diversity of views, it seems clear that given a chance to say so a substantial majority of leaders wanted a federation of French West Africa. De Gaulle, like the leaders of French Governments before, favoured the views of Houphouët and in the referendum of 1958 offered either autonomous colonial units linked with France in the Community (Houphouët's policy) or total independence and complete severance of assistance from and relations with France (nobody's policy). No opportunity was given to vote for African federations of any description. De Gaulle and his advisers had estimated astutely that continued association with France would win, because the federalists would fear independence as leading to permanent balkanisation, and judge that only by continued association with France could the association of West African states be assured. The choice before African voters in the referendum was an enlarged self-government under France or balkanised independence. However, Houphouët's party was not united behind him. At the RDA's Bamako conference of 1957 Sékou Touré, the RDA leader in Guinea, championed Senghor's views and went over Houphouët's head to persuade the party to fight to strengthen the federal executive. In early 1958 the RDA-dominated federal council in Dakar, with the sole exception of the Ivoirean delegate, voted to recommend strengthening the federal executive. In July 1958 Senghor called a congress in Cotonou which represented most of the major parties, except the RDA, of French West Africa. The Cotonou Conference passed a resolution advocating inde-

*An official government poster in Dakar urging a 'Yes' vote in the 1958 referendum.*

pendence, recorded its approval of a strong federation and appeared ready, if led, to vote 'No' (for independence) in De Gaulle's referendum. However, Senghor called for a 'Yes' to De Gaulle, hoping for an independent federation later.

Sékou Touré came to the opposite conclusion, that France was the major obstacle to federation, that it must be eliminated from West African politics and that only when the eight states were independent could Africans fashion the federal union they desired. Touré, therefore, persuaded Guinea to vote 'No' (for independence) when all other prominent leaders, except Bakary of Niger, were deciding to vote 'Yes' (for continued association with France).

The referendum at first appeared an unbelievable triumph for De Gaulle. Who had imagined that if colonies were given a chance to vote for independence they would, with only one exception, choose continued colonial rule? In British West Africa the results of the referendum were received with shocked disbelief. Despite close proximity British and French West Africans knew very little about each other's movements towards independence. English-speaking West Africans knew virtually nothing at this time about the issue of federation versus balkanisation. To English-speaking West Africans Sékou Touré was the only French-speaking African who could be compared with their own 'nationalist' leaders. However, Guinea's brave declaration for total independence mobilised popular enthusiasm for independence in every other colony. Sékou Touré's suddenly inflated popularity was a threat to all other political leaders who had to either ride the tide of enthusiasm or be eclipsed.

The example of independent Guinea throughout French West Africa plus that of independent Ghana ultimately convinced Senghor and Houphouët and even the French that independence could not be resisted. Senghor secured the agreement of Soudan (Mali), Upper Volta and Dahomey to join Senegal in the Mali Federation and then persuaded De Gaulle, with some reluctance but with good grace, to grant independence. Houphouët, startled by his eclipse and isolation, sought the aid of France in detaching Dahomey and Upper Volta from the proposed Mali Federation. This was easy enough to do since France financed both the governments of these poor countries. In addition it made no economic sense for Dahomey to join a grouping which did not embrace Niger, its natural hinterland, or for Upper Volta to join one excluding Ivory Coast, its natural outlet to the sea. Houphouët created instead the Entente Council, a loose economic and political alliance, not a federation, of Ivory Coast, Upper Volta, Niger and Dahomey and requested independence for the Entente states. This was granted in 1960 and in the same year, fortunately for Houphouët, the truncated Mali Federation of Senegal and Mali broke apart, thus appearing to justify his balkanisation policy. Houphouët thus protected Ivory Coast's revenues from being spent to help develop its poorer neighbours.

By 1960 the French West Africa and Equatorial Africa federations had been dismantled and all the former French colonies became independent.

### Guinea's path to independence—Samorism and socialism

In 1947 the RDA formed a branch in Guinea, the *Parti Démocratique de Guinée* with a directorate composed of representatives of all ethnic groups. Sékou Touré represented the Mandinka. In 1951 he was a candidate for election but was roundly beaten by the old alliance of French officials, chiefly elite and Ponty graduates. By 1953 Guinea was experiencing the new economic surge in bauxite, iron ore and diamonds and Sékou Touré (a trade union leader) organised a record-breaking 66-day strike for higher wages and shorter working hours. As a consequence he lost his civil service job but became the overnight hero of the workers and the poor. Out of fear of his rising popularity, the old ethnic parties formed a Bloc (alliance) to fight the *Parti Démocratique* in the election of 1954. Given a reasonably fair election the Parti Démocratique would likely have won but the French administration openly threw itself behind the bloc as it had never had to do before. It gave civil servants paid leave and the use of official transport to campaign for the bloc. It added 72,000 names to the voters' register in the pro-bloc Futa Jalon and struck off 11,000 names in the pro-Touré forest region. The chiefs distributed voting cards and sat at the polling booths where no effort was made to maintain secrecy. There was little surprise that the bloc won the election.

Such behaviour discredited the French, their institutions, the chiefs and the Ponty elite. The election of 1954 was a powerful boost to the opposition. The colonial administration no longer had the acquiescence of the people. The choice for the French in Guinea, as in much of the rest of French West Africa, was either to bring in the troops as in Indo China and Algeria or permit the growth of the new forces which leaders like Sékou Touré represented. By 1956 the Paris government had decided to abandon the chiefs and throw its weight behind the RDA, thereby hoping either to turn it into a tool of French

*Sékou Touré, who led Guinea to independence in 1958 by rejecting De Gaulle's constitutional proposals of the same year.*

control or watch it break up into ethnic factions or 'Unions of those who feather their nests'. As a result of the new policy of keeping French hands out of the elections, the Parti Démocratique won all the municipal elections in 1956 and in the following year 56 of the 60 seats in the Guinea state assembly. In line with the provisions of the *Loi Cadre* Sékou Touré became chief minister.

One major problem Sékou Touré had to try to overcome in Guinea was ethnicity. The original parties had been openly ethnic unions and even the Parti Démocratique was preoccupied with ethnic balance. Its four strong men were Touré (Mandinka), Sayfoulaye Diallo (Fulani), B. Lansana (forest) and B. Camar (coastal Susu). Sékou Touré continually sought inter-ethnic harmony. As a trade unionist he had warned against the harmful and divisive effects of ethnicity among workers. As leader of the Parti Démocratique his major task was conciliation of the Fulani of Futa Jalon, the leading ethnic group of Guinea (30 per cent of the population) and the hard core of opposition. In this he was assisted by Diallo, his second in command, and a Fulani of high chiefly status in the Futa Jalon. When his supporters in Conakry were singing anti-Fulani songs Touré warned, 'Do not play the song again ... Forget the song. The Fula is your brother.... You are Fula. You are all races.' He attacked ethnic exclusiveness by appealing to the brotherhood of Islam, '... at sunset when you pray to God say over and over that each man is a brother, and that all men are equal'. He stressed the oneness of humanity and the race.

> If I wore a grey boubou and were called Amadou Gueye and spoke Wolof you would think me Senegalese. If I wore a white cloth and spoke Bambara and were called Mamadou Sissoko you would think me Soudanese.... If I wore Khaki trousers and spoke Ewe you would think me Togolese. ... The clothes can change and the language can be learned. I am like you; I am a man like you; my race is African.

Samori became the historic symbol of unity. Sékou Touré, a great-grandson of Samori, consciously emphasised the historical parallel of resistance to French rule. Samori was an effective symbol. He had not clashed with the Fulani of the Futa Jalon; his own people, the Mandinka, had unitedly fought the French. They had not, as in the Tokolor empire, divided between collaborators and resisters. When the French had pushed him eastward into modern Ivory Coast, Samori imposed himself on non-Mandinka peoples.

Two groups in Guinea looked back upon Samori with distaste. One was the people of the forest whom Samori sought to Islamise through conquest, selling into slavery those who resisted. The other

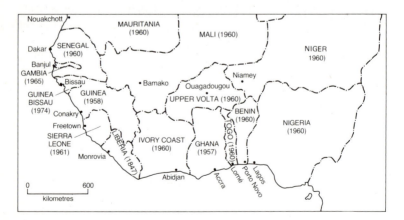

38   *Independent West Africa.*

was the people of the slave villages in the Futa Jalon whose ancestors had been sold to the Fulani chiefs by Samori's commercial monopoly. An elderly villager in the forest once asked Sékou Touré, 'You will not sell us into slavery?' In the Futa Jalon the Parti Démocratique argued, 'If Samori Touré can make you slaves, Sékou Touré can make you free.' Strangely enough these two areas were the earliest centres of Sékou Touré's political strength. The Parti Démocratique won its first victories among the forest peoples and its first votes in the Futa Jalon from the former slave villages. Sékou Touré had repeatedly proved his egalitarianism in his struggle for the workers within the trade unions and in the anti-chiefly, anti-privilege policies of his party. In his opposition to the privileged classes he resembled his great-grandfather whose centralised authority suppressed the chiefs and who drew his popularity and strength from under-privileged groups in Mandinka society.

Among the Mandinka, Samorism brought support to the Parti Démocratique from the Diula trading class to which Samori belonged, the descendants of his army sofa and the Muslim scholars upon whom Samori had depended for his programme of conversion. One of these was Grand Sherif Fanta Mady of Kankan whose father had been Samori's principal spiritual guide and chaplain to the sofa. Fanta Mady, a mystic and recluse, received from his followers a vast tribute which he redistributed to the poor, an action which the Parti Démocratique readily admired. When the Grand Sherif died in 1955 Sékou Touré called him 'the living example of a being who believes in God . . . and who treats as equal every man, regardless of his colour or origins'.

Members of the Tall family were influential in the area around Dinguiray from which al-Hajj Umar had launched his jihad in the nineteenth century. The Parti Démocratique sought their support. One descendant of Umar, Habib Tall, was elected vice-president of the Guinea assembly, and another, a wealthy merchant, became president of the government's economic council.

In Guinea successful political parties after the Second World War turned to history to stimulate and revive resistance to the French among the descendants of those who had resisted them in the nineteenth century.

# PART SIX

# Independent West Africa 1960-78

## CHAPTER TWENTY-SIX

# Ghana since independence

Nkrumah's rule between 1957 and 1966 can be divided into two clear periods, the period from March 1957 to July 1960 and from July 1960 to the coup in February 1966. July 1960 not only saw the adoption of the new republican constitution but also marks the shift in Nkrumah's policies from right to left, from Western capitalism to African socialism or Nkrumaism.

### Nkrumah's rule 1957-60

During the period 1957-60 Nkrumah consolidated the position of himself, his party and his government. The Convention People's Party had won 71 out of the 104 seats in the July 1956 elections, but it had polled 398,000 votes against as many as 299,000 for the Opposition parties.

The CPP was, therefore, not all that strong in the country as a whole. Moreover, the government had little authority in certain regions, notably in Volta where the Togoland Congress refused to accept the result of the plebiscite to join Togoland to Ghana, and in Asante, where the threat of violence meant no government minister could visit Asante. In an attempt to solve these problems, Nkrumah carried out a number of measures during his first period. Firstly, the government suspended the NLM-dominated Kumasi Municipal Council. Secondly, it appointed CPP politicians instead of civil servants as Chief Regional Commissioners. Thirdly, it dismissed anti-CPP chiefs, such as Nana Ofori Atta, Paramount chief of Akyem Abuakwa. Fourthly, it moved against the largely regionalist opposition parties by the 1957 Avoidance of Discrimination Act, which banned 'Tribal, radical and religious groups ... which were used for political purposes'. Finally, the Trade Union Congress, the National Cooperative Council and the United Ghana Farmers Council were all made parts of the CPP.

The measures failed, however, to weaken the opposition parties or strengthen the hold of the CPP in the country as a whole. On the contrary, the Avoidance of Discrimination Act inspired the NLM, the NPC and others to unite to form the United Party (October 1957). The UP soon began to spread throughout the country and challenge the CPP. Therefore, Nkrumah's government introduced the Preventive Detention Bill (July 1958), which empowered the government 'to imprison without trial, any person suspected of activities prejudicial to the state's security'. This act was primarily meant to cripple the UP in Accra.

Regional assemblies had been established by the independence constitution as a compromise between a unitary system advocated by the CPP and a federal system desired by the NLM. The government used parliament to reduce the powers of the assemblies to advisory functions and held elections to them in October 1958. The opposition UP unwisely boycotted the elections in protest at their reduced powers, and the CPP gained control of all of them. The first and only act of the new assemblies at their first meeting was to vote themselves out of existence. By destroying the regional assemblies and detaining some of the leading opposition members of parliament, Nkrumah had launched himself on the suicidal road towards personal dictatorship by the end of the 1950s.

What did Nkrumah and his government do in the economic field from 1957 to 1960? The economy of Ghana at independence was dominated by foreign firms and companies. Over 90 per cent of the country's import trade was in the hands of foreign firms. All the seven gold mines were owned by foreign companies. Two British banks controlled 90 per cent of all banking business. Manufacturing and construction industries were also dominated by expatriate firms, as was the marketing of agricultural products. Ghanaian retail traders were facing stiff competition from Lebanese, Syrian, Indian and British firms. In short, the economy of Ghana at independence was a typical colonial economy, controlled and dominated by expatriate firms to the advantage of their shareholders in Europe. However, during the first phase of his post-independence rule, Nkrumah hardly introduced any fundamental changes in the economy. His policy during this period was *laissez-faire*. The number of Syrians and

Lebanese operating in the retail field actually increased between 1957 and 1960. Expatriate firms during this period were exporting more capital from Ghana than they were bringing in, and the annual loss averaged about 21.3 million dollars. The government resisted pressures for radical change in ownership of industry. It gave grants to expatriate companies operating mines of marginal profit value, and increased only from ten to thirteen the number of government-owned factories. Between 1957 and 1960 foreign companies pulled out of the cocoa-buying field, but not because they were pushed out by the Ghana government. The main reason was their failure in competition with the United Ghana Farmers Council.

It is surprising, at first glance, that Nkrumah, a socialist, should have followed a policy favouring the foreign capitalist. After all, Nkrumah had been converted to socialism as early as the late 1930s. In his *Towards Colonial Freedom*, published in London in 1947, he had advocated economic planning and control of the means of production by the people. The CPP's constitution described the party as a 'nationalist, democratic and socialist movement'. But there is a straightforward explanation for Nkrumah's policy of *laissez-faire* and financial freedom from 1957 to 1960. This was the need for foreign investment. Above all else Nkrumah was determined to carry out the Volta River Project which to him was the key to industrialisation in the country. But it could not be done without massive foreign capital.

Nkrumah's achievements in the social field in the first period of independence were quite considerable, especially in education. The number of government and approved secondary schools increased from 38 in 1957 to 59 in 1960 and that of private schools from 22 to 52. The total enrolment in these secondary schools rose from 12,119 to 20,000 between 1957 and 1960. Every assistance was also given to the two university colleges and steps were taken during this period which led to the granting of full university status to both institutions in 1961. Equally active were the steps taken in health, housing, water supply and electricity. In the second development plan, 1959-64, huge sums were allocated for the provision of services in these fields.

But even more spectacular, indeed revolutionary, were the activities of the government in the field of foreign policy. Nkrumah's foreign policy during this period was governed by three basic principles: pan-Africanism, non-alignment or neutralism, and world peace. Pan-Africanism was his main preoccupation. He aimed at achieving the total liberation of the African continent from colonial domination and the political union of African states. Indeed, on the eve of independence, Nkrumah declared that 'the independence of Ghana is meaningless unless it is linked up with total liberation of the African continent'. On the question of African unity, he stated in July 1959, 'unless we work toward ... some form of constitutional Union of Africa, our continent will remain what it is today—a balkanised mass of small individual units, used as a political and economic pawn by those external forces which seek to keep us divided and backward'.

The first practical step Nkrumah took towards African unity was the convening in Accra of the Conference of Independent African States in April 1958. This conference was attended by the heads or their representatives of all independent African states, then only eight. Little was achieved beyond general agreement on the desirability of setting up a permanent machinery for co-operation between African states. In December 1958 Nkrumah convened a second All-African People's Conference (AAPC). This was a much larger conference attended by more than 200 delegates representing 62 African nationalist organisations in 28 African countries. In November 1959 a third all-African conference, the All-African Trade Union Federation (AATUF) was also held in Accra.

The effects of these Accra conferences on both pan-Africanism and the liberation struggle in Africa were dramatic. Pan-Africanism moved from Europe and America where it had been since the 1900s in the words of Nkrumah 'to the African Continent where it really belonged'. For the first time in history, leaders of independent African states met in Africa to discuss problems of common interest and to formulate common policies affecting economic, political and cultural matters. As Tom Mboya of Kenya put it, the two conferences 'marked the rediscovery of Africa'. The second effect was the building of a political bridge across the Sahara, since of the eight countries that attended the first conference five were from across the Sahara. The fourth and most important effect, especially of the AAPC, was to inspire liberation movements throughout the continent, as delegates returned home determined to do battle with colonialism. Nkrumah also followed the conference up by giving grants to freedom fighters and political parties in many colonial countries.

However, Nkrumah did not confine himself merely to preaching African unity. He also made some practical moves towards its realisation. These moves were the formation of the Ghana-Guinea Union in November 1958 and the Ghana-Guinea-Mali Union in 1961 (see Chapter 30).

By the end of the period 1957-60, Nkrumah's African policy had been very successful. His name and that of Ghana had become houschold words throughout Africa and Accra had become the Mecca of freedom fighters and pan-Africanists.

What about Nkrumah's policies towards the great powers during this period? Here he was guided by two clear principles: world peace and neutralism or non-alignment. In the interests of world peace, he opposed the establishment of foreign military bases in Africa, the manufacture of nuclear weapons and the testing of atomic bombs. Nkrumah not only condemned the first French atomic tests in the Sahara, but he also froze French assets in Ghana. In the interests of neutralism, he established firm relations with America as well as the USSR and the socialist countries. He paid an official visit to the United States in June 1958. He also began contacts with the Soviet bloc though his moves here were rather slow. A Russian ambassador did not arrive until September 1959, while the Ghana Embassy in Moscow was not opened until January 1960. However, it was a neutrality which had a very strong pro-Western bias. The reason for this was Nkrumah's desire to get from the United States the huge foreign capital needed for the Volta River Project. Finally, during this period Nkrumah made firm contacts with the Third World. When he visited India in 1958 he was hailed in the Indian papers as 'Africa's man of destiny'.

By July 1960 Nkrumah was at the peak of his fame, popularity and influence in Africa in particular and the world in general. He had become the idol of all blacks and freedom fighters everywhere. Unfortunately, during the next six years his policies and methods changed and brought disaster to Ghana and to his hopes of a united Africa.

## Nkrumah and socialism 1960-66

Politically the change in Nkrumah's policies began with the adoption first of a republican constitution and then a one party system of government. Economically, there was a change-over from the policy of *laissez-faire*, private enterprise and capitalism to a rigid state control or partnership in the economy and an emphasis on industrialisation. Secondly, everything was geared towards a socialist reconstruction of Ghanaian society. Externally, non-alignment was retained in theory, though in practice it was given a bias towards the left. In short, there was a turn to the left and the governing principles of Nkrumah's policies became Marxist socialism adapted to suit African conditions, which he called first African socialism, then Nkrumaism and finally consciencism.

Nkrumah had been a socialist since the late 1930s. By the end of 1960 he felt able to apply socialism to Ghana. By then, the Americans had committed themselves to financing the Volta River Project, on which Nkrumah virtually staked the economic future of the country. Secondly, the new republican constitution of July 1960, which made Nkrumah President, also gave him all the powers he needed to bulldoze through socialist measures and to rule by decree and to appoint or dismiss any member of the public service. Thirdly, by then he had a sufficient number of socialists (or at least people who called themselves socialists) who could be appointed to key posts. The Ideological Institute created at Winneba in 1960-1 provided socialist education to CPP activists, TUC officials, civil servants and freedom fighters. In 1960 and 1961 Nkrumah pushed socialists into key positions such as TUC general secretary, editor of the *Ghanaian Times*, CPP general secretary, and as bank directors and to senior posts in the civil service. Strong advocates of capitalism were forced out of office. Gbedemah was transferred from the ministry of finance in May 1961 to the less important ministry of health. On 16 October he spoke out against Nkrumah in parliament and fled into exile that very day. Finally, by July 1960 the news media had also come under the complete control of Nkrumah and his close supporters. The *Evening News* and the *Ghanaian Times* were owned by them. The independent *Daily Graphic* was bought by the government in July 1962. The *Ashanti Pioneer* was placed under censorship. The all-powerful fanatical socialist Tawia Adamafio was made minister of information and broadcasting in October 1961.

The July 1960 constitution gave Nkrumah dictatorial powers. He also retained the Preventive Detention Act and extended it indefinitely in 1962. It was also applied more ruthlessly. Between September and December 1960, 178 people were detained, 311 in 1961, 254 in 1962, 586 in 1963, 37 in 1964 and 13 in 1965. Attempts to assassinate Nkrumah in 1962 and 1963 and bomb explosions in Accra in the same years mainly account for the large number of arrests. But whatever the reasons, the continued use of the Preventive Detention Act turned the whole country into one concentration camp of fear, insecurity and uncertainty.

The Kulungugu incident in August 1962 was an unsuccessful attempt on the life of Nkrumah when a hand grenade was thrown at him. He sustained serious injuries and a young girl was killed. The incident led to the arrest and trial of innocent men like Adamafio, Kofi Crabbe and Ako Adjei, to the dismissal of the chief justice and the judges who acquitted Adamafio in the first trial, and to the setting up of a new presidential security system. The Presidential Detail Department under the Russians and the Special Intelligence unit under the semi-literate Ambrose Yankey spread a network of spies all over the country. Their false reports led to the detention of hundreds of Ghanaians.

A second attempt on Nkrumah's life in December 1963 by a policeman, Ametewee, led to the detention of the opposition leaders, Danquah and William Ofori-Atta, and some senior police officers.

Next, in the January 1964 plebiscite, voters were asked to decide whether Ghana was to become a one-party state and whether the president should have powers to dismiss judges of the High Court 'at any time for reasons which appear to himself sufficient'. The votes were 2,773,920 in favour and only 2,452 against. Clearly, the plebiscite was a nonsensical farce.

Finally to crown it all, on the day of elections to parliament in 1965 Nkrumah announced on the radio the names of people whom he had selected as MPs and for which constituencies. Some of them did not even know where their constituencies were.

Nkrumah destroyed democracy in Ghana. What did he achieve for Ghana's benefit after 1960? In education, both the university colleges of Legon and Kumasi became full universities in 1961 while a new university college was built at Cape Coast. In 1965-6 the number of teacher-training colleges almost doubled from 44 to 80. However, technical and agricultural education was neglected. Moreover, with the turn to the left, there was unwarranted interference in the affairs of the universities. Nkrumah assumed the right to terminate contracts of academic staff and to appoint professors, against brave resistance by the Vice-Chancellor Dr Conor Cruise O'Brien (later an Irish cabinet minister). This trend of affairs made it very difficult for the universities to pursue research and learning.

On the other hand, in the cultural field, a new dynamism began to be felt on all fronts during the second phase of Nkrumah's independence government. He and his government did much to popularise the doctrine of African personality. Active steps were taken to revive Ghanaian music, dancing, art and literature, while tremendous resources were sunk into the development of sports. Ghana became the champion boxing country during the 1962 Commonwealth Games in Perth, and the champion football country in Africa in 1963. The Ghana Dance Ensemble won international fame on its journeys abroad. The revival of Ghana's culture was undoubtedly one of Nkrumah's greatest achievements.

In the economic field, Nkrumah and his government pursued a

very dynamic policy from 1961 to 1965, putting restraints on foreign enterprises and increasing the state sector of the economy. By 1966, a number of successes had been achieved. The mining industry and cocoa marketing had become the exclusive monopolies of the state. The state had acquired the lion's share of banking and insurance. Fifty per cent of the import trade was controlled by the Ghana National Trading Company, while construction was dominated by the Ghana National Construction Corporation. In agriculture, the State Farms Corporation set up a number of state farms using large quantities of agricultural machinery, especially tractors imported mainly from eastern countries. In an attempt to diversify the agricultural economy, the government set up palm oil and rubber plantations in the western region. By 1965 the number of state-run factories had risen from 13 to 22. Finally, on 23 January 1966, the government-owned Volta Dam Project was officially opened. The socialist reconstruction of the economy was really well on the road to success. However, there were some notable failures, which were partly to account for Nkrumah's downfall.

Firstly, an acute shortage of essential goods hit the country in 1964 and continued until the coup. This resulted in very high prices for drugs, sugar, milk, rice, baby food, flour, cement, raw materials for factories and spare parts for vehicles. There was even a period when

*The Volta Dam. The Volta River Project, completed in 1966, was regarded by Nkrumah as the keystone of Ghanaian industrialisation.*

basic medicines like anti-snake bite serum ran out completely and people died for lack of antibiotics. Secondly, the state-owned industries and corporations failed. By 1965 only two state-owned factories were running at a profit. All the rest were running at a loss, partly due to bad management and lack of skilled labour, but mainly because of inadequate capital and lack of raw materials. Thirdly, by the end of 1964 Ghana was completely bankrupt. The national foreign debt grew from 64 million dollars in 1959 to 524 million in 1957 and to 770 million in 1964.

It must be admitted that the economic problems facing Nkrumah were partly due to the disastrous fall in the overseas price of cocoa, which was the principal foreign exchange earner (almost 60 per cent). The world price fell as follows:

| 1954 | £474 per tonne |
| 1957 | £251 per tonne |
| 1960 | £230 per tonne |
| 1965 | £142 per tonne |

However, Nkrumah still cannot be free from blame. Realising the drop in the income from cocoa, he should have trimmed his economic projects accordingly. But the more cocoa prices dropped, the more new projects he authorised. If he had adopted a realistic policy and heeded the warnings of his economic advisers to reduce his industrialisation programme, he could have saved the country from bankruptcy.

Moreover, while Nkrumah urged the ordinary people to tighten their belts, he and his ministers led a life of luxury, rode in huge cars, and erected buildings in the main towns from funds received from corrupt deals and bribes.

Nkrumah's foreign policy from 1960 to 1966, after initial successes, ended in failure. The Congo crisis broke out in July 1960 with the mutiny of the security forces and the secession of Katanga (Shaba) under Moise Tshombe. Nkrumah sent the Ghanaian army to help to end the Katanga secession. Later, with the arrival of the United Nations in the Congo, he placed the Ghana contingent under UN command. He saw the UN as the main means of keeping the great powers out of Africa and of restoring order and peace in the Congo. He was undoubtedly right, and his Congo policy was successful. However, Nkrumah failed in his main foreign policy aim: to create a truly united Africa.

Throughout the period from 1960 to 1966 Nkrumah preached the need for a union government of all Africa and an African high command. He vigorously opposed all the regional groupings, especially the proposed East African Federation, on the grounds that they would be 'just another form of balkanisation'. However, the OAU formed in 1963 fell short of Nkrumah's dream of a true political union with a pan-African parliament of two houses and an African common market. Instead, the OAU was a loose association of states. Nkrumah constantly quarrelled with other African heads of state, the vast majority of whom opposed his strong pan-African policy, and feared Nkrumah's open desire to become president of Africa. By 1965, Nkrumah, by his over-ambition, had become the greatest obstacle to unity in Africa.

In his policy towards the great powers 1960-66, Nkrumah veered more and more towards the East. In December 1960, the Ghana-Soviet Agreement for economic and technical co-operation was signed. This was followed in February 1961 by the visit of the Soviet leader Leonid Brezhnev. Then from July to September 1961 Nkrumah toured the communist countries of eastern Europe and China. However, in order to give the impression that he was still non-aligned, and especially since President Kennedy's final decision on the VRP was still to be made, Nkrumah arranged Queen Elizabeth's visit to Ghana in November. But from then on, Nkrumah turned more and more to the East, especially as he relied increasingly on the Russians for his security. His contacts with America cooled off, especially after the assassination of Kennedy whom Nkrumah admired, and his blaming of the CIA for the second attempt on his life by Ametewee. When Britain refused to use force to crush the white settler rebellion in Rhodesia in 1965, Nkrumah broke off diplomatic relations with Britain and began to talk of sending Ghanaian forces to Rhodesia.

However, the Ghanaian forces stayed at home. On 21 February 1966, Nkrumah left for Vietnam in an attempt to settle the Vietnam question as a member of the Commonwealth peace mission. Three days later, on 24 February, the army seized power in Ghana. The coup was almost bloodless, with no resistance from anyone except the presidential guard in Flagstaff House in Accra. The coup provoked spontaneous jubilation by virtually the entire Ghanaian nation. Why was Nkrumah so easily overthrown and the coup so welcome?

The first obvious reason for the coup was a change in the character and personality of Nkrumah himself. Up to about 1960 he was a humble, selfless, tolerant, frugal and morally upright man. However, from about 1960 onwards he grew steadily intolerant, proud, dictatorial, corrupt and immoral. He began to acquire more and more mistresses and girl-friends on whom he lavished fantastic presents in money, cars and buildings. By the time of the coup his wealth had increased to a total of £2,322,000, whereas his lawful earnings from 1951 to 1966 amounted to only £134,000. While he continued to place funds in foreign banks from 1962, he made the holding of foreign accounts abroad illegal.

Nkrumah's megalomania and power-drunkenness were partly caused by the flattery and personal idolatry he received from his colleagues and advisers, who showered upon him ridiculous titles such as 'Showboy', 'His Messianic Dedication', 'Osagyefo', 'Fount of Honour', etc. His megalomania made him see himself as the man destined by God to become the first president of a united Africa. It also drove him to excessive use of the Preventive Detention Act and the use of spies on his own people. The death in the condemned cell of the highly respected Dr Danquah in February 1965 turned more Ghanaians against Nkrumah than any other single episode. The Ghana Young Pioneers, established in 1960 to replace the Boy Scouts Movement and to train the young in Nkrumaism, became one of the most effective instruments of spying, with children reporting their parents for anti-government utterances.

All classes of Ghana's population turned against Nkrumah. His major mistake was to neglect and threaten the position of the army. The army was alarmed by the expansion of the presidential company, formed in 1960, into a well equipped battalion under Russian officers. They felt that Nkrumah had planned, in the words of Ocran, the commander of the First Brigade, 'gradually to strangle the regular army to death'. By 1965 Nkrumah's private army was well dressed and well equipped with modern weapons while the regular armed forces were going about in 'tattered uniforms, often without boots on their feet', and with rickety equipment and vehicles. Of the armoured vehicles, only 40 per cent were roadworthy by 1966. And Nkrumah was proposing to send the army to Rhodesia in this condition! Another factor that led to the army decision to take over was the sudden forced retirement with no reason given of Major-General Otu, the then Chief of Defence Staff, and his deputy, Lieutenant-General Ankrah, in August 1965.

The police had become demoralised and alarmed when they were disarmed, eight senior officers were dismissed, and two were detained after Ametewee's assassination attempt. Under their commissioner, J. W. K. Harley, they co-ordinated with the army colonels Kotoka and Ocran and Major Afrifa to carry out the coup. The army and police forces were not acting solely for their own benefit, but to help all the people of Ghana. A coup or an assassination were the only means of removing Nkrumah. His departure for Hanoi was not the cause of the coup but a convenient occasion for it.

After the coup Nkrumah went to live in Guinea where Sékou Touré proclaimed him co-president. Nkrumah spent the first year of exile broadcasting futile appeals to the people of Ghana to rebel against the military. Eventually he settled down to writing books and learning French. On 27 April 1972 he died in Rumania where he was receiving treatment for cancer. He was buried first in Guinea but later his body was flown to Ghana for a state funeral at his birthplace.

Thus ended the life and career of Kwame Nkrumah, the man who shook and inspired the world of black people in a way that nobody had done since Marcus Garvey, the man who became the first African politician of world stature in this century. He was a great African and future generations will find him even greater still. But as a Ghanaian leader he was in the end a failure. Obsessed with his dream of African unity he lost touch with reality in Ghana.

## Ghana after Nkrumah: the National Liberation Council 1966-9

The National Liberation Council that began to rule Ghana in February 1966 consisted of eight senior army and police officers, headed by Lieutenant-General Ankrah as chairman. It managed the affairs of the country until it voluntarily handed over to a civilian government on 1 October 1969. It inherited enormous problems.

The NLC's first task was to rescue the economy. In this it was only partly successful. Large loans were negotiated from the International Monetary Fund (IMF) to help to repay debts incurred by the Nkrumah regime. Agreements were also made with western and eastern creditor nations about rescheduling loan repayments. A policy of austerity was adopted, and prestige projects like the Accra-Tema motorway and the Nkrumah Tower were stopped. Ministries were reduced from thirty-two to seventeen. The number of Ghana's foreign missions was reduced by about 40 per cent. State corporations were placed under competent management and redundant labour was sacked. As a result of these and other austerity measures Ghana's trade showed a surplus of ₵ 28.5 million in the first half of 1966.

To relieve the financial pressure on Ghanaians, the first budget of the NLC abolished or reduced the duty on essential food items, reduced prices of motor spirits and inland postage, gave income tax

*Members of the National Liberation Council, February 1966. From left to right: Colonel A. A. Afrifa; Deputy Commissioner of Police B. A. Yacubu; Brigadier A. K. Ocran; Commissioner of Police J. W. K. Harley; Lieutenant-General J. A. Ankrah; Major-General E. K. Kotoka; Deputy Commissioner (C.I.D.) A. K. Deku; Assistant Commissioner of Police J. E. O. Nunoo.*

exemption to the poorer paid, and raised the price of cocoa. Similar policies were continued in 1968 and 1969. By 1969 essential goods were once more in good supply, and inflation had been reduced. A great deal of attention was paid to the development of rural areas, especially water schemes.

However, the NLC's economic measures were very unpopular in some respects. The removal of redundant labour in corporations and ministries increased unemployment. The devaluation of the cedi in 1967, to increase budget receipts more than expenditure, led to a great increase in the cost of imported goods. Above all, the NLC never repudiated the huge debts incurred by Nkrumah's regime, and thus had to concentrate on repaying them to the exclusion of development. Moreover, cocoa prices remained low.

Politically, the NLC was on the whole successful. Its first act was to release all political detainees. Revenge was not taken on CPP supporters in the administration, most of whom kept their jobs. The civil service was not interfered with. Complete freedom of the press was restored. Above all, early steps were taken to return the country to civilian rule, when in September 1966 a constitutional commission was set up under the chairmanship of Chief Justice Edward Akufo-Addo. In 1967 an electoral commission was set up and started to register voters. In the same year fourteen civilians were appointed commissioners to head ministries. Finally, in 1968 the NLC entrusted a 150-member constituent assembly with the task of discussing the draft constitution submitted by the constitutional commission and preparing a final constitution for the Second Republic.

In April 1969 Brigadier Afrifa took over the chairmanship of the NLC from Ankrah who resigned after confessing to collecting money from foreign firms to organise a political party of his own. Afrifa was a strong supporter of an early return of the army to its barracks. He feared that growing personal and regional dissensions within the NLC might lead to another counter-coup like that attempted in April 1967 by soldiers at Ho barracks, when General Kotoka, the driving force of the NLC, was killed. Afrifa believed an early return to civilian rule would maintain and strengthen stability in the country. Therefore, soon after becoming chairman he lifted the ban on party political activities and fixed dates for a general election and the return to civilian government.

## The return to civilian government 1969-72

The elections of August 1969 resulted in a massive victory for the Progress Party (PP) of Dr Kofi Busia, an eminent scholar and well-known opponent of Nkrumah since 1949. The PP won 105 of the 140 seats. Second were the National Alliance of Liberals (NAL) under K. A. Gbedemah, with 29 seats. Though a brilliant organiser and administrator, Gbedemah was severely handicapped by his long

*Dr Kofi Busia, Prime Minister of Ghana from August 1969 to January 1972.*

experience as Nkrumah's finance minister until 1961. The public remembered less his break with Nkrumah than his long service for him, and they tended to identify the NAL with the CPP.

The return to civilian rule and Busia's assumption of the prime ministership in October 1969 show that, in spite of what has generally happened in African states, an orderly transition from military to civilian rule is possible. During the short period that Busia's government remained in power, it achieved a great deal but also made many mistakes. One of its greatest achievements for which it will long be remembered was the effort made to improve the living conditions of the people in the rural areas. This helped to narrow the gap between the urban and rural populations. Within the period from October 1969 to June 1971, the government completed thirty-three water projects to give people good drinking water, and had as many as sixty-four under construction in rural areas. The government launched the Rural Electrification Scheme under which fifty-eight villages and small towns were provided with electricity and street lighting by June 1971. A vigorous housing policy was pursued while sixty-four health posts were completed or were under construction throughout the country. Far more feeder roads were constructed during the short period of the Busia administration than at any period since independence. To enable Ghanaians to gain control over certain aspects of the economy of the country and to promote employment, the government introduced the Ghanaian Business (Promotions) Act and the Aliens Compliance Order. Above all, the government launched well-planned agricultural schemes, especially in the northern and upper regions, to produce more food for the people. The Busia administration also started industries operating again. But the government made some mistakes. The rather inhuman way in which the Aliens Compliance Order was enforced caused a great deal of hardship to the aliens and antagonised countries like Nigeria. Some of his ministers became corrupt and began to acquire property, while others offended Ghanaians by their arrogance, snobbish attitude and by parading about in large new cars. There is no doubt too that the regime intensified ethnicism and regionalism. Busia showed some of the dictatorial tendencies of Nkrumah by arbitrarily dismissing an editor of one of the government-owned daily newspapers and by his 'No court' speech. His attempt to disband the TUC and to harass its leadership caused a great deal of concern. Furthermore, Busia shocked African nationalist feeling throughout the continent by his friendly policy towards South Africa.

He offended the army by cutting its budget in an attempt to solve Ghana's economic problems. His devaluation of the cedi by 44 per cent in December 1971, instead of the 20-25 per cent suggested by experts and foreign creditors, alarmed the nation and was the final straw. Probably, had Busia been given a little more time, he would have corrected some of these mistakes. But he was not. On 13 January 1972, only twenty-seven months after his assumption of office, Busia was overthrown in a second coup organised by Colonel Ignatius Acheampong and was replaced by the National Redemption Council. He died in exile in England in October 1978 and was given a state burial in Ghana. The second coup marked the failure of Ghana's second attempt at parliamentary democracy.

## The National Redemption Council 1972-78

Acheampong's government was received with surprise and scepticism by a majority of Ghanaians. However, during the first two, or even three, years of his term of office, Acheampong surprised even the sceptics by his activities and achievements. The new leader introduced programmes such as self-reliance and Operation Feed Yourself, and certainly brought the cost of food down during that period. He revised the devaluation which helped to reduce the cost of imported goods. He certainly succeeded in generating a sense of dynamism and enthusiasm, especially among university and secondary school students, and he succeeded in calming down some of the people such as the Ewe. He won a great deal of support when he boldly repudiated some of the foreign debts and insisted on and obtained some very favourable terms. But from the fourth year of his rule Acheampong began to lose control of events while economic conditions grew from bad to worse. From 1976 the country began to face acute shortages of imported goods as well as of locally produced foodstuffs despite the Operation Feed Yourself programme. Galloping inflation meant that a tuber of yam, for instance, came to cost the equivalent of the official minimum daily wage. Price controls proved almost impossible to enforce as they ran into opposition from traders.

By the middle of 1978 inflation was raging at about 200 per cent. Some parts of the country were facing starvation and most industries had stopped operating due to a lack of raw materials. Smuggling and hoarding on a massive scale led to severe shortages of essential commodities such as wheat, salt, sugar, soap and spare parts. While

Acheampong's military administrators and civilian advisers became steadily more corrupt and irresponsible he assumed wide dictatorial powers and began to run the country like his own private estate.

In the middle of this serious economic crisis, Acheampong launched his idealistic Union Government proposal, whereby the next constitutional government was to be composed of the army, the police and civilians; it was to be elected, but not on the basis of political parties which were to remain banned. Instead of paying attention to·the economic crisis and inflation which were growing worse daily, Acheampong devoted the manpower and financial resources of the country to sell his unpopular Union Government scheme to Ghanaians and to let them vote on it in a national plebiscite on 30 March 1978.

Opposition to Acheampong, and especially to his Union Government proposal, was universal and was spearheaded first by the students and the professional groups and later by political organisations like the Peoples Movement for Freedom and Justice (PMFJ), the Third Force (TF) and the Front for the Prevention of Dictatorship in Ghana (FPDG). The Association of Recognised Professional Bodies made up of such groups as the Bar Association, the Ghana Association of University Teachers, the Nurses Association and the Ghana Medical Association embarked on strike action to demand the resignation of Acheampong while students in three universities boycotted classes from February 1978 in opposition to Union Government proposals. The referendum of 30 March 1978 revealed the extent of opposition to Union Government. The official voting figures were 1,103,423 in favour of Union Government and 880,255 against it. However, there was general doubt about the accuracy of the figures. The opposition claimed 1,399,330 had voted in favour and 1,600,294 against. Suspicion was aroused when on the day of the referendum High Court Justice Abban, who was the Electoral Commissioner in charge of the referendum, went into hiding after a night-time visit by soldiers. After the referendum the government detained about 300 of its leading civilian opponents. This detention antagonised practically every group in the country including the Christian Council, the Catholic Secretariat and even some traditional rulers. It was not surprising therefore when General Acheampong was forced to resign on 15 July 1978 in a palace coup led by younger officers. They were angered and alarmed by his universal unpopularity, the corruption going on among the senior-officer ranks, the rigging of the referendum and above all the failure to deal with economic difficulties. Acheampong was succeeded as head of the military council by his deputy and Chief of Defence Staff, Lieutenant-General Frederick Akuffo. Ghanaians welcomed this change, but in a calm manner because they wanted to see the departure of all the soldiers and a return to complete civilian rule. The new government, the Supreme Military Council, released all political detainees and confirmed the earlier decision to return the country to civilian rule in July 1979. However, it decided to retain the Union Government idea in a slightly modified form. But even now the idea has had to be abandoned so that the country could be returned to full civilian rule, on the basis of political parties and parliamentary democracy, in July 1979.

## CHAPTER TWENTY-SEVEN

# Nigeria since independence

## Nigeria at independence

The new federal government of Nigeria inherited stable international boundaries but the British left serious unresolved internal problems covering every aspect of the nation's political, social and economic life.

In the political arena there was an uneasy balance between the three regions. They had been held together more by the need for political unity in the achievement of independence than by respect for or acceptance of the constitution. One major region, the West, was effectively excluded from the policy decisions of the federal government. The political experience in the business of government of the elected members of both federal and regional parliaments was short and the voting population had the highest expectations of their leaders' ability to fulfil the promises which they had been told at the election would be fulfilled by the achievement of independence.

It was against this political background that the federal government was expected to undertake rapid modernisation of a country whose people were among the poorest in the world. Over 75 per cent of all Nigerians were illiterate and techniques of production in agriculture, though effective in a peasant society, were centuries old and tied to traditional laws of land tenure. Many people suffered from ill-health and infant mortality was high.

The tools for this modernisation were largely absent. The ability to buy skills and materials from abroad was limited by foreign revenues of only £164 million, earned largely from labour intensive agricultural production of groundnuts, palm oil, cocoa, cotton and timber, with a small mineral contribution from the Plateau. Oil production was in its early stages and was largely exploited by foreign companies who absorbed most of the oil revenue in development costs. The number of Nigerian graduates, particularly in the skilled technical, engineering, scientific and medical fields, represented a tiny fraction of the nations' need and there were only two full universities, under two hundred secondary schools, mainly without sixth forms, and a handful of technical colleges and polytechnics. At the beginning of 1961 few of the main centres were linked by metalled roads, internal air services were intermittent and unreliable, telephone systems, when they worked, linked only the privileged few and electricity and piped water supplies were available only in the larger cities.

Under the economic principles of the British colonial system Nigeria, like other colonies, had until shortly before independence been expected to supply raw materials to Britain and other developed countries and to purchase manufactured goods in exchange. Thus, at independence there was virtually no industrial base in Nigeria. Even the simplest manufactured goods like tinned food, toilet paper and shoes were mainly imported from abroad and less than 2 per cent of the labour force was in industrial employment. This not only wasted the potential skills of Nigerian workers but used valuable foreign exchange for things that could have been made in Nigeria.

It is against this background of the need for development in all areas that the economic and political events of post-independence Nigeria must be considered.

## Political events in 1960–66

At independence the federal government led by Sir Abubakur Tafawa Balewa was composed of a coalition of the mainly Northern NPC and the mainly Eastern NCNC. The Yoruba peoples of the West were largely without a voice in the federal government and the leader of the Action Group, Chief Awolowo, had left regional politics to become leader of the opposition in the federal parliament.

The federal government appears, in the years after independence, to have set out to punish the AG for its tactics in the 1959 election, when the AG won support from the ethnic minorities. In April 1961 the federal government passed a motion to create a Mid-West state around Benin thus taking the non-Yoruba speaking area out of the opposition controlled Western Region. Since neither the NPC nor the NCNC supported new states in the country as a whole their action in creating the Mid-West was certainly, in part, directed against the AG. A year later Awolowo and many of his principal lieutenants were arrested and jailed on charges of conspiracy and a commission of inquiry was set up to probe the Action Group leaders' financial affairs. As a result a large group of Westerners, feeling isolated from the mainstream of policy making, determined to find a way back into the central federal councils.

This group was led by the Western Premier, Chief S. L. Akintola, who, backed by the Sardauna of Sokoto, Premier of the North and leader of the NPC, formed a new party, the Nigerian National Democratic Party (NNDP), in opposition to the Action Group and the NCNC. Akintola was able, through defections from other parties and federal government intervention, to gain control of the Western House of Assembly.

In February 1964 the results of the federal census held in 1962 were announced which showed that of a total population of 55 million well over half were resident in the Northern Region. The political implication of this was to confirm the Northern domination of the Federal House of Assembly and as a result the NCNC Governments of the East and Mid-West rejected the census in its entirety. Since political power at the centre was determined by the voting power in the regions the NCNC and the AG felt compelled to reject the census (which in any case was probably inaccurate) since they greatly feared the potential domination of the whole country by the North. The Eastern and Mid-Western Regions were particularly alarmed since these regions were almost entirely Christian and feared a modern extension of the nineteenth century Muslim jihad from the North.

As a result of the census a realignment of political forces took place. The NCNC in the East and Mid-West allied themselves with the predominantly Western Action Group and the opposition parties of the North to form the United Progressive Grand Alliance (UPGA) for the purpose of fighting the 1964–5 federal election. This group was opposed by the Nigerian National Alliance (NNA) composed of the NPC, the traditional party of the North and the NNDP, the new Western party splintered from the AG and the NCNC.

The election itself has become notorious for its electoral malpractice. The political stakes were so high that all parties indulged in questionable practices to ensure the election of their candidates. The result, though technically securing overall victory for the NNA was considered by many, particularly in the South, to be so dubious that President Azikiwe declined to invite the NNA to form a government. Balewa, always a peace-maker and seeker of compromise, eventually agreed to form a national government involving all parties including UPGA but by this time inter-regional trust and understanding had reached a very low ebb and sporadic violence and unrest, particularly in the West, was making physical control of the country by the police increasingly difficult.

This position became even more serious during the regional elections of 1965. In the West the election was reduced more to a physical battle between the opposing NNDP and UPGA groups than a democratic ballot and it became almost impossible to restore civil order. Balewa was unwilling to declare a state of emergency without full support from his own party leader, the Sardauna of Sokoto, head of the NPC, who was wholeheartedly committed to the NNA alliance and Northern control of the federal government. Lawlessness and violence thus continued, particularly in the West.

## The National Development Plan 1962–68

Despite these political problems the Development Plan announced in April 1962 co-ordinated the development objectives of the four regions of Nigeria. Its aim was to provide as fast as possible, an economic base for overcoming the nation's lack of development, and it provided for capital expenditure of N1,353 million over the six year period. Special emphasis was given in the plan to agricultural development, industry and technical education.

*The Kainji Dam and Lake (above) and nearby power station were built as the first phase of the Niger Dams Project which aimed to provide power for expanding industries.*

347

Compared with the Third Development Plan noted below this plan was of a modest nature allowing just under N4 of capital expenditure for every Nigerian in each year of the plan. Furthermore, much of the development money had to be borrowed from abroad as Nigeria's internal finances at that time, even with growing oil revenues, could provide only a little over half the required sum. It was nevertheless hoped that the plan would provide a basis for future development and that growth in the economy would proceed faster than growth in population, thus helping to raise the standard of living of all citizens.

In the event fulfilment of the plan was overtaken by political events but much useful work was done, particularly in building the Kainji hydro-electric project, in the extension of metalled roads and in building new schools and hospitals. The plan failed however, to increase agricultural production.

## Coup d'état 1966

Late in 1965 and early in 1966 there were rumours that the army was to be used to restore civil order but before this could happen the army itself determined to impose a solution and on 15th January 1966 groups of middle ranking army officers attempted a coup d'état. The mutineers secured control in Kaduna and Ibadan, killing the Sardauna of Sokoto and Chief S. L. Akintola, Premier of the West. In Lagos the mutineers succeeded in assassinating Sir Abubakar Tafawa Balewa, the Federal Prime Minister and Chief Okotie-Eboh, Finance Minister, but failed to take over the federal government machinery. However, the survivors of the federal cabinet felt compelled to hand over power to the head of the army, Major-General J. T. A. Aguiyi-Ironsi. The mutineers, admitting their failure, surrendered to Ironsi and the 'loyal' section of the army and were placed in protective custody. Thus, while the coup was successful in establishing the army's political authority, power did not fall into the hands of the officers, led by Major Nzeogwu in the North and Major Ifeajuna in Lagos, who had planned the coup.

Although the Nigerian people welcomed the army as an alternative to the discredited political regime there was considerable unease. First, neither the Igbo political leadership nor, the Igbo military leadership had been touched. Second, Tafawa, unlike the Sardauna and Akintola, had not resisted arrest, and therefore his assassination was interpreted as deliberate despite the mutineers claim that they had sought to avoid bloodshed. Third, the new head of state was

*Yakubu Gowon, Nigerian army chief under Ironsi, who assumed control of the army and government on 1 August 1966.*

surrounding himself with Igbo advisors.

In May 1966 General Ironsi decreeed the abolition of the federal structure of the government which was widely interpreted in the North as an attempt to bring that region under Southern control. As a result there was a wave of killings of Southerners resident in the North and later, in July, a mutiny within the army which resulted in the death of General Ironsi and numerous other officers of Southern origin. On 1st August 1966 Lieutenant Colonel Yakubu Gowon, Nigerian army chief of staff under Ironsi, a Northerner of Plateau origin and a Christian, assumed control of the army and of the government.

## Causes of the civil war

The Nigerian civil or 'Biafran' war has been presented, popularly, as being rooted in ethnic and religious distrust between the three major groups; Yoruba, Igbo and Hausa/Fulani. While it is hardly surprising that such distrust should exist in some measure among people of such widely divergent cultures and religions it is important to look further for the causes of the war. Many countries have similar or even more serious problems but manage to live in harmony. The ability to do so depends on having a satisfactory constitutional base, the political flexibility to make it work and an adequate economic base from which to govern. Nigeria had none of these. The federal constitution, left by the British, gave an absolute majority to one region, the political parties had become regionally rather than nationally based and therefore self-interested and in a generally poor agricultural economy the one really valuable asset for future development, oil, lay in only one part of the country. It was thus inevitable that underlying passions should be awakened and, once the army had entered the political arena, that the final settlement should be through military confrontation.

Upon assumption of power Gowon released Awolowo and restored the federal form of government. He also began planning for a conference to review the constitution. However, these moves did not quieten fears in the North, and the number of attacks on Southerners led to many of them fleeing to their home areas. As more and more refugees arrived in towns such as Port Harcourt and Onitsha their stories encouraged reprisal attacks on Northerners, which in turn resulted in an even fiercer wave of attacks on Southerners in the North, culminating in a mutiny by troops in Kano, who carried out a terrifying massacre of civilians.

These acts received no official encouragement, either from the military governor of the East, Odumegwu Ojukwu, nor from the governor of the North, Hassan Katsina, but the situation was out of their control. Many thousands of Southerners, mostly from the Eastern Region, were killed and finally most of those remaining fled.

These events were an important factor in the creation of Biafra which brought the country nearer to the possibility of civil war. As a result of them the Eastern Region withdrew from the constitutional conference in Lagos, and demanded sovereign rights for the Regions. Major concessions on this issue were made by Gowon at a meeting in Aburi, Ghana, Ojukwu having refused to come to Lagos through fears for his safety. However, differences of interpretation over the agreement caused its failure.

The stage was now set for secession, which drew much closer in May 1967 when General Gowon decreed the division of Nigeria into twelve states. One aim of this move was to reduce the power of the majority over the minority ethnic groups, by creating states in which the minority groups held power. It was a policy which many Igbo had ardently advocated. However, the Igbo's enthusiasm for a structure which would not leave them with access to the oil in the Delta and coastal waters had diminished and they interpreted the move as directed against themselves. There can be little doubt that the presence of oil not only made the Easterners feel that they would be

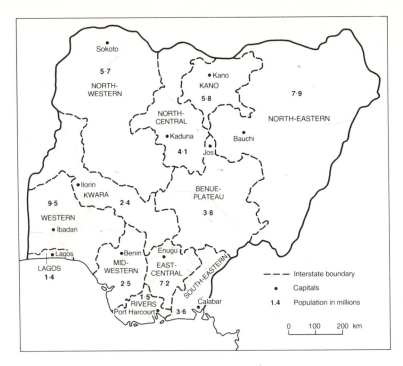

39  *The twelve Nigerian states created in 1967.*

economically secure if they did secede, but actually encouraged them to do so, as they saw a prosperous future for the region if the oil revenues did not have to be shared with the rest of Nigeria.

### The course of the war

The proclamation of the 'Republic of Biafra' was made soon after, on the 30th May 1967. For a time the possibility existed of the complete break-up of the federation, as Awolowo had claimed that, if the Eastern Region was allowed to secede, the West should be given the opportunity to follow them. However, this possibility faded with the overthrow of the government of the Mid-West by the 'Biafrans', which was followed by an invasion of the West, the climax of which was intended to be the capture of Ibadan and Lagos. 'Biafran' troops penetrated as far as Ore in the Western Region, where a fierce battle took place. The 'Biafrans' were eventually defeated, and had to withdraw to the Mid-West. As a result of this invasion, the resolve of the people of the Western Region to stay within the federation and conclude the war in partnership with the rest of Nigeria was greatly strengthened.

Building on the success of the battle of Ore, Gowon ordered full-scale military operations against 'Biafra'. Attacks were mounted from the West and the North which recaptured Benin and then struck as far as Asaba on the Niger, other armies moved in from the North to capture Nsukka and Enugu and advance South to Ikom. Soon after, Calabar was captured by a combined naval and military operation and by May 1968, when Port Harcourt was taken, the 'Biafrans' were enclosed, with no access to the sea, within the heart of Igboland. Now eleven of Nigeria's twelve states were able to function within the federal framework.

For the next eighteen months the Biafrans continued determinedly to resist the advance of the federal armies, partly because they were convinced by their leaders that they would all be killed if they were defeated, and partly because they were given aid in the form of finance and arms by sympathisers from outside the country, who had been persuaded by a very well organised propaganda campaign that the 'Biafran' cause was just. Some states, such as Tanzania and Ivory Coast, even granted recognition to 'Biafra', and this encouraged the belief that, if they fought on despite the increasing suffering of the people, the whole world would come to see that they were in the right. However, in the end the much greater strength of the federal armies won the day, and in January 1970 the 'Biafran' army surrendered and Ojukwu fled to the Ivory Coast. After the surrender there was no genocide, instead a relief programme was mounted by the federal government. Only a few of the Biafran officers were imprisoned, and

*Odumegwu Ojukwu (right) with Philip Effiong, his deputy, who negotiated the end of the war following Ojukwu's flight from 'Biafra' in January 1970.*

all were later released. Many Igbos were reabsorbed into the federal administration, some into the jobs they had held before the war and gradually many of those who had left the North at the time of the massacres returned to their old homes. Gowon's policy of reconciling the defeated secessionists with the rest of the nation was one of his greatest achievements, and left Nigeria in many ways more united than it had been before the war.

## Post war reconstruction and development

Although the civil war placed heavy burdens on the national economy and the internal economy of the 'Biafra' area was temporarily destroyed, the natural resilience of the Nigerian farmers and increasing revenues from oil production made rapid recovery possible.

Following on from the First National Development Plan, two major National Development Plans covering the periods 1970–74 and 1975–80 were prepared by the Federal Military Government. Both these plans, particularly the Third Development Plan, were aimed at accelerating both economic and social development. The Third Development Plan provided for total expenditure of N32 billion (N32,000,000,000) or around N500 per every Nigerian during the period of the plan. This huge sum, more than six times the amount provided in the Second Plan, was all to be found from Nigerian resources, principally from oil revenue, and was to provide development which would result in the income of every Nigerian citizen rising from an average of N295 per year to over N400 in the plan period and to over N700 in the 1990s. The plan, as in previous plans, gave priority to agricultural development of crops and livestock farming, of forest resources and of fisheries. With basic agricultural development, the Third Plan made provision for the transformation of the country's poor communications by road, rail and air and of telecommunications. It promised implementation of universal free primary education and enhanced secondary and higher education systems to meet the nation's needs for skilled manpower. Great improvements in the health and social welfare facilities of the people together with major changes in the structure of the Nigerian manufacturing, construction and extractive industries were planned as well as a modernised defence force that would provide protection for the nation and would ensure that Nigeria's voice was respected internationally.

*This inner ring road was built to relieve traffic congestion in Lagos and was completed in 1978.*

## Oil

While the Nigerian economic planners laid great stress on the development of traditional sources of wealth and on the creation of new industries the foundation of their plans, and by far the largest source of investment funds, lay in revenues from the nation's oil resources. The tenfold increase in planned investment in the Third Development Plan was almost entirely the result of the trebling of the price of crude oil following the meetings of the Organisation of Petroleum Exporting Countries (OPEC), of which Nigeria had become a full member, late in 1973. The value of Nigeria's oil exports rose immediately from N2 billion to N5.5 billion contributing some 90 per cent of the total revenue.

Use of the oil revenues for Nigerian economic development could only be ensured, however, through the assertion of government control over the international companies who were extracting the oil and exporting it to overseas markets. The 1972 agreements with the companies gave the government 55 per cent of their profits, and in June 1973 the government took a 35 per cent share of the ownership of Shell/BP, increasing this to 55 per cent a year later, when similar shares were also taken in other key companies. These shares were held by the Nigerian National Oil Corporation (NNOC), which by 1975 was also producing its own oil. By the late 1970s, therefore, a high proportion of the profits, as well as policy decisions about the price of oil and the rate of its extraction were securely in the hands of the Nigerian Government.

Although the price of oil continued to rise after 1973, to a price of $30 a barrel by 1979, the income obtained from oil by the government did not increase at the same rate. Because the demand for oil in the world dropped between 1975 and 1978, and because of the developments of new oil fields, such as those in Alaska and the North Sea, Nigeria had to cut its production, and this affected the rate at which it was possible to carry out the Third Development Plan. After the middle of 1978, however, output steadily increased again and by 1979 with further price increases, Nigeria's oil revenues amounted to over N9.0 billion per annum.

*Port Harcourt oil refinery.*

### Post war political developments

After the reconciliation which followed the civil war the Federal Military Government turned to two major objectives, the development of the country and a return to democratic rule.

With the release of vast sums earned from oil and the application of this money to nation building both employment on development projects and the growth in general business resulting from the new wealth gave Nigerians economic opportunities on a scale never previously experienced. While there was much purposeful development with new buildings, institutions and businesses springing up in both the public and private sectors of the economy there was also

355

much waste and as a result of inexperience in dealing with economic growth on a very large scale, much inefficiency and unhealthy corruption among many people in positions of authority. This resulted, inevitably, in a high rate of inflation which meant that although people were earning much more particularly after the Udoji Commission on public service pay in 1974 prices rose even faster than salaries.

The credibility and authority of General Gowon's government was further undermined by its inability to deal with problems largely created through the tremendous post war economic expansion. Such problems were periodic outbursts of lawlessness, especially in the cities, despite public execution of the criminals; the breakdown in internal and external telephone systems; massive traffic jams in all the cities; frequent and persistent breakdowns of electricity and water supplies; frustration induced by a bureaucracy unequipped to deal with a greatly increased volume of work and congestion in the docks culminating in the 'cement crisis' of 1975. The ports became blocked by hundreds of ships bringing cement from all over the world and foreign and local racketeers were able to make fortunes without even delivering their goods while imports, essential to economic development and the welfare of the people, lay idle on the ships.

Having already announced, late in 1974, the postponement of the return to civilian rule in order to allow time for the Federal Military Government to eliminate corruption, combat inflation and improve the economic and social life of the country, Gowon's failure to make the desired improvements led to dissatisfaction with the military regime. In July 1975, while Gowon was at an OAU summit conference in Uganda, senior army officers, led by Brigadier-General Murtala Mohammed, took over in a bloodless coup.

General Mohammed, who had been commissioner of communication in Gowon's government, set about solving the problems which had caused Gowon's downfall. Civil servants and military officers accused of inefficiency and corrupt practice were dismissed, efforts were made to resolve the traffic service and other public service problems of Lagos and the programme for the new capital at Abuja was accelerated. To combat ethnicism and provide a more secure political future the number of states was increased from twelve to nineteen and, most important, Mohammed promised a return to civilian rule in 1979. It was a severe shock to the whole of Nigeria when Mohammed was murdered in February 1976 during an unsuccessful and apparently aimless attempted coup led by Colonel B. S. Dimka who was later executed. Although it was widely held that

*Brigadier-General Murtala Moham-med, who became Head of the Federal Military Government in July 1975. He was tragically assassinated on 13 February 1976.*

*Lieutenant-General Olusegun Ob-asanjo, who continued Mohammed's programme of constitutional reform and return to civilian government.*

General Gowon was implicated in the attempted coup firm evidence was not made public. Mohammed was succeeded as Head of State by General Olusegun Obasanjo who pledged himself to complete Mohammed's reforms and to return the country to civilian rule as planned.

## Nigeria and the outside world

During the civil war, Nigeria's international diplomacy was aimed chiefly at winning support for her cause from the major powers and other African countries, and in this she was largely successful. In the immediate post war years, despite her increasing wealth, Nigeria continued to play a relatively low-key role on the international stage. However, her initiative in the establishment of the Economic Community of West African States (ECOWAS), which was designed to create greater political and economic co-operation among both French and English speaking countries in West Africa, confirmed her position as an important power in the region. Her growing influence was highlighted in 1969 when she intervened in Chad to bring together the combatants for peace negotiations to end a bitter civil war.

Nigeria also emerged into a position of leadership in the Organisation of African Unity in the second half of the seventies, and her support for Agostinho Neto's MPLA in Angola during the civil war there after the departure of the Portuguese was influential in securing the OAU's backing for the MPLA, the eventual victors in the conflict. Nigeria continued, however, to uphold the OAU principle that no African nation should intervene directly in the internal affairs of another nation, and opposed the Tanzanian invasion of Uganda in 1979 on these grounds.

Nigeria's new wealth also increased her political strength in the wider world. She became a leading figure among those countries in OPEC which sought to obtain the highest possible price for their oil, and she showed how far she was prepared to use her strength when in 1979 the British Government seemed likely to recognise the government of Bishop Muzorewa in Zimbabwe. The assets of the BP oil company in Nigeria were nationalised, a ban was temporarily placed on the award of contracts to British firms, and wider commercial sanctions were threatened. These moves helped to ensure that Britain eventually took the decision to try to bring about a solution to the Zimbabwe conflict which was acceptable to the African nations.

### Return to civilian rule

A constituent assembly began considering a draft constitution written by a committee headed by Chief Rotimi Williams, an eminent lawyer, in October 1977. The assembly consisted of members elected by local councillors throughout Nigeria, together with members representing special interests such as trade unions, students, commerce and industry. There was much discussion in the assembly over whether the constitution should give the president executive power on the United States model, or whether there should be a figurehead president with a prime minister at the head of government. There were also some who felt that only one party should be allowed, while others argued that there should be a multi-party system. At one point the assembly almost broke up in disagreement over the issue of whether the Muslim Sharia courts should be given equal status with the ordinary courts, but in the end a compromise was achieved on this issue and the assembly produced its constitutional recommendations, which with minor changes were approved by the government. This gave the president executive power, and a senate and house of representatives legislative powers, with executive and legislative power at state level in the hands of governors and houses of assembly. By making sure that power was divided between the federal government and the nineteen states, the new constitution aimed to ensure the continuance of Nigeria's federal system on a more stable political base.

Only those parties which were able to prove to the Federal Electoral Commision that they had organisations in at least thirteen out of the nineteen states were permitted to register and stand for election. The aim of this provision was to make sure that none of the parties was exclusively based on one region of the country. Five parties were given approval to fight the elections in 1979. They were the Nigerian Peoples Congress, the Nigerian Peoples Party, the Great Nigeria Peoples Party, the Peoples Redemption Party and the United Party of Nigeria. Although all these parties won support throughout Nigeria, each of them had their main strength in one of the old regions—the NPC, GNPP and PRP in the North, the NPP in the East and UPN in the West—and, although there were differences of emphasis between them, all believed in maintaining the existing social and economic system in Nigeria.

*Alhaji Shehu Shagari, who took office as the first President of the Second Republic in October 1979.*

359

Five elections took place in July and August 1979—for the Senate, House of Representatives, State House of Assembly and Governors, and for the Presidency. In all the national elections the NPC obtained more votes than its rivals, and its leader Alhaji Shehu Shagari, was elected President, ahead of Obafemi Awolowo of UPN, and Nnamdi Azikiwe, of NPP. He took office as the first President of the Second Republic in October 1979.

## CHAPTER TWENTY-EIGHT

# Sierra Leone, Gambia and Liberia

## Triumph of the protectorate—Sierra Leone 1946-64

The Sierra Leone constitution of 1924 provided for three elected Creoles from the colony, normally National Congress supporters, and three nominated paramount chiefs, two Mende and one Temne, from the protectorate. As elsewhere in British West Africa during the Second World War, loyalty to the empire was combined with a desire for increased autonomy when the war was over.

In 1947 the British proposed that the central legislative council be given an unofficial majority and an African majority of 14 to 10, of whom four were to be elected from the colony and nine by the recently-created protectorate assembly. Creoles were led into a futile opposition to protectorate predominance in 1950 by a revived National Congress, under the name National Council, which pro-claimed, 'We object to *foreigners* predominating in *our* legislative council' (authors' italics). In 1952 the Council leader, Bankole-Bright, moved a motion in the legislative council asking for separate independence for the colony. Creole stubbornness produced solidar-ity in the protectorate. Milton Margai, the Mende leader, lashed out at the Creoles. 'Our forefathers, I regret very much to say . . . [gave] shelter to a handful of foreigners who have no will to co-operate with us and imagine themselves to be our superiors because they are aping the western mode of living, and have never breathed the true spirit of independence.'

Opposition to Creole ambitions brought diverse elements—the chiefly and professional elite, the Mende and Temne—together to form the Sierra Leone Peoples' Party (SLPP) in 1951. Through chiefly pressure, Margai was chosen as leader. Chiefs were also strongly represented in the party executive. Wisely Margai left the door open for reconciliation with the colony by appointing two Creoles to the party executive.

In 1951 the British introduced a new constitution with an African majority in both the legislative and executive councils. In an election the same year the SLPP won six seats against five for the National Council. By allying with the chiefs and independents it controlled 41 seats against nine for the opposition. The connection between the SLPP and the chiefly elite was striking. In 1957, 72 per cent of all its candidates for election had chiefly kinship ties. The chiefs and their local governments acted as agencies for recruiting party support.

By 1960 Creole solidarity had been broken. Five Creole legislators supported the SLPP government and four sat in opposition. The Creoles had been 'submerged' and were being governed by men from the protectorate for whom, only a decade earlier, they had displayed so much contempt. However, the Creoles were only submerged politically. Thanks to their command of Western education and to their superior position in commerce, the Creoles played a much greater part in Sierra Leone public life than their small numbers warranted. In 1960 the largest national groups held approximately the number of legislative seats that their population percentage allowed. The Mende, with 31 per cent of the total population of Sierra Leone, held 35 seats in the legislature; the Temne, 30 per cent of the population, 23 per cent of the seats; and the Kono, 5 per cent of the population, 6 per cent of the seats. However, the Creoles alone were unique in holding 22 per cent of the seats while comprising only two per cent of the population. In addition Creoles predominated in the civil service, the corporations and in educational institutions such as Fourah Bay College. Thus while the nineteenth may have been the great century of Creole achievement, the gains of the century were still making themselves felt in modern times. Despite their fears, Creoles were about to play a greater role 'submerged' in an African-controlled state than they had ever done from their 'privileged' position in colonial Sierra Leone.

Sierra Leone achieved independence in 1961 but the achievement was marred by growing political tension between the SLPP and the new All Peoples Congress (APC) which was formed in 1960 by Siaka Stevens, a former trade unionist and a Limba of part-Mende ancestry. The APC appealed to the youths, clerks and teachers of the towns who disliked the chiefly connections of the SLPP, to Temne, and other ethnic groups who resented what they believed was Mende domination of the government party, and to the lower- and middle-class Creoles of Freetown who opposed the extravagant consumption and high life of the political class. The APC also had the approval of the intellectuals who were concerned about the economic chaos into which the SLPP appeared to be leading the country accompanied by open and rampant corruption, bribery and

*Sir Milton Margai arriving at Marlborough House, London, to attend the Commonwealth Conference, 1962.*

nepotism. Shortly after its formation the APC won the Freetown municipal elections. However, in 1960-1, there was political violence by thugs from both parties, as Stevens unsuccessfully agitated for elections before independence. He was arrested and detained.

In the 1962 elections the APC won 20 seats and the SLPP 29. As in previous elections Milton Margai remained in power by combining with the independents and twelve chiefs in the legislature to control 54 of the total 74 seats. The distribution of the APC votes indicated the pattern for the future. Their votes were nation-wide except for Mende areas.

In 1964 Sir Milton Margai died. He was widely respected and held the aura of the man who had achieved independence. However, his brother and successor, Albert, appeared unwilling and ill-equipped to handle the new nation's growing problems. Indeed, Albert Margai's leadership promoted the growth of the opposition.

Between 1964 and 1967 Albert Margai's government destroyed the relatively harmonious country inherited from Sir Milton. The most noticeable, if not the most important, factor was the extravagant living of the political class despite the worsening economic situation, which could not be maintained solely from legitimate salaries. Unlike his brother, Albert Margai did not himself set an example, but enjoyed ostentatious display of luxury.

Furthermore, Albert Margai's tendency to autocracy aroused fear and hostility. For example, he had expanded the Freetown City

Council by three appointed members to deprive the APC of its elected majority and give control to the SLPP. Despite Nkrumah's overthrow and the exposures of the one-party state in Ghana, Albert continued to advocate it. The proposed abolition of appeals to the Privy Council aroused fears for the independence of the judiciary, particularly since Albert had appointed his own strong supporter, Gershon Collier, as chief justice.

The greatest failure of the SLPP government under Albert Margai was the way it allowed ethnic antagonisms to develop in Sierra Leone. Even more than the corruption of the political and chiefly classes, the lack of sound economic planning or the tendency to autocracy, this discredited the party and led to the election crisis and army takeover in 1967. Sierra Leone had not experienced the same degree of ethnic antagonism which dominated Nigeria. For example, there had been a considerable degree of inter-ethnic marriage. In addition, Krio, the mother tongue of the Creoles, was used as a *linga franca* throughout the country. Yet Albert Margai's rule led to increased ethnic tensions.

Albert Margai inherited a party and government from Sir Milton which was probably as much Sierra Leonean in composition as possible in a democratic society. But under Albert the party became first a Mende-Creole coalition and then by 1967 a Mende party. Albert's succession to the leadership in 1964 was done behind the back of the Northern members. It caused a revolt of 21 of the 58 SLPP members of the House plus the resignation of four non-Mende cabinet ministers. This fissure was partially healed but Northerners had hoped that Sir Milton's successor might be non-Mende. All the more reason for Albert to have wooed the non-Mende by important concessions, but he failed to do this.

## The people, the politicians and the army

The 1967 election for the Sierra Leonean House of Representatives was to be in two stages. On 17 March the people were to elect 66 ordinary members and on 21 March the paramount chiefs were to select 12 of their own number, one to represent each of the twelve districts. Sensing their declining popularity the SLPP instructed civil servants and the electoral officers that it was their duty to assure its return to office in the forthcoming poll.

The election results confirmed the growing ethnic tensions. The North and the old colony (Western area) gave all their seats to the

APC, except those uncontested. In 1962 the SLPP could rightly claim to represent Sierra Leone since it held seats in every district except two and among all ethnic groups except the Kono. Following the 1967 election the SLPP had become a Mende party. The final results were SLPP 28, APC 32 and independents six. Tension mounted as the government delayed publication of the results, and then claimed quite dishonestly that the six independents had declared for the governing party. The government news media were thus claiming 34 seats to 32 for the opposition. The APC supporters began to prepare to resort to physical violence. A situation of impending civil war rapidly built up.

The governor-general, wishing to stabilise the situation, quickly called on Margai and Stevens to form a coalition. When this failed and the chiefs were still voting, the governor-general, with the sympathy of the Creole commissioner of police, William Leigh, swore in Siaka Stevens of the APC as prime minister. The commander of the armed forces, David Lansana (a Mende), believing the governor-general had acted unconstitutionally because he had not waited for the advice of the elected chiefs, declared martial law and placed the governor-general and Stevens under house arrest. Ten of the twelve elected paramounts declared support for the SLPP and Lansana appeared to be moving towards the reinstatement of Margai. To forestall civil war, the officers of the army, led by Major Charles Blake, arrested Lansana and placed Margai along with Stevens and the governor-general under restriction. The officers set up a National Council composed of two military or police representatives from each of the provinces and the Western Area, headed by Lieutenant-Colonel Juxon-Smith.

All parties in the post-election drama justified their actions by their interpretation of the constitution. The governor-general appointed Stevens who enjoyed majority popular support. The governor-general believed that the chiefs, who did not stand for election under party labels, were expected to support the government chosen by the people. On the other hand, Lansana, supported later by Juxon-Smith and legal opinion, argued that the chiefly members had as much right to political choice as the ordinary members of the House of Representatives. Since the governor-general and the commissioner of police were Creole, it was inevitable that the Mende should believe that they were partial to the APC, the party the Creoles now favoured. On the other hand, Lansana moved to defend legality because he was as determined as Albert Margai that the SLPP must win. Lansana miscalculated that the army would not move against him. In the circumstances the action of the officers—the most completely illegal of all—was the most sensible. Since they were politically divided, a move to support either party would have split the army on the Nigerian pattern. To abolish the political establishment, organise a neutral government and investigate the election was the wisest alternative.

The officers took early and firm measures to suppress inter-ethnic tensions. They proscribed the use of a man's ethnic affiliations on government documents or in the press. The National Reformation Council was carefully balanced with two representatives from each of the four administrative divisions of the country and, as in the Gowon government of Nigeria, the minor ethnic groups were given stronger representation.

However easy it appeared to turn over power to Siaka Stevens and the APC, Juxon-Smith's government hesitated to do so. Juxon-Smith himself appeared anxious to prolong his period of power. In fact he planned in secret to detain all APC leaders and announce the continuation of army rule. This was forestalled by an army mutiny in April 1968 which jailed all senior officers and called back Colonel John Bangura and Lieutenant-Colonel Ambrose Genda from Guinea and Liberia respectively. With great swiftness members of parliament were assembled and Siaka Stevens chosen as premier.

As prime minister at last, Stevens called new elections in March 1969, in which the APC obtained a larger majority. Stevens' rule of

*Siaka Stevens, Prime Minister of Sierra Leone (1968-71) and subsequently President of the Republic.*

Sierra Leone has been marked by a move to the left, and violent but unsuccessful challenges to his government. He established state control over much of the diamond mining industry, and arranged for aid from the Soviet Union as well as the West. In 1970 the opposition United Democratic Party (UDP) alleged corruption and diamond smuggling by members of the government, and there was violence by thugs from both the APC and the UDP. In September Stevens declared a state of emergency, arrested UDP leaders and some soldiers, and had them tried on charges of plotting to overthrow the government. In 1971 there were two attempts to assassinate Stevens and an unsuccessful attempt to carry out a coup. In March Guinean forces were sent to Sierra Leone, at the prime minister's request, to forestall a possible coup. In April 1971 Sierra Leone became a Republic with Stevens as president, and he was re-elected in 1976.

## Political re-awakening in Gambia 1946-65

In the inter-war period Gambian political activities centred on the Creole, Edward Small, who organised the Gambia branch of the National Congress of British West Africa.

The constitution of 1954 provided for a legislative council including seven elected from the colony, seven from the protectorate and seven by the chiefs. A new constitution in 1959 increased the protectorate constituencies to twelve.

Until 1960 politics were dominated by the Creoles and Wolofs of Bathurst and particularly by the old-timers, the Rev. J. C. Faye (Wolof-Serer) and I. M. Garba-Jahumpa (Wolof). In 1951 Faye organised the Democratic Party and in 1952 Garba-Jahumpa organised the Muslim Congress Party. These basically religious parties were defeated in the 1960 election when the United Party (UP) of Pierre N'Jie won five of the seven colony seats.

The protectorate took longer to awake politically, but was brought into the mainstream of Gambian political life by the People's Progressive Party (PPP) formed by a Mandinka labour contractor, Sanjali Bojane, in 1959. Leadership soon passed to Dawda Jawara, a Christian Mandinka and son of a Muslim trader. Jawara was assisted by two prominent Muslim Mandinka, Sherif Sekuba Sesay and Sherif Mustafa Dibba. These men later became the top three in the post-independence movement of the Gambia. They campaigned on a PPP programme of hostility to the chiefs, the long Bathurst neglect of the protectorate, and the ethnic pride of the Mandinka. In two ways the party differed from Milton Margai's Sierra Leone Peoples' Party. The PPP was anti-chief and it was built on a narrow ethnic base. Moreover, the SLPP shrank into a Mende party after 1964, whereas the PPP, particularly after 1962, broadened out from its narrow Mandinka beginnings.

In the 1960 election the results were: PPP eight, United Party six and chiefs eight. The chiefs, determined to exclude the PPP from power, chose to support the colony-based United Party, and the governor called N'Jie as chief minister. This arrangement clearly subverted the people's choice, so constitutional conferences were held in Bathurst and London. Under the self-government constitution of 1962 the colony was to have eight seats, the protectorate 25, and the chiefs four.

The 1962 election began to show a division on ethnic lines. The PPP won 17 seats in the protectorate, drawing particular support from the Mandinka, and one seat in the colony. The United Party took five seats in the colony and eight in the protectorate, largely in non-Mandinka areas. The United Party, for example, won four of the six contested seats among the Fulani and Serahuli along the upper river. However, there was little inter-ethnic tension or tension between the colony and the protectorate. Following the election, the United Party could not control the House of Representatives even with the backing of the chiefs. Jawara became Prime Minister, Sesay finance minister and Dibba minister of local government; the three

*Sir Dawda Jawara.*

strong men thus held the three most important cabinet posts. After the election a number of United Party supporters defected to the PPP and widened the government's ethnic base; the Fula, Camara, became minister of education in 1963, the Wolof, Kebba Kah, became minister of health in 1965 and the Wolof, Bandara N'Jie, became foreign affairs minister after independence.

The Gambia secured internal self-government in October 1963, and independence on 18 February 1965. In the general election of May 1966 the PPP government confirmed its popularity by winning 24 of the 32 seats.

Once the march to independence got under way, the issue of association with Senegal was raised because of the Gambia's precarious economic situation. Association was popular with the Wolof because they were the dominant people of Senegal and because it would permit a greater flow of imports and exports through Banjul, by which its Wolof population would gain. It was once believed that Pierre N'Jie would have moved quicker towards association not only because he was a Wolof but also because his cousin Valdiodio N'Diaye was minister of the interior and Senegal's third most important politician. When Pierre N'jie was chief minister, a joint Senegalese-Gambian ministerial committee was set up which asked the United Nations to study Senegambian association. However, once in opposition, Pierre N'jie vigorously opposed closer association possibly because he feared the PPP might commit the Gambia to becoming an eighth region of Senegal.

In 1964 the UN Commission rejected integration as unrealistic and recommended closer association in easy stages. By this time, Jawara's predominantly Mandinka government was in power in Banjul. It was cautious about association. The Mandinka formed a very minor ethnic group, in many ways an 'outside group', in Senegal. On Gambian independence day, the Gambia and Senegal signed three agreements on defence, common foreign representation and co-operation on the development of the Gambia River. Later an office was set up in Bathurst which was the secretariat of the Senegalo-Gambian International Committee to handle all matters regarding association. Senegal later signed an agreement with Mauritania, Mali and Guinea to develop the Senegal River, which will probably leave the Gambia River undeveloped for the foreseeable future.

The Gambia had certain advantages at independence. There was no Christian-Muslim division following ethnic lines as between the Mende and Temne in Sierra Leone. Islam tended to blur ethnic differences and Gambia resembled Senegal, where ethnic tension was less, rather than its English-speaking West African neighbours. Because of the Islamic revolutions and the peculiar nature of British 'indirect rule', the chiefly elite, frequently a focus of ethnic loyalty, had less influence than in Sierra Leone or Nigeria. Nor have Gambian politicians steeped themselves in corruption and luxurious living. And of course, the Gambia had no army.

Another significant factor was that neither the small intelligentsia nor organised labour became deeply involved in politics. The intelligentsia was small in number, but in having remained detached from politics, it was unique in English-speaking West Africa. In many states the most sophisticated of the intellectuals marshalled the ethnic battalions. It was they, with their pretensions to superior knowledge and insight, who claimed to see threats of domination from other ethnic groups. It was they who plotted for their own ethnic domination as in Nigeria under the slogan of demanding a fair share of the 'national cake'. The disease of seeing the government as a national cake over which the ethnic groups did battle has not yet spread to the Gambia.


## Liberia since 1944—national unification

The presidency of William Tubman, from 1944 to his death in 1971, created a new era in Liberia, an era of confidence and improved harmony among various sections of the population.

The Tubman administration overcame the long-standing financial problem which arose after the collapse of the merchant princes in the nineteenth century. Government revenue expanded from less than one million dollars when Tubman came to power to over twenty million in 1959. This was the result of the Open Door economic policy which encouraged investment in Liberia by foreign capitalists. When Tubman came to power there was one foreign investor, the Firestone Rubber Company, which had controlled the economy since 1925. By 1960 there were 25, and by 1966, 38. The Open Door created a surge of economic activity—artificial harbours at Monrovia and other ports, two railways into the interior, a growing road network, large iron mining operations at Bomi Hills, in the Nimba mountains and in other areas, and light manufacturing industries producing cement and coffee. In addition, while Firestone still produced 87 per cent of the rubber exported, the number of small Liberian producers grew.

The new development had uneven effects, shifting economic

*The inauguration of President William Tubman of Liberia, 1944. Tubman remained in office until his death in 1971.*

activity away from the Kru coast, and the Americo-Liberian settlements there, to the interior along the Monrovia-Ganta highway. This left the Kru area more depressed than before the Second World War and would ultimately help to shift political power from the coast to the interior in the same way that roads and railways did in Sierra Leone and Nigeria.

There has also been economic diversification. Iron ore reduced dependence on rubber. Capital no longer came solely from America and American trade declined as a proportion of the total. In 1950 the United States took 90 per cent of Liberia's exports and provided 71 per cent of her imports. A decade later these figures had dropped to 61 and 47 per cent respectively. Liberia's economic and political development was now more closely paralleling that of other West African states. More adequate revenues had brought Liberia out of the shadow of American economic colonialism just as the rest of West Africa was emerging from colonial status. No longer was Liberia associated with debts and loans.

Adequate revenue to provide for an expanding bureaucracy had given the president an opportunity to advance the African new elite into state positions at a rate never before contemplated. Some had even been promoted into those sacred precincts of the old oligarchy, the supreme court and the cabinet. This enrichment of the Americo-Liberian community by African blood and brains was beginning to close the old cleavage between the descendants of the settlers and the indigenous people. No longer did an African have to hide his origin, change his name and live in fear of exposure. Tubman himself took an African name, appeared in African dress and showed an appreciation of African art and dancing.

Before 1964 Liberia administered the interior provinces through the chiefs and indirect rule. In the coastal counties about 50 per cent of Africans lived under chiefly authority much as in the provinces. In 1958 there were 65 townships in the counties containing the remaining half of the population. The townships paid taxes directly to the central government, had limited local government, came under magistrate courts, and were administered by Western-educated officers, normally of local origin and paid by the central government. The majority of the townships had grown out of the Americo-Liberian settlements but are today mainly African in population. In addition those Africans who wished were allowed to move out of chiefly-controlled towns and create new settlements nearby, seeking government recognition as a township. In the late 1950s there were thirteen such Kru townships. Kru urban areas were thus often distinguished by a dual settlement pattern, the old town under the chiefs and the new town under Western-educated leaders. In 1958 in Grand Cess, for example, the old town had a population of about 500, while the new town contained almost 1,500 people.

In 1964 the interior provinces were abolished and replaced by counties, thus extending to Africans in the interior the choice of the kind of administration under which they wished to live. This was likely to undermine indirect rule—in harmony with the climate of opinion elsewhere in English-speaking West Africa—especially in those areas of rapid economic development. It also enlarged the number of local government positions available for Western-educated Africans. By 1966 it could be said that Western-educated Africans had 'virtually taken over the running of their counties'. In the 1967 general election almost half of the candidates who contested seats in the legislature were of full African descent. However, the legislature, indicated above, was not a major instrument of Liberian government and the large number of Africans in the legislature did not mean that they were about to achieve political power.

President Tubman made it a practice to hold periodic executive councils in the provincial headquarters—Albert Margai instituted the same precedent in Sierra Leone—where Africans were encouraged to come forward and lay complaints against the civil service. Justice was meted out to officials who collected illegal taxes, demanded free labour, acquired land or took wives without dowry payments. Errant district commissioners were dismissed, including close relatives of the president. Tubman was genuinely popular and physical resistance to Americo-Liberian rule ceased. The rapid absorption of the new African elite into the administration, the emphasis upon justice in the interior and the willingness to permit Africans to be 'African', were all part of the policy of national unification, of closing the gap between Americo-Liberians and Africans which was best described by Tubman.

> We must destroy all ideologies that tend to divide us. Americo-Liberianism must be forgotten and all of us must register a new era of justice, equality, fair dealing and equal opportunity for everyone from every part of the country, regardless of tribe, clan, element, creed or economic status.

There were political limits to how fast Tubman could push national unification. Some of the Americo-Liberian oligarchy, frightened by the submergence of the Creoles in Sierra Leone, believed that the president was moving towards integration too quickly, while impatient Africans inspired by Mende-Temne rule in Sierra Leone felt that he was moving too slowly. 'There are still a few die-hards on both sides,' Tubman warned, 'opposing the unification programme in the hope that one element will overcome or exterminate the other.' Part of Tubman's political strength arose from his position midway between the extremists and accounted for the relief which was apparent each time he agreed to stand for re-election.

Tubman had been able to continue to receive support from the oligarchy because of his entrenched political position and because it was being 'bought off' in the sense that its members benefited enormously financially from the Open Door policy. While on the one hand the political gap between Africans and Americo-Liberians had been closing, on the other the economic gap between the oligarchy and the rest of the population, which included Africans and the majority of Americo-Liberians, had been steadily widening. A related weakness was the failure of Liberia to follow other West African states in actively fostering an indigenous mercantile and industrial class. Such a class with independent resources and free of the patronage and of the control of the oligarchy might be feared as the basis of an opposition political party. One observer has warned of the dangers of an alien-dominated economy. In the long run the failure of the government to insist upon Liberianisation of the economy may be detrimental to the ruling Americo-Liberian ruling class and the foreign economic interests.

## CHAPTER TWENTY-NINE

# French-speaking West Africa since independence

De Gaulle was reluctant to concede independence in 1960, but he was aware that there could be no real change in the power relations between France and her former colonies so long as France underwrote the ordinary operating expenses of these new 'independent' states. Mali made a determined bid to make its independence real, like Guinea's, but was forced by economic realities to come back under French financial direction. Ivory Coast, because of its economic development, had had more opportunity than others to emerge from under the French shadow, but since independence President Houphouët-Boigny has not been the leader of a movement of Ivoirean economic emancipation. Rather, he has tied his country's development closely to French capitalism. President Senghor of Senegal has shown his personal awareness of the problem of economic dependence on France. In 1963 he said, 'Independence does not become a reality except through *economic* independence. . . . From this point of view, let us dare say it, we are not yet *de-colonised*.'

However, in practice, Senghor has been able to do little to reduce Senegal's over-dependence on groundnut exports to France, and he has even been unwilling to reduce dependence on France in the administration.

The balkanisation of French West Africa in 1958 by De Gaulle, aided enthusiastically by Houphouët and reluctantly by Senghor (see Chapter 25), has created serious problems for the new states. Senegal has never been able to afford its expensive former federal capital of Dakar. The break-up of the federation immediately struck a blow at Senegal's infant manufacturing industry by severely limiting its market. Even in Ivory Coast, despite the inflow of capital and continued economic boom, the same factor of a limited market is beginning to check industrial expansion.

Mali's potential as the granary of West Africa was destroyed when the break-up of the federation left it landlocked, and by the failure of the Mali Federation with Senegal in 1960. Mali left the French currency zone in 1962 in an effort to assert economic independence.

However, its franc was not acceptable among its neighbours and Mali was virtually excluded from trade with them.

For Guinea a separate·unattached currency was less of a problem since it was not landlocked and its mineral exports earned dollars in the international market.

In both Ivory Coast and Senegal the most lucrative commercial and industrial enterprises are in the hands of Europeans, and a large share of the profits is repatriated to France. European industries' finances are kept in European-owned banks. Large salaries are paid to European managers who spend it on European food and in clothing shops, European cafés, night clubs and cinemas; all of which, in turn, make their own remittances back to France. A small share filters through via taxation and in the wages of unskilled labour into African hands. Much of the tax finances schools from which African youths emerge to find the commercial firms uninterested in them and that the most readily available jobs are in the civil service. Thus the government expands its bureaucracy—until, as in Senegal, two thirds of its revenue is spent on salaries—to absorb the school-leavers because of the threat to political stability which the educated unemployed create. In Ivory Coast a policy of limiting educational opportunities has been followed.

Both states have been primarily dependent upon one or two export crops to earn foreign exchange. But with the constant downward price trend of primary products and the upward trend of industrial products, a continual balance of payments problem is likely to result. In addition, the French subsidies for these exports have been gradually withdrawn. This was to be compensated for by association with the European Economic Community (EEC), which was expected to provide a larger market and permit expansion of production. This has not taken place and discontent has spread among the African associates of the EEC. Senegal and Ivory Coast remain heavily dependent upon French 'aid', either private or governmental, and neither has been able to diversify its sources of aid. Fortunately French 'aid' has so far been maintained, France being the only country to equal and even surpass the level of aid suggested by the United Nations for the industrialised states.

## Guinea—standing on one's own feet

In 1959 Guinea came forcibly to world attention by voting 'No' in De Gaulle's constitutional referendum, thereby becoming abruptly independent. Four thousand French civil servants, including doctors, teachers, judges and technicians, were withdrawn within a month. Before they left they cut phone lines, cleared hospital shelves of drugs, threw office equipment into the lagoon, cracked state dishes and even removed light bulbs from their sockets. France also cut off all trade with Guinea. Ghana gave an interest-free loan of £10,000,000. Both the Americans and the Russians offered assistance. The Americans feared French childishness would force Guinea into the world socialist bloc and the Russians sympathised with the ideological position of Sékou Touré. Americans provided charitable assistance, i.e. rice, wheat and edible oils; the Russians provided a loan of £12m.

Sékou Touré maintained very friendly and close relations with the Communist countries from 1958 to 1961. He brought in 1,500 Russian technical advisers to help Guinea in its struggle to survive after the French departure and economic boycott. The Russians helped to develop Guinea's rich mineral resources, notably bauxite. Chinese experts helped in the setting up of a rice-development project. However, Sékou Touré was not, and is not, a Communist. He is an African socialist, and a devout Muslim. He accepted communist aid because it was freely given at a time of national crisis. It is true that he nationalised Guinea's export and import trade, banking and insurance. But he was not copying communism and destroying capitalism. He was setting up new economic institutions to help develop the country, which had been one of the most neglected of the French colonies. Sékou Touré expelled the Russians in 1961 when it appeared they might have been involved in the 'teachers' plot' against him. He then turned increasingly to the USA for development aid, especially in the mining industry. He also resumed relations with France after a few years, when France indicated she was prepared to treat Guinea as an equal. Touré's policy was not to align with any of the great powers, but to accept aid from any of them.

Guinea is the only former French colony that has not had to depend economically on France. Exports to France declined from 69 per cent in 1958 to 17.8 per cent in 1961, and imports from France went down from 78 per cent in 1958 to only 12.1 per cent in 1961. Even when relations with France were resumed, Sékou Touré was careful to ensure that the former pattern of dependence on the French was not restored. In 1970 Guinea's leading trading partners were Russia, Czechoslovakia, Poland, the USA, and in fifth place France.

At independence, Guinea's exports consisted almost entirely of cash crops: bananas, palm produce, coffee and cocoa. However, by 1972 the main export was alumina, made from bauxite. Both the

Russians and the Americans helped Guinea develop the world's largest known deposit of high quality bauxite at Fria. Iron ore, gold and diamonds were also mined in exportable quantities.

Income from the mining industry helped Sékou Touré to restore the economy of Guinea, and also to embark on massive new schemes of social development, such as education, hospitals and cultural and sports activities. From 1967 he began a cultural revolution, aiming not only to spread African socialist ideas throughout the population, but also to boost African culture. Already, in 1959, the Guinean national ballet had been created, and within a few years had turned professional. Since the mid-1960s the ballet has spent most of each year travelling abroad, to Europe, America and China. At home, the government actively assisted the development of African theatre, traditional music, painting, folklore and so on. Guinea won first position at the pan-African Cultural Festival in Algiers in 1969.

Sékou Touré's government has strongly discouraged ethnicism, and taken imaginative steps to build a spirit of national unity. Touré's party, the Parti Démocratique de Guinée, was supported at independence by all ethnic groups except the Fula of Futa Jalon. Touré formed a government of national unity and gave cabinet posts to leading Fula. Educational policy has been adapted to serve the needs of national unity. Secondary school students are required to board in schools outside their ethnic regions.

In his African policy, Sékou Touré has been a consistently radical pan-Africanist, a close ally of Nkrumah and opponent of balkanisation. He helped make the Ghana-Guinea Union in 1958, to which Mali was added in 1961. If Touré, Nkrumah and Keita were unable to establish an effective political union, the main factor was geography. However, at least they kept the flickering flames of pan-Africanism alive by a symbol of unity in a rapidly balkanising continent. When Nkrumah was overthrown in Ghana in 1966, Sékou Touré gave him a home in Guinea and made him a co-president—a gesture of support not for his domestic policies but for his strong pan-Africanism.

Touré's policies have not always been successful and have aroused considerable opposition. One major problem was the lack of educated personnel to man schools, hospitals, corporations and the administration. Massive inefficiency did not begin to be overcome until the 1970s, when the products of the educational expansion of the early 1960s were available. Many Guineans did not share their leader's vision of a socialist society. Smuggling and buying and selling on the black market have been rife. The doctrine of 'human investment', i.e. using unemployed young men to build schools, hospitals and so on, is no different from colonial forced labour if the spirit is not willing. Sékou Touré has dealt ruthlessly with opponents of his policies, and as a result thousands of Guineans, many of them educated, have fled into exile into neighbouring countries.

In November 1970 Guinean opponents of his regime allied with the colonial government of Portuguese Guinea to invade Conakry. The Guinean army defeated and expelled the invaders after several days of heavy fighting. The Portuguese were retaliating for Sékou Touré's open aid to the PAIGC freedom fighters in their territory. The final victory of the PAIGC and the expulsion of the Portuguese from Bissau in 1974 was also a victory for Sékou Touré, who contributed so much to it in terms of bases, military supplies and financial assistance. Sékou Touré deserves due credit for his role as a liberator of more than one country. It remains to be seen, however, how he will cope in the future with the considerable opposition from Guinean exiles and from opponents from within his own country.

## Ivory Coast—French capitalism and African capitalism

If Sékou Touré's Guinea is a symbol of socialism, its south-eastern neighbour, Ivory Coast, represents the triumph of capitalism in post-colonial West Africa. Houphouët-Boigny's policy has been to obtain the assistance of French capitalism for the development of Ivoirean capitalism. The policy has been for the Ivory Coast government to invest in new French businesses, and then later sell its investments to private Ivoirean businessmen. Industrial expansion has been stupendous. From 1960 to 1970 industrial production grew at an annual average rate of 18 per cent. Factories were set up for making cigarettes and cigars from locally-grown tobacco, textiles from local and imported cotton, for canning fruit, fish and vegetable oils, for making fertilisers and even for assembling cars.

In agriculture, efforts by African capitalist cash crop farmers to diversify production away from the original two exports of coffee and cocoa have been highly successful. Bananas, pineapples, sugar cane, palm oil and rubber are now major exports. By 1970 the period of dependence on coffee and cocoa had gone. Rice production increased so that by the late 1970s it was no longer necessary to import it. A massive programme of public works turned Abidjan into Africa's most modern city (complete with an ice-skating rink for the French community), provided a huge new port at San Pedro in the south-west, and led to the construction of a large dam at Kossou.

There are, however, several blemishes in the Ivory Coast success story. Firstly, even as late as the late 1970s foreign capitalism still dominates the economy at the expense of Ivoirean capitalism, and not just in industry. The number of French and Levantine commercial firms has increased since independence. Secondly, education has been neglected, not for lack of funds but because the government hopes to co-ordinate educational expansion with the rate of increase of new job opportunities in the economy. Education is not regarded as a fundamental right of each individual. Thirdly, Houphouët-Boigny's regime is a dictatorship with a record of repression of the young elite, many with socialist ideas, who want a radical change in the government's pro-French and pro-expatriate and anti-pan-African policy. In 1963 two plots to overthrow the government were discovered, and several cabinet ministers and many MPs and civil servants were detained or dismissed, most of them only on suspicion. The conservative leadership of the ruling single party, the PDCI, relies not on argument or debate to maintain its authority, but on a 6,000-strong party militia, well armed to guard against an army coup. On the credit side, though, Houphouët-Boigny has kept the lid on ethnic tensions that in the 1940s and 1950s threatened to blow Ivory Coast to pieces, particularly when they were deliberately fostered by the French administration. He has constantly maintained an ethnic balance in the government and administration.

### Senegal—French capitalism and African Socialism

Senghor, the apostle of West African federation, reluctantly advised his people to vote 'Yes' in De Gaulle's balkanisation referendum in 1958, so that Senegal's only important export crop, groundnuts, would continue to be subsidised by the French Government, and French aid and technical assistance to Senegal would also continue. Senghor, an apostle also of African Socialism, has in practice strongly supported French capitalist enterprise in Senegal's post-independence economy. His socialism has been applied not in the economic field but in his support for traditional African culture.

Senegal became independent in July 1960 as part of the Mali Federation, which broke up after only two months when Senghor refused to accept Malian President Keita's demands for a strong unitary government, Africanisation of the civil service, and expulsion of French armed forces, and when neither country could agree on whose leader should be overall president.

Senghor's policies have changed little since 1960. Africanisation of the civil service has been extremely slow. The number of Frenchmen in the administration actually increased after independence, to more than 1,500 in 1966, and their number has gone down only slowly since. The French army remained in Senegal until 1965, partly to provide security for the regime against internal socialist opposition, and partly for the economic advantages its presence brought. Senghor hoped that Senegal's associate membership of the European Economic Community would have provided a larger market for Senegal's exports, but this hope has not been fulfilled. Some attempt had been made to diversify the rural economy away from its heavy reliance on groundnuts, but little has been achieved. In education, the French classical system, of which Senghor himself is West Africa's most successful product, has been preserved, at the expense of much needed scientific and technical education. Moreover, many French teachers have had to be imported.

Until February 1978 Senghor could fairly be classified as a benevolent dictator. He suppressed opposition thoroughly but not ruthlessly. The prime minister, the brilliant young Mamadou Dia, was arrested and imprisoned for his alleged part in the abortive coup of December 1962. The 1963 referendum considerably strengthened the president's constitutional powers. From 1966 to 1978 Senegal was in practice a one-party state. Student demonstrations at Dakar University against Senghor's conservative and pro-French policies were regularly suppressed. But the national and presidential elections of 26 February 1978 marked a new development in Senegalese politics.

*President Senghor photographed in Lisbon in January 1979 with the general secretary of the Portuguese Socialist Party, Mario Soares.*

380

In 1977 Senghor drew up plans for a multi-party political system in Senegal. In December the ruling *Union Progressiste Sénégalais* (UPS) was renamed the *Parti Socialiste* (PS) and prepared to fight an election against two newly legalised opposition parties. Senghor's plans provided for three parliamentary parties, one to advocate liberal democratic or right-of-centre policies, another to support social democratic or slightly left-of-centre policies, and a third to fight for extreme left-wing Marxist policies. The PS reserved for itself the social democratic slot. The liberal democratic slot was taken by the *Parti Démocratique Sénégalais* (PDS), led by the barrister Abdoulaye Wade. The Marxist-Leninist slot was taken by the *Parti Africain d'Indépendance* (PAI), led by Majmout Diop. The main electoral opposition to the PS came from the PDS, and Wade stood against Senghor as a candidate for president.

The elections of 26 February were a remarkable experiment of significance to all Africa—the first example of a one-party state turning itself by a deliberate act of policy into a multi-party democracy. During the election campaign the legal opposition parties were given the opportunity to express their views on public issues and to criticise the ruling party. There was almost total press freedom during the election. Senghor won a third seven-year term as president, with 82.02 per cent of the vote against Wade's 17.38 per cent. In the elections for the national assembly, the ruling PS gained 82.45 per cent of the votes, the PDS obtained 17.12 per cent and the PAI received less than one per cent. Under the system of proportional representation introduced by the new electoral law, the opposition PDS won 17 seats in the assembly and the PS won 83 seats.

One positive effect of the elections was to reinvigorate the decaying ruling party. The PS now held regular national and local meetings and the youth section was revived and expanded. The ruling party does, however, face a number of problems. The first is the intolerance shown by some PS local branch officials to the opposition. Another problem is the association of the ruling party with some elements in the governing elite who do not share the party's socialist principles. A third problem is the refusal of the government to recognise the *Rassemblement National Démocratique* (RND) led by the lecturer and author, Cheik Anta Diop. The socialist and nationalist RND has strong support among Dakar's intellectuals and educated youth, and possibly among other elements of the population as well. It is significant that as many as 37 per cent of registered voters abstained in the elections.

CHAPTER THIRTY

# West Africa and African unity

## Nkrumah's early leadership

There can be little doubt that pan-Africanism—the movement towards African unity—has suffered severe setbacks as well as achieving a few triumphs in the first twenty years after Ghana's independence in 1957. West African states inevitably took the lead in the pan-African movement from the 1950s, because most of them attained independence before countries in the rest of sub-Saharan Africa. Therefore, a study of the successes and failures of West Africa's attempts to achieve African unity is also a study of Africa's efforts as a whole.

The driving force at the 1945 Pan-African Conference in London was supplied by the energy of two men, Kwame Nkrumah of Ghana and George Padmore, a socialist intellectual born in Trinidad who attached himself to the cause of African liberation and unity, and settled in Ghana on its independence. Padmore was Nkrumah's adviser in pan-African affairs until his death in 1959. Nkrumah and Padmore also spearheaded the movement towards African unity after 1957, with the two Accra Conferences of

*Kwame Nkrumah presiding at the Conference of Independent African States in Accra, April 1958.*

1958, the Conference of Independent African States in April and the All-African People's Conference in December. These were followed by the All-African Trade Union Federation Conference in November 1959, also held in Accra. These conferences marked a decisive shift in pan-Africanism away from a concern with the grievances of the black man in the world in general, to a practical concern with liberation of the rest of the continent still under colonial rule and the unity of the newly-emerging independent African states.

## The Ghana-Guinea Union

Kwame Nkrumah wanted not just an independent Ghana but a united Africa. He believed Africa could never be truly independent of the colonial powers unless it was strong, and it could only be strong if it was politically and economically united. These ideas are expressed in his book *Neo-Colonialism*, published in 1965.

The independence of Guinea in October 1958 gave Nkrumah an opportunity to try out an experiment in the political union of African states. Guinea faced the possibility of collapse with the immediate withdrawal of all French personnel as well as financial subsidies. Nkrumah believed that such a collapse would be a very severe blow to the independence movement then gathering momentum in Africa. He also saw the chance of laying foundations for his passionate dream, African unity. He not only offered Guinea a loan of £10 million for ten years, but also offered to form a union with it. Sékou Touré, President of Guinea, was both desperate for aid and also a keen believer in radical pan-Africanism himself. So he accepted both of Nkrumah's offers in November 1958. In May 1959 a declaration of basic principles on which the Ghana-Guinea Union was based was signed by the two leaders. Under this, their union was to be the nucleus of a 'Union of Independent African States', which was to be open to all others who wished to join. The union was to have a flag, an anthem, and a motto which was to be 'Independence and unity', and a union citizenship. There were to be a common defence policy, a union bank, a common economic policy and co-ordinated language teaching and cultural activities. Nkrumah talked in the Ghana National Assembly of his

> deep sense of pride ... that I have been an instrument in this movement. This new Africa of ours is emerging into a world of great combinations—a world where the weak and the small are pushed aside unless they unite their forces.

383

*West Africa* hailed the union as 'the first check to the progress of disintegration in West Africa which has been going on for years'.

It is very doubtful, however, whether Sékou Touré took union as seriously as did Nkrumah. It appears that the union was the price he had to pay for the loan. Also, the Guinean president regarded the union as primarily of symbolic value. When Mali joined the union in December 1960, Sékou Touré explained, 'It was a psychological coming together at a critical time.' The critical time was the crisis in the Congo, when that state broke up in civil war and the United Nations sent a peacekeeping force there.

The union never really got off the ground. Ghana lacked common frontiers with the other two states. No common institutions were developed, either political or economic, in spite of the hopes of May 1959. The most that was achieved was the occasional attendance of cabinet ministers of one country at cabinet meetings of another. The language barrier of French versus English, in particular, was not overcome. Ministers spoke either French or English but no common language, whether European or African. The Ghana-Guinea-Mali Union was less a union than an alliance of states with similar policies. Nkrumah, Touré and President Modibo Keita of Mali all followed socialist policies at home and favoured a strongly united Africa. Even this alliance broke up when Nkrumah and Keita were removed from power by military coups in 1966 and 1968 respectively.


## The Mali Federation

Keita had earlier played a major role in the formation and break-up of another political union in West Africa, the abortive Mali Federation from January 1959 to August 1960.

We saw, in Chapter 25, how the French West African Federation was 'balkanised', i.e. broken up into many smaller states, at independence. However, there was an attempt to preserve the federation after independence. The leaders of four states out of eight—Senegal, Soudan (later Mali), Upper Volta and Dahomey— proposed to federate. But Upper Volta and Dahomey withdrew from the scheme when their assemblies failed to ratify the federation's constitution. Dahomey voted 'No' to federation because of distance from the other states, and because Niger was its economic hinterland. Upper Volta backed out because it was linked economically and by railway to Abidjan in Ivory Coast. Only Senegal and Soudan ratified the January 1959 constitution.

384

The Mali Federation, like the Ghana-Guinea Union, failed to get off the ground. It also broke up sooner. Trouble began in March 1959 when the Senegalese and Soudanese politicians tried to come to grips with the problems of uniting their political parties into a common party, the proposed Parti de la Fédération Africaine (PFA). Senegal was a multi-party state, with several parties, and there was a long tradition of open political debate and liberty of expression going back to the days of nineteenth-century politics in the four communes. In contrast, the Soudanese branch of the RDA was all-powerful in a one-party state, and was run with ruthless discipline with few opportunities for discussion. The Senegalese and Soudanese party officials found it almost impossible to work with each other.

Then again, the leaders had widely differing policies. Senghor of Senegal opposed Keita's demands for a strong unitary government. Senghor wanted a loose federal structure which could then attract other states. Senghor also rejected Keita's plans to rapidly Africanise the civil service and to expel French armed forces. Above all, Senghor and Keita were two strong personalities who displayed different brands of socialism. Keita wanted to nationalise foreign firms, whereas Senghor's African Socialism was more concerned with preservation and fostering of African culture.

Senegal and Soudan were also divided by disputes over material interests like money and jobs. Senegal was richer than Soudan and felt she would have to subsidise it. The Senegalese complained that the Soudanese took most of the good jobs in the federal administration, in spite of their lack of educated men. Finally, there was disagreement over who should be federal president, when the Soudanese refused to accept the dominant figure of Senghor and proposed a lesser Senegalese politician.

Senegal and Soudan became independent on 20 June 1960. Exactly two months later, on 20 August, the Senegalese police, acting on Senghor's orders, arrested Keita and other Soudanese ministers in Dakar and deported them to Bamako. Thus the Mali Federation was stillborn, but Soudan renamed itself Mali, and in December 1960 joined its radical socialist allies Guinea and Ghana.

## The Casablanca and Monrovia groups

The break-up of the Mali Federation before it had even elected a president was followed by the division of African states into two opposing groups which were not brought together until May 1963.

These groups became known as the Casablanca and Monrovia groups. The Casablanca group consisted of radical states such as Ghana, Guinea, Mali, Algeria and Egypt who met at Casablanca. They supported a strong political union in Africa. In the Congo crisis of the time they favoured a strong central government under the radical Patrice Lumumba and opposed the Katanga secessionist movement of the pro-capitalist Moise Tshombe. The Monrovia group consisted of states that favoured a loose association of independent states in Africa and a loose federation of provinces in the Congo. The members of the Monrovia group were nearly all the French-speaking states (except Guinea and Mali), Liberia and Nigeria. The division between the Casablanca and Monrovia groups became clear at the Second Conference of Independent African States held in Addis Ababa in June 1960. The leader of the Nigerian delegation opposed the Casablanca group's proposed Union of African States, put forward by Nkrumah, as premature. He said:

We feel such a move is too radical—perhaps too ambitious—to be of lasting benefit. Gradual development of ideas and thoughts is more lasting ... We must first prepare the minds of the different countries—we must start from the known to the unknown. At the moment we in Nigeria cannot afford to form union by government with any African States by surrendering our sovereignty.

The Monrovia group also greatly feared Nkrumah's ambition, especially in the light of growing dictatorship in Ghana. The same Nigerian delegate warned:

If anybody makes the mistake of feeling that he is a Messiah who has got a mission to lead Africa the whole purpose of pan-Africanism will, I fear, be defeated.

In fact, the other members of the Casablanca group turned against Nkrumah's proposals, published in his new book *Africa Must Unite*, for a common African foreign policy, joint economic planning, a common currency, a common defence system, and a union legislature with an upper and a lower house. Sékou Touré of Guinea and Nasser of Egypt began to work with members of the Monrovia group and with Haile Selassie of Ethiopia to secure a loose association of all African states. As a result of their efforts a conference of all independent African states was held at Addis Ababa in May 1963, and the Organisation of African Unity (OAU) was born.

# The Organisation of African Unity

The May 1963 conference in Addis Ababa did succeed in reconciling the Casablanca and Monrovia groups into a single union and a common charter was signed by all on 26 May 1963. Under this charter, the aims of the OAU were stated: to promote the unity and solidarity of the African states, to defend their sovereignty, their territorial integrity and independence, and to eradicate all forms of colonialism from Africa. The signatories agreed to harmonise and co-ordinate their general policies in the field of political and diplomatic co-operation, economic co-operation including transport and communications, educational and cultural co-operation, scientific and technical co-operation and co-operation for defence and security. The members of the OAU were to observe the following principles: the sovereign equality of all member states; non-interference in the internal affairs of states; respect for the sovereignty and territorial integrity of each member state and for its inalienable right to independent existence; unreserved condemnation, in all its forms, of political assassination as well as of subversive activities on the part of neighbouring states or any other states; absolute dedication to the total emancipation of the African territories which were still dependent; and the affirmation of a policy of non-alignment with regard to all blocs. The following organs were set up: the Assembly of Heads of State and Government which was to be the supreme organ of the organisation and was to meet at least once a year, the Council of Ministers to meet twice a year, the general

*Africa Hall, Addis Ababa, the home of the Organisation of African Unity.*

secretariat with an administrative general secretary and a number of assistant general secretaries, and finally a commission of mediation, conciliation and arbitration. A number of specialised commissions were to be established by the assembly, among which were the Economic and Social Commission, the Educational and Cultural Commission, the Health, Sanitation and Nutrition Commission, the Defence Commission and the Scientific, Technical and Research Commission. Finally the budget of the organisation was to be provided by contributions from member states.

The formation of the OAU as a loose association of states was a heavy defeat for Nkrumah's strong union policy. The Ghanaian president never stopped advocating such a policy until his death. He even went as far as consistently breaking those OAU principles against interference by one state in the internal affairs of another and against subversive activity by one state against another. He set up guerrilla training camps in Ghana not only for freedom fighters from countries still under colonial rule, but also for political exiles from independent African countries such as Nigeria, Niger, Ivory Coast, Cameroon and Zaire. This kind of subversive activity turned nearly all other African heads of states against Nkrumah, and made him the greatest obstacle to the African unity he desired so much.

It is difficult to see how Nkrumah's policy of union government and a military high command could have been put into practice. The progress of the OAU since 1963 has been limited, and its failures are at least as many as its successes. It has done considerable work for refugees, but it has been able to do little to prevent or end the civil wars in African states that create refugees, though it did play a key role in ending the Sudanese Civil War in 1972. The OAU can do little to prevent new divisions between African states, and it reflects these divisions. It could not prevent Ivory Coast, Gabon, Tanzania and Zambia supporting 'Biafra' in the Nigerian Civil War. It could not prevent the division of African states over a policy of dialogue with South Africa or a policy of sanctions against that state. The OAU simply has no authority over the policies of each member state. For instance, Dr Busia of Ghana supported dialogue with South Africa (i.e. trying to bring about change in South Africa by discussion with its leaders). But Ghana abandoned the policy as soon as its government changed: Colonel Acheampong, who overthrew Busia in the 1972 coup, immediately rejected dialogue with South Africa.

The OAU is composed of states divided between civilian and military systems of government; radical and moderate states; socialist and mixed-economy states; those close to the West in foreign policy and those close to the East, and a few genuine non-aligned states; French-speaking versus English-speaking states; and between states with a considerable measure of political freedom, others which can only be described as brutal dictatorships, and a large number which fall somewhere between these two extremes.

## Economic unions

In addition to the political obstacles to African unity, there are the problems of inadequate inter-African economic co-operation and major communications links. If Africa is ever to be truly united, it is probably most sensible to start from the bottom upwards, rather than from the top downwards, i.e. to start with economic unity on a regional basis, then move on to political unity. A most hopeful development along these lines was the formation in Lagos in May 1975 of the Economic Community of West African States (ECOWAS).

All fifteen West African states are members of ECOWAS. They have pledged themselves to set up a customs union over fifteen years by progressive reduction of import duties. The whole of West Africa would then become a free trade area, with free movement also of people, services and capital. Industrial development will be co-ordinated, so as to avoid duplication of resources and capital. The first two years of ECOWAS's existence were spent establishing its organisation and gathering essential economic information.

It is to be hoped that ECOWAS prospers. It will need to improve on OCAM, the organisation of most French-speaking states in Africa that was set up in 1965 to co-ordinate their economic planning and development. In practice, OCAM has been a paper organisation. ECOWAS will also have to guard against the possibility of disintegration caused by ideological differences, as has happened to the East African Community of Kenya, Uganda and Tanzania with the splitting up of common communications services and the erection of higher tariffs between the three states.

Regional economic unions may well in the long run play a major role in securing the economic unity which is essential to political union. Thus, they may well prove to be of more practical value than the OAU in progress towards African unity. Paradoxically, however, ECOWAS could not have been set up without the OAU. The fact that the OAU exists has helped African states to get together and plan and co-ordinate some of their activities. Much of the groundwork for the creation of ECOWAS was done through the OAU.

# Further reading

## A  General books

These are designed for students' use and cover large sections of the syllabus.

AJAYI, J. F. A. and ESPIE, I., *A Thousand Years of African History*, IUP and Nelson, 1966.
AGBODEKA, F., *The Rise of the Nation States*, Nelson, 1969.
BOAHEN, A. A., *Topics in West African History*, Longman, 1966.
CROWDER, M., *West Africa: An Introduction to its History*, Longman, 1977.
FAGE, J. D., *A History of West Africa*, CUP, rev. ed. 1969.
FAGE, J. D., *An Atlas of African History*, Arnold, 1958.
LATHAM, N., *A Sketchmap History of West Africa*, Hulton, 1962.
OLIVER, R. and FAGE, J. D., *A Short History of Africa*, Penguin, 5th ed. 1975.
OSAE, T. A. and ODUNSI, A. T. O. *A Short History of West Africa, A.D. 1800 to the present day*, Hodder and Stoughton, 1973.
PARRY, K. J., *Study for Success: Revision Guide: Essay Writing in West African History*, Longman, 1979.
THATCHER, P. F. *Longman Certificate Notes: West African History*, Longman, 1974.

## B  More specialised books

These give detailed coverage of certain parts of the syllabus. They are useful for reference purposes and for teachers' use.

ABRAHAM, A., *Topics in Sierra Leone History*, Leone Publishers, 1976.
ADAMOLEKUN, L., *Sékou Touré's Guinea*, Methuen, 1976.
ADELEYE, R. A., *Power and Diplomacy in Northern Nigeria*, Longman, 1971.
AFIGBO, A. E., *The Warrant Chiefs*, Longman, 1972.
AFRIFA, A. A., *The Ghana Coup*, Frank Cass, 1966.

AGBODEKA, F., *African Politics and British Policy in the Gold Coast 1868-1900*, Longman, 1971.

AJAYI, J. F. A., *Christian Missions in Nigeria 1841-1891*, Longman, 1965.

AJAYI, J. F. A. and CROWDER, M. (eds.) *History of West Africa*, Volume Two, Longman, 1974.

AJAYI, J. F. A. and SMITH, R. S., *Yoruba Warfare in the Nineteenth Century*, CUP, 1964.

AKINTOYE, S. A., *Revolution and Power Politics in Yorubaland, 1840-1893*, Longman, 1971.

AKINTOYE, S. A., *Emergent African States*, Longman, 1976.

ALAGOA, E. J., *The Small Brave City State*, IUP, 1964.

ANENE, J. C., *Southern Nigeria in Transition*, CUP, 1966.

ASIWAJU, A. I., *Western Yorubaland under European Rule 1889-1945*, Longman, 1976.

ATANDA, J. A., *The New Oyo Empire*, Longman, 1973.

AUSTIN, D. G., *Politics in Ghana 1946-1960*, OUP, 1964.

AWOLOWO, O., *Awo*, CUP, 1960.

AYANDELE, E. A., *The Missionary Impact on Modern Nigeria, 1842-1914*, Longman, 1966.

AZIKIWE, N., *My Odyssey; an Autobiography*, Hurst, 1971.

BELLO, SIR A., *My Life*, CUP, 1962.

BIOBAKU, S. O., *The Egba and Their Neighbours 1842-1872*, OUP, 1957.

BOAHEN, A. A., *Britain, the Sahara, and the Western Sudan, 1788-1861*, OUP, 1964.

BOAHEN, A. A., *Ghana: evolution and change in the nineteenth and twentieth centuries*, Longman, 1975.

BRENNER, L., *The Shehus of Kukawa*, OUP, 1973.

CROWDER, M., *Senegal*, Methuen, 1967.

CROWDER, M., *West African Resistance*, Hutchinson, 1971.

CROWDER, M. and IKIME, O., *West African Chiefs*, University of Ife, 1970.

DAVIDSON, B., *Black Star: A View of the Life and Times of Kwame Nkrumah*, Allen Lane, 1973.

DIKE, K. O., *Trade and Politics in the Niger Delta*, OUP, 1956.

EKECHI, F. K., *Missionary Enterprise and Rivalry in Igboland 1857-1914*, Cass, 1971.

EKUNDARE, R. O., *An Economic History of Nigeria 1860-1960*, Methuen, 1973.

FLINT, J. E., *Sir George Goldie and the Making of Nigeria*, OUP, 1960.

FYFE, C., *A Short History of Sierra Leone*, Longman, 1962.

391

FYFE, C., *Sierra Leone Inheritance*, OUP, 1964.

FYFE, C., *Africanus Horton*, OUP, 1972.

GAILEY, H. R., *A History of the Gambia*, Routledge, 1964.

GRAY, J. M., *A History of the Gambia*, Cass, 1966.

HALIBURTON, G. M., *The Prophet Harris*, Longman, 1971.

HALLETT, R., *Africa to 1875*, Heinemann, 1974.

HALLETT, R., *Africa since 1875*, Heinemann, 1974.

HARGREAVES, J. D., *Prelude to the Partition of West Africa*, Macmillan, 1963.

HARGREAVES, J. D., *West Africa: the Former French States*, Prentice-Hall, 1967.

HATCH, J., *A History of Post-War Africa*, Deutsch, 1965.

HODGKIN, T., *Nigerian Perspectives*, OUP, new edition, 1975.

HOPKINS, A. G., *An Economic History of West Africa*, Longman, 1973.

IKIME, O., *Niger Delta Rivalry*, Longman, 1969.

IKIME, O., *Merchant Prince of the Niger Delta*, Heinemann, 1968.

IKIME, O., *The Fall of Nigeria*, Heinemann, 1977.

IKIME, O., *Leadership in Nineteenth Century Africa*, Longman, 1974.

ISICHEI, E., *The Ibo People and the Europeans*, Faber and Faber, 1973.

JOHNSON, G. W., *The Emergence of Black Politics in Senegal*, Stanford, 1971.

JONES, T., *Ghana's First Republic 1960-1966*, Methuen, 1976.

KANYA-FORSTNER, A. S., *The Conquest of the Western Sudan*, CUP, 1969.

KILSON, *Political Change in a West African State* (Sierra Leone), Harvard, 1966.

KIMBLE, D., *A Political History of Ghana 1850-1928*, OUP, 1963.

LANGLEY, J. A., *Pan-Africanism and Nationalism in West Africa*, OUP, 1973.

LAST, M., *The Sokoto Caliphate*, Longman, 1977.

MINERS, N. J., *The Nigerian Army 1956-1966*, Methuen, 1971.

MORTIMER, E., *France and the Africans, 1944-1960*, Faber and Faber, 1969.

NKRUMAH, K., *Ghana: The Autobiography of Kwame Nkrumah*, Nelson, 1957.

NICOLSON, I. F., *The Administration of Nigeria 1900-1960*, OUP, 1969.

OLORUNTIMEHIN, B. O., *The Segu Tukulor Empire*, Longman, 1972.

OLUSANYA, G. O., *The Second World War and Politics in Nigeria, 1939-1953*, Evans, 19.

OMARI, T. P., *Kwame Nkrumah*, Hurst, 1970.

PINKNEY, R., *Ghana Under Military Rule 1966-1969*, Methuen, 1972.

PORTER, A., *Creoledom*, OUP, 1963.

POST, K. and VICKERS, S. M., *Structure and Conflict in Nigeria 1960-1965*, University of Wisconsin Press, 1974.

POST, K. and JENKINS, G. D., *The Price of Liberty*, CUP, 1973.

SMITH, R. S., *Kingdoms of the Yoruba*, Methuen, rev. ed. 1976.

TAMUNO, T. N., *The Evolution of the Nigerian State*, Longman, 1972.

TRIMINGHAM, J. S., *A History of Islam in West Africa*, OUP, rev. ed. 1970.

WARD, W. E. F., *A History of Ghana*, Allen and Unwin, 1963.

WEBSTER, J. B., *African Churches among the Yoruba*, OUP, 1964.

WILKS, I., *The Northern Factor in Ashanti History*, Legon, 1961.

WOLFSON, F., *Pageant of Ghana*, OUP, 1959.

## C   Journals

The following journals also include much useful material:

*Journal of African History*
*Journal of the Historical Society of Nigeria*
*Journal of Modern African Studies*
*Tarikh*
*Transactions of the Historical Society of Ghana*

# Questions

These questions can be used for examination practice. Many are based on questions set in the West African School Certificate Examination, which also provide useful practice for examination at a higher level. Since examination questions frequently require the use of material from several different sections of a syllabus, it would be unrealistic to list questions strictly under chapter headings. But these questions have been arranged in about the same order as the contents of the book so that it should be easy to find questions dealing with any particular section of the book.

1   Write an account of the importance of the career of *either*
    a) Uthman dan Fodio, *or*
    b) Al-Hajj Umar   (WASC June '74).

2   What important contributions did Muhammad Bello, son of Uthman dan Fodio, make to the history of 'Northern Nigeria'?   (WASC June '75).

3   Give an account of the rise and organisation of Samori Touré's first empire.

4   Assess the importance of al-Kanami for the history of nineteenth-century Borno.

5   Write an account of the changing fortunes of the trans-Saharan trade in the nineteenth century.

6   Give an account of the nature and importance of the trade which replaced the trans-Atlantic slave trade in West Africa in the nineteenth century.   (WASC June '74).

7   Show why and how the empire of Old Oyo collapsed in the early nineteenth century.

8   Describe the system of central government in nineteenth-century Dahomey.

9   Would you say that the Asante were justified in coming several times into conflict with the British on the coast of modern Ghana in the nineteenth century?   (WASC June '75).

10 Show the importance of the Awka and Arochukwu oracles in the history of the peoples of south-eastern Nigeria in the nineteenth century.

11 What political problems faced Liberia in the nineteenth century? (WASC June '76).

12 Why has it been said that the Creoles of Sierra Leone were the leaders of West African society from about 1850 to 1918? (WASC June '73).

13 Write briefly on two of the following:
a) The career of Alali in Bonny
b) The Blood Men of Calabar
c) The career of Olomu in Itsekiriland
d) The career of Jaja before the Partition.

14 Why and how was the Fante Confederation formed? Why and how did it collapse?

15 Explain the economic reasons why European powers partitioned West Africa in the 1880s and 1890s.

16 Describe how the activities of the Royal Niger Company influenced the political and economic history of Nigeria in the second half of the nineteenth century. (WASC June '73).

17 Why was Samori Touré able to resist the French invasion for so long?

18 Show, by use of examples, how disputes between West Africans prevented them from co-operating with each other against European invasion 1880-1905.

19 Why did indirect rule 'work' in Northern Nigeria but not in Southern Nigeria?

20 Describe and assess the effects of how the French administered their colonies in West Africa up to 1946. (WASC June '74).

21 Show how the European colonial power both developed and exploited the economy of *one* West African country.

22 Assess the importance of Blaise Diagne in the history of French West Africa.

23 Assess the importance of Marcus Garvey in the history of West Africa.

24 Outline the aims of the Congress of British West Africa. How far had these aims been fulfilled by 1930? (WASC June '75).

25 What important contributions did either Tete-Ansa or James Aggrey make to the development of modern Ghana?

26 What common features were there in the struggle for independence in the Commonwealth countries of West Africa? (WASC June '73).

27 Show the main stages in the transition of the Gold Coast into Ghana between 1945 and 1959.

28 Briefly trace the history of the formation of Rassemblement Démocratique Africain (RDA) and outline its aims, influence and difficulties. (WASC November '73).

29 Show how party politics in Nigeria was bedevilled by regionalism between 1945 and independence in 1960.

30 Show the main stages in the constitutional and political development of Gambia from 1945 to independence.

31 'His place in history has been assured'. Do you think
either
a) President Tubman of Liberia, or
b) Dr Kwame Nkrumah of Ghana, deserves this praise? (WASC June '74).

32 Show why and how the army took over the government of Nigeria in January 1966.

33 Describe and explain the political problems Sierra Leone had to face in the first ten years after independence.

34 Describe and assess the career since 1958 of either Senghor of Senegal or Houphouët-Boigny of the Ivory Coast or Sékou Touré of Guinea.

35 Drawing your examples from any one West African country, explain why its leaders have been unable to maintain throughout, the British or French type of representative government since the attainment of the country's independence. (WASC June '75).

36 Show why and how the Ghana-Guinea-Mali Union and the Mali Federation were formed, and show why and how they collapsed.

# Index

Abd al-Salam, 8
Abeokuta, 72, 203
Abidjan, 378; Lycée, 221
Abiodun (Alafin), 64
Abok (Igbo), 110
Abomey, 74, 76; court of law, 82
Aborigines Protection Society, 208, 267
Aborigines Rights Protection Society (ARPS), 246, 247
Abyssinia (*see* Ethiopia)
Accra, 88, 263, 264; riots (1948), 287; Conferences (1958), 382–3
*Accra Evening News*, 288, 290
*Accra Morning Post*, 298
Acheampong, General, 341–3, 388
Achimota College, 208, 220, 221, 254, 255, 265
Action Group (AG), 280, 305, 307–8, 310–11, 345–6 (*and see* Nigeria)
Adamafio, Tawia, 331
Addis Ababa, 386
Afonja (of Oyo), 64–5
*Africa Must Unite*, 386
Africa, Scramble for, 73, 133–4, 167, 168, 170, 176 (*and see* Berlin Conference; Partition)
African and Eastern Trading Corporation, 231
African Association, 52, 230
African armies, 177, 275, 276
African Baptists, 237
'Africanisation' policy, 208–9, 221, 283, 293, 380, 385
*African Morning Post*, 244
*African Standard*, 270
African Students' Association, 261
African Workers' Union, 244
Agades, 2–3
Agaja (King of Dahomey), 74
Agbala oracle, 107
Age-sets, 104, 106, 107
Aggrey (King of Cape Coast), 158, 160
Aggrey, Kodwo, K., 254–5
Agriculture: cash crops, 12; wheat trade, 42; planning (Dahomey), 83–4; Creoles, 117; prices, 281 (*and see* Cocoa); Ghana, 292 (*and see* Ghana); Guinea, 376–7; Ivory

Coast, 378
Agyeman (*see* Prempe)
Ahmad, 180
Ahmad (son of al-Hajj Umar), 22–3
Ahmad II (son of Ahmad Lobbo, q.v.), 17
Akans, 284; language, 281–2
Akintola, Chief, 346, 348
Akuffo, General, 343
Aladaxonus, 80, 216
Alafin (of Oyo), 62–4, 202 (*and see* Oyo)
Alali, Regent, 143–4
Aliens' Compliance Order (Ghana), 340
Alkalawa, 5, 6
Al-Kanami, 9, 38–9
All-Africa Peoples' Conference, 329, 383
All-Africa Trade Union Federation, 329, 383
All Peoples' Congress (APC), 362–3
Almami, 33, 185
Al-Muktar, 15
Ama-ala, 101, 102, 103, 104, 204
America: slave traders, 53, 57
American Colonisation Society, 123, 124, 125, 128, 136
Americo-Liberians, 124, 126, 129, 130, 131, 371
*Amir al-Muminin*, 11, 200, 201, 306
Anderson, Benjamin, 126
Anglicans, 150
Anglo-Brazilian Treaty, 57
Angoulvant, Governor, 188, 227
Ankrah, General, 336, 337, 339
Anti-Slavery and Aborigines Protection Society, 246
Anti-Slave Trade Squadron (British), 57, 140–1 (*and see* Britain)
Arabic, language, 14, 89 (*and see* Islam)
Archibong I, 147
Arden-Clarke, Sir Charles, 290, 295
Aro people, 108, 109, 110, 192; slave traders, 108–9
Arochuku oracle, 107–10, 192
Artillery, 180, 183 (*and see* Firearms)
Artisans, 44; taxes on, 84

Asante: Empire, 85–97; administration, 91; decline, 91ff.; wars with British: (1824), 90, 93, (1826), 93, (1863), 93–4, (1873), 94–5, 165; becomes British Protectorate, 97, 193–4; treaty with Britain, 154
Asantehene, 85
*Ashanti Pioneer*, 331
Assimilation, 197; Liberal, 132; British policy of, 212–14, 217, 222 (*and see* France)
*Association* (*see* France: colonial policy)
Atebutu, 97
Atiba, Alafin, 68
Atlantic Charter, 277
Attahiru, 189–90
Attlee, Clement, 277, 278
Avoidance of Discrimination Act, 327
Awka, 107, 108, 110
Awolowo, O., 277, 301, 305, 308–12, 345, 351, 360
Ayew, John, 270, 271
Azikiwe, Nnamdi, 244, 272, 276, 280, 298–9, 300, 303–4, 307, 309–11, 346, 360

Baako, Kofi, 290
Ba Bemba, 185
Baffoe, E. Y., 296
Bai Bureh, 194–5
Baikie, Dr., 54, 148 (*and see* Quinine)
Bambara, 180
Bamako, 54, 385; Lycée, 221; 1946 Conference, 313; 1957 Conference, 320
Banjul, 26, 28, 120, 121, 209, 210
Bank of West Africa, 135–6
Baoule people, 177, 187, 317; revolt, 188, 314
Barra: and British, 120–1
Barth, Heinrich, 47, 49, 50, 53
Basel Missionary Society, 155–6
Bashorun (of Oyo), 63
Bathurst (*see* Banjul)
Bathurst Native Association, 122
Bauxite, 376–7
Belgium, 168, 169
Bello, Ahmadu,.306, 309
Bello, Muhammad, 5, 7–10, 19
Bende, 108, 109
Benghazi, 45
Benin, 73, 190; and Biafran War, 352
Berlin Conference, 170, 171
Biafra, 309, 349–53
Bini political system, 190
Bisandugu, Treaty of, 181–2
Bismarck, German Chancellor, 167, 168, 169, 171
Bissau, 378
Black Star Shipping Line, 258 (*and see* Steamship lines)

*Bloc Démocratique Sénégalais*, 317
Blyden, E. W., 126, 128, 129, 175, 176
Bond (of 1844), 156–7
Bonny, 58, 61, 108, 109, 141, 143–6, 152
Bonsaso, 90
Bordeaux Agreement, 247–8
Borno, 9, 13, 35–45; Mai of, 35–6 — and Sokoto *jihad*, 37–8; decline, 40–5
Botsio, K., 288
Braid, Garrick, 239–41
Brass (port), 141, 148, 149, 150, 152, 192
Brazil: and slave trade, 57, 147
Brazzaville Conference (1944), 278
Brezhnev, Leonid, 335
Britain: expedition against Baddibu, 28; exploration policy, 52–3; defeat of Ijebu, 71; defeat of Asante, 91ff., 154 (*and see* Asante); Atebutu Protectorate, 97; acts against slave trade, 111, 113, 124 (*and see* Anti-Slavery Squadron, Slave Trade, Wilberforce); colonial expansion, 166ff.; occupation of Egypt, 168, 170, 174; rivalry with France, 174–5, 176; colonial policy, 212ff.
Bronzes (Benin), 190
Burmi, battle of, 190
Burton, Richard, 173
Burns Constitution (Gold Coast), 278, 285, 286
Busia, Dr Kofi, 294, 295, 296, 339, 340, 388
Buxton, Fowell, 53

Cadell, Major, 135
Caillié, René, 48
Calabar, 143, 146–7
Camel, 54
Cameron, Governor Donald, 206
Cameroons (German), 234
Camwood, 126, 133
Canoes, war, 138, 192
Cape Coast, 153, 154, 155, 156, 159, 160
*Cape Coast Daily Mail*, 290
Cape Mesurado, 130
Caravan trade, 43, 44–5, 46ff.; decline of, 51–4
Cardew, Governor, 174, 194, 196, 209, 213–14
Carter, Governor, 71, 174, 188
Casablanca Group, 385–6
Casely Hayford, J. E., 208, 263, 266, 268, 269, 271
Catholicism, 205, 242, 243
Cattle trade, 13
Cedi: devaluation of, 341, 342
Censor of Public Morals, 17, 18
Censorship (Ghana), 331, 338
Census: Dahomey, 83; Nigeria, 346

Cesaire, Aimé, 260
Chad, Lake, 43, 45, 181
Chief system, 198–9, 203, 209, 210, 211, 278; and French policy, 216, 314; and Christianity, 241; in Ghana, 293; among Yoruba, 304; in Gambia, 368, 370
Christ Army, 240, 241
Christianity, 72, 117, 175–6, 240–1; in Liberia, 130–1; in Niger Delta, 149–52
Christiansborg Castle, 159
Christie and Davis Co., 173
Church Missionary Society (CMS), 238, 239
Churches, African, 237–43
Churchill, Winston, 277
Clapperton, Commander, 47, 49
Clark, J. P., 67
Clarkson, Thomas, 56
Clifford, Governor, 204
*Climats*, 315
Coal mines, 280 (*and see* Enugu)
Cocoa, 227–8; prices, 231, 272, 290, 334, 338; industry, 290–1 (*and see* Gold Coast; Ghana)
'Cocoa Hold-Up', 272
Cocoa Purchasing Co., 291
Coffee: Liberia, 126, 133; Ivory Coast, 227, 316
Coker, J. K., 270
Collier, Gershon, 364
Colonial Office, 164, 165, 197
Colonial Pact (French), 223, 224
Combo, 121
Commercial War (1856–86), 147–9
Committee on Youth Organisation, 288 (*and see* Ghana)
*Comptoir Français de l'Afrique Occidentale* (CFAO), 230–1 (*and see* Grands Comptoirs)
Conakry, 378
Condiment trade, 84
Conference of Independent African States, 382, 386
Congreve rockets, 93
Conran, Governor, 160
Convention People's Party (CPP), 280, 285ff., 326; foundation, 289 (*and see* Ghana)
Co-operative movement, 236, 271
Copper trade, 43; deposits of, 172
Cotonou, 82, 250; Conference, 283, 320–1
Coussey, Sir Henry, 287
Coussey Committee, 289
Creoles, 115, 196, 197, 213–14; 'civilisation', 115–19; and Sierra Leone, 269, 361, 362, 365
Cross River clans, 105–6
Crowther, Dandeson, 150, 152
Crowther, Bishop Samuel Ajayi, 116, 117, 119, 150, 151, 152, 237, 238, 239, 240
Crummell, Alexander, 126
Cugoano, Ottobah, 59
Culture: Senegal, 261; Ghana, 332; Guinea, 377
Customs duties, 165, 190 (*and see* Taxes)

Dabakala, 183, 185
Dadie, Bernard, 260
Dahomey, 58, 66, 71–3, 230, 250–1; attacks Abeokuta, 72–3; administration of, 74–84; army, 75–7; and palm-oil trade, 82; occupied by France, 186–7
*Daily Graphic*, 331
*Daily Service*, 305, 309
Dakar, 374; School, 221; port, 225; University, 380
Danquah, Dr J. B., 262, 269, 280, 286, 336
Dawodu, W. A., 225
Denkyira, 159, 161
De Gaulle, General, 278, 319, 320, 374; and referendum (1958), 319–22, 379
De Lokpon, 250
Democratic Party (Nigeria), 268
Denmark, 88; coastal forts, 157
Depression (1930s), 132–3, 235–6, 249
Devany, Francis, 126
Dia, Mamadou, 380
Diagne, Blaise, 247–9, 250, 259
Dinguiray, 20, 31
Diop, Cheik Anta, 381
Diop, Majmout, 381
Diula traders, 29, 133, 280, 325
Dodowah, 93
Dodds, General, 187
Dubois, Felix, 49
Dubois, Dr W. E., 256–9
Dunama (son of Al-Kanami, q.v.), 38, 39, 40–1
Dysentery, 94

*Eastern Nigerian Guardian*, 302
Eboué, Félix, 211, 278
Ebrohimi, 191
Economic Community of West African States (ECOWAS), 389
Economic imperialism, 171–2
Economic policies, 223ff.; self-sufficiency policy, 279; boom of 1950s, 280–1; in Ghana, 327–8, 332–4, 338
Economic Unions, 389
Education, 2–3, 10, 14, 114; made compulsory, 32; Borno, 39; Creoles, 116; Freetown, 119; Liberia, 132, 134; and Efiks, 150; Western-style and Westernised elite, 200, 202, 207, 208, Chapter 18,

243–4, 302; Igbo, 205, 206; Ghana, 207, 208, 288, 292, 293, 328; Sierra Leone, 209, 362; Gambia, 210; French colonial policy, 215–16, 218–22, 244; British colonial policy, 218–22; Phelps Stokes Commissions, 254; Guinea, 377; Ivory Coast, 379; Senegal, 380 (and see Emma Jaja; Missionaries)

Efik, 150

Egba, 70, 71, 189

Egbe Omo Oduduwa, 304

Egypt: British occupation of, 168, 170, 174

Ekiti-Parapo alliance, 70–1

Ekpe people, 147

Ekpe secret society, 105, 106, 107

Ekumeku, 192

Eleko, 266, 267

Elmina, 88, 90, 91, 92, 94, 95, 193

Enahoro, Anthony, 308

Entente Council, 321, 322

Enugu: coal mines, 272–3, 280; revolts, 272–3, 280, 300

Equiano, Olaudah, 59

Ethiopia, 262–3, 267

Ethiopianism, 237, 238, 240

Ethnic groups, 26, 370

European Economic Community (EEC), 375

*Evening News*, 331

Ewe people, 263, 296, 342

Eyo Ita, 268

Faidherbe, General Louis, 21, 28, 53, 61

Family Compact rule, 305–6

Fante people, 87–8; Confederation (annexed by Osei Bonsu), 90–1; Confederation, 158–64, 207

Farmers' Unions, 270

Faye, Rev. J. C., 367

Finance (colonial development), 224 (and see Economics)

Firearms, 7, 20, 30, 32, 76, 92, 122, 171, 177, 188, 194; local manufactures, 21, 177, 183; trade with Tripoli, 42; first large-scale imports, 50; smuggling, 71; supplies for Asante, 88; breech-loading rifles, 94; Bathurst trade, 121; machine guns, 177, 188; and King Glele, 186–7

Firestone Co., 227, 370

Fodeba, Keita, 260

Fomena, Treaty of, 95

Fourah Bay College, 116, 362

Fourn, Governor, 250–1

Franc Zone, 374–5

France, 20, 28, 197, 260; suppresses Medina revolt, 25; occupies Wadai, 51; exploration policies, 52–3; occupies Senegal, 53, 61, 197; occupies Porto Novo, 82; conquest of Dahomey, 83, 84; conquest of Ivory Coast, 97; destroys Freetown, (1794), 112; and the Gambia, 122; and Niger trade, 149; expansion policy, 169, 179–81; indirect rule, 210–11; colonial policy, 214–16; colonial education (see education); Free French armies, 278; citizenship laws, 278–9; and colonies' independence, Chapters 25 and 29; aid programmes, 375 (and see De Gaulle)

Franchise, 265, 279

Freeman, Thomas Birch, 156

Freetown, 32, 59, 112, 114, 117, 118, 119, 196, 209, 225, 363

Fulani, 2, 189, 323, 324, 377; and Hausa, 9–10

Futa Jalon, 323, 324, 377; French invasion, 185; revolts, 210, 251

Gabon, 318, 319

Gadeau, Cofi, 260

Galliéni, J. S., 179, 186

Gambia, the, 26–8, 120–2, 209, 210, 367–70; indirect rule, 209–10; 1962 Constitution, 368; independence (1965), 369

Gandhi, Mohandas K., 277

Garvey, Marcus, 250, 255–8

*Gaskiya Ta Fi Gwabo*, 303

Gatling gun, 177

Gbedemah, K. A., 288, 290, 291, 331, 339

Germany, 133, 276; expansion in Africa, 169, 171; palm-oil imports, 240

Gezo, King, 71, 75, 79, 81, 82, 83, 84

Ghana, Chapters 14 and 23; forts, 157; British annexation (1874), 165; 'indirect rule', 207–9; cocoa production, 227; Constitution (1951), 289; Constitution (1954), 293–5; and regionalism, 295–7; political parties, 295; since independence, Chapter 26; foreign policy, 328–30, 334–5; Army, 336; police, 336–7; civil government, 339–41

Ghana-Guinea Union, 383–4

Ghanaian Business (Promotions) Act, 340

*Ghanaian Times*, 331

Ghana National Construction Corporation, 333

Ghana National Trading Co., 333

Ghana Young Pioneers, 336

Ghartey, King of Winneba, 162, 163

Gin trade, 240

Glassmaking, 43

Glele, King, 72, 73, 79, 80, 81, 83, 84, 186, 187
Gobir, 4–5
Gold, 50, 52; Rand deposits, 172; Asante fields, 232–3, 234
Gold Coast, 95, 160; renamed Ghana, 284 (*and see* Ghana)
*Gold Coast Aborigines* (newspaper), 246
Gold Coast Federation of Cocoa Farmers, 271
*Gold Coast Independent*, 244, 263
Gold Coast Youth Conference, 269
Golden Stool (of Asante), 85, 91, 95, 96, 97, 178, 194, 207
Goldie, Sir George Taubman, 54, 61, 149, 170, 173, 174, 177, 192
Gowon, General, 349–53, 356–7
*Grammar and Vocabulary of the Yoruba language*, 119
Grand Bassa, 123
Grand Bonny, 137, 144
*Grands Comptoirs*, 230–1, 270, 271, 279
Grant, George A., 286
Grebo tribe, 130–1
Groundnut trade, 59, 60, 61, 121, 122; and Senegal, 223–4, 227, 228–9, 247, 248, 249, 374, 379
Guerilla warfare, 177, 192, 194, 196
Guggisberg, Governor Sir Gordon, 207–8, 220, 221, 225
Guinea, 321, 322–5, 375–8; unemployment, 375, 377
Gulama, Ella Koblo, 364

Haile Selassie, Emperor, 262
Hamalliyya Brotherhood, 211
Hamdullahi, 21
Harris, William Wade, 126, 237, 238, 241–3; deported to Liberia, 243
Harris Movement, 241–3, 314
Hausaland, 51
*Hijra*, 5, 16, 20
Hill, Captain, 156–7
*History of the Yoruba*, 119
Hodgson, Governor, 194
Holland, 88; in Southern Ghana, 157–8; agreement with British on fort exchange, 161, 163; withdrawal from Ghana, 164
Horton, J. B. 'Africanus', 116, 119, 162
Houphouët-Boigny, Felix, 280, 283, 313, 315, 316, 317, 374, 378, 379
'House' system, 138–40, 152
Housing (Ghana), 292
Howard, President, 132
Humanitarianism, 56, 57, 93, 111
Hunkarin, Louis, 250–1
Hut tax, 194
Hutton Co., 81

Ibadan, 348, 351; rise and fall of Empire, 67–71; and British, 189, 203;

Conference (1950), 301
Ibadan Planters' Union, 271
Ideological Institute, 331
Ife, 202
Igbo, 140, 192, 205, 303; indirect rule, 204–6; nationalism, 302–4; Unions, 303–4; and Biafra, 350, 352–3
Igboland, 98–110, 205
Ijaye war, 69–70
Ijebu, 70–1; British conquest of, 189
*Ikuba*, 151, 152
Ilorin, 71
Imams, 32
*Indigénat*, 215, 216, 250
Indirect rule: 1948 Commission of Enquiry, 209; Cardew's policy, 213–14 (*and see* Cardew; Lugard)
Industrial and Commercial Bank, 270
Industrial revolution (Britain), 60, 171
Industrialisation policies, 279–80
Inflation, 279–80; Ghana, 333–4, 337–8, 342; Nigeria, 356 (*and see* Economics)
Influenza epidemic (1918), 234
International Association, 169
International Monetary Fund (IMF), 337
Ironsi, General, 348–9
Islam: and Hausaland, 3–4; reforms in, 39; unifying force, 178; and Samori Touré, 186; northern Nigeria, 201–2 (*and see* Koran; Law)
Italy, 51, 262
Itsekiri, 191
Ivory trade, 13
Ivory Coast, 97, 187–8, 313–17, 378–9; Church, 237–8, 241–3; 1951 Election, 315; education, 316, 379; economic boom, 316–17; cocoa exports, 316; industrialisation, 378

Jaja, Emma, 126–7
Jaja of Opobo, 144, 145, 146, 151, 152, 190–1
Jamaica, 112
Jenne, 16
*Jihad*, 4, 5, 6, 7, 39–40
Johnson, Elijah, 125
Johnson, G. W., 175
Johnson, H. R., 129, 131
Johnson, Bishop James, 239
Johnson, J. W. de Graft, 261
Johnson, Rev. Samuel, 71, 119
Johnston, Harry (Consul), 190–1
Justice (*see* Law)
Juxon-Smith, Colonel, 364–5, 366

Kaduna, 348
Kamwana, Elliot, 238
Kano, 12, 13, 49; population, 49; cloth trade, 49–50; railway link, 227; riots, 310; Army mutiny, 352

Katanga, 172
Katsina, 49
Keita, Modibo, 379, 384, 385
Kennedy, Governor, 120
Kennedy, President J. F., 335
Kenyatta, Jomo, 262
Ketu, 72, 73, 82
Kimbangu, Simon, 238
Kitab al-Farq, 5
Kofi Karikari, 94, 95
Kolak, 41, 44
Kola nut trade, 13, 43, 50, 229, 232
Konate, Momadou, 282
Kong, 29, 184, 185
Kono, the, 362
Koran, 17
Koranic law, 2
Koranic schools, 2
Kossou Dam, 378
Krio language, 115, 364
Kru people, 130, 131; revolts, 131–2,
   134; and Liberia, 371, 372
Kukawa, 44, 50
Kumasi, 94, 95, 97, 193; and
   Convention Peoples' Party, 290;
   University, 292–3; riots, 296
Kurunmi (of Ijaye), 68
Kwaku Dua I, 94
Kwaku Dua II, 95
Kwaku Dua III, 96

Labour: forced, 233, 234, 272; African,
   272–3; Nigeria, 302
Lagos, 58, 61, 81; mosque, 119; port,
   356
Lagos Daily News, 271
Lagos Weekly Record, 245
Lagos Weekly Times, 176
Laird, Macgregor, 53, 54, 61, 148–9
Laissez-faire economic policy, 327, 330
Lamine Gueye, 215, 317
Lamptey, Kwesi, 294
Land: law, 233, 245, 246; rights,
   245–7; rights compensation, 266
Lander brothers, 148
Languages, 281–2, 283; English v.
   French, 384, 388
Lansana, David, 365, 366
Latrille, Governor, 314
Law, 9, 10; Islamic, 14, 17, 39 (and see
   Koranic); Borno, 36; Dahomey,
   79–81; Asante, 90, 94; Igbo, 102–3;
   Southern Ghana, 154, 155, 156–7;
   Liberia, 372
Lebanese traders, 231, 232, 328, 379
L'Eclaireur de la Cote d'Ivoire, 245
Le Guide du Dahomey, 245
Leopold, King, 168, 169, 170, 174
Lewis, Sir Samuel, 116
Liberia, 123–36, 370–3; politics in,
   127–30; economic collapse, 133–6,
   227; and Booker T. Washington

Institute, 254; education, 372
Liberia College, 126, 128, 129
Liberian Herald, 126
Liberian Rubber Corporation, 135
Libraries, 14
Ligue des Droits de l'Homme, 250
Lincoln, President, 57, 61
Literature, 14
Literacy, 89
Liverpool, 141
Lobbo, Ahmad (also known as Hamad
   Bari or Seku Ahmadu), 13, 15, 16, 32
Loi Cadre (Guinea), 323
Loi Diagne, 247
Loi Lamine Gueye, 215
Lott Carey, 123, 125
Lugard, Lord, 173, 179, 188, 189, 190,
   199, 200, 205; indirect rule policy,
   198ff.; and the Yoruba, 204; and
   Chiefs system, 206, 211; and
   educational system, 221–2
Lumumba, Patrice, 386
Lycée Faidherbe, 221

Maba Diakhou Ba: jihad, 26–8, 121
Macarthy, Sir Charles, 90, 114; killed
   by the Asante, 90, 93
Macaulay, Herbert, 176, 266–7, 299,
   300
Macina, 15–18
Maclean, George, 93, 113–16, 158, 161
Macpherson Constitution (Nigeria),
   301, 305–7
Mahdi, the, 181
Malaria, 148, 173, 213, 234, 246
Mali, 374, 384; Federation, 374–5,
   384–5
Mandinka, 26–34, 325, 368, 369; war
   with France, 182–5
Mankessim, 161, 163
Marabout Wars, 209
Margai, Albert, 363, 364, 365, 366
Margai, Milton, 361, 363
Maria Theresa dollar, 44
Marketing Boards, 279, 311
Markham, J. G., 290
Maroons, 112, 113
Masonic secret societies, 128
Maxim gun, 177
Mboya, Tom, 329
Mecca, 20
Medina revolt, 25
Mende people, 195–6, 209, 361, 362,
   363, 364, 365
Mensa Bonsu, 95
Metal working, 12
Methodist Times, 246
Mfantsipim school, 156
Mid-West Coup (Nigeria), 351
Miller Brothers, 231
Missionaries, 176, 190, 202, 241;
   schools, 200, 210, 221

Mohammed, General Murtala, 356–7
Monrovia, 123, 132; 1847 Convention, 125; Group, 385–6
Moor, Consul, 191
'Morocco' leather, 12
Moro Naba, 210–11
Mossi, 211
Muhammed Shitta Bey, 119
Mulattoes, 128, 129
Musa Mollah, 209
Muslims (*see* Islam)
Muslim Congress Party, 367
Mussolini, Benito, 262

Nafata, Sultan, 5
Nana of Itsekiri, 191–2
Nana Ofori Atta, 208, 263, 266, 268, 269, 326
*Narrative of a Journey to Musardu*, 126
National Association for the Advancement of Coloured Peoples (NAACP), 256
National Bank of Nigeria, 272
National Congress of British West Africa (NCBWA), 263, 264, 265, 270, 367
National Council of Nigeria and the Cameroons (NCNC), 280, 299ff., 345
Nationalism, 172–4; ethnic, 281–2
National Liberation Council (Ghana), 337–9
National Liberation Movement (NLM), 295, 296
National Redemption Council (Ghana), 341–3
National Reformation Council (Sierra Leone), 366
Native Authorities, 293
Native Pastorate Church, 116
Negritude, 259–61
*Negro World,* 250, 258
Neilson, Karl, 95
*Neo-Colonialism,* 383
Neto, Agostinho, 222
Ngazargamu, Birni, 50
Nigerian Baptist Missions, 126
*Nigerian Daily Service,* 277
*Nigerian Daily Telegraph,* 244
Nigerian National Alliance, 346, 347
Nigerian National Democratic Party, 267
Nigerian Youth League, 268
Nigerian Youth Movement (NYM), 268, 269, 270, 304, 305
Nigeria, 263, 281; and Britain, 188–92; Northern — indirect rule, 200–2; palm-oil trade, 240; land law, 246; National Congress, 266–7; 1922 Constitution, 267; independence, Chapter 24; Northern Region, 306–11; 1953 Constitutional

Conference, 309–10; 1954 elections, 311; minorities in, 310–12; economic boom, 311; Minorities Commission (1957), 311; after independence, Chapter 27; 1964 elections, 346–7; mutiny (1966), 348–51; twelve-state division (1967), 350–1 (*and see* Biafra)
Niger Delta states, Chapter 13
Niger Delta Pastorate, 238–9
Niger Mission, 150, 238
Niger River, 53–4
N'Jie, Pierre, 367, 368, 369
Nkrumah, Kwame, 280, 283, 286, 287, 288, 289, 293, 294, 386; imprisoned, 290; rule 1957–60, 326–37; dismissed in coup, 335–6, 377; death, 337; early leadership years, 382–4; Pan-Africanism, 382–4, 388
Non-Alignment policy, 281, 330
Northern Elements Progressive Union (NEPU), 305–6
Northern Peoples' Congress (NPC), 306, 307, 310, 345–7, 359–60
Noufflard, Governor Charles, 250
Nova Scotia slaves, 111, 112; Sierra Leone rebellion, 113
Nupe cavalry, 177
Nyampa, 146

Obasanjo, General, 357
OCAM, 389
Oil resources (Nigeria), 354–5, 358; production, 344, 353–5
Ojukwu, General, 352, 353, (*and see* Biafra)
Okojumbo, 151, 152
Olympio, O., 263
Oni (of Ife), 202
Onitsha, 206
Open Door Economic policy (Liberia), 370, 373
Operation Feed Yourself (Ghana), 341–2
Opoku Ware, 91
Order of Blood Men, 147
Ore, Battle of, 351–2
Organisation of African Unity (OAU), 335, 356, 386, 387–9
Osei Bonsu, 88, 89–91
Osei Kwadwo, 91
Osei Tutu, 91, 92
Osei Yaw Akoto, 93
Osemwede, Oba, 73
Oshogbo, Battle of, 7
Ostrich feather trade, 50
Ouidah, 81, 82, 186
Ovonramwen, Oba of Benin, 73, 190
Oyo, 7, 202, 203; Empire's decline, 62–5; political system, 62–4; and Afonja's revolt, 64–6
Ozo people, 107

Padmore, George, 382
PAIGC (Guinea-Bissau), 378
Palm-oil trade, 59–60, 81, 141, 145,
  146, 147–9, 224; Ibadan, 69;
  Dahomey, 81–3, 187, 226; Bonny,
  109; Liberia, 126, 133; Niger Delta,
  190–1
Pan-African Congresses, 259, 260
Pan-African Cultural Festival, 377
Pan-Africanism, 382–4
'Panyarring', 154, 157
Paris-Dakar (newspaper), 244
Parkes, J. C., 209
Parti Africain d'Indépendance (PAI),
  381
Parti de la Fédération Africaine (PFA),
  385
Parti Démocratique de Guinée, 282,
  322, 325, 377
Parti Démocratique Sénégalais, 381
Partition policies, 166–76
Parti Socialiste (PS), 381
PDCI, 379
Pechoux, Governor, 314, 315
Peoples' Union, 246
Peoples' Progressive Party (PPP), 367,
  368, 369
Pepper trade, 84
Peters, Thomas, 111, 112
Phelps Stokes Commissions
  (Education), 254
Phillips, Acting Consul, 190
Phillips, Rev. C., 71
Pine, Richard, 93, 94, 160
'Political Blueprint', 299
Poll Tax Ordinance, 157–8, 159–60
Ponty, William, 211 (and see William
  Ponty School)
Pope-Hennessy, Governor, 117
Poro Society, 133, 196
Port Harcourt, 352, 355
Porto Novo, 81, 82, 186, 250
Portugal, 148, 378
Potash trade, 43
Pottery, 13
Prempe, Agyeman, 95–7, 193, 207, 208
Presbyterians, 149, 150
Press, the, 245, 381 (and see
  Censorship)
Preventive Detention Bill (Ghana), 327
Preventive Detention Act (Ghana),
  331, 336
Preventive Squadron (see Anti-Slavery
  Squadron)
Price-fixing, 271–2 (and see Cocoa)
Privy Council, 266, 267, 364
Progressive Unions, 206
Progress Party (PP), Ghana, 339

Qadis, 32–3
Qadiriyya Brotherhood, 14, 19, 20, 21,
  24, 45, 184, 282

Quinine, 54, 148, 173, 246 (and see
  Dr Baikie)

Rabeh, 181
Racialism, 172
Railways, 187, 224, 225, 226, 227, 232,
  234, 291
Rand goldfields, 172, 174
Raffia fibre trade, 126, 133
Rassemblement Démocratique Africain
  (RDA), 280, 313–17, 318, 319
Rassemblement National Démocratique
  (RND), 381
Reade, Winwood, 173
Recaptives, 113–15, 117
Reffell, Joseph, 120, 122
Reffell, Thomas, 120
Regis et Cie., 81
Religion: syncretism, 27; freedom of,
  152 (and see various denominations)
Resident Commissioners, 200–1
Rhodesia problem, 335
Rice, 229
Richards, Governor, 299
Richards, J. B., 120
Richards Constitution (Nigeria), 278,
  299–300, 305
Rifle Volunteer Corps, 161
Road systems, 225, 226, 291
Roberts, President, 125, 126, 127, 128
Roosevelt, Franklin, 277
Roosevelt, Theodore, 135
Royal African Corps, 114, 120
Royal Niger Co., 54, 149, 174, 192
Roye, E. J., 126, 128
Rubber trade, 227, 370, 371 (and see
  Liberia)

Salmon, Administrator, 164
Salt trade, 42–3; Dahomey monopoly,
Samori Touré, 29–34, 177, 187, 324;
  political organisation, 32–4, 216;
  war with France, 181–6; military
  strength, 182–3; death, 185
Sanusiyya Brotherhood, 44–5, 52,
  181
Sardauna, the, 306, 346–8
Sartre, Jean-Paul, 261
Savage, R. A., 263
Schneider rifle, 71
'Scorched earth' policy, 183
Secret societies, 79, 105, 192, 196 (and
  see Ekpe; Poro)
Sefawa dynasty, 41–2
Segmentary societies, 99–100
Sekou Touré, 282, 320, 321, 323, 324,
  325, 337, 376, 378, 383, 384
Select Committee of 1865, 160
Senegal, 53, 197, 214–16, 282, 374,
  379–81; education, 221; groundnut
  production (see Groundnuts);
  'four communes', 247–9, 251;

economic dominance, 317; *Loi Cadre* reforms, 318 (*and see* France)
Senghor, Léopold, 260, 280, 283, 318, 319, 374, 379, 380, 385
Sere Burlay, 30
Shagari, Alhaji Shehu, 359, 360
Shanahan, Bishop, 205
Sharp, Granville, 56, 111
Sherman, R. A., 126
Sierra Leone, 57, 119, 124, 194–6, 269, 270, 361–7; indirect rule, 209–10; Constitution of 1945, 278; 1967 elections, 364–5; army mutiny, 364
Sierra Leone Co., 111
Sierra Leone Peoples' Party (SLPP), 361ff.
*Sierra Leone Weekly*, 245
Sikasso, 177, 182, 185
Slave trade, 13, 50; abolition of, 51–2, 61, 138–9; trans-Atlantic, 55–9; Dahomey, 82; via Bonny, 138–9 (*and see* Anti-Slavery; Wilberforce)
Smallpox, 119, 192
*Société Commerciale de l'Ouest Africain* (SCOA), 230–1
Sofas (soldiers), 33, 182
Sokoto, 5–6, 189; and Emirates, 10–11; and the Sudan, 11–12
Solanke, Ladipo, 261
Soudan, 385
South Africa, Republic of, 388
*Southern Nigerian Defender*, 278
Soyinka, Wole, 260
State Farms Corporation, 333
Steamship lines, 141, 231, 258
Stevens, Siaka, 362, 364, 365, 366, 367
Strikes: Dahomey, 250; 1920s, 273; 1940s, 280; Ghana, 290, 342–3 (*and see* Enugu)
Sudanese Civil War, 388
Suez Canal, 168
Sugar trade, 55–6; Liberia, 133
Swanzy, 231
Syncretism, 27
Syrian traders, 231, 232, 327, 379

Tafawa Balewa, Abubakar, 306–7, 309, 311, 345, 346, 347, 348, 349
Takoradi (port of), 225, 291
Talbot, P. A., 240
Taxes, 4, 10, 84, 375; palm-oil, 83; Liberia, 130; imposed by RNC, 149; Southern Ghana, 157–8, 159–60; 'head tax', 187; 'hut tax', 194; Igboland, 206; Nigeria, 246; Ivory Coast, 314
Temne people, 112, 113, 194–5, 209, 361, 362
Tete-Ansa, Musa, 270, 271, 272
*The Dual Mandate in Tropical Africa*, 198, 204, 205
*The Future of Africa*, 126

*The Lagos Weekly Record*, 126
*The Medical Topography of the West Coast of Africa*, 119
Thorpe, John, 116
Tieba (of Sikasso), 185
Tijaniyya Brotherhood, 14, 19, 20, 21, 24, 25, 27, 30, 32, 45, 184, 211, 282, 306
Timbuctu, 17, 48–9, 50, 181
*Times of Nigeria*, 204
Tofa, King, 249, 250
Togo, 263, 297
Tokolor, 179, 180; army, 23–4
*Towards Colonial Freedom*, 328
*Towards Nationhood in West Africa*, 261
Trade routes, Chapter 5; trans-Saharan, 13, 201 (*and see* Caravans)
Trade Unions, 273
Trade Union Congress (Ghana), 340
True Whigs (Liberia), 128, 129, 136
Tsetse fly, 292
Tshombe, Moise, 386
Tubman, President, 370, 372, 373

Umar (of Borno), 41–2
Umar Tall, al-Hajj, 19–22, 27, 32, 325; creates Tokolor Empire, 20–1; and the French, 21–2, 53–4; death, 22; and other Islamic reformers, 24–5
Unemployment, 285, 375, 377
Union Government (Ghana), 342–3
*Union Progressiste Sénégalais*, (UPS), 381
*Union Soudanaise*, 282
United Africa Coy. (UAC), 54, 149, 230–1, 271
United African Methodists, 237
United Democratic Party (UDP), Sierra Leone, 367
United Ghana Farmers' Council, 328
United Gold Coast Convention (UGCC), 280, 285ff.
United Native African Church, 237, 239
United Native Church, 237
United Nations Organisation (UNO), 277, 334; Commission (Gambia), 369
United Party (UP), Ghana, 327, 368, 369
United Progressive Grand Alliance (UPGA), Nigeria, 346–7
*United West Africa at the bar of the Family of Nations*, 261
Universal Negro Improvement Association (UNIA), 258
Universal Primary Education scheme (UPE), 353
Universities, 222, 316, 332, 343
USA (*see* America)
USSR: Agreement with Ghana, 335; aid to Sierra Leone, 367; aid to Guinea, 376
Uthman dan Fodio, 4, 201; death (1817), 7

Vai script, 130
Vegetable oil trade, 59–61
Vichy Government, 278
Vietnam, 335
Village government, 100–4
Volta River Project, 328, 330, 331, 333

Wadai, 42, 44, 45, 51
Waddell Hope Institute, 149–50
Wade, Abdoulaye, 381
Wage rates, 234–5
Wallace Johnson, Isaac, 244, 269, 270
Warrant Chiefs, 206 (*and see* Chiefs)
Washington, Booker T., 135, 253–4;
  Institute, 254
*Wathiquat Ahl al-Sud*
Watson Commiss'
Wesleyan Missio'
*West Africa*, 384
West African A
  270
West African (
  270
*West African C*
  162
*West African Pi*

West African Students' Union
  (WASU), 261, 262
West African Youth League, 244,
  269–70
Whale-oil, 224
Wilberforce, W., 56, 61, 111
William Ponty School, 221, 244, 322
Williams, H. Sylvester, 259
Wolof, the, 369
Wolseley, Sir Garnet, 94
Women's Riots (Aba), 206
World Festival of Negro Arts
  (Senegal), 261
World War II, 236

  ɔwaa, 194
  ʹe, 268
  vogana, 78
  ʹ5; new States arise,
  adan, 67–9; indirect
  Muslims, 250, 251;
  independence, 304–5,
  n, 304–5
  s, 267–70

  rench control of,